Lecture Notes in Computer Science　　13658

Founding Editors

Gerhard Goos
Karlsruhe Institute of Technology, Karlsruhe, Germany

Juris Hartmanis
Cornell University, Ithaca, NY, USA

Editorial Board Members

Elisa Bertino
Purdue University, West Lafayette, IN, USA

Wen Gao
Peking University, Beijing, China

Bernhard Steffen
TU Dortmund University, Dortmund, Germany

Moti Yung
Columbia University, New York, NY, USA

More information about this series at https://link.springer.com/bookseries/558

Ilya Sergey (Ed.)

Programming Languages and Systems

20th Asian Symposium, APLAS 2022
Auckland, New Zealand, December 5, 2022
Proceedings

 Springer

Editor
Ilya Sergey (ID)
National University of Singapore
Singapore, Singapore

ISSN 0302-9743 ISSN 1611-3349 (electronic)
Lecture Notes in Computer Science
ISBN 978-3-031-21036-5 ISBN 978-3-031-21037-2 (eBook)
https://doi.org/10.1007/978-3-031-21037-2

This Springer imprint is published by the registered company Springer Nature Switzerland AG
The registered company address is: Gewerbestrasse 11, 6330 Cham, Switzerland

Preface

This volume contains the papers presented at the 20th Asian Symposium on Programming Languages and Systems (APLAS 2022), co-located with SPLASH 2022 and held on December 5, 2022, in Auckland, New Zealand.

The 10 papers in this volume were selected by the Program Committee (PC) from 22 submissions. We were also honored to include the invited talk by Shankaranarayan Krishna (IIT Bombay) on the topic of "Verification of Concurrent Programs under Release-Acquire Concurrency".

Each of the regular APLAS 2022 submissions received between three and four reviews. After having received the initial reviews, the authors had a chance to respond to questions and clarify misunderstandings of the reviewers. After the author response period, the papers were discussed electronically using the HotCRP system by the 25 Program Committee members and seven external reviewers. One paper, for which the PC chair had a conflict of interest, was kindly managed by Eric Koskinen. The reviewing for APLAS 2022 was double-anonymous, and only authors of the eventually accepted papers have been revealed.

Following the example set by other major conferences in programming languages, for the first time in its history, APLAS featured optional artifact evaluation. Authors of the accepted manuscripts were invited to submit artifacts, such as code, datasets, and mechanized proofs, that supported the conclusions of their papers. Members of the Artifact Evaluation Committee (AEC) read the papers and explored the artifacts, assessing their quality and checking that they support the reported results. The authors of seven of the accepted papers submitted artifacts, which were evaluated by 21 AEC members, with each artifact receiving at least four reviews. Authors of papers with accepted artifacts were assigned unique artifact evaluation badges, designed specifically for APLAS by Kiran Gopinathan. The badges indicate that the authors have taken the extra time and have undergone the extra scrutiny to prepare a useful artifact. APLAS 2022 AEC awarded Accessible, Verified, and Expandable badges. All submitted artifacts were deemed Accessible and Verified, and five were found to be Expandable.

My sincere thanks to all who contributed to the success of the conference and to its exciting program. This includes the authors of the submitted papers; the external reviewers, who provided timely expert reviews; the members of AEC and its chairs, Arpita Dutta and Jan de Muijnck-Hughes, who took great care of this new aspect of APLAS; and, of course, the members of the APLAS 2022 Program Committee. Finally, I would like to thank Alex Potanin (SPLASH 2022 General Chair), Andreea Costea (SPLASH 2022 Publicity Chair), Hakjoo Oh (the PC chair of APLAS 2021), and Atsushi Igarashi (the Chair of Asian Association for Foundation of Software), for their advice and support.

October 2022   Ilya Sergey

Organization

Program Committee Chair

Ilya Sergey   National University of Singapore, Singapore

Program Committee

Anders Miltner	Simon Fraser University, Canada
Andrzej Murawski	University of Oxford, UK
Anton Podkopaev	JetBrains Research, The Netherlands
Arie Gurfinkel	University of Waterloo, Canada
Beniamino Accattoli	Inria and Ecole Polytechnique, France
Casper Bach Poulsen	Delft University of Technology, The Netherlands
Elena Zucca	University of Genoa, Italy
Eric Koskinen	Stevens Institute of Technology, USA
Farzaneh Derakhshan	Carnegie Mellon University, USA
Isao Sasano	Shibaura Institute of Technology, Japan
Jan de Muijnck-Hughes	University of Glasgow, UK
Jihyeok Park	Oracle Labs, Australia
Marco Gaboardi	Boston University, USA
Marco Patrignani	University of Trento, Italy
Meenakshi D'Souza	IIIT Bangalore, India
Nengkun Yu	University of Technology Sydney, Australia
Ondrej Lengal	Brno University of Technology, Czech Republic
Pierre-Marie Pédrot	Inria, France
Rumyana Neykova	Brunel University London, UK
Shachar Itzhaky	Technion, Israel
Thi Thu Ha Doan	University of Freiburg, Germany
Umang Mathur	National University of Singapore, Singapore
Xuan Bach Le	Singapore Management University, Singapore
Youyou Cong	Tokyo Institute of Technology, Japan
Zhenjiang Hu	Peking University, China

Additional Reviewers

Adam Chen	Stevens Institute of Technology, USA
Adam Rogalewicz	Brno University of Technology, Czech Republic
Cyrus Liu	Stevens Institute of Technology, USA

Hongfei Fu	Shanghai Jiao Tong University, China
Julien Lange	Royal Holloway, University of London, UK
Juneyoung Lee	Seoul National University, Republic of Korea
Tiago Cogumbreiro	University of Massachusetts Boston, USA

Artifact Evaluation Committee Chairs

Arpita Dutta	National University of Singapore, Singapore
Jan de Muijnck-Hughes	University of Glasgow, UK

Artifact Evaluation Committee

Ankan Mullick	IIT Kharagpur, India
Baber Rehman	University of Hong Kong, Hong Kong
Fabrizio Fornari	University of Camerino, Italy
Kai-Oliver Prott	Kiel University, Germany
Krishna Narasimhan	TU Darmstadt, Germany
Lilia Georgieva	Heriot-Watt University, UK
Luyu Cheng	HKUST, Hong Kong
Mário Pereira	Universidade NOVA de Lisboa, Portugal
Martin Lester	University of Reading, UK
Matt Griffin	University of Surrey, UK
Neea Rusch	Augusta University, USA
Pranesh Santikellur	Technology Innovation Institute, Abu Dhabi, UAE
Ridwan Shariffdeen	National University of Singapore, Singapore
Salwa Souaf	CEA List, France
Sankalp Gambhir	EPFL, Switzerland
Shouvick Mondal	Concordia University, Canada
Sourav Das	IIT Kharagpur, India
Yaozhu Sun	University of Hong Kong, Hong Kong
Yunjeong Lee	National University of Singapore, Singapore
Yuyi Zhong	National University of Singapore, Singapore
Ziyi Yang	National University of Singapore, Singapore

Verification of Concurrent Programs Under Release Acquire (Invited Talk)

Shankaranarayan Krishna

IIT Bombay
krishnas@iitb.ac.in

Abstract. This is an overview of some recent work on the verification of concurrent programs. Traditionally concurrent programs are interpreted under sequential consistency (SC). Eventhough SC is very intuitive and easy to use, modern multiprocessors do not employ SC for performance reasons, and instead use so called "weak memory models". Some of the well known weak memory models in vogue among modern multiprcessor architectures are Intel x-86, IBM POWER and ARM. The use of weak memory is also prevelant in the C11 model, leading to the release acquire fragment of C11. This talk is on the verification of concurrent programs under the release acquire (RA) semantics.

The main focus of the talk will be on non parameterized programs under RA, and I will briefly discuss results in the parameterized setting.

In the non parameterized setting, the reachability problem for RA is undecidable even in the case where the input program is finite-state. What works well for this class is under approximate reachability, in the form of bounded view switching, an analogue of bounded context switching, relevant to RA. In the parameterized setting, the first observation is that the semantics of RA can be simplified, lending to a better complexity for verification. Further, safety verification is pspace-complete for the case where the distinguished threads are loop-free, and jumps to nexptime-complete for the setting where an unrestricted distinguished ego thread interacts with the environment threads.

Contents

Semantics and Analysis

An Algebraic Theory for Shared-State Concurrency 3
  Yotam Dvir, Ohad Kammar, and Ori Lahav

Decoupling the Ascending and Descending Phases in Abstract
Interpretation 25
  Vincenzo Arceri, Isabella Mastroeni, and Enea Zaffanella

Inferring Region Types via an Abstract Notion of Environment
Transformation 45
  Ulrich Schöpp and Chuangjie Xu

Testing and Verification

RHLE: Modular Deductive Verification of Relational ∀∃ Properties 67
  *Robert Dickerson, Qianchuan Ye, Michael K. Zhang,
  and Benjamin Delaware*

Automated Temporal Verification for Algebraic Effects 88
  Yahui Song, Darius Foo, and Wei-Ngan Chin

Model-Based Fault Classification for Automotive Software 110
  *Mike Becker, Roland Meyer, Tobias Runge, Ina Schaefer,
  Sören van der Wall, and Sebastian Wolff*

Types

Characterizing Functions Mappable over GADTs 135
  Patricia Johann and Pierre Cagne

Applicative Intersection Types 155
  Xu Xue, Bruno C. d. S. Oliveira, and Ningning Xie

A Calculus with Recursive Types, Record Concatenation and Subtyping 175
  Yaoda Zhou, Bruno C. d. S. Oliveira, and Andong Fan

Novice Type Error Diagnosis with Natural Language Models 196
   *Chuqin Geng, Haolin Ye, Yixuan Li, Tianyu Han, Brigitte Pientka,
   and Xujie Si*

Author Index 215

Semantics and Analysis

An Algebraic Theory for Shared-State Concurrency

Yotam Dvir[1]($\boxtimes$) (ID), Ohad Kammar[2] (ID), and Ori Lahav[1] (ID)

[1] Blavatnik School of Computer Science, Tel Aviv University, Tel Aviv, Israel
yotamdvir@mail.tau.ac.il, orilahav@tau.ac.il
[2] School of Informatics, University of Edinburgh, Edinburgh, Scotland
ohad.kammar@ed.ac.uk

Abstract. We present a monadic denotational semantics for a higher-order programming language with shared-state concurrency, i.e. global-state in the presence of interleaving concurrency. Central to our approach is the use of Plotkin and Power's algebraic effect methodology: designing an equational theory that captures the intended semantics, and proving a monadic representation theorem for it. We use Hyland et al.'s equational theory of resumptions that extends non-deterministic global-state with an operator for yielding to the environment. The representation is based on Brookes-style traces. Based on this representation we define a denotational semantics that is directionally adequate with respect to a standard operational semantics. We use this semantics to justify compiler transformations of interest: redundant access eliminations, each following from a mundane algebraic calculation; while structural transformations follow from reasoning over the monad's interface.

Keywords: Shared state · Concurrency · Denotational semantics · Monads · Equational theory · Program refinement · Program equivalence · Compiler transformations · Compiler optimisations

1 Introduction

Denotational semantics $[\![-]\!]$ associates every program M with its meaning, i.e. its denotation, $[\![M]\!]$. A key feature of a denotational semantics is compositionality: the denotation of a program depends only on the denotations of its constituents.

As a concrete example, consider an imperative language that manipulates a memory store $\sigma \in S$, and denotational semantics for it that associates with each program M a denotation $[\![M]\!] : S \to S$ modelling how M transforms the store. For example – denoting by $\sigma[a \mapsto v]$ the store that is the same as σ but with its value at a changed to v – we have $[\![a := v]\!]\sigma = \sigma[a \mapsto v]$. Compositionality

Supported by the Israel Science Foundation (grant numbers 1566/18 and 814/22) and the European Research Council (ERC) under the European Union's Horizon 2020 research and innovation programme (grant agreement no. 851811); and by a Royal Society University Research Fellowship and Enhancement Award.

I. Sergey (Ed.): APLAS 2022, LNCS 13658, pp. 3–24, 2022.
https://doi.org/10.1007/978-3-031-21037-2_1

manifests in the semantics of program sequencing: $[\![M \mathbin{;} N]\!]\sigma = [\![N]\!]\,([\![M]\!]\sigma)$. Thus $[\![\mathsf{a} \coloneqq 0 \mathbin{;} \mathsf{a} \coloneqq 1]\!]\sigma = [\![\mathsf{a} \coloneqq 1]\!]\,([\![\mathsf{a} \coloneqq 0]\!]\sigma) = (\sigma\,[\mathsf{a} \mapsto 0])\,[\mathsf{a} \mapsto 1] = \sigma\,[\mathsf{a} \mapsto 1]$. Incidentally, we also have $[\![\mathsf{a} \coloneqq 1]\!]\sigma = \sigma\,[\mathsf{a} \mapsto 1]$, and so $[\![\mathsf{a} \coloneqq 0 \mathbin{;} \mathsf{a} \coloneqq 1]\!] = [\![\mathsf{a} \coloneqq 1]\!]$.

A desirable property of a denotational semantics $[\![-]\!]$ is *adequacy*, meaning that $[\![M]\!] = [\![N]\!]$ implies that M and N are contextually equivalent: replacing N with M within some larger program does not affect the possible results of executing that program. Contextual equivalence is useful for optimizations: for example, M could have better runtime performance than N. Adequate denotational semantics can justify optimizations without quantifying over all program contexts, serving in this way as a basis for validating compiler optimizations.

Returning to the example above, although $[\![\mathsf{a} \coloneqq 0 \mathbin{;} \mathsf{a} \coloneqq 1]\!] = [\![\mathsf{a} \coloneqq 1]\!]$, in the presence of concurrency a:=0;a:=1 and a:=1 are not contextually equivalent. For example, if b:=a? (read from a and write the result to b) is executed concurrently, it could write 0 to b only with the first program. Therefore, the semantics we defined is inadequate for a concurrent programming language; differentiating between these programs requires a more sophisticated denotational semantics.

Moreover, the *transformation* $\mathsf{a} \coloneqq 0 \mathbin{;} \mathsf{a} \coloneqq 1 \twoheadrightarrow \mathsf{a} \coloneqq 1$ eliminating the first, redundant memory access is valid in the presence of concurrency, even though the programs are not equivalent. Indeed, a compiler applying this simplification within a program would not introduce any additional possible results (though it may eliminate some), and in particular it would conserve the correctness of the program. We would like our semantics to be able to justify such transformations.

This leads us to the concept of *directional adequacy*, a useful refinement of adequacy. Given a partial order $\leqslant$ on the set of denotations, the denotational semantics is directionally adequate (w.r.t. $\leqslant$) if $[\![M]\!] \leqslant [\![N]\!]$ implies that M contextually refines N: replacing N with M within some larger program does not introduce new possible results of executing that program. Thus, directional adequacy can justify the transformation $N \twoheadrightarrow M$ even if it is not an equivalence.

In this paper we define directionally-adequate denotational semantics for a higher-order language, subsuming the imperative language above, that justifies the above transformation along with other standard memory access eliminations:

$$\ell \coloneqq w \mathbin{;} \ell \coloneqq v \;\twoheadrightarrow\; \ell \coloneqq v \qquad\qquad \text{(write ; write)}$$
$$\ell \coloneqq v \mathbin{;} \ell? \;\twoheadrightarrow\; \ell \coloneqq v \mathbin{;} v \qquad\qquad \text{(write ; read)}$$
$$\mathsf{let}\ x = \ell?\ \mathsf{in}\ \ell \coloneqq x \mathbin{;} x \;\twoheadrightarrow\; \ell? \qquad\qquad \text{(read ; write)}$$
$$\mathsf{let}\ x = \ell?\ \mathsf{in}\ \mathsf{let}\ y = \ell?\ \mathsf{in}\ \langle x, y \rangle \;\twoheadrightarrow\; \mathsf{let}\ x = \ell?\ \mathsf{in}\ \langle x, x \rangle \qquad \text{(read ; read)}$$
$$\ell? \mathbin{;} M \;\twoheadrightarrow\; M \qquad\qquad \text{(irrelevant read)}$$

Other transformations and equivalences this semantics validates are structural ones, such as **if** M **then** N **else** $N \cong M \mathbin{;} N$; and concurrency-related ones, such as $(M \parallel N) \mathbin{;} K \twoheadrightarrow M \mathbin{;} N \mathbin{;} K$.

None of these transformations are novel. Rather, the contribution of this paper is in the methodology that is used to justify them, fitting shared-state concurrency semantics into a general, uniform model structure. In particular, each memory access eliminations is proven correct via a mundane algebraic calculation; and the structural transformations can be justified using simple structural arguments that abstract away the details of our particular semantics.

Methodology. The use of monads to study the denotational semantics of effects [30] has proven fruitful, especially with its recent refinement with algebraic operators and equational theories [9, 10, 23, 35, 36]. We follow the algebraic approach to define denotational semantics for a simple higher-order concurrent programming language, using an equational theory extending non-deterministic global-state with a single unary algebraic operator for yielding computation to a concurrently running program [1]. We find a concrete representation of the monad this theory induces based on sets of traces [4, 6], and use it to define a directionally adequate denotational semantics. From this adequacy result we deduce various program transformations via routine calculations.

The advantages of denotational semantics defined with this approach include:

Uniformity. Theories are stated using the same general framework. This uniformity means that many theoretical results can be stated in general terms, applying to all theories. Even if a theorem, like adequacy, must be proven separately for each theory, it is likely that a similar proof technique can be used, and experience can guide the construction of the proof.

Comparability. Comparing and contrasting theories is convenient due to uniformity [23]. While our language and semantics is very different from Abadi and Plotkin's [1], the equational theory we obtain easily compares to theirs.

Modularity. Since the theories are stated algebraically, using operators and equations, they are amenable to be combined to form larger theories. Some combinations are the result of general theory-combinators, such as the theory of non-deterministic global-state resulting from combining the theory of global-state [34] with the theory of non-determinism [14]. In this combined theory, equations that are provable in each separate theory remain provable. Even if the combination is bespoke, using an algebraic theory breaks down the problem into smaller components [8].

Abstraction. The semantics we define for the fragment of our language without shared-state is identical in form to the standard semantics, by using the monad operations. Therefore, any structural transformation proven using these abstractions remains valid in the language extended with shared-state.

Implementability. Monads are ubiquitous as a computational device in functional programming languages, such as Haskell. Thus a theory based on a monad may in the future form a bridge to implementation.

Outline. The remaining sections are as follows. The next section provides background to the problem and overviews our results in a simplified manner. Then we dive into the weeds, starting with a succinct presentation of the equational theory and related notions (Sect. 3). We then work our way gradually to define the induced monad's concrete representation (Sect. 4). Next we define the denotations using this representation (Sect. 5). With everything in place, we present our metatheoretical results and use them to justify program transformations and equivalences (Sect. 6). We conclude with a discussion of related work and future prospects (Sect. 7).

2 Overview

Our setting is a simple programming language with state. We fix a finite set of *locations* $\mathbb{L} := \{1_1, \ldots, 1_{\bar{n}}\}$ and a finite set of *(storable) values* $\mathbb{V} := \{v_1, \ldots, v_{\bar{m}}\}$. A *store* σ is an element of $\mathbb{S} := \mathbb{L} \to \mathbb{V}$, where $\sigma[\ell \mapsto v]$ is the store that is equal to σ except (perhaps) at ℓ, where it takes the value v. We use subscripts to apply stores to locations, i.e. we write σ_ℓ instead of $\sigma\ell$. In examples we often assume $\mathbb{L} = \{a, b, c\}$ and $\mathbb{V} = \{0, 1\}$, and write stores in matrix notation, e.g. $\left(\begin{smallmatrix} a & b & c \\ 1 & 0 & 1 \end{smallmatrix}\right)$.

The language is based on a standard extension of Moggi's [30] computational lambda calculus with products and variants (labelled sums), further extended with three shared-state constructs. Many other constructs are defined using syntactic sugar, such as if-statements and booleans, let-bindings, and program sequencing. The core syntax is presented below (where $n \geq 0$):

$$G ::= (G_1 * \cdots * G_n) \mid \{\iota_1 \text{ of } G_1 \mid \cdots \mid \iota_n \text{ of } G_n\} \qquad \text{(Ground types)}$$
$$A, B ::= (A_1 * \cdots * A_n) \mid \{\iota_1 \text{ of } A_1 \mid \cdots \mid \iota_n \text{ of } A_n\} \mid A \mathrel{-}> B \qquad \text{(Types)}$$
$$V, W ::= \langle V_1, \ldots, V_n \rangle \mid \iota V \mid \lambda \mathsf{x}.\, M \qquad \text{(Values)}$$
$$M, N ::= \mathsf{x} \mid \langle M_1, \ldots, M_n \rangle \mid \iota M \mid \lambda \mathsf{x}.\, M \mid MN \qquad \text{(Terms)}$$
$$\mid \textbf{match}\, M\, \textbf{with}\, \langle \mathsf{x}_1, \ldots, \mathsf{x}_n \rangle \mathrel{-}> N$$
$$\mid \textbf{case}\, M\, \textbf{of}\, \{\iota_1\, \mathsf{x}_1 \mathrel{-}> N_1 \mid \cdots \mid \iota_n\, \mathsf{x}_n \mathrel{-}> N_n\}$$
$$\mid M? \mid M := N \mid M \parallel N$$

The typing rules for the shared-state constructs appear at the top of Fig. 1, where we define $\textbf{Loc} := \{1_1 \textbf{ of } () \mid \cdots \mid 1_{\bar{n}} \textbf{ of } ()\}$ and $\textbf{Val} := \{v_1 \textbf{ of } () \mid \cdots \mid v_{\bar{m}} \textbf{ of } ()\}$.

The language is equipped with a call-by-value, small-step operational semantics $\sigma, M \rightsquigarrow \rho, N$, meaning that the program M executed from store σ progresses to N with store ρ. The operational semantics for the shared-state constructs appears at the bottom of Fig. 1. Parallel execution is interpreted via a standard interleaving semantics, ultimately returning the pair of the results of each side, and synchronizing on their completion. The reflexive-transitive closure of $\rightsquigarrow$ is denoted by $\rightsquigarrow*$. The operational semantics can be seen in action in Example 2.

2.1 Global-State (for Sequential Computation)

To make this exposition more accessible, we focus on sequential computation before advancing to denotational semantics of concurrent computation. Sequential computations with global state cause two kinds of side-effects: looking a

$$\boxed{\Gamma \vdash M : A}$$

$$\frac{\Gamma \vdash M : \mathbf{Loc}}{\Gamma \vdash M? : \mathbf{Val}} \qquad \frac{\Gamma \vdash M : \mathbf{Loc} \qquad \Gamma \vdash N : \mathbf{Val}}{\Gamma \vdash M := N : ()} \qquad \frac{\Gamma \vdash M : A \qquad \Gamma \vdash N : B}{\Gamma \vdash M \parallel N : (A * B)}$$

$$\boxed{\sigma, M \rightsquigarrow \sigma', M'}$$

$$\frac{\sigma, M \rightsquigarrow \sigma', M'}{\sigma, M? \rightsquigarrow \sigma', M'?} \qquad \overline{\sigma, \ell? \rightsquigarrow \sigma, \sigma_\ell} \qquad \frac{\sigma, M \rightsquigarrow \sigma', M'}{\sigma, M := N \rightsquigarrow \sigma', M' := N}$$

$$\frac{\sigma, N \rightsquigarrow \sigma', N'}{\sigma, V := N \rightsquigarrow \sigma', V := N'} \qquad \overline{\sigma, \ell := v \rightsquigarrow \sigma\,[\ell \mapsto v]\,, \langle\rangle} \qquad \frac{\sigma, M \rightsquigarrow \sigma', M'}{\sigma, M \parallel N \rightsquigarrow \sigma', M' \parallel N}$$

$$\frac{\sigma, N \rightsquigarrow \sigma', N'}{\sigma, M \parallel N \rightsquigarrow \sigma', M \parallel N'} \qquad \overline{\sigma, V \parallel W \rightsquigarrow \sigma, \langle V, W \rangle}$$

Fig. 1. Typing and operational semantics of the shared-state constructs.

value up in the store, and updating a value in the store. Plotkin and Power [34] propose a corresponding equational theory with two operators:

Lookup. Suppose $\ell \in \mathbb{L}$, and $(t_v)_{v \in \mathbb{V}}$ is a $\mathbb{V}$-indexed sequence of terms. Then $L_\ell\,(t_v)_{v \in \mathbb{V}}$ is a term representing looking the value in ℓ up, calling it v, and continuing the computation with t_v. We write $L_\ell\,(v.\,t_v)$ instead of $L_\ell\,(t_v)_{v \in \mathbb{V}}$.

Update. Suppose $\ell \in \mathbb{L}$, $v \in \mathbb{V}$, and t is a term. Then $U_{\ell,v}t$ is a term representing updating the value in ℓ to v and continuing the computation with t.

The equations of the theory of global-state are generated by taking the closure of the axioms – listed at the top of Fig. 2 – under reflexivity, symmetry, transitivity, and substitution. The grayed-out axioms happen to be derivable, and are included for presentation's sake. The theory of global-state can be used to define adequate denotational semantics for the sequential fragment of our language, obtained by removing concurrent execution ($\parallel$).

Example 1. Global-state includes the following Eq. (1) which, when considering sequential programs, represents the program equivalence (2):

$$L_b\,(v.\,U_{a,v}L_c\,(w.\,U_{a,w}\,\langle\rangle)) = L_c\,(w.\,U_{a,w}\,\langle\rangle) \tag{1}$$

$$a := b?\,;\,a := c? \cong a := c? \tag{2}$$

2.2   Shared-State

The equivalence (2) from Example 1 fails in the concurrent setting, since the two program can be differentiated by program contexts with concurrency:

Global-State

UL-det	$U_{\ell,w} L_\ell (v.\, x_v) = U_{\ell,w} x_w$	
UU-last	$U_{\ell,v} U_{\ell,w} x = U_{\ell,w} x$	
LU-noop	$L_\ell (v.\, U_{\ell,v} x) = x$	
LL-diag	$L_\ell (v.\, L_\ell (w.\, x_{v,w})) = L_\ell (v.\, x_{v,v})$	
UU-comm	$U_{\ell,v} U_{\ell',w} x = U_{\ell',w} U_{\ell,v} x$	$\ell \neq \ell'$
LU-comm	$L_\ell (v.\, U_{\ell',w} x_v) = U_{\ell',w} L_\ell (v.\, x_v)$	$\ell \neq \ell'$
LL-comm	$L_\ell (v.\, L_{\ell'} (w.\, x_{v,w})) = L_{\ell'} (w.\, L_\ell (v.\, x_{v,w}))$	

Non-Determinism

ND-return	$\bigvee_{\iota<1} x = x$	
ND-epi	$\bigvee_{j<\beta} x_j = \bigvee_{\iota<\alpha} x_{\varphi\iota}$	surjective $\varphi : \alpha \to \beta$
ND-join	$\bigvee_{\iota<\alpha} \bigvee_{j<\beta_\iota} x_{\iota,j} = \bigvee_{j<\sum_{\iota<\alpha} \beta_\iota} x_{\varphi j}$	bijective $\varphi : \sum_{\iota<\alpha} \beta_\iota \to \coprod_{\iota<\alpha} \beta_\iota$

Interaction with Non-Determinism

ND-L	$\bigvee_{\iota<\alpha} L_\ell (v.\, x_{v,\iota}) = L_\ell (v.\, \bigvee_{\iota<\alpha} x_{v,\iota})$
ND-U	$\bigvee_{\iota<\alpha} U_{\ell,v} x_\iota = U_{\ell,v} \bigvee_{\iota<\alpha} x_\iota$
ND-Y	$\bigvee_{\iota<\alpha} Y x_\iota = Y \bigvee_{\iota<\alpha} x_\iota$

Fig. 2. The axiomatization of the algebraic theory

Example 2. Consider the program context $\Xi\,[-] = [-] \parallel \mathsf{a?}$, i.e. executing each program in parallel to a thread dereferencing the location a. Then there is no execution of $\Xi\,[\mathsf{a} := \mathsf{c?}]$ that starts with the store $\left(\begin{smallmatrix}\mathsf{a}&\mathsf{b}&\mathsf{c}\\1&0&1\end{smallmatrix}\right)$ and returns $\langle\langle\rangle, 0\rangle$, but there is such a execution of $\Xi\,[\mathsf{a} := \mathsf{b?}\,;\,\mathsf{a} := \mathsf{c?}]$:

$$\left(\begin{smallmatrix}\mathsf{a}&\mathsf{b}&\mathsf{c}\\1&0&1\end{smallmatrix}\right), \mathsf{a} := \mathsf{b?}\,;\,\mathsf{a} := \mathsf{c?} \parallel \mathsf{a?} \rightsquigarrow^* \left(\begin{smallmatrix}\mathsf{a}&\mathsf{b}&\mathsf{c}\\0&0&1\end{smallmatrix}\right), \mathsf{a} := \mathsf{c?} \parallel \mathsf{a?} \rightsquigarrow$$

$$\left(\begin{smallmatrix}\mathsf{a}&\mathsf{b}&\mathsf{c}\\0&0&1\end{smallmatrix}\right), \mathsf{a} := \mathsf{c?} \parallel 0 \rightsquigarrow^* \left(\begin{smallmatrix}\mathsf{a}&\mathsf{b}&\mathsf{c}\\1&0&1\end{smallmatrix}\right), \langle\rangle \parallel 0 \rightsquigarrow \left(\begin{smallmatrix}\mathsf{a}&\mathsf{b}&\mathsf{c}\\1&0&1\end{smallmatrix}\right), \langle\langle\rangle, 0\rangle$$

Therefore, the aforementioned denotational semantics defined using the theory of global-state cannot be extended with a denotation for $(\parallel)$ while preserving adequacy. More sophistication is needed in the concurrent setting: the denotations, even of sequential programs, must account for environment effects.

We thus extend the global-state theory with a single unary operator:

Yield. Suppose t is a term. Then Yt is a term. Its intended meaning is to let the environment read and write and then continue with the computation t.

We also need to account for the non-determinism inherent in parallel executions. We do so by extending the resulting theory with operators for finite non-determinism with their equational theory, and further standard equations axiomatizing commutative interaction with the other operators [14]:

Choice. For every $\alpha \in \mathbb{N}$ there is a respective choice operator. Suppose $(t_\iota)_{\iota<\alpha}$ is a sequence of terms $t_0, \ldots, t_{\alpha-1}$. Then $\bigvee_\alpha (t_\iota)_{\iota<\alpha}$ is a term. Its intended meaning is to choose $\iota < \alpha$ non-deterministically and continue with the computation t_ι. We write $\bigvee_{\iota<\alpha} t_\iota$ instead of $\bigvee_\alpha (t_\iota)_{\iota<\alpha}$; and when $\alpha = 2$ we use infix notation, i.e. instead of $\bigvee_{\iota<2} t_\iota$ we may write $t_0 \vee t_1$.

The axioms of the resulting theory of resumptions RES [1,14,30] are listed in Fig. 2. The novelty is not in the equational theory, but rather in the way we use it to define denotations. We compare to related work in Sect. 7.

2.3 Denotations

In Sect. 5 we define denotations of programs, but for the sake of this discussion we simplify, defining the denotation $[\![M]\!]$ of a program M to be an equivalence class $|t|$ of a particular term t in RES. Our actual denotations defined in Sect. 5 will use the concrete representation of the monad (developed in Sect. 4.3), similar to how state transformers represent equivalence classes of terms of global-state.

Dereference & Assignment. We use the monadic bind $)\!\!\!=$ (defined in Sect. 4.3), which we can think of as "sequencing"; and *possible yields* $Y^? t \eqcirc t \vee Yt$:

$$[\![M?]\!] := [\![M]\!])\!\!\!= \lambda\ell. \left| L_\ell \left(v. Y^? v \right) \right|$$

$$[\![M := N]\!] := [\![M]\!])\!\!\!= \lambda\ell. [\![N]\!])\!\!\!= \lambda v. \left| U_{\ell,v} Y^? \langle\rangle \right|$$

The main idea is to intersperse possible yields to block the use of global-state equations such as in (1) and to allow computations to interleave. Although Eq. (1) still holds in RES, it does not imply the program equivalence (2) because the programs in (2) do not map to the algebraic terms in (1). Rather:

Example 3. The denotations of the programs in Example 1 are:

$$[\![a := c?]\!] = \left| L_c \left(v. Y^? v \right) \right|)\!\!\!= \lambda v. \left| U_{a,v} Y^? \langle\rangle \right| = \left| L_c \left(v. Y^? U_{a,v} Y^? \langle\rangle \right) \right| \qquad (3)$$

$$[\![a := b? \, ; \, a := c?]\!] = \left| L_b \left(w. Y^? U_{a,w} Y^? L_c \left(v. Y^? U_{a,v} Y^? \langle\rangle \right) \right) \right| \qquad (4)$$

So the denotation (3) looks c up finding a value v, then possibly yields, then updates a to v, then possibly yields, and finally returns the empty tuple. The concrete representation (Theorem 1) immediately proves that (3) and (4) are not equal, in contrast to the situation in Example 1.

Parallel Execution. Computations interleave using the yield operator. Interleaving execution of programs suggests, for example, the following calculation:

$$[\![\ell? \parallel \ell := 0]\!] = \left| L_\ell \left(v. Y^? [\![v \parallel \ell := 0]\!] \right) \vee U_{\ell,0} Y^? [\![\ell? \parallel \langle\rangle]\!] \right|$$

$$= \left| L_\ell \left(v. Y^? U_{\ell,0} Y^? [\![v \parallel \langle\rangle]\!] \right) \vee U_{\ell,0} Y^? L_\ell \left(v. Y^? [\![v \parallel \langle\rangle]\!] \right) \right|$$

$$= \left| L_\ell \left(v. Y^? U_{\ell,0} Y^? \langle v, \langle\rangle\rangle \right) \vee U_{\ell,0} Y^? L_\ell \left(v. Y^? \langle v, \langle\rangle\rangle \right) \right|$$

The problem with the above is that is lacks compositionality: $[\![\ell? \parallel \ell := 0]\!]$ should be defined in terms of $[\![\ell?]\!]$ and $[\![\ell := 0]\!]$, without referring to the underlying programs. In Sect. 4.6 we define a function $(\|\|\|)$ such that $[\![M \parallel N]\!] = [\![M]\!] \, \|\|\| \, [\![N]\!]$. This definition relies on the concrete representation from Sect. 4.3.

2.4   Program Transformations

Our main result is directional adequacy (Theorem 5). Under this simplified view it can be stated, in terms of the partial-order on our denotations generated by $|t| \leqslant |t \vee s|$, as follows: if $[\![M]\!] \leqslant [\![N]\!]$ then the transformation $N \twoheadrightarrow M$ is valid in the concurrent setting. The following example illustrates how directional-adequacy can be used to validate program transformations of interest, of the relatively few that are valid in the strong memory-model we consider here.

Example 4. We validate (write ; read) (see also Example 9):

$$[\![\ell := v \, ; \, \ell?]\!] = \left| U_{\ell,v} Y^? L_\ell \left(w. \, Y^? w \right) \right| \geqslant \left| U_{\ell,v} L_\ell \left(w. \, Y^? w \right) \right| = \left| U_{\ell,v} Y^? v \right| = [\![\ell := v \, ; \, v]\!]$$

We can similarly validate the other memory access eliminations from Sect. 1. By using $Y^?$ rather than Y in the denotations, the cases where the environment is known to not interleave are taken into accounted explicitly. The relevant global-state equation can then be exploited to eliminate the redundant memory access.

2.5   Caveats and Limitations

Our goal in this work is to fit concurrency semantics on equal footing with other semantic models of computational effects. As a consequence, the proposed model has its fair share of fine print, which we bring to the front:

Memory Model. We study a very strong memory model: sequential consistency. Modern architectures adhere to much weaker memory-models, where further program transformations are valid.

Concurrency Model. Our semantics involves a simple form of concurrency in which threads interleave their computation without restriction, acting on a shared memory store. This is in contrast to a well-established line of work in which models include a causal partial-order in which incomparable events denote "truly" parallel execution [31]. These causal models are showing promise in modelling sophisticated (i.e. weak) shared-state models [7,16,17,25]. We hope further work would fit these causal models into a relatable semantic footing that easily accommodates higher-order structure.

Features. Our analysis lacks many valuable features that appear in related work, such as recursion [1], higher-order state [4], probabilities [41], and infinitely many locations/values. This simplification is intended: we took to reductionism, finding a minimal model still accounting for core features of shared state. The benefit of the algebraic approach is that this model can be modularly combined with other features, hopefully using standard technology such as sum-and-tensor [14], domain-enrichment [27], and functor categories [21,32,33,38]. For example, to support recursion our model may be integrated with one of the known powerdomain theory-combinators [42]. This requires making a semantic-design choice that is orthogonal to shared-state concurrency, each with different trade-offs. We avoid making such choices.

Semantic Precision. The equational theory and denotational semantics based on it leave much room for improvement in terms of precision and abstraction. For example, our denotational model does not support the *introduction* of irrelevant reads, i.e. it does not justify the valid transformation $M \twoheadrightarrow \ell? \,;\, M$. Indeed, taking $M = \langle\rangle$, we have $[\![\ell? \,;\, \langle\rangle]\!] = \left| L_\ell \left(v.\, Y^? \langle\rangle\right)\right| = \left|Y^? \langle\rangle\right| \nleqslant |\langle\rangle| = [\![\langle\rangle]\!]$. The problem stems from a "counting" issue: even though the value being looked-up in ℓ is discarded, the additional possible-yield remains. We hope further work could address this semantic inaccuracy.

Full Abstraction. Brookes's seminal work [1,6] defined denotational semantics for concurrency that is fully-abstract, meaning that the converse of adequacy holds: programs that are replaceable in every context have equal denotations. Our semantics is far from being fully-abstract: there is a first-order valid equivalence, $M \cong \ell? \,;\, M$, that our semantics does not support. Moreover, we do not include atomic block executions in our language as Brookes did, which was crucial for the proof of full-abstraction. However, even if our model was precise enough to capture the first-order equivalences, and even if we were to include atomic block executions, we still would not expect to obtain full-abstraction, since this result is infamously elusive for higher-order languages (see Abramsky's recent overview on the full-abstraction problem of PCF [2]).

3   Equational Theory

At the foundation of our approach is the equational theory of resumptions RES [1, 14,30] presented in Sect. 2, consisting of operators and equational axioms over them. We succinctly fill-in the formalities below, followed by related definitions.

The signature of RES consists of the following parameterized operators. The notation $O : A \langle P \rangle$ means that the arity of the operator O is the set A and it is parameterized over the set P:

$L : \mathbb{V} \langle \mathbb{L} \rangle$ lookup $Y : \mathbb{1} \langle \mathbb{1} \rangle$ yield

$U : \mathbb{1} \langle \mathbb{L} \times \mathbb{V} \rangle$ update $\bigvee_\alpha : \alpha \langle \mathbb{1} \rangle$ non-deterministic choice for every $\alpha \in \mathbb{N}$

From now on, whenever we refer to an *operator*, we mean an operator of RES. We denote the set of terms freely generated by the signature over X by $\mathrm{Term}X$.

Figure 2 lists the axioms of RES, classified as follows: an axiomatization of the equational theory of global-state [34]; the standard axiomatization of non-determinism; and an axiomatization of the commutative interaction of non-determinism with the other operators [13] via the tensor [14].

A RES-*algebra* $\mathcal{A}$ consists of a carrier set $\underline{A}$ together with interpretations $\tilde{O}^{\mathcal{A}} : \underline{A}^A \times P \to \underline{A}$ for each operator $O : A \langle P \rangle$. We elide the superscript if it is clear from context. For a set X, a RES-*algebra on X* consists of a RES-algebra $\mathcal{A}$ and a function $\mathrm{env} : X \to \underline{A}$; which extends to $\mathrm{eval} : \mathrm{Term}X \to \underline{A}$ homomorphically along the inclusion $X \hookrightarrow \mathrm{Term}X$. A RES-*model on X* is a RES-algebra on X that satisfies each axiom of RES, i.e. the same element of $\underline{A}$ is obtained by applying eval to either side of the axiom.

In the following, we abbreviate using $\vec{L}\left(\sigma.\, t_\sigma\right) := L_{1_1}\left(v_1.\, \ldots L_{1_{\bar{n}}}\left(v_{\bar{n}}.\, t_{\lambda 1_i.\, v_i}\right)\right)$ and $\vec{U}_\sigma t := U_{1_1, \sigma_{1_1}} \ldots U_{1_{\bar{n}}, \sigma_{1_{\bar{n}}}} t$, in addition to $Y^? t := t \vee Yt$ that we saw in Sect. 2.3. For example, $\vec{L}\left(\sigma.\, \vec{U}_{\left(\begin{smallmatrix} a & b & c \\ 1 & 0 & \sigma_b \end{smallmatrix}\right)} Y^? t_{\sigma_c}\right) = L_a\left(v.\, L_b\left(w.\, L_c\left(u.\, U_{a,1} U_{b,0} U_{c,w}\left(t_u \vee Yt_u\right)\right)\right)\right)$.
We use similar shorthands with interpretations of operators as well.

4   A Monad for Shared-State

The next part in our denotational semantics is a monad whose elements represent equivalence classes of RES. The monad can be obtained via a universal construction [28] (by quotienting the terms by the equational theory), but a concrete representation is crucial to reason about it; for example, to show that two denotations are different.

4.1   Difficulty of Term Normalization

To motivate the definitions building up to this concrete representation, we first find a representative for each equivalence class in $\mathrm{Term}X/\mathrm{RES}$, by taking an arbitrary $t \in \mathrm{Term}X$ and transforming it via equations in RES to a particular form – a normal form – such that there is only one term of this form equal to t.

Consider an algebraic term $t \in \mathrm{Term}X$. Using LU-noop once for each location, a sequence of LU-comm, and ND-return, we find that $t = \vec{L}\left(\sigma.\, \bigvee_{i<1} \vec{U}_\sigma t\right)$. Note:

$$\vec{U}_\sigma L_\ell\left(v.\, s_v\right) \overset{\mathrm{RES}}{=} \vec{U}_\sigma s_{\sigma_\ell} \qquad \vec{U}_\sigma U_{\ell, v} s \overset{\mathrm{RES}}{=} \vec{U}_{\sigma[\ell \mapsto v]} s \qquad \vec{U}_\sigma \bigvee_{i<\alpha} s_i \overset{\mathrm{RES}}{=} \bigvee_{i<\alpha} \vec{U}_\sigma s_i$$

By applying these equalities left-to-right as long as possible, and applying ND-join and ND-epi to rearrange the sums, we find that t is equal to a term of the form $\vec{L}\left(\sigma.\, \bigvee_{i<\alpha_\sigma} \vec{U}_{\rho_{i,\sigma}} s_{i,\sigma}\right)$, where $s_{i,\sigma}$ is either in X or is of the form $Y s'_{i,\sigma}$.

For every σ, we can rearrange the sum according to common prefixes, thus we find that t is equal to a term of the form: $\vec{L}\left(\sigma.\, \bigvee_{\rho \in S} \vec{U}_\rho \bigvee_{J < \alpha_{\rho, \sigma}} s_{J, \rho, \sigma}\right)$ where $s_{i, \rho, \sigma}$ is either in X or is of the form $Y s'_{i, \rho, \sigma}$ (we can take $\alpha_{\rho, \sigma} = 0$ when the prefix $\vec{U}_\rho$ did not appear in t). For every ρ, we can rearrange to obtain the form:

$$\vec{L}\left(\sigma.\, \bigvee_{\rho \in S} \vec{U}_\rho\left(Yr_{\rho, \sigma} \vee \bigvee_{J < \beta_{\rho, \sigma}} x_{J, \rho, \sigma}\right)\right) \tag{5}$$

This is not yet a normal form, which to obtain would require recursively applying this procedure to $r_{\rho, \sigma}$ and propagating empty choice operators outward. Were we to continue in this way to find a normal form, we would still need to prove uniqueness and completeness. One standard way to achieve this is to show that this procedure equates the sides of every axiom and respects the deduction rules of equational logic. This requires a careful proof-theoretic analysis of this normalization procedure. Instead, we take a model-theoretic approach, akin to normalization-by-evaluation, constructing for every set a concrete representation of the free RES-model over it. This representation is based on finite sets of traces.

4.2   Traces

Brookes [6] defined a trace to be a non-empty sequence of transitions, where a *transition* is a pairs of stores; e.g. $\langle\langle\begin{smallmatrix}a&b&c\\1&0&1\end{smallmatrix}\rangle,\langle\begin{smallmatrix}a&b&c\\0&0&1\end{smallmatrix}\rangle\rangle\,\langle\langle\begin{smallmatrix}a&b&c\\0&1&1\end{smallmatrix}\rangle,\langle\begin{smallmatrix}a&b&c\\1&0&1\end{smallmatrix}\rangle\rangle$. Brookes used traces to define a denotational semantics for an imperative concurrent programming language. In Brookes's semantics, traces denote interrupted executions, where each transition corresponds to an uninterrupted sequence of computation steps that starts with the first store and end with the second store. The breaks between transitions are where the computation yields to the environment.

The concept was adapted by many, including Benton et al. [4], to define denotational semantics for a functional language, where they have added an additional value at the end of the sequence to refer to the value the computation returns. A *trace* in this paper will refer to this concept: a non-empty sequence of transitions followed by an additional return value. If we wish to specify X as the set of the return values, we will call it an X-*trace*. For example, if $x \in X$ then $\langle\langle\begin{smallmatrix}a&b&c\\1&0&1\end{smallmatrix}\rangle,\langle\begin{smallmatrix}a&b&c\\0&0&1\end{smallmatrix}\rangle\rangle\,\langle\langle\begin{smallmatrix}a&b&c\\0&1&1\end{smallmatrix}\rangle,\langle\begin{smallmatrix}a&b&c\\1&0&1\end{smallmatrix}\rangle\rangle\,x$ is an X-trace.

For sets Y, Z, we denote by Y^* the set of sequences over Y, by Y^+ the set of non-empty sequences over Y, and $Y \cdot Z := \{yz \mid y \in Y, z \in Z\}$. That is, $(\cdot)$ is just notation for $(\times)$ which suggests that the elements of the set are written in sequence, eliding the tuple notation. Thus $(S \times S)^+ \cdot X$ is the set of X-traces.

Following our discussion in Sect. 4.1, our representation will use finite sets of traces instead of the algebraic syntax. In particular, the form we have found in (5) suggests the recursive definition:

$$\operatorname{rep} t := \{\langle\sigma, \rho\rangle \tau \mid \sigma, \rho \in S, \tau \in \operatorname{rep} r_{\rho,\sigma}\} \cup \{\langle\sigma, \rho\rangle\, x_{\jmath,\rho,\sigma} \mid \sigma, \rho \in S, \jmath < \beta_{\rho,\sigma}\} \quad (6)$$

The model-theoretic approach we use below obviates the need for the syntactic manipulation that leads to the form in (5) as part of finding the representation. In the model definition, eval will play the role of rep.

4.3   Model Definition

We represent elements of $\operatorname{Term} X/\text{RES}$ by $\underline{\mathcal{T}}X := \mathcal{P}_{\text{fin}}\left((S \times S)^+ \cdot X\right)$, i.e. finite sets of X-traces. We equip $\underline{\mathcal{T}}X$ with a RES-algebra structure $\mathcal{F}X$:

$$\tilde{\mathrm{L}}_\ell\,(v.\,P_v) := \{\langle\sigma, \rho\rangle\,\tau \mid \langle\sigma, \rho\rangle\,\tau \in P_{\sigma_\ell}\} \qquad \widetilde{\bigvee_{\imath<\alpha}} P_\imath := \bigcup_{\imath<\alpha} P_\imath$$

$$\tilde{\mathrm{U}}_{\ell,v}P := \{\langle\sigma, \rho\rangle\,\tau \mid \langle\sigma\,[\ell \mapsto v], \rho\rangle\,\tau \in P\} \qquad \tilde{\mathrm{Y}}P := \{\langle\sigma, \sigma\rangle\,\tau \mid \sigma \in S, \tau \in P\}$$

We further equip it with $\operatorname{env} x := \{\langle\sigma, \sigma\rangle\,x \mid \sigma \in S\}$ to make it a RES-algebra over X. We denote $\operatorname{env} x$ by $\operatorname{return} x$, or $\tilde{x}$ for shorthand. This RES-algebra is in fact a RES-model over X by virtue of satisfying the axioms of RES:

Example 5. We verify that $\langle\mathcal{F}X, \operatorname{return}\rangle$ satisfies the axiom LU-noop:

$$\operatorname{eval}\left(\mathrm{L}_\ell\,(v.\,\mathrm{U}_{\ell,v}x)\right) = \tilde{\mathrm{L}}_\ell\left(v.\,\tilde{\mathrm{U}}_{\ell,v}\tilde{x}\right) = \tilde{\mathrm{L}}_\ell\,(v.\,\{\langle\sigma, \sigma\,[\ell \mapsto v]\rangle\,x \mid \sigma \in S\})$$

$$= \{\langle\sigma, \sigma\,[\ell \mapsto \sigma_\ell]\rangle\,x \mid \sigma \in S\} = \{\langle\sigma, \sigma\rangle\,x \mid \sigma \in S\} = \tilde{x} = \operatorname{eval} x$$

4.4   Correspondence to Non-deterministic Global-State

The theory of non-deterministic global-state (the fragment of RES excluding
Y) admits a concrete representation using non-deterministic state transformers
$S \to \mathcal{P}_{\mathrm{fin}}(SX)$ [14]. This representation corresponds to the one we have defined
in an interesting way. Namely, there is a bijection between $\mathcal{T}X$ and the set of
functions mapping stores to finite sets of X-traces-with-the-first-store-removed:

$$\lambda P \in \mathcal{T}X. \, \lambda \sigma \in S. \, \{\rho\tau \in S \cdot (S \times S)^* \cdot X \mid \langle \sigma, \rho \rangle \tau \in P\}$$

$$\lambda \psi \in S \to \mathcal{P}_{\mathrm{fin}}(S \cdot (S \times S)^* \cdot X). \bigcup_{\sigma \in S} \{\langle \sigma, \rho \rangle \tau \in (S \times S)^+ \cdot X \mid \rho\tau \in \psi\sigma\}$$

Implicitly identifying the two, the model from Sect. 4.3 can be defined using
formulas that look exactly like the non-deterministic global-state ones:

$$\tilde{\mathrm{L}}_\ell(v. \, P_v) := \lambda\sigma. \, P_{\sigma_\ell}\sigma \qquad\qquad \bigvee_{\imath < \alpha} P_\imath := \lambda\sigma. \bigcup_{\imath < \alpha} P_\imath\sigma$$

$$\tilde{\mathrm{U}}_{\ell,v}P := \lambda\sigma. \, P(\sigma[\ell \mapsto v]) \qquad\qquad \tilde{x} := \lambda\sigma. \, \{\sigma x\}$$

However, these are not the same formulas – they are defined for different elements (sets of traces as opposed to non-deterministic state transformers).

Using this identification for the yield operator, we obtained the definition
$\tilde{\mathrm{Y}}P := \lambda\sigma. \, \{\sigma\tau \mid \tau \in P\}$, which we understand as "the thread does not modify the
state, then allows the environment to intervene, and then continues as before."

4.5   Representation Theorem

The model $\langle \mathcal{F}X, \mathrm{return} \rangle$ defined in Sect. 4.3 *represents* Term$X$/RES because –
according to the representation theorem – this is a *free* RES-model on X, and
therefore equivalent to the model of equivalence classes we used in Sect. 2 or the
model of syntactic normal forms to which we have alluded in Sect. 4.1.

To prove that the model is free we first equip the family of sets $\mathcal{T}$ with
a monad structure. For every RES-model $\mathcal{A}$ and function $f : X \to \underline{\mathcal{A}}$, define
$- \Vvdash f : \mathcal{T}X \to \underline{\mathcal{A}}$, the homomorphic extension of f along return, recursively;
where $R_P^{\langle \sigma, \rho \rangle} := \{\tau \in (S \times S)^+ \cdot X \mid \langle \sigma, \rho \rangle \tau \in P\}$ and $X_{P,f}^{\langle \sigma, \rho \rangle} := \bigvee_{\langle \sigma, \rho \rangle x \in P}^{\mathcal{A}} fx$:

$$\varnothing \Vvdash f := \bigvee_0^{\mathcal{A}} \varnothing \qquad P \Vvdash f := \vec{\tilde{\mathrm{L}}}^{\mathcal{A}} \left(\sigma. \bigvee_{\rho \in S}^{\mathcal{A}} \vec{\tilde{\mathrm{U}}}_\rho^{\mathcal{A}} \left(\tilde{\mathrm{Y}}^{\mathcal{A}} \left(R_P^{\langle \sigma, \rho \rangle} \Vvdash f \right) \tilde{\vee}^{\mathcal{A}} X_{P,f}^{\langle \sigma, \rho \rangle} \right) \right)$$

A simpler definition is available when there exists a set Y such that $\mathcal{A} = \mathcal{F}Y$:

$$\varnothing \Vvdash f := \varnothing \qquad P \Vvdash f := \{\alpha \langle \sigma, \varsigma \rangle \tau \mid \exists \rho. \, \alpha \langle \sigma, \rho \rangle x \in P \wedge \langle \rho, \varsigma \rangle \tau \in fx\}$$

The recursion is well-founded since $R_P^{\langle \sigma, \rho \rangle}$ is smaller than P when measured by
the length of the longest trace in the set.

Thus we have our monad structure $\mathcal{T} := \langle \mathcal{T}, \mathrm{return}, \Vvdash \rangle$. We show it is induced
by the aforementioned family of free RES-models:

Theorem 1 (Representation for shared-state). *The pair $\langle \mathcal{F}X, return \rangle$ is a free* RES-*model on X: for every* RES-*model $\mathcal{A}$ and $f : X \to \underline{\mathcal{A}}$, the function $-\,\rangle\!\!= f : \mathcal{T}X \to \underline{\mathcal{A}}$ is the unique homomorphism g satisfying $f = g \circ return$.*

As a direct consequence:

Corollary 1 (Model is sound and complete). *Terms over X are equal in* RES *iff they have the same representation in $\langle \mathcal{F}X, return \rangle$.*

4.6 Synchronization

To define the denotational semantics of ($\|$) in Sect. 5, we will define a corresponding function ($\|\|$) on elements of the monad. To this end we first define the *trace synchronization*, an inductively defined relation $\tau_1 \parallel \tau_2 \Rightarrow \tau$ presented below, that relates $\tau_i \in (\mathbb{S} \times \mathbb{S})^+ \cdot X_i$ and $\tau \in (\mathbb{S} \times \mathbb{S})^+ \cdot (X_1 \times X_2)$, representing the fact that τ_1 and τ_2 can synchronize to form τ:

$$\boxed{\tau \parallel \pi \Rightarrow \omega} \qquad \frac{}{\langle \sigma, \rho \rangle\, x \parallel \langle \rho, \varsigma \rangle\, \beta y \Rightarrow \langle \sigma, \varsigma \rangle\, \beta \langle x, y \rangle} \text{ (VAR-LEFT)}$$

$$\frac{\tau \parallel \pi \Rightarrow \omega}{\langle \sigma, \rho \rangle\, \tau \parallel \pi \Rightarrow \langle \sigma, \rho \rangle\, \omega} \text{ (BRK-LEFT)} \qquad \frac{\tau \parallel \pi \Rightarrow \langle \rho, \varsigma \rangle\, \omega}{\langle \sigma, \rho \rangle\, \tau \parallel \pi \Rightarrow \langle \sigma, \varsigma \rangle\, \omega} \text{ (SEQ-LEFT)}$$

Symmetrically: (VAR-RIGHT)   (BRK-RIGHT)   (SEQ-RIGHT)

One way to understand these rules is to concentrate on the first transition on the left trace $\tau_1 = \langle \sigma, \rho \rangle\, \tau'_1$; the right-sided rules are treated symmetrically. If the first transition is also the last, i.e. $\tau'_1 \in X$, then ρ must be the initial store when the execution continues (recall that only a break *between transitions* reflects a yield to the environment). This is why VAR-LEFT combines the transitions as it does. The value in τ_3 is the pair of the values in τ_1 and τ_2, reflecting the operational semantics of ($\|$) returning the pair of the results. If, on the other hand, the first transition is not the last, then we may combine the transition with the continuation of the computation (SEQ-LEFT), or we may not (BRK-LEFT). The first option means the yield was used-up in this synchronization; while in the second option yield remains available to ambient synchronizations.

From this relation we derive the *semantic synchronization* function:

$$(\|\|) : \mathcal{T}X \times \mathcal{T}Y \to \mathcal{T}(X \times Y) \qquad P \parallel\!\!\!\parallel Q := \{\omega \mid \exists \tau \in P, \pi \in Q.\ \tau \parallel \pi \Rightarrow \omega\}$$

Example 6. For $\sigma, \rho \in \mathbb{S}$, we may synchronize $\langle \sigma, \rho \rangle\, \langle \rho, \sigma \rangle\, \langle\rangle$ and $\langle \rho, \rho \rangle\, 0$ so:

$$\cfrac{\cfrac{}{\langle \rho, \sigma \rangle\, \langle\rangle \parallel \langle \rho, \rho \rangle\, 0 \Rightarrow \langle \rho, \sigma \rangle\, \langle\langle\rangle, 0\rangle} \text{ VAR-RIGHT}}{\langle \sigma, \rho \rangle\, \langle \rho, \sigma \rangle\, \langle\rangle \parallel \langle \rho, \rho \rangle\, 0 \Rightarrow \langle \sigma, \sigma \rangle\, \langle\langle\rangle, 0\rangle} \text{ SEQ-LEFT}$$

Therefore, if $\langle \sigma, \rho \rangle \langle \rho, \sigma \rangle \langle \rangle \in P$ and $\langle \rho, \rho \rangle \, 0 \in Q$, then $\langle \sigma, \sigma \rangle \langle \langle \rangle, 0 \rangle \in P \mathbin{|||} Q$.

The use of SEQ-LEFT was possible since the stores happen to match, resulting in a trace that does not allow the environment to interfere. By using BRK-LEFT we could find a different synchronization, one that does yield to the environment.

5   Denotational Semantics

With the monad in place, denotations of types and contexts are standard [30]:

$$\llbracket (A_1 * \cdots * A_n) \rrbracket := \llbracket A_1 \rrbracket \times \cdots \times \llbracket A_n \rrbracket \qquad \llbracket A \to B \rrbracket := \llbracket A \rrbracket \to \mathcal{T} \llbracket B \rrbracket$$
$$\llbracket \{\iota_1 \text{ of } A_1 \mid \cdots \mid \iota_n \text{ of } A_n \} \rrbracket := \bigcup_{i=1}^{n} \{\iota_i\} \times \llbracket A_i \rrbracket \qquad \llbracket \Gamma \rrbracket := \prod_{(x:A)\in\Gamma} \llbracket A \rrbracket$$

Define the extension of $\gamma \in \llbracket \Gamma \rrbracket$ to $\gamma \, [x \mapsto y] \in \llbracket \Gamma, x : A \rrbracket$ by $\gamma \, [x \mapsto y] \, x := y$.

On the above we base two kinds of denotations for programs $\Gamma \vdash M : A$:

Computational. $\llbracket M \rrbracket^c : \llbracket \Gamma \rrbracket \to \mathcal{T} \llbracket A \rrbracket$. When Γ is empty we may write $\llbracket M \rrbracket^c$ instead of $\llbracket M \rrbracket^c \langle \rangle$. We write $\llbracket M \rrbracket^c \subseteq \llbracket N \rrbracket^c$ for $\forall \gamma \in \llbracket \Gamma \rrbracket$. $\llbracket M \rrbracket^c \gamma \subseteq \llbracket N \rrbracket^c \gamma$.

Valuational. $\llbracket V \rrbracket^v : \llbracket \Gamma \rrbracket \to \llbracket A \rrbracket$ defined solely for values, and satisfying $\llbracket V \rrbracket^c \gamma = \text{return} \, (\llbracket V \rrbracket^v \gamma)$. When Γ is empty we may write $\llbracket V \rrbracket^v$ instead of $\llbracket V \rrbracket^v \langle \rangle$; and if furthermore A is a ground type, we may write V instead of $\llbracket V \rrbracket^v$, noting that the restriction of $\llbracket - \rrbracket^v$ to closed programs of ground type is a bijection.

Most denotations of programs are standard as well, such as:

$$\llbracket \langle \rangle \rrbracket^v \gamma := \langle \rangle \qquad\qquad \llbracket \lambda x. \, M \rrbracket^v \gamma := \lambda y. \; \llbracket M \rrbracket^c \gamma \, [x \mapsto y]$$
$$\llbracket x \rrbracket^v \gamma := \gamma x \qquad\qquad \llbracket NM \rrbracket^c \gamma := \llbracket N \rrbracket^c \gamma \mathbin{\!\!\rangle\!\!=} \lambda f. \; \llbracket M \rrbracket^c \gamma \mathbin{\!\!\rangle\!\!=} f$$

The denotations of the state effects allow the environment to intervene:

$$\llbracket M? \rrbracket^c \gamma := \llbracket M \rrbracket^c \gamma \mathbin{\!\!\rangle\!\!=} \lambda \ell. \; \tilde{L}_\ell \left(v. \; \tilde{Y}^? \tilde{v} \right)$$
$$\llbracket M := N \rrbracket^c \gamma := \llbracket M \rrbracket^c \gamma \mathbin{\!\!\rangle\!\!=} \lambda \ell. \; \llbracket N \rrbracket^c \gamma \mathbin{\!\!\rangle\!\!=} \lambda v. \; \tilde{U}_{\ell,v} \tilde{Y}^? \tilde{\langle \rangle}$$
$$\llbracket M \parallel N \rrbracket^c \gamma := \llbracket M \rrbracket^c \gamma \mathbin{|||} \llbracket N \rrbracket^c \gamma$$

Example 7. With the definitions above, we can state the denotations from Example 3 precisely. For instance, (4) becomes:

$$\llbracket a := b? \, ; \, a := c? \rrbracket^c = \tilde{L}_b \left(w. \; \tilde{Y}^? \tilde{U}_{a,w} \tilde{Y}^? \tilde{L}_c \left(v. \; \tilde{Y}^? \tilde{U}_{a,v} \tilde{Y}^? \tilde{\langle \rangle} \right) \right)$$

Example 8. We can explain the execution of a := b? ; a := c? ∥ a? from Example 2 in denotational terms. First we find traces to synchronize:

$$\langle (\begin{smallmatrix} a & b & c \\ 1 & 0 & 1 \end{smallmatrix}), (\begin{smallmatrix} a & b & c \\ 0 & 0 & 1 \end{smallmatrix}) \rangle \, \langle (\begin{smallmatrix} a & b & c \\ 0 & 0 & 1 \end{smallmatrix}), (\begin{smallmatrix} a & b & c \\ 1 & 0 & 1 \end{smallmatrix}) \rangle \, \langle \rangle \in \llbracket a := b? \, ; \, a := c? \rrbracket^c$$
$$\langle (\begin{smallmatrix} a & b & c \\ 0 & 0 & 1 \end{smallmatrix}), (\begin{smallmatrix} a & b & c \\ 0 & 0 & 1 \end{smallmatrix}) \rangle \, 0 \in \llbracket a? \rrbracket^c$$

Following from the derivation in Example 6 with $\sigma = (\begin{smallmatrix} a & b & c \\ 1 & 0 & 1 \end{smallmatrix})$ and $\rho = (\begin{smallmatrix} a & b & c \\ 0 & 0 & 1 \end{smallmatrix})$:

$$\langle (\begin{smallmatrix} a & b & c \\ 1 & 0 & 1 \end{smallmatrix}), (\begin{smallmatrix} a & b & c \\ 1 & 0 & 1 \end{smallmatrix}) \rangle \, \langle 0, \langle \rangle \rangle \in \llbracket a := b? \, ; \, a := c? \parallel a? \rrbracket^c$$

This trace corresponds to the (uninterrupted) execution presented in Example 2.

6   Metatheoretical Results

First we find that the single-transition traces in the denotation of a program account for the possible executions of that program:

Theorem 2 (Soundness). *If $\sigma, M \rightsquigarrow* \rho, V$ then $\langle \sigma, \rho \rangle \llbracket V \rrbracket^v \in \llbracket M \rrbracket^c$.*

For the proof, omitted for brevity, we instrument the operational-semantics with *actions*, elements of $\{U_{\ell,v}, L_\ell, \varepsilon\}$ signifying the effect caused by the step, to analyse the change to the denotation of the program as it runs.

Working our way up to the fundamental lemma, we define a unary logical relation: functions $\mathcal{V}(\!|-|\!)$ and $\mathcal{E}(\!|-|\!)$ from types to sets of closed programs by mutual recursion. Specifically, $\mathcal{V}(\!|A|\!)$ is a set of closed values of type A, and $\mathcal{E}(\!|A|\!)$ is a set of closed programs of type A. The definition of $\mathcal{V}(\!|-|\!)$ is standard:

$$\mathcal{V}(\!|A \to B|\!) := \{\lambda x. M \mid \forall V \in \mathcal{V}(\!|A|\!). M[V/x] \in \mathcal{E}(\!|B|\!)\}$$
$$\mathcal{V}(\!|(A_1 * \cdots * A_n)|\!) := \{\langle V_1, \ldots, V_n \rangle \mid \forall i. V_i \in \mathcal{V}(\!|A_i|\!)\}$$
$$\mathcal{V}(\!|\{\iota_1 \text{ of } A_1 \mid \cdots \mid \iota_n \text{ of } A_n\}|\!) := \bigcup_i \{\iota_i V \mid V \in \mathcal{V}(\!|A_i|\!)\}$$

The definition of $\mathcal{E}(\!|-|\!)$ is also standard in that it ensures programs in $\mathcal{E}(\!|A|\!)$ compute to values in $\mathcal{V}(\!|A|\!)$, but bespoke in its requirement about *how* they compute. This requirement is based on the way traces specify interrupted executions, a notion we have discussed in Sect. 4.2 and now make precise. For a non-empty sequences $\alpha = \langle \sigma_1, \rho_1 \rangle \ldots \langle \sigma_m, \rho_m \rangle$ we write $M \xrightarrow{\alpha} N$ when there exist $M = M_1, M_2 \ldots M_m, M_{m+1} = N$ such that $\sigma_i, M_i \rightsquigarrow* \rho_i, M_{i+1}$ for all $i \in \{1, \ldots, m\}$. We write $M \xrightarrow{\alpha x} V$ when $M \xrightarrow{\alpha} V$ and $\llbracket V \rrbracket^v = x$. We now define:

$$\mathcal{E}(\!|A|\!) := \left\{ M \in \cdot \vdash A \mid \forall \tau \in \llbracket M \rrbracket^c \, \exists V \in \mathcal{V}(\!|A|\!). M \xrightarrow{\tau} V \right\}$$

The last component needed is the function $\mathcal{G}(\!|-|\!)$ from typing contexts to sets of program substitutions: $\mathcal{G}(\!|\Gamma|\!) := \{\Theta \mid \forall (x : A) \in \Gamma. \Theta x \in \mathcal{V}(\!|A|\!)\}$ The *semantic typing judgment* $\Gamma \models M : A$ is then defined as: $\forall \Theta \in \mathcal{G}(\!|\Gamma|\!). \Theta M \in \mathcal{E}(\!|A|\!)$

Theorem 3 (Fundamental Lemma). *If $\Gamma \vdash M : A$ then $\Gamma \models M : A$.*

This brings us one step closer to proving the theorem of directional adequacy. One piece is still missing: since the theorem assumes set inclusion of denotations rather than equality, we will need a different form of compositionality of the denotations than the one that holds by definition.

To state this form of compositionality we first define the standard notion of a program with holes. A function $\Xi [-] : \Gamma \vdash A \to \Delta \vdash B$ is a *program context* (or *context* for short) if, in the language extended with a program $\bullet$ and additional axioms $\Gamma' \vdash \bullet : A$ for all $\Gamma' \geq \Gamma$, we have $\Delta \vdash \Xi [\bullet] : B$; and if $\Gamma \vdash M : A$, then $\Xi [M]$ is obtained from $\Xi [\bullet]$ by replacing every occurrence of $\bullet$ with M.

Theorem 4 (Compositionality). *Let $\Xi[-] : \Gamma \vdash A \to \cdot \vdash G$ be a context for ground G, and $M, N \in \Gamma \vdash A$. If $[\![M]\!]^c \subseteq [\![N]\!]^c$ then $[\![\Xi[M]]\!]^c \subseteq [\![\Xi[N]]\!]^c$.*

The condition that the context be closed and ground is necessary, so an attempt to prove directly by induction on the structure of the context fails. The proof, omitted for brevity, instead uses a binary logical relation approximating containment that identifies with it on ground types; the main ingredient being:

$$\mathcal{E}^\circ (\!|A|\!) := \{ \langle P, Q \rangle \in \mathcal{T}[\![A]\!] \times \mathcal{T}[\![A]\!] \mid \forall \, \alpha x \in P \, \exists \, \beta y \in Q. \, \alpha = \beta \wedge \langle x, y \rangle \in \mathcal{V}^\circ (\!|A|\!) \}$$

With this compositionality in hand we are finally ready to prove the main result of this paper, that we will then use to justify program transformation. To state it we first spell out the standard definition of contextual refinement.

Suppose that $M, N \in \Gamma \vdash A$. We say that M *refines* N, and write $M \sqsubseteq N$, if $\sigma, \Xi[M] \leadsto_* \rho, V$ implies $\sigma, \Xi[N] \leadsto_* \rho, V$ whenever $\Xi[-] : \Gamma \vdash A \to \cdot \vdash G$ is a context for ground G. This justifies the transformation $N \twoheadrightarrow M$, since replacing N with M within a larger program introduces no additional behaviours.

Theorem 5 (Directional Adequacy). *If $[\![M]\!]^c \subseteq [\![N]\!]^c$ then $M \sqsubseteq N$.*

Proof. Let $\Xi[-] : \Gamma \vdash A \to \cdot \vdash G$ be a program context for some ground G, and assume $\sigma, \Xi[M] \leadsto_* \rho, V$ for some V. By soundness, $\langle \sigma, \rho \rangle [\![V]\!]^v \in [\![\Xi[M]]\!]^c$. Using compositionality, by assumption $\langle \sigma, \rho \rangle [\![V]\!]^v \in [\![\Xi[N]]\!]^c$. By the fundamental lemma, $\Xi[N] \xrightarrow{\langle \sigma, \rho \rangle} W$ for some W such that $[\![W]\!]^v = [\![V]\!]^v$. They are of ground type, so $W = V$. Therefore, $\sigma, \Xi[N] \leadsto_* \rho, V$. ∎

6.1 Example Transformations

Thanks to directional adequacy, we can now justify various transformations and equivalences using rather mundane calculations, requiring no reasoning about the context in which these transformations are to take place.

Example 9. We make the reasoning from Example 4 precise.

Denote $\Gamma := x : \mathbf{Loc}, y : \mathbf{Val}$. We have $\Gamma \vdash x := y \, ; x? : \mathbf{Val}$ and $\Gamma \vdash x := y \, ; y : \mathbf{Val}$. Let $\gamma \in [\![\Gamma]\!]$, and denote $\ell := \gamma x$ and $v := \gamma y$. Calculating, we have:

$$[\![x := y \, ; x?]\!]^c \gamma = \tilde{\mathsf{U}}_{\ell, v} \tilde{\mathsf{Y}}^? \tilde{\mathsf{L}}_\ell \left(w. \, \tilde{\mathsf{Y}}^? \tilde{w} \right) \supseteq \tilde{\mathsf{U}}_{\ell, v} \tilde{\mathsf{Y}}^? \tilde{v} = [\![x := y \, ; y]\!]^c \gamma$$

By directional adequacy, $x := y \, ; y \sqsubseteq x := y \, ; x?$.

Example 10. We validate elimination of irrelevant reads, i.e. $M \sqsubseteq x? \, ; M$:

$$[\![x? \, ; M]\!]^c \gamma = [\![(\lambda \_. \, M) \, x?]\!]^c \gamma = [\![x?]\!]^c \gamma \mathbin{)\!\!=} \lambda v. \, [\![M]\!]^c \gamma = \tilde{\mathsf{Y}}^? ([\![M]\!]^c \gamma) \supseteq [\![M]\!]^c \gamma$$

As mentioned in Sect. 2.5, the semantics does not validate *introduction* of irrelevant reads, i.e. we have $[\![x? \, ; M]\!]^c \not\subseteq [\![M]\!]^c$ even though $x? \, ; M \sqsubseteq M$.

Example 11. Thanks to our use of standard monad-based semantics, structural transformations and equivalences follow from structural reasoning, avoiding considerations relating to shared-state. For instance:

$$[\![\text{if } y \text{ then } \lambda x. K_{\text{true}} \text{ else } \lambda x. K_{\text{false}}]\!]^c \gamma = [\![\lambda x. K_{\gamma y}]\!]^c \gamma$$

$$= \text{return } \lambda z. \ [\![K_{\gamma y}]\!]^c (\gamma [x \mapsto z]) = [\![\lambda x. \text{if } y \text{ then } K_{\text{true}} \text{ else } K_{\text{false}}]\!]^c \gamma$$

Therefore, **if** y **then** λx. K_{true} **else** λx. $K_{\text{false}} \cong \lambda$x. **if** y **then** K_{true} **else** K_{false} .

Finally, adequacy can help validate expected transformations involving ($\|$):

Example 12. Defining map $\psi P := \{\alpha (\psi x) \mid \alpha x \in P\}$ we have:

$$[\![\langle M, N \rangle]\!]^c \gamma \subseteq [\![M \| N]\!]^c \gamma \tag{Sequencing}$$

$$[\![M \| V]\!]^c \gamma = \text{map} (\lambda x. \ \langle x, [\![V]\!]^v \rangle) ([\![M]\!]^c \gamma) \tag{Neutrality}$$

$$[\![M \| N]\!]^c \gamma = \text{map} (\lambda \langle y, x \rangle. \ \langle x, y \rangle) ([\![N \| M]\!]^c \gamma) \tag{Symm.}$$

$$[\![(M \| N) \| K]\!]^c \gamma = \text{map} (\lambda \langle x, \langle y, z \rangle \rangle. \ \langle \langle x, y \rangle, z \rangle) ([\![M \| (N \| K)]\!]^c \gamma) \tag{Assoc.}$$

Unlike the previous examples, proving the above involves careful reasoning at the level of the traces. We still gain the benefit of justifying equivalences and transformations of programs – even open ones – without resorting to analysis under arbitrary program contexts and substitutions:

$$\langle M, N \rangle \sqsubseteq M \| N \tag{Sequencing}$$

$$\langle M, V \rangle \cong M \| V \tag{Neutrality}$$

$$M \| N \cong \textbf{match } N \| M \textbf{ with } \langle y, x \rangle \rightarrow \langle x, y \rangle \tag{Symm.}$$

$$(M \| N) \| K \cong \textbf{match } M \| (N \| K) \textbf{ with } \langle \langle x, \langle y, z \rangle \rangle \rangle \rightarrow \langle x, y \rangle , z \tag{Assoc.}$$

Coordinating the returned values make these somewhat awkward. More convenient but less informative forms are derivable, such as $M ; N ; K \sqsubseteq (M \| N) ; K$ (mentioned as a transformation in Sect. 1) which is a consequence of (Sequencing).

7   Conclusion, Related Work, and Future Work

We have defined a monad-based denotational semantics for a language for shared-state providing standard higher-order semantics supporting standard meta-theoretic development. This monad is a representation of the one induced by the equational theory of resumptions, which extends non-deterministic global-state with a delaying/yielding operator [14].

Abadi and Plotkin [1] design a modification for the theory of resumptions to define a denotational semantics for a concurrent imperative programming language with cooperative asynchronous threads. We have shown that the theory of resumptions can be used as-is to define denotational semantics for concurrency, albeit of a different kind. It is interesting to note that they interpret the unary operator analogously to our interpretation of $Y^?$, rather than Y. By decomposing into a sum we were able to validate transformations that are not equivalences.

Benton et al. [4] also define a monad for higher-order shared-state, with additional features such as recursion and abstract locations, using Brookes's style of semantics. Contrasting, the monad we defined is presented algebraically, and has finite sets of traces, whereas Benton et al.'s denotations are infinite even for recursion-free programs. Although this finiteness makes our definition simpler, we saw in Example 10 that it leads to a resumption-counting issue, thus less abstract semantics. It would be interesting to analyse their semantic model from the algebraic perspective as it may lead to more abstract semantics.

Like in previous work, including those mentioned above, our semantics is based on the sets of traces, originally used by Brookes [6] to define denotational semantics for an imperative concurrent language. Brookes proved that this semantics is not only directionally adequate, but also fully abstract. The proof makes crucial use of atomic execution blocks which we have not included.

Birkedal et al. [5] provide an interesting related model, given by logical relations (step-indexed, Kripke, etc.) over syntactic terms as semantics. Their language is substantially more expressive including higher-order local store, and accounts for a type-and-effect system semantics. A more precise model could lead to a monadic account that reproduces these results less syntactically.

Also of note are process calculi and algebraic laws concerning the structure of programs. Hoare and van Staden [12] give such an account for concurrent programs, unifying previous work. Their laws are much more general, parameterizing over the notions of sequencing programs and running programs in parallel. It would be interesting to discover if and how our semantics is an instance of theirs. There is also a lot of work on semantics of "while" languages where all information flows through the state, which support more advanced features such as probabilistic choice [3,11,41]. Others approach the study of concurrency through game semantics, such as Jaber and Murawski's [15] study of the semantics of a higher-order call-by-value concurrent language. Trace semantics features in their study too, though their traces are quite different, being sequences of player/opponent actions that incrementally transform configurations.

In the future we plan to refine the type system into a type-and-effect system [18,20,22,29,39,40], by annotating the typing judgments with the allowed effects. The denotations then depend on the effect annotations, with each annotation having its own associated equational theory. This may allow additional transformations that are currently beyond this model's reach. For example, the converse of (Sequencing) under certain syntactic and static guarantees would enable compiler parallelism.

Atomic constructs that disallow interference from the environment are a common feature of concurrent languages. Adding such constructs may be a simple matter, since we have a dedicated operator, yield, for allowing interference. Nevertheless, in the spirit of reductionism, we leave this investigation to future work.

We would also like to see how well our approach extends to weak-memory models. In particular, we believe that the timestamp-based operational semantics of the release-acquire memory model [19,24,26,37] is amenable to a similar treatment by using more sophisticated traces.

Acknowledgments. We thank Andrés Goens for providing his perspective on a previous version of this paper, and the anonymous APLAS reviewers for their helpful feedback.

References

1. Abadi, M., Plotkin, G.D.: A model of cooperative threads. Log. Methods Comput. Sci. **6**(4) (2010)..https://doi.org/10.2168/LMCS-6(4:2)2010, https://doi.org/10.2168/LMCS-6(4:2)2010

2. Abramsky, S.: Intensionality, definability and computation. In: Baltag, A., Smets, S. (eds.) Johan van Benthem on Logic and Information Dynamics. OCL, vol. 5, pp. 121–142. Springer, Cham (2014). https://doi.org/10.1007/978-3-319-06025-5_5

3. Anderson, C.J., et al.: NetKAT: semantic foundations for networks. In: Jagannathan, S., Sewell, P. (eds.) The 41st Annual ACM SIGPLAN-SIGACT Symposium on Principles of Programming Languages, POPL 2014, San Diego, CA, USA, 20–21 January 2014. pp. 113–126. ACM (2014). https://doi.org/10.1145/2535838.2535862, https://doi.org/10.1145/2535838.2535862

4. Benton, N., Hofmann, M., Nigam, V.: Effect-dependent transformations for concurrent programs. In: Cheney, J., Vidal, G. (eds.) Proceedings of the 18th International Symposium on Principles and Practice of Declarative Programming, Edinburgh, United Kingdom, 5–7 September 2016. pp. 188–201. ACM (2016). https://doi.org/10.1145/2967973.2968602, https://doi.org/10.1145/2967973.2968602

5. Birkedal, L., Sieczkowski, F., Thamsborg, J.: A Concurrent logical relation. In: Cégielski, P., Durand, A. (eds.) Computer Science Logic (CSL'12) - 26th International Workshop/21st Annual Conference of the EACSL. Leibniz International Proceedings in Informatics (LIPIcs), vol. 16, pp. 107–121. Schloss Dagstuhl-Leibniz-Zentrum fuer Informatik, Dagstuhl, Germany (2012). https://doi.org/10.4230/LIPIcs.CSL.2012.107, http://drops.dagstuhl.de/opus/volltexte/2012/3667

6. Brookes, S.D.: Full abstraction for a shared-variable parallel language. Inf. Comput. **127**(2), 145–163 (1996). https://doi.org/10.1006/inco.1996.0056, https://doi.org/10.1006/inco.1996.0056

7. Castellan, S.: Weak memory models using event structures. In: Signoles, J. (ed.) Vingt-septimes Journées Francophones des Langages Applicatifs (JFLA 2016). Saint-Malo, France, January 2016. https://hal.inria.fr/hal-01333582

8. Fiore, M., Saville, P.: List objects with algebraic structure. In: Miller, D. (ed.) 2nd International Conference on Formal Structures for Computation and Deduction, FSCD 2017, 3–9 September 2017, Oxford, UK. LIPIcs, vol. 84, pp. 16:1–16:18. Schloss Dagstuhl - Leibniz-Zentrum für Informatik (2017). https://doi.org/10.4230/LIPIcs.FSCD.2017.16, https://doi.org/10.4230/LIPIcs.FSCD.2017.16

9. Forster, Y., Kammar, O., Lindley, S., Pretnar, M.: On the expressive power of user-defined effects: effect handlers, monadic reflection, delimited control. J. Funct. Program. **29**, e15 (2019). https://doi.org/10.1017/S0956796819000121, https://doi.org/10.1017/S0956796819000121

10. Gibbons, J., Hinze, R.: Just do it: simple monadic equational reasoning. In: Chakravarty, M.M.T., Hu, Z., Danvy, O. (eds.) Proceeding of the 16th ACM SIGPLAN international conference on Functional Programming, ICFP 2011, Tokyo,

Japan, 19–21 September 2011, pp. 2–14. ACM (2011). https://doi.org/10.1145/2034773.2034777, https://doi.org/10.1145/2034773.2034777

11. Gibbons, J., Hinze, R.: Just do it: simple monadic equational reasoning. In: Chakravarty, M.M.T., Hu, Z., Danvy, O. (eds.) Proceeding of the 16th ACM SIG-PLAN International Conference on Functional Programming, ICFP 2011, Tokyo, Japan, 19–21 September 2011, pp. 2–14. ACM (2011). https://doi.org/10.1145/2034773.2034777, https://doi.org/10.1145/2034773.2034777

12. Hoare, T., van Staden, S.: The laws of programming unify process calculi. Sci. Comput. Program. **85**, 102–114 (2014). https://doi.org/10.1016/j.scico.2013.08.012, https://doi.org/10.1016/j.scico.2013.08.012

13. Hyland, M., Levy, P.B., Plotkin, G.D., Power, J.: Combining algebraic effects with continuations. Theor. Comput. Sci. **375**(1-3), 20–40 (2007). https://doi.org/10.1016/j.tcs.2006.12.026, https://doi.org/10.1016/j.tcs.2006.12.026

14. Hyland, M., Plotkin, G.D., Power, J.: Combining effects: Sum and tensor. Theor. Comput. Sci. **357**(1-3), 70–99 (2006). https://doi.org/10.1016/j.tcs.2006.03.013, https://doi.org/10.1016/j.tcs.2006.03.013

15. Jaber, G., Murawski, A.S.: Complete trace models of state and control. In: ESOP 2021. LNCS, vol. 12648, pp. 348–374. Springer, Cham (2021). https://doi.org/10.1007/978-3-030-72019-3_13

16. Jagadeesan, R., Jeffrey, A., Riely, J.: Pomsets with preconditions: a simple model of relaxed memory. Proc. ACM Program. Lang. **4**(OOPSLA) (nov 2020). https://doi.org/10.1145/3428262, https://doi.org/10.1145/3428262

17. Jeffrey, A., Riely, J., Batty, M., Cooksey, S., Kaysin, I., Podkopaev, A.: The leaky semicolon: Compositional semantic dependencies for relaxed-memory concurrency. Proc. ACM Program. Lang. **6**(POPL) (2022). https://doi.org/10.1145/3498716, https://doi.org/10.1145/3498716

18. Jouvelot, P., Gifford, D.K.: Algebraic reconstruction of types and effects. In: Wise, D.S. (ed.) Conference Record of the Eighteenth Annual ACM Symposium on Principles of Programming Languages, Orlando, Florida, USA, 21–23 January 1991. pp. 303–310. ACM Press (1991). https://doi.org/10.1145/99583.99623, https://doi.org/10.1145/99583.99623

19. Kaiser, J., Dang, H., Dreyer, D., Lahav, O., Vafeiadis, V.: Strong logic for weak memory: reasoning about release-acquire consistency in iris. In: Müller, P. (ed.) 31st European Conference on Object-Oriented Programming, ECOOP 2017, 19–23 June 2017, Barcelona, Spain. LIPIcs, vol. 74, pp. 17:1–17:29. Schloss Dagstuhl - Leibniz-Zentrum für Informatik (2017). https://doi.org/10.4230/LIPIcs.ECOOP.2017.17, https://doi.org/10.4230/LIPIcs.ECOOP.2017.17

20. Kammar, O.: Algebraic theory of type-and-effect systems. Ph.D. thesis, University of Edinburgh, UK (2014). http://hdl.handle.net/1842/8910

21. Kammar, O., Levy, P.B., Moss, S.K., Staton, S.: A monad for full ground reference cells. In: 32nd Annual ACM/IEEE Symposium on Logic in Computer Science, LICS 2017, Reykjavik, Iceland, 20–23 June 2017, pp. 1–12. IEEE Computer Society (2017). https://doi.org/10.1109/LICS.2017.8005109, https://doi.org/10.1109/LICS.2017.8005109

22. Kammar, O., McDermott, D.: Factorisation systems for logical relations and monadic lifting in type-and-effect system semantics. In: Staton, S. (ed.) Proceedings of the Thirty-Fourth Conference on the Mathematical Foundations of Programming Semantics, MFPS 2018, Dalhousie University, Halifax, Canada, June 6–9, 2018. Electronic Notes in Theoretical Computer Science, vol. 341, pp. 239–260. Elsevier (2018). https://doi.org/10.1016/j.entcs.2018.11.012, https://doi.org/10.1016/j.entcs.2018.11.012

23. Kammar, O., Plotkin, G.D.: Algebraic foundations for effect-dependent opti-
    misations. In: Field, J., Hicks, M. (eds.) Proceedings of the 39th ACM
    SIGPLAN-SIGACT Symposium on Principles of Programming Languages, POPL
    2012, Philadelphia, Pennsylvania, USA, 22–28 January 2012, pp. 349–360.
    ACM (2012). https://doi.org/10.1145/2103656.2103698, https://doi.org/10.1145/
    2103656.2103698
24. Kang, J., Hur, C., Lahav, O., Vafeiadis, V., Dreyer, D.: A promising semantics for
    relaxed-memory concurrency. In: Castagna, G., Gordon, A.D. (eds.) Proceedings
    of the 44th ACM SIGPLAN Symposium on Principles of Programming Languages,
    POPL 2017, Paris, France, 18–20 January 2017, pp. 175–189. ACM (2017). https://
    doi.org/10.1145/3009837.3009850, https://doi.org/10.1145/3009837.3009850
25. Kavanagh, R., Brookes, S.: A denotational semantics for sparc tso. Elec-
    tronic Notes in Theoretical Computer Science **336**, 223–239 (2018). https://doi.
    org/10.1016/j.entcs.2018.03.025, https://www.sciencedirect.com/science/article/
    pii/S1571066118300288, the Thirty-third Conference on the Mathematical Foun-
    dations of Programming Semantics (MFPS XXXIII)
26. Lahav, O., Giannarakis, N., Vafeiadis, V.: Taming release-acquire consistency. In:
    Bodík, R., Majumdar, R. (eds.) Proceedings of the 43rd Annual ACM SIGPLAN-
    SIGACT Symposium on Principles of Programming Languages, POPL 2016, St.
    Petersburg, FL, USA, 20–22 January 2016, pp. 649–662. ACM (2016). https://doi.
    org/10.1145/2837614.2837643, https://doi.org/10.1145/2837614.2837643
27. Levy, P.B.: Call-By-Push-Value: A Functional/Imperative Synthesis, Semantics
    Structures in Computation, vol. 2. Springer, Dordrecht (2004). https://doi.org/
    10.1007/978-94-007-0954-6
28. Linton, F.E.J.: An outline of functorial semantics. In: Eckmann, B. (ed.) Seminar
    on Triples and Categorical Homology Theory. LNM, vol. 80, pp. 7–52. Springer,
    Heidelberg (1969). https://doi.org/10.1007/BFb0083080
29. Lucassen, J.M., Gifford, D.K.: Polymorphic effect systems. In: Ferrante, J., Mager,
    P. (eds.) Conference Record of the Fifteenth Annual ACM Symposium on Princi-
    ples of Programming Languages, San Diego, California, USA, 10–13 January 1988,
    pp. 47–57. ACM Press (1988). https://doi.org/10.1145/73560.73564, https://doi.
    org/10.1145/73560.73564
30. Moggi, E.: Notions of computation and monads. Inf. Comput. **93**(1), 55–92
    (1991). https://doi.org/10.1016/0890-5401(91)90052-4, https://doi.org/10.1016/
    0890-5401(91)90052-4
31. Nielsen, M., Plotkin, G.D., Winskel, G.: Petri nets, event structures and domains,
    part I. Theor. Comput. Sci. **13**, 85–108 (1981). https://doi.org/10.1016/0304-
    3975(81)90112-2, https://doi.org/10.1016/0304-3975(81)90112-2
32. Oles, F.J.: A Category-Theoretic Approach to the Semantics of Programming Lan-
    guages. Ph.D. thesis (1983)
33. Oles, F.J.: Type algebras, functor categories, and block structure. DAIMI Report
    Series (156) (1983)
34. Plotkin, G., Power, J.: Notions of computation determine monads. In: Nielsen,
    M., Engberg, U. (eds.) FoSSaCS 2002. LNCS, vol. 2303, pp. 342–356. Springer,
    Heidelberg (2002). https://doi.org/10.1007/3-540-45931-6_24
35. Plotkin, G.D., Power, J.: Algebraic operations and generic effects. Appl. Cat-
    egorical Struct. **11**(1), 69–94 (2003). https://doi.org/10.1023/A:1023064908962,
    https://doi.org/10.1023/A:1023064908962
36. Plotkin, G., Pretnar, M.: Handlers of algebraic effects. In: Castagna, G. (ed.) ESOP
    2009. LNCS, vol. 5502, pp. 80–94. Springer, Heidelberg (2009). https://doi.org/10.
    1007/978-3-642-00590-9_7

37. Podkopaev, A., Sergey, I., Nanevski, A.: Operational aspects of C/C++ concurrency. CoRR abs/1606.01400 (2016), http://arxiv.org/abs/1606.01400

38. Reynolds, J.C.: The essence of algol. In: de Bakker, J.W., van Vliet, J.C. (eds.) Algorithmic Languages. pp. 345–372. International Symposium on Algorithmic Languages, Amsterdam; New York: North-Holland Pub. Co. (1981)

39. Talpin, J., Jouvelot, P.: Polymorphic type, region and effect inference. J. Funct. Program. **2**(3), 245–271 (1992). https://doi.org/10.1017/S0956796800000393, https://doi.org/10.1017/S0956796800000393

40. Talpin, J., Jouvelot, P.: The type and effect discipline. Inf. Comput. **111**(2), 245–296 (1994). https://doi.org/10.1006/inco.1994.1046, https://doi.org/10.1006/inco.1994.1046

41. Wagemaker, J., Foster, N., Kappé, T., Kozen, D., Rot, J., Silva, A.: Concurrent netKAT: modeling and analyzing stateful, concurrent networks. CoRR abs/2201.10485 (2022). https://arxiv.org/abs/2201.10485

42. Winskel, G.: On powerdomains and modality. Theor. Comput. Sci. **36**, 127–137 (1985). https://doi.org/10.1016/0304-3975(85)90037-4, https://doi.org/10.1016/0304-3975(85)90037-4

Decoupling the Ascending and Descending Phases in Abstract Interpretation

Vincenzo Arceri[1]([⊠]) [iD], Isabella Mastroeni[2] [iD], and Enea Zaffanella[1] [iD]

[1] University of Parma, Parma, Italy
{vincenzo.arceri,enea.zaffanella}@unipr.it
[2] University of Verona, Verona, Italy
isabella.mastroeni@univr.it

Abstract. Abstract Interpretation approximates the semantics of a program by mimicking its concrete fixpoint computation on an abstract domain $\mathbb{A}$. The abstract (post-) fixpoint computation is classically divided into two phases: the *ascending* phase, using widenings as extrapolation operators to enforce termination, is followed by a *descending* phase, using narrowings as interpolation operators, so as to mitigate the effect of the precision losses introduced by widenings. In this paper we propose a simple variation of this classical approach where, to more effectively recover precision, we *decouple* the two phases: in particular, before starting the descending phase, we replace the domain $\mathbb{A}$ with a more precise abstract domain $\mathbb{D}$. The correctness of the approach is justified by casting it as an instance of the A^2I framework. After demonstrating the new technique on a simple example, we summarize the results of a preliminary experimental evaluation, showing that it is able to obtain significant precision improvements for several choices of the domains $\mathbb{A}$ and $\mathbb{D}$.

Keywords: Abstract interpretation · Static analysis · Widening · Narrowing

1 Introduction

Abstract interpretation [17] is a framework for designing approximate semantics, with the aim of gathering information about programs in order to provide conservative/sound answers to questions about their run-time behaviors. In other words, the purpose of abstract interpretation is to formally design automatic program analyses by approximating program semantics for statically determining dynamic properties. The design of static analyzers consists in automatizing the computation of such approximations, and in this case the answer can only be partial or imprecise, due to the undecidability of program termination. Abstract/approximated semantics are computed by mimicking the monotonic (ascending) concrete semantics computation, obtained by Kleene iteration reaching fixpoint. Unfortunately, it is well known that Kleene fixpoint computation may

I. Sergey (Ed.): APLAS 2022, LNCS 13658, pp. 25–44, 2022.
https://doi.org/10.1007/978-3-031-21037-2_2

not terminate. In the static analysis framework this issue has been tackled by introducing fixpoint accelerators, namely new operators (called widenings) built on the computational abstract domain, allowing to accelerate the fixpoint computation at the price of potentially reaching a post-fixpoint, namely at the price of losing precision in the answer. For this reason, it is common in static analysis to design another operator (called narrowing) performing a descending path in order to try to recover some precision by refining the reached post-fixpoint.

The precision of the result depends both on the ability of the widening operator to *guess* a limit of the increasing sequence, and on the information gathered during the decreasing phase. Intuitively, the increasing sequence extrapolates the behavior of the program from the first steps of its execution, while the decreasing sequence gathers information about the end of the execution of the program [13]. Moreover, a naive application of the classical approach may lead to an inadequate analysis, which is too expensive or too imprecise, meaning that there is a strong need for mechanisms that can effectively tune the precision/efficiency tradeoff. In order to improve this ratio, we could either improve efficiency (usually to the detriment of precision) by choosing a simpler (less precise) domain or by changing the fixpoint construction (e.g., replacing precise abstract operators with cheaper over-approximations), or improve precision (usually to the detriment of efficiency) by choosing a more precise/costly domain or again by changing the fixpoint construction (clearly in the opposite direction, see techniques discussed in Sect. 5).

In this work, we propose to combine these improvement approaches by choosing to use different domains (with different precision degrees) depending on the analysis phase: we use a potentially less precise domain in the fixpoint computation exploiting a widening operator for reaching a post-fixpoint in the ascending phase, and therefore potentially sensitively losing precision, and we use a more precise domain in the descending (narrowing) phase for trying to improve the gain of precision of such phase. The idea is rather simple but, to the best of our knowledge, it was never proposed before; also, since it is orthogonal with respect to similar approaches, it can be used in combination with them (rather than as an alternative to them). The intuition beyond the gain of precision without a relevant loss of efficiency is based on the idea that in the descending phase we do not need to use the more expensive operations. Such intuition is supported by our initial experimental evaluation, showing that the proposed approach is surely promising, being able to improve precision in a significant number of cases.

Paper Structure. Section 2 gives basics in order theory, Abstract Interpretation, and the classical approach for static analysis by Abstract Interpretation. Section 3 presents our proposal for decoupling the ascending and descending phases with two different abstract domains. Section 4 reports a preliminary experimental evaluation of our approach. Section 5 discusses most related works. Section 6 concludes.

2 Background

Order Theory. We denote by $\wp(S)$ the powerset of a set S. A poset $\langle L, \sqsubseteq_L \rangle$ is a set L equipped with a partial order $\sqsubseteq_L \in \wp(L \times L)$, i.e., a reflexive, transitive and anti-symmetric binary relation; in the following we will omit subscripts when clear from context. A poset is a join semi-lattice if, for each $l_1, l_2 \in L$, the lub (least upper bound) $l_1 \sqcup l_2$ belongs to L; similarly, it is a meet semi-lattice if the glb (greatest lower bound) $l_1 \sqcap l_2$ belongs to L; when both properties hold, we have a lattice $\langle L, \sqsubseteq, \sqcup, \sqcap \rangle$. A lattice is complete if $\forall X \subseteq L, \bigsqcup X$ and $\bigsqcap X$ belong to L; a complete lattice with bottom element $\bot$ and top element $\top$ is denoted $\langle L, \sqsubseteq, \sqcup, \sqcap, \bot, \top \rangle$. A poset $\langle L, \sqsubseteq \rangle$ satisfies the ascending chain condition (ACC) iff each infinite sequence $l_0 \sqsubseteq l_1 \sqsubseteq \cdots \sqsubseteq l_i \sqsubseteq \ldots$ of elements of L is not strictly increasing, i.e., $\exists k \geq 0, \forall j \geq k : l_k = l_j$. Dually the poset satisfies the descending chain condition (DCC) iff each infinite sequence $l_0 \sqsupseteq l_1 \sqsupseteq \cdots \sqsupseteq l_i \sqsupseteq \ldots$ of elements of L is not strictly decreasing, that is $\exists k \geq 0, \forall j \geq k : l_k = l_j$.

A function $f : L \to L$ on poset $\langle L, \sqsubseteq \rangle$ is monotone if, for all $l_1, l_2 \in L, l_1 \sqsubseteq l_2$ implies $f(l_1) \sqsubseteq f(l_2)$. We denote $\text{post}(f)$ the set of post-fixpoints of f, i.e., those elements $x \in L$ satisfying $f(x) \sqsupseteq x$; similarly, $\text{pre}(f)$ is the set of pre-fixpoints of f, satisfying $f(x) \sqsubseteq x$; the set of fixpoints of f, satisfying $f(x) = x$, is thus $\text{fix}(f) = \text{pre}(f) \cap \text{post}(f)$. Given a function $f : L \to L$ we recursively define the iterates/iterations of f from $x \in L$ as $f^0(x) = x$ and $f^{i+1}(x) = f(f^i(x))$. The Kleene fixpoint theorem says that a continuous function $f : L \to L$ on a complete lattice $\langle L, \sqsubseteq, \sqcup, \sqcap, \bot, \top \rangle$ has a least fixpoint $\text{lfp}(f) \in L$, which can be obtained as the lub of the increasing sequence $f^0(\bot) \sqsubseteq f^1(\bot) \sqsubseteq \cdots \sqsubseteq f^i(\bot) \sqsubseteq \ldots$ [18].

Abstract Interpretation (AI). Abstract Interpretation [17,18] is a theory to soundly approximate program semantics, focusing on some run-time property of interest. In the classical setting, the concrete and the abstract semantics are defined over two complete lattices, respectively called the concrete domain C and the abstract domain A. A pair of monotone functions $\alpha : C \to A$ and $\gamma : A \to C$ forms a *Galois Connection* (GC) if $\forall c \in C, \forall a \in A : \alpha(c) \sqsubseteq_A a \Leftrightarrow c \sqsubseteq_C \gamma(a)$. If C and A are related by a GC, denoted $C \xleftrightarrow[\alpha]{\gamma} A$, then an abstract function $f_A : A \to A$ is a correct approximation of a concrete function $f_C : C \to C$ if and only if $\forall c \in C : \alpha(f_C(c)) \sqsubseteq_A f_A(\alpha(c))$ or equivalently $\forall a \in A : f_C(\gamma(a)) \sqsubseteq_C \gamma(f_A(a))$; the *best correct approximation* of f_C is $f_A^\sharp = (\alpha \circ f_C \circ \gamma)$.

Static Program Analysis via Abstract Interpretation. It is possible to represent a program of interest as a control-flow graph (CFG for short). A CFG is a graph $\langle N, E \rangle$ such that $N = \{n_1, n_2, \ldots, n_m\}$ is a finite set of nodes corresponding to the control points of the program, and $E \subseteq N \times N$ is a finite set of edges. It is possible to compute the CFG associated with a certain program with standard techniques [37].

Let us denote by A the abstract domain approximating the concrete domain C, used to analyze programs of interest. With each node $n \in N$ is associated a function transformer $f_n : A^m \to A$ capturing the effects of the node

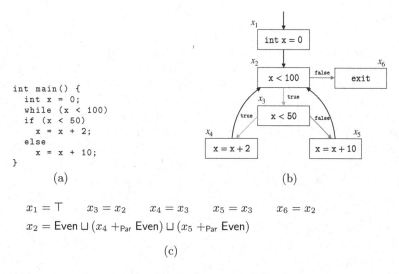

```
int main () {
    int x = 0;
    while (x < 100)
    if (x < 50)
        x = x + 2;
    else
        x = x + 10;
}
```

(a)

(b)

$$x_1 = \top \qquad x_3 = x_2 \qquad x_4 = x_3 \qquad x_5 = x_3 \qquad x_6 = x_2$$
$$x_2 = \mathsf{Even} \sqcup (x_4 +_{\mathsf{Par}} \mathsf{Even}) \sqcup (x_5 +_{\mathsf{Par}} \mathsf{Even})$$

(c)

Fig. 1. (a) C function example, (b) associated CFG, (c) associated system of equations with the Par abstract domain.

n, i.e., the abstract semantics. Analyzing a given CFG $C = \langle N, E \rangle$, where $N = \{n_1, n_2, \ldots, n_m\}$ means to resolve the following system of equations[1]

$$F = \big\{\, x_i = f_i(x_1, x_2, \ldots, x_m) \mid i = 1, 2, \ldots, m \,\big\}$$

The goal of AI-based static analysis, using an abstract domain A, is to compute the least solution of the equation set F as the limit of a Kleene iteration on A, i.e., $x^{\mathrm{lfp}(F)} \triangleq (x_1^{\mathrm{lfp}(F)}, \ldots, x_m^{\mathrm{lfp}(F)})$ starting from the bottom elements of A, i.e., $\forall i \in [1, m].\, x_i = \bot$.

Example 1. Consider the C function of Fig. 1a and the corresponding CFG, shown in Fig. 1b. We intuitively describe the analysis of this program using the abstract domain Par [18, Example 10.1.0.3], tracking the parity of numerical variables:

$$\mathsf{Par} = \langle \{\bot, \top, \mathsf{Even}, \mathsf{Odd}\}, \sqsubseteq, \sqcup, \sqcap, \bot, \top \rangle,$$

where the partial order is defined by $\bot \sqsubseteq x \sqsubseteq \top$, for each $x \in \mathsf{Par}$. The system of equations is reported in Fig. 1c; Note that the equation defining x_i is intuitively describing the values that are possibly *entering* the corresponding node of the CFG (also labeled x_i for convenience); for instance, the right hand side of the equation defining x_2 computes the lub of the abstract values *exiting* from nodes x_1, x_4 and x_5, respectively. For space reasons, we leave to intuition the abstract functions modeling the semantics of each CFG node (e.g., function $+_{\mathsf{Par}} \colon \mathsf{Par} \times \mathsf{Par} \to \mathsf{Par}$ modeling addition on the Par domain). The least solution for the system is $x_1 = \top$ and $x_i = \mathsf{Even}$ for $i = 2, \ldots, 6$.   □

---

[1] In general, the least fixpoint on the concrete domain C is not finitely computable. Hence, the idea is to compute an abstract fixpoint, over an abstract domain A, that correctly approximates the concrete one.

The ascending sequence over the system of equations F may fail to (finitely) converge for abstract domains that do not satisfy the ACC. A converge guarantee can be provided by widening operators, which over-approximate the least fixpoint solution $x^{\text{lfp}(F)}$ by effectively computing a post-fixpoint of F. A widening $\nabla \colon A \times A \to A$ is an operator such that:

- for each $a_1, a_2 \in A$, $a_1 \sqsubseteq a_1 \nabla a_2$ and $a_2 \sqsubseteq a_1 \nabla a_2$;
- for all ascending sequences $a_0 \sqsubseteq \cdots \sqsubseteq a_{i+1} \sqsubseteq \ldots$, the ascending sequence $x_0 \sqsubseteq \cdots \sqsubseteq x_{i+1} \sqsubseteq \ldots$ defined by $x_0 = a_0$ and $x_{i+1} = x_i \nabla a_{i+1}$ is not strictly increasing.

In principle, widening can be applied to all equations of the system F, which however would lead to a gross over-approximation; following [12], it is sufficient that the widening is applied on one node in each cycle of the CFG; for instance, in Fig. 1b we can use x_3 as the one and only widening point. We denote $WP \subseteq N$ the set of *widening points*, i.e., the nodes of the CFG where widening is applied, leading to the system of equations F^∇:

$$\begin{cases} x_i = x_i \ \nabla \ f_i(x_1, x_2, \ldots, x_m), & \text{if } i \in WP; \\ x_i = x_i \ \sqcup \ f_i(x_1, x_2, \ldots, x_m), & \text{otherwise.} \end{cases} \tag{1}$$

In order to mitigate the loss of precision introduced by widenings, the *ascending phase* computing the post-fixpoint x^∇ of F can be followed by another Kleene iteration on the system F, starting from x^∇ and descending towards a fixpoint of F (not necessarily the least one). If the abstract domain A does not satisfy the DCC, this descending sequence may fail to converge; a convergence guarantee can be obtained by using a narrowing operator $\Delta \colon A \times A \to A$, satisfying:

- for each $a_1, a_2 \in A$, $a_1 \sqsupseteq a_1 \Delta a_2 \sqsupseteq a_1 \sqcap a_2$;
- for all descending sequences $a_0 \sqsupseteq \cdots \sqsupseteq a_{i+1} \sqsupseteq \ldots$, the descending sequence $x_0 \sqsupseteq \cdots \sqsupseteq x_{i+1} \sqsupseteq \ldots$ defined by $x_0 = a_0$ and $x_{i+1} = x_i \Delta a_{i+1}$ is not strictly decreasing.

As before, the application of narrowings can be limited to WP, leading to the system of equations F^Δ used during the *descending phase*:

$$\begin{cases} x_i = x_i \ \Delta \ f_i(x_1, x_2, \ldots, x_m), & \text{if } i \in WP; \\ x_i = x_i \ \sqcap \ f_i(x_1, x_2, \ldots, x_m), & \text{otherwise.} \end{cases} \tag{2}$$

In general, the descending sequence with narrowing will compute a post-fixpoint x^Δ of F (not necessarily a fixpoint), satisfying $x^\Delta \sqsubseteq x^\nabla$. A graphical representation of the ascending and descending phases over the abstract domain A is reported in Fig. 2. Note that a "glb-based" narrowing operator can be easily defined by computing the domain glb and forcing the descending sequence to stop as soon as reaching a fixed, finite number $k \in \mathbb{N}$ of iterations. For this reason, several abstract domains do not implement a proper narrowing operator.

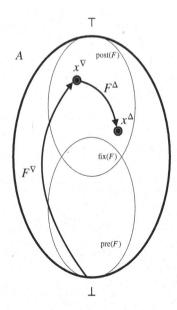

Fig. 2. The ascending and descending phases over abstract domain A.

Example 2. The domain of integral intervals [22] (or 1-dimension integral boxes) is an example of complete lattice satisfying neither the ACC nor the DCC:

$$\mathsf{Itv} = \{\bot, \top\} \cup \{[\ell, u] \mid \ell, u \in \mathbb{Z}, \ell \leq u\} \cup \{[-\infty, u] \mid u \in \mathbb{Z}\} \cup \{[\ell, +\infty] \mid \ell \in \mathbb{Z}\},$$

where $\bot$ is the bottom element (denoting the empty interval), $\top = [-\infty, +\infty]$ is the top element (denoting $\mathbb{Z}$) and the partial order, lub and glb operators consistently model the usual containment relation. The interval widening operator [22] $\nabla \colon \mathsf{Itv} \times \mathsf{Itv} \to \mathsf{Itv}$ is defined, for each $x \in \mathsf{Itv}$, by $\bot \nabla x = x \nabla \bot = x$ and

$$[\ell_0, u_0] \nabla [\ell_1, u_1] = [(\ell_1 < \ell_0 ? -\infty : \ell_0), (u_0 < u_1 ? +\infty : u_0)].$$

Similarly, the interval narrowing operator [22] $\Delta \colon \mathsf{Itv} \times \mathsf{Itv} \to \mathsf{Itv}$ is defined, for each $x \in \mathsf{Itv}$, by $\bot \Delta x = x \Delta \bot = \bot$ and

$$[\ell_0, u_0] \Delta [\ell_1, u_1] = [(\ell_0 = -\infty ? \ell_1 : \ell_0), (u_0 = +\infty ? u_1 : u_0)].$$

Considering again the C function in Fig. 1a, the corresponding system of equations for the domain Itv is shown in Fig. 3a (where $+_{\mathsf{Itv}} \colon \mathsf{Itv} \times \mathsf{Itv} \to \mathsf{Itv}$ models addition on the Itv domain). The computation of the ascending and descending sequences is shown in Fig. 3b, where in the 2nd column we have highlighted the only widening point x_3; in particular, the 4th and 6th columns show the post-fixpoint and the fixpoint obtained at the end of the ascending and the descending phases, respectively. □

$$x_1 = \top$$
$$x_2 = [0,0] \sqcup (x_4 +_{\mathsf{ltv}} [2,2]) \sqcup (x_5 +_{\mathsf{ltv}} [10,10])$$
$$x_3 = x_2 \sqcap [-\infty, 99]$$

$$x_4 = x_3 \sqcap [-\infty, 49]$$
$$x_5 = x_3 \sqcap [50, +\infty]$$
$$x_6 = x_2 \sqcap [100, +\infty]$$

(a)

N	WP	ascending phase iter		descending phase iter	
		1st	2nd $(= x_{\mathsf{ltv}}^{\triangledown})$	1st	2nd $(= x_{\mathsf{ltv}}^{\triangle})$
x_1		$\top$	$\top$	$\top$	$\top$
x_2		$[0,0]$	$[0, +\infty]$	$[0, +\infty]$	$[0, 109]$
x_3	$\checkmark$	$[0,0]$	$[0, +\infty]$	$[0, 99]$	$[0, 99]$
x_4		$[0,0]$	$[0, 49]$	$[0, 49]$	$[0, 49]$
x_5		$\bot$	$[50, +\infty]$	$[50, 99]$	$[50, 99]$
x_6		$\bot$	$[100, +\infty]$	$[100, +\infty]$	$[100, 109]$

(b)

Fig. 3. (a) Equations for CFG in Fig. 1b using ltv, (b) interval results.

Powerset Domains. Many abstract domains (e.g., numerical domains whose elements are convex sets) are unable to precisely describe disjunctive information, thereby incurring significant precision losses whenever the abstract semantic construction needs to merge different control flow paths. To avoid these losses, it is possible to lift the domain using a disjunctive domain refinement operator [18]. In the following we will consider the finite powerset [6] of an abstract domain A, which is the join-semilattice $\mathsf{Set}_{\mathsf{fn}}(A) = \langle \wp_{\mathsf{fn}}(A), \sqsubseteq_{\mathsf{fn}}, \sqcup_{\mathsf{fn}}, \bot_{\mathsf{fn}} \rangle$, where:

- the carrier $\wp_{\mathsf{fn}}(A)$ is the set of the *finite* and *non-redundant* subsets of A (an element $a_1 \in A$ is redundant in $S \subseteq A$ iff $a_1 = \bot_A$ or $\exists a_2 \in S . a_1 \sqsubseteq_A a_2$);
- the partial order $S_1 \sqsubseteq_{\mathsf{fn}} S_2$ is defined by $\forall a_1 \in S_1, \exists a_2 \in S_2 . a_1 \sqsubseteq_A a_2$;
- the (binary) least upper bound $S_1 \sqcup_{\mathsf{fn}} S_2$ is computed by removing the redundant elements from the set union $S_1 \cup S_2$;
- the bottom element is $\bot_{\mathsf{fn}} = \emptyset$.

For space reasons we omit a more thorough discussion of powerset domains (e.g., the lifting of the abstract semantic operators defined on A), referring the interested reader to [6,18].

3   Decoupling the Ascending and Descending Phases

In the previous section we have recalled the classical approach used in static analysis based on abstract interpretation, which can be summarized as follows: (a) fix an abstract domain A such that $C \xrightleftharpoons[\alpha]{\gamma} A$ and a corresponding, correct system of abstract equations F_A; (b) approximate the concrete semantics by computing a post-fixpoint of F_A in the ascending phase (with widening); (c)

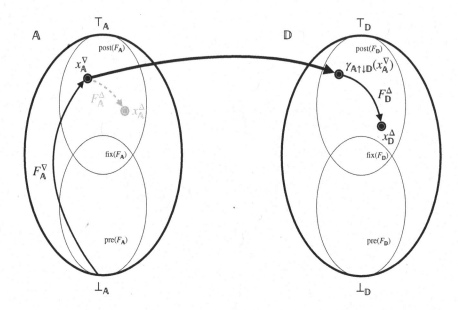

Fig. 4. The ascending and descending phases over $\mathbb{A}$ and $\mathbb{D}$, respectively.

improve the result in the descending phase (with narrowing). What is worth noting is that the two phases (b) and (c) are computed on the same domain A.

Moving from the observation that the only goal of the descending phase is to improve precision, we propose to *decouple* it from the ascending phase: that is, we compute the descending sequence on a different, more precise abstract domain, so as to increase the chances of a significant precision improvement. Clearly, the adoption of a more precise domain likely incurs some penalty in terms of the efficiency of the analysis; however, since in our proposal this domain is only used in the descending phase, it should be simpler to achieve a good tradeoff between precision and efficiency, because the descending phase can be stopped after any number of iterations and still provide a correct result.

In the following we will denote $\mathbb{A}$ and $\mathbb{D}$ the abstract domains used in the ascending and descending phases, respectively, and use the notation $\mathbb{A} \uparrow\downarrow \mathbb{D}$ to refer to this decoupled approach. The correctness/precision relation between the concrete domain and the two abstract domains is formalized by requiring $C \xleftrightarrow[\alpha_{\mathbb{D}}]{\gamma_{\mathbb{D}}} \mathbb{D} \xleftrightarrow[\alpha_{\mathbb{A}\uparrow\downarrow\mathbb{D}}]{\gamma_{\mathbb{A}\uparrow\downarrow\mathbb{D}}} \mathbb{A}$; we also require that the concretization function $\gamma_{\mathbb{A}\uparrow\downarrow\mathbb{D}}$ is effectively computable.

Our decoupled approach is graphically represented in Fig. 4. The (concrete) system of equations F_C is correctly approximated on domain $\mathbb{D}$ by the (abstract) system of equations $F_{\mathbb{D}}$, which is further approximated on domain $\mathbb{A}$ by the system of equations $F_{\mathbb{A}}$. We first compute a post-fixpoint $x_{\mathbb{A}}^{\nabla} \in \mathbb{A}$ using the system of equations $F_{\mathbb{A}}^{\nabla}$ (with widening); instead of descending on the same abstract domain, as done in Sect. 2, we transfer the post-fixpoint $x_{\mathbb{A}}^{\nabla}$ to the more precise domain $\mathbb{D}$, using the concretization function $\gamma_{\mathbb{A} \uparrow\downarrow \mathbb{D}}$ (which is computable); hence, the descending phase will use the system of equations $F_{\mathbb{D}}^{\Delta}$ (with narrowing) on domain $\mathbb{D}$, starting from $\gamma_{\mathbb{A} \uparrow\downarrow \mathbb{D}}(x_{\mathbb{A}}^{\nabla})$ and obtaining an improved post-fixpoint $x_{\mathbb{D}}^{\Delta} \in \mathbb{D}$.

The next lemma states that the post-fixpoint $x_{\mathbb{A}}^{\nabla} \in \mathbb{A}$ corresponds to a post-fixpoint for $F_{\mathbb{D}}$, necessary for starting the descending phase on $\mathbb{D}$.

Lemma 1. *Consider* $\mathbb{D} \xrightleftharpoons[\alpha_{\mathbb{A}\uparrow\downarrow\mathbb{D}}]{\gamma_{\mathbb{A}\uparrow\downarrow\mathbb{D}}} \mathbb{A}$ *and let* $F_{\mathbb{A}} : \mathbb{A} \to \mathbb{A}$ *be a correct approximation of* $F_{\mathbb{D}} : \mathbb{D} \to \mathbb{D}$. *Then,*

$$x_{\mathbb{A}}^{\nabla} \in \mathrm{post}(F_{\mathbb{A}}) \implies \gamma_{\mathbb{A}\uparrow\downarrow\mathbb{D}}(x_{\mathbb{A}}^{\nabla}) \in \mathrm{post}(F_{\mathbb{D}}).$$

It would be desirable to prove that the final result $x_{\mathbb{D}}^{\Delta}$ obtained when using the decoupled approach $\mathbb{A} \uparrow\downarrow \mathbb{D}$ systematically improves on the final result $x_{\mathbb{A}}^{\Delta}$ obtained by the classical approach, i.e., $x_{\mathbb{D}}^{\Delta} \sqsubseteq_{\mathbb{D}} \gamma_{\mathbb{A}\uparrow\downarrow\mathbb{D}}(x_{\mathbb{A}}^{\Delta})$. However, in general this property does not hold, due to the use of different, unrelated, possibly non-monotonic narrowing operators on the domains $\mathbb{A}$ and $\mathbb{D}$. We can prove the desired result provided we force both domains to use the glb-based narrowing (with the same threshold value).

Proposition 1. *Consider* $\mathbb{D} \xrightleftharpoons[\alpha_{\mathbb{A}\uparrow\downarrow\mathbb{D}}]{\gamma_{\mathbb{A}\uparrow\downarrow\mathbb{D}}} \mathbb{A}$ *and let* $F_{\mathbb{A}} : \mathbb{A} \to \mathbb{A}$ *be a correct approximation of* $F_{\mathbb{D}} : \mathbb{D} \to \mathbb{D}$; *let also* $x_{\mathbb{A}}^{\nabla} \in \mathrm{post}(F_{\mathbb{A}})$. *Then, for each* $k \in \mathbb{N}$,

$$F_{\mathbb{D}}^{k}(\gamma_{\mathbb{A}\uparrow\downarrow\mathbb{D}}(x_{\mathbb{A}}^{\nabla})) \sqsubseteq_{\mathbb{D}} \gamma_{\mathbb{A}\uparrow\downarrow\mathbb{D}}(F_{\mathbb{A}}^{k}(x_{\mathbb{A}}^{\nabla})).$$

Note that Lemma 1 and Proposition 1 are well-known results. Intuitively, the correctness of the decoupled approach is easily justified by viewing it as an instance of the $\mathrm{A}^2\mathrm{I}$ framework [20]: starting from a classical analysis using the more precise domain $\mathbb{D}$, we further abstract part of its computation (the ascending phase), approximating it on domain $\mathbb{A}$.

On the Galois Connection Requirement. When formalizing our decoupled proposal, we have assumed that all the considered domains (concrete, ascending and descending) are related by GCs: this corresponds to an ideal situation where for each element x of the more precise domain (resp., each semantic transformer f) we can identify the corresponding best correct approximation on the less precise domain $\alpha(x)$ (resp., $\alpha \circ f \circ \gamma$). However, there are well-known abstract domains (e.g., the domain convex polyhedra [21] approximating sets of reals or the deterministic finite-state automata domain [4] approximating sets of strings) that cannot be related to the concrete domain using a GC. This is not a real concern because, as discussed at length in [19], one can adopt a slightly weaker theoretical framework and still ensure the correctness of the analysis. As a matter of fact, in the experimental evaluation we will implicitly relax the GC assumption.

N	transfer $\gamma_{Itv\uparrow\downarrow ISet}(x^\nabla_{Itv})$	descending phase		
		1st iter	2nd iter	
x_1	$\{\top_{Itv}\}$	$\{\top_{Itv}\}$	$\{\top_{Itv}\}$	
x_2	$\{[0,+\infty]\}$	$\{[0,0],[2,51],[60,+\infty]\}$	$\{[0,0],[2,2],[4,51],[60,61],[70,109]\}$	✓
x_3	$\{[0,+\infty]\}$	$\{[0,0],[2,51],[60,99]\}$	$\{[0,0],[2,2],[4,51],[60,61],[70,99]\}$	✓
x_4	$\{[0,49]\}$	$\{[0,0],[2,49]\}$	$\{[0,0],[2,2],[4,49]\}$	✓
x_5	$\{[50,99]\}$	$\{[50,51],[60,99]\}$	$\{[50,51],[60,61],[70,99]\}$	✓
x_6	$\{[100,+\infty]\}$	$\{[100,+\infty]\}$	$\{[100,109]\}$	

Fig. 5. Computing the descending phase on $Itv\uparrow\downarrow ISet$.

Example 3. We now reconsider the C program in Fig. 1a and show how the decoupled approach can be used to improve on the results computed by the classical analysis on domain Itv (see Example 2 and Fig. 3b). To this end, while keeping the domain Itv for the ascending phase, we will compute the descending phase on the powerset domain $ISet = Set_{fn}(Itv)$, i.e., we will adopt the combination $Itv\uparrow\downarrow ISet$.

Before starting the descending phase, the post-fixpoint x^∇_{Itv} computed in the ascending phase using Itv (see the 4th column of Fig. 3b) is transferred to $ISet$ using $\gamma_{Itv\uparrow\downarrow ISet} : Itv \rightarrow ISet$, obtaining the (singleton) sets of intervals shown in the 2nd column of Fig. 5. Then the descending phase on $ISet$ is started: note that we use the glb-based narrowing, with a threshold value $k = 2$ on the number of iterations; the results computed by the two iterations are shown in the 3rd and 4th columns of Fig. 5.

It is now possible to perform a precision comparison of the results obtained on domain Itv using the classical approach (last column in Fig. 3b) with respect to the results obtained with the $Itv\uparrow\downarrow ISet$ combination (4th column of Fig. 5): for convenience, in the last column we show a checkmark (✓) on the CFG nodes where we actually obtain a precision improvement. Note that the post-fixpoint computed on $ISet$ is not a fixpoint: hence, the precision could be refined further by increasing the threshold value $k \in \mathbb{N}$.   □

4   Experimental Evaluation

In order to obtain a preliminary experimental evaluation of the precision gains resulting from the proposed analysis technique, we have modified the open source static analysis tool PAGAI [32] to allow for decoupling the ascending and descending iteration phases; in particular, we have added program options to select a different abstract domain for the descending phase, as well as to select a threshold value for the number of descending iterations (this threshold is set to 3).[2] In our experiments we configured PAGAI to perform a *simple* static analysis: hence, we disregard more sophisticated approaches, such as *path focusing*,

---

[2] By design, PAGAI does not use proper narrowing operators to enforce the termination of the decreasing sequence; rather, it stops when the iteration count reaches the threshold value (or earlier, if a fixpoint is detected).

and we disabled those LLVM bitcode instrumentation passes that heavily modify the CFG in order to potentially detect overflows and other runtime errors.

PAGAI is interfaced with the Apron library [33], which provides several numeric domains, among which boxes [17] (Box), octagons [35] (Oct) and convex polyhedra [21] (Pol); these non-disjunctive domains all implement the corresponding "standard" widening operator. We extended Apron interface by adding a modified version of the PPLite library [10] which, besides its enhanced implementation of the domain of convex polyhedra [7,8], also includes a prototype implementation of the finite powerset $\mathsf{PSet} = \mathsf{Set}_{\mathsf{fn}}(\mathsf{Pol})$ of convex polyhedra [6]; since this prototype is not (yet) provided with a widening operator, it can only be used in the descending phase of the analysis. Note that PAGAI features a variant analysis technique that is meant to compute disjunctive invariants, but this would yield an analysis which is quite different from the direct adoption of a powerset domain; for instance, one would be forced to choose in advance the maximal number of disjuncts that are allowed.

The experimental evaluation considers 35 C source files distributed with PAGAI, which are variants of benchmarks taken from the SNU real-time benchmark suite for worst-case execution time analysis. PAGAI can be configured to perform a precision comparison among two different abstract domains (DOM_1 and DOM_2): in this case, the analyzer records the invariant properties computed by the two domains for each widening point (WP); then it compares them and provides a final report made of four numbers, counting the widening points on which the invariant computed by the first domain is, respectively, equivalent (EQ), stronger (LT), weaker (GT) and uncomparable (UN) with respect to the invariant computed by the second domain. The results of the precision comparisons have been summarized in Tables 1 and 2; note that, for readability, the tables show the percentages of widening points, rather than absolute values.[3]

Table 1. Precision comparison for non-disjunctive domains.

		% WP				
DOM_1	DOM_2	EQ	LT	GT	UN	ΔEQ
Box	Oct	**66.5**	0.7	32.4	0.4	
Box	Box↑↓Oct	83.6	0.4	**16.0**	0.0	
Box↑↓Oct	Oct	**73.0**	0.7	26.3	0.0	**6.4**
Box	Pol	**53.7**	3.6	37.0	5.7	
Box	Box↑↓Pol	76.5	0.4	**23.1**	0.0	
Box↑↓Pol	Pol	**59.8**	5.7	31.3	3.2	**6.0**
Oct	Pol	**69.4**	6.8	21.4	2.5	
Oct	Oct↑↓Pol	87.2	0.0	**12.8**	0.0	
Oct↑↓Pol	Pol	**72.2**	8.2	18.5	1.1	**2.8**

---

[3] The total number of widening points is 281.

Consider first Table 1, which is meant to evaluate the effectiveness of the new approach when both abstract domains are non-disjunctive. Note that the rows in the table are divided in three groups (three rows per group); let us focus on the first group, which is evaluating the precision improvements obtained when using the abstract domain Box⇅Oct. The first row in the group provides the *baseline* for the precision comparison: in particular, the value in column EQ (highlighted in boldface) informs us that the domain Box achieves the same precision as Oct on 66.5% of the widening points; this means that only the remaining 33.5% of widening points are further *improvable*. The second row in the group, in particular the value in column GT, shows us that Box⇅Oct is able to improve the precision of Box on 16% of all widening points. The third row in the group, in particular the value in column EQ, informs us that Box⇅Oct is able to achieve the same precision of Oct on 73% of the widening points: this corresponds to an increase by 6.4% (reported in the column labeled ΔEQ) with respect to the baseline EQ value (in the first row).

It is worth stressing that the percentages highlighted in the second and third row of the group are computed with respect to the total number of widening points, which might mislead the reader towards an underestimation of the effectiveness of the approach. One should observe that a precision gain on 16.0% of *all* the widening points corresponds to a precision gain on almost one half (16.0/33.5 = 47.9%) of the *improvable* widening points. The same reasoning applies to the 6.4% value of ΔEQ, which corresponds to almost 20% of the improvable widening points.

Similar observations can be derived from the second and third group of rows in Table 1, where we evaluate the abstract domain combinations Box⇅Pol and Oct⇅Pol, respectively. For instance, the third group of rows in Table 1 informs us that Oct⇅Pol is able to improve precision on 12.8% of all the widening points with respect to Oct and that it increases by 2.8% the percentage of widening points on which the same precision as Pol is obtained.

Table 2. Precision comparison when using PSet in the descending phase.

		% WP				Time (s)	
DOM₁	DOM₂	EQ	LT	GT	UN	DOM₁	DOM₂
Box	Box⇅PSet	52.3	0.4	**47.3**	0.0	6.20	6.76
Oct	Oct⇅PSet	56.2	0.0	**43.8**	0.0	12.70	8.93
Pol	Pol⇅PSet	64.8	0.0	**35.2**	0.0	7.03	7.53

In Table 2 we provide the summary for the precision comparisons between the three non-disjunctive domains Box, Oct and Pol and the corresponding enhanced combinations using the finite powerset of polyhedra PSet in the descending phase. Note that, in contrast with what we did in Table 1, in this case we cannot provide a *baseline* comparison with PSet because, as said before, this domain is missing a widening operator and hence cannot be used in the ascending phase of the analysis. The use of a powerset domain in the descending phase is of particular interest because it should be able to avoid the over-approximations that are incurred by the non-disjunctive domains when merging control flow paths. In fact, the values in column GT show us that the number of widening points where a precision improvement is obtained is significantly higher than those of Table 1, ranging from 35.2% to 47.3%. In summary, the results in Tables 1 and 2 provide an evidence that the adoption of a more precise abstract domain in the descending phase of the analysis is able to significantly improve precision. Intuitively, this is due to the fact that, by changing the abstract domain, we are potentially improving the precision of all the abstract semantic operators used in the descending phase (i.e., all operators except widening).

Note that we do not perform a proper efficiency comparison, because the considered benchmark suite seems inadequate to the purpose; also, PAGAI is a static analyzer meant to simplify experiments, rather than achieve maximum efficiency. Hence, we merely report in the last two columns of Table 2 the overall time spent on the 35 tests. A meaningful efficiency comparison will be the subject of future work.

A Note on the Relative Precision of Abstract Domains. A non-expert but attentive reader may be wondering how it is possible that the more precise abstract domain Pol can sometimes compute weaker invariants when compared to the less precise domain Box (more generally, why column LT is not always zero). A first reason is that widening operators are not monotonic; another reason is that the two domains may be adopting different approximation strategies for some of the semantic operators (e.g., when modeling non-linear tests/assignments and when taking into account the integrality of program variables).

A Technical Note on the Precision Comparison. When comparing the invariants computed by different abstract domains, PAGAI calls a third-party model checking tool based on SMT (Satisfiability Modulo Theory), which also takes into account the integrality of program variables. Hence, when comparing the abstract elements of different domains, we are *not* counting those "dummy" precision improvements that are simply induced by the real relaxation step. As a concrete example, when x is an integral variable, the Box value $x \in [0, 2]$, the Pol value $\{0 \leq x \leq 2\}$ and the PSet value $\{ \{x = 0\}, \{x = 1\}, \{x = 2\} \}$ are all considered equivalent (note that the last two would not be considered equivalent when compared in the more precise domain PSet).

4.1   A Detailed Example

In Fig. 6 we show a simplified version of one of the tests distributed with PAGAI; assuming $N > 1$, function `fib(N)` computes the $(N + 1)$-th element of the Fibonacci sequence $0, 1, 1, 2, 3, 5, 8, \ldots$. In Table 3 we show the abstract values computed for the one and only widening point (whose position in the code is highlighted using a comment), first with the classical Box domain and then

```
int fib(int N) {
  int P = 0, F = 1;
  for (int K = 2; K < N; ++K) {
    /* widening point */
    int tmp = F;
    F += P;
    P = tmp;
  }
  return F;
}

int main() { return fib(7); }
```

Fig. 6. A simplified version of `fibcall.c`

using the Box↑↓PSet combination, i.e., using the finite powerset of polyhedra in the descending phase. For this example, the threshold value for the number of downward iterations is set to 10.

When using the Box domain, the ascending phase ends on the 4th iteration: due to the use of widenings, the computed post-fixpoint has no upper bound for variable K; the upper bound 6 is easily recovered in the first iteration of the descending phase, which is then detected to be an abstract fixpoint on Box. When using the Box↑↓PSet combination, the ascending phase is computed exactly as before but, before starting the descending phase, the post-fixpoint on Box is transferred to the PSet domain using the concretization function γ: Box → PSet, obtaining a singleton set of polyhedra (see row labeled 'dsc/0'). Then the analysis proceeds by computing the descending iterates using the more precise domain PSet; the descending sequence is able to improve precision by computing several disjuncts, detecting the fixpoint on the 6th downward iteration.

It is worth stressing that, in this specific example, the descending sequence is able to reach a fixpoint on PSet only because function `fib` is called with a constant argument ($N = 7$). If instead the value of the argument was unknown, the descending sequence on PSet would be non-stabilizing, generating a new disjunct at each iteration. This is not a real issue because, as we already said, once started the descending phase the static analysis can be stopped at any iteration and still preserve correctness; a precision improvement with respect to the Box decreasing sequence is obtained even when computing a single downward iterate. Note that, for this detailed example, we have chosen the domain combination Box↑↓PSet and the constant value $N = 7$ merely for exposition purposes, since the computed abstract values turn out to be simpler. For instance, if using the combination Box↑↓Pol and stopping after the 3rd downward iteration, we would obtain as post-fixpoint the following abstract value:

$$\{2 \le K \le 6, 3K - 3P + 2F \ge 8, 7K - 7P - 13F \le 1, K + 12P - 8F \le 7,$$
$$K + 4P - 4F \le 3, 3K - 16P + 8F \le 14, 3K - 6P - 2F \le 4\}.$$

Table 3. Abstract values computed using Box and Box↑↓PSet.

Domain	Phase/Iter	Abstract value
Box	asc/1	$P \in [0,0], F \in [1,1], K \in [2,2]$
Box	asc/2	$P \in [0,+\infty], F \in [1,1], K \in [2,+\infty]$
Box	asc/3	$P \in [0,+\infty], F \in [1,+\infty], K \in [2,+\infty]$
Box	asc/4	Same value (detected post-fixpoint in Box)
Box	dsc/1	$P \in [0,+\infty], F \in [1,+\infty], K \in [2,6]$
Box	dsc/2	Same value (detected fixpoint in Box)
PSet	dsc/0	$\{ \{P \geq 0, F \geq 1, K \geq 2\} \}$
PSet	dsc/1	$\{ \{P = 0, F = 1, K = 2\}, \{P \geq 1, F \geq P, 3 \leq K \leq 6\} \}$
PSet	dsc/2	$\{ \{P = 0, F = 1, K = 2\}, \{P = 1, F = 1, K = 3\},$ $\{P + 1 \leq F \leq 2P, 4 \leq K \leq 6\} \}$
PSet	dsc/3	$\{ \{P = 0, F = 1, K = 2\}, \{P = 1, F = 1, K = 3\},$ $\{P = 1, F = 2, K = 4\}, \{3P \leq 2F, F \leq 2P - 1, 5 \leq K \leq 6\} \}$
PSet	dsc/4	$\{ \{P = 0, F = 1, K = 2\}, \{P = 1, F = 1, K = 3\},$ $\{P = 1, F = 2, K = 4\}, \{P = 2, F = 3, K = 5\},$ $\{3P + 1 \leq 2F, 3F \leq 5P, K = 6\} \}$
PSet	dsc/5	$\{ \{P = 0, F = 1, K = 2\}, \{P = 1, F = 1, K = 3\},$ $\{P = 1, F = 2, K = 4\}, \{P = 2, F = 3, K = 5\},$ $\{P = 3, F = 5, K = 6\} \}$
PSet	dsc/6	Same value (detected fixpoint in PSet)

5   Related Work

Widening operators are quite often necessary to enforce the stabilization of the ascending iteration sequence. Sometimes they are used even in abstract domains having no infinite ascending chains, to accelerate convergence, rather than enforcing it. In restricted cases, the use of widenings can be avoided even though the domain has infinite ascending chains: sometimes it is possible to apply fixpoint acceleration techniques [25] or strategy/policy iteration [23,24] so as to compute the *exact* abstract fixpoint.

When widening operators are actually used, they also are one of the main sources of imprecision for the static analysis. As a consequence, many techniques try to mitigate the corresponding precision loss: [31] proposes the *widening up-to* technique, which tries to preserve precision by using a fixed set of constraints, used as *widening hints*; a similar approach (*widening with thresholds*) is used in [11]; in [5] a framework is proposed to improve the precision of any given widening operator using several heuristics, while still guaranteeing termination; other generic techniques include widening with landmarks [38], lookahead widening [26], guided static analysis [27], and stratified widening [36]. Note that all of the approaches above focus on the ascending sequence and hence are in principle orthogonal with respect to (i.e., they can be combined with) our proposal.

The computation of the descending sequence with narrowing is just another technique (as a matter of fact, the very first one proposed in the literature) to mitigate the imprecision of widenings. However, narrowings have received fewer attention,[4] and it is often believed that the descending sequence can hardly improve precision after a few iterations. Such a belief is probably justified when considering abstract domains whose elements are expressible as template polyhedra. In particular, for the case of template polyhedra with integral bounds (including integral boxes and octagons), [1] first shows that the abstract join operation can be safely replaced by its *left strict* variant; then they prove that, when using this join operator, the computed descending sequence cannot be infinite. However, as witnessed by the `fibcall.c` example shown in Fig. 6, when adopting more precise domains the descending sequence can improve the precision of the analysis well beyond the first few iterations. This seems to be the case, in particular, for domains such as the finite powerset of polyhedra.

[2,3] propose a technique to intertwine the computation of widenings and narrowing (i.e., the computation of ascending and descending chains) during the analysis, aiming at improving the precision of the post-fixpoint computed when the CFG has nested loops. [13,29] propose a technique to improve the precision of the analysis by restarting, possibly several times, the abstract (ascending and descending) iteration sequence from a perturbation of the computed post-fixpoint. In the proposals recalled above the abstract domain is fixed during the runs of the analysis, i.e., the same domain is used in the ascending and descending iteration phases; hence, once again, these approaches are orthogonal with respect to the proposal of this paper. We plan to better investigate the potential synergies arising by integrating the intertwining of widening and narrowing of [3] (implemented for instance in IKOS [14] and SeaHorn [28]) with our decoupling of the ascending and descending phases: in practice, for the combination $\mathbb{A} \uparrow \downarrow \mathbb{D}$, besides using the concretization function $\gamma \colon \mathbb{A} \to \mathbb{D}$ to transfer the ascending post-fixpoint to domain $\mathbb{D}$ (as in the current proposal), we will also be using the abstraction function $\alpha \colon \mathbb{D} \to \mathbb{A}$ to transfer back the descending post-fixpoint whenever restarting the ascending phase on $\mathbb{A}$.

As mentioned previously, a formal justification for the correctness of our proposal is easily obtained by casting it as a meta-abstract interpretation (the so-called A^2I framework [20]). The pre-analysis of the CFG proposed in [12] to reduce the number widening points can be interpreted as a very early instance of the offline A^2I approach. More recently, [34] propose an offline pre-analysis to tailor the configuration of the static analysis tool to the specific program being analyzed. Online (i.e., dynamically computed) meta-analyses include, for instance, variable partitioning techniques [30,39] and the optimized implementation of semantic operators using *boxed polyhedra* [9]. While there certainly are static analysis tools that perform a *non-uniform* analysis (i.e., they use different abstract domains for different portions of the program being analyzed), to the best of our knowledge our approach is the first example of an analysis where the

---

[4] Probably, this is due to the fact that the abstract domain glb operator implements a correct narrowing as soon as we can enforce a finite number of applications.

whole abstract domain (and not just one of its operators) is changed *during* the analysis of a single portion of code.

6   Conclusion

In this paper we have proposed a novel yet simple variation of the typical approach used in static analysis by abstract interpretation, where we decouple the ascending and descending phases of the abstract semantics computation. We use an abstract domain combination denoted $A{\uparrow}{\downarrow}D$, meaning that the ascending phase uses an (ascending) abstract domain A, while the descending phase uses a strictly more precise (descending) abstract domain D. We have implemented our approach by extending the static analysis tool PAGAI and studied its effectiveness on several, different choices for A and D of classical numerical abstract domains, including boxes, octagons, convex polyhedra and sets of polyhedra. Our preliminary experimental results show that decoupling the ascending and descending phases in $A{\uparrow}{\downarrow}D$ allows to obtain significant precision improvements when compared with a classical static analysis computing on A. In particular, the choice of a disjunctive domain for the descending phase seems promising.

Even though this preliminary experimental evaluation is not adequate for assessing the impact on efficiency (in particular, scalability) of the proposed approach, we conjecture that the idea of using a more precise domain D only in the descending phase naturally leads to a more easily tunable efficiency/-precision tradeoff. We would also like to stress that our approach is not really meant to be used *uniformly* on all the code being analyzed; rather, the idea is to selectively enable it on those portions of the program where a precision gain would be desirable, but scalability issues likely prevent to perform the whole analysis using the more precise (and usually less efficient) domain D. As a consequence, an interesting problem that will be studied in future work is how to automatically identify those parts of the program where the decoupled approach is going to be more helpful. In particular, we plan to investigate the effectiveness of simple heuristics (e.g., suitable metrics on the CFG of a function) as well as more sophisticated approaches possibly based on machine learning techniques. Going even further, we could not only select *where* to enable the more concrete descending domain D, but also *drive* the choice of the descending domain D. In particular, we can observe that precision of static analysis is an intensional property, namely it depends on the way the program is written [15,16]. This implies that, we can drive the choice of the descending domain depending on the syntactic characteristics of expressions (guards and assignments) that, in the program, we effectively aim to analyze, since precisely these expressions are the program elements determining the precision of the analyzer [16].

By studying the results of the experimental evaluation, one can also observe that, in a high percentage of cases, the analysis with $A{\uparrow}{\downarrow}D$ is able to produce the same analysis results of the more precise domain D (e.g., Box ${\uparrow}{\downarrow}$ Oct obtains the same results of Oct in 73% of the widening points for the considered benchmarks). This suggests an alternative usage of the decoupled approach, starting from rather different motivations: instead of improving the precision of a classical analysis on $\mathbb{A}$ using the more precise combination $\mathbb{A} \uparrow\downarrow \mathbb{D}$ (as discussed above), one may try to improve the efficiency of a classical analysis on $\mathbb{D}$ by adopting the less precise combination $\mathbb{A} \uparrow\downarrow \mathbb{D}$. In such a context, one would be interested in identifying those portions of the program where the decoupled approach is anyway as precise as the classical approach using $\mathbb{D}$; once again, from a practical point of view, this problem can be addressed using heuristics and/or machine learning techniques. The same problem can also be addressed from a more theoretical point of view, leading to the following research question: *"For a program P and an abstract domain $\mathbb{D}$, which is the less precise domain $\mathbb{A}$ such that the decoupled approach $\mathbb{A} \uparrow\downarrow \mathbb{D}$ yields the same results of $\mathbb{D}$ on P?"*

References

1. Amato, G., Di Nardo Di Maio, S., Meo, M.C., Scozzari, F.: Descending chains and narrowing on template abstract domains. Acta Informatica **55**(6), 521–545 (2017). https://doi.org/10.1007/s00236-016-0291-0
2. Amato, G., Scozzari, F.: Localizing widening and narrowing. In: Logozzo, F., Fähndrich, M. (eds.) SAS 2013. LNCS, vol. 7935, pp. 25–42. Springer, Heidelberg (2013). https://doi.org/10.1007/978-3-642-38856-9_4
3. Amato, G., Scozzari, F., Seidl, H., Apinis, K., Vojdani, V.: Efficiently intertwining widening and narrowing. Sci. Comput. Program. **120**, 1–24 (2016). https://doi.org/10.1016/j.scico.2015.12.005
4. Arceri, V., Mastroeni, I., Xu, S.: Static analysis for ECMAScript string manipulation programs. Appl. Sci. **10**, 3525 (2020). https://doi.org/10.3390/app10103525
5. Bagnara, R., Hill, P., Ricci, E., Zaffanella, E.: Precise widening operators for convex polyhedra. Sci. Comput. Program. **58**(1–2), 28–56 (2005). https://doi.org/10.1016/j.scico.2005.02.003
6. Bagnara, R., Hill, P., Zaffanella, E.: Widening operators for powerset domains. Int. J. Softw. Tools Technol. Transf. **8**(4–5), 449–466 (2006). https://doi.org/10.1007/s10009-005-0215-8
7. Becchi, A., Zaffanella, E.: A direct encoding for nnc polyhedra. In: Chockler, H., Weissenbacher, G. (eds.) CAV 2018. LNCS, vol. 10981, pp. 230–248. Springer, Cham (2018). https://doi.org/10.1007/978-3-319-96145-3_13
8. Becchi, A., Zaffanella, E.: An efficient abstract domain for not necessarily closed polyhedra. In: Podelski, A. (ed.) SAS 2018. LNCS, vol. 11002, pp. 146–165. Springer, Cham (2018). https://doi.org/10.1007/978-3-319-99725-4_11
9. Becchi, A., Zaffanella, E.: Revisiting polyhedral analysis for hybrid systems. In: Chang, B.-Y.E. (ed.) SAS 2019. LNCS, vol. 11822, pp. 183–202. Springer, Cham (2019). https://doi.org/10.1007/978-3-030-32304-2_10
10. Becchi, A., Zaffanella, E.: PPLite: zero-overhead encoding of NNC polyhedra. Inf. Comput. **275**, 104620 (2020). https://doi.org/10.1016/j.ic.2020.104620
11. Blanchet, B., et al.: A static analyzer for large safety-critical software. In: Cytron, R., Gupta, R. (eds.) Proceedings of the ACM SIGPLAN 2003 Conference on Programming Language Design and Implementation 2003, San Diego, California, USA, 9–11 June 2003, pp. 196–207. ACM (2003). https://doi.org/10.1145/781131.781153
12. Bourdoncle, F.: Efficient chaotic iteration strategies with widenings. In: Bjørner, D., Broy, M., Pottosin, I.V. (eds.) FMP&TA 1993. LNCS, vol. 735, pp. 128–141. Springer, Heidelberg (1993). https://doi.org/10.1007/BFb0039704

13. Boutonnet, R., Halbwachs, N.: Improving the results of program analysis by abstract interpretation beyond the decreasing sequence. Formal Methods Syst. Des. **53**(3), 384–406 (2017). https://doi.org/10.1007/s10703-017-0310-y

14. Brat, G., Navas, J.A., Shi, N., Venet, A.: IKOS: a framework for static analysis based on abstract interpretation. In: Giannakopoulou, D., Salaün, G. (eds.) SEFM 2014. LNCS, vol. 8702, pp. 271–277. Springer, Cham (2014). https://doi.org/10.1007/978-3-319-10431-7_20

15. Bruni, R., Giacobazzi, R., Gori, R., Garcia-Contreras, I., Pavlovic, D.: Abstract extensionality: on the properties of incomplete abstract interpretations. Proc. ACM Program. Lang. **4**(POPL), 28:1–28:28 (2020)

16. Bruni, R., Giacobazzi, R., Gori, R., Ranzato, F.: A logic for locally complete abstract interpretations. In: 36th Annual ACM/IEEE Symposium on Logic in Computer Science, LICS 2021, Rome, Italy, June 29–July 2, 2021, pp. 1–13. IEEE (2021)

17. Cousot, P., Cousot, R.: Abstract interpretation: a unified lattice model for static analysis of programs by construction or approximation of fixpoints. In: Conference Record of the Fourth ACM Symposium on Principles of Programming Languages, Los Angeles, California, USA, January 1977, pp. 238–252 (1977)

18. Cousot, P., Cousot, R.: Systematic design of program analysis frameworks. In: Conference Record of the Sixth Annual ACM Symposium on Principles of Programming Languages, San Antonio, Texas, USA, January 1979, pp. 269–282 (1979)

19. Cousot, P., Cousot, R.: Abstract interpretation frameworks. J. Log. Comput. **2**(4), 511–547 (1992). https://doi.org/10.1093/logcom/2.4.511

20. Cousot, P., Giacobazzi, R., Ranzato, F.: A^2I: abstract^2 interpretation. Proc. ACM Program. Lang. **3**(POPL), 42:1–42:31 (2019). https://doi.org/10.1145/3290355

21. Cousot, P., Halbwachs, N.: Automatic discovery of linear restraints among variables of a program. In: Aho, A., Zilles, S., Szymanski, T. (eds.) Conference Record of the Fifth Annual ACM Symposium on Principles of Programming Languages, Tucson, Arizona, USA, January 1978, pp. 84–96. ACM Press (1978). https://doi.org/10.1145/512760.512770

22. Cousot, P., Cousot, R.: Comparing the Galois connection and widening/narrowing approaches to abstract interpretation. In: Bruynooghe, M., Wirsing, M. (eds.) PLILP 1992. LNCS, vol. 631, pp. 269–295. Springer, Heidelberg (1992). https://doi.org/10.1007/3-540-55844-6_142

23. Gaubert, S., Goubault, E., Taly, A., Zennou, S.: Static analysis by policy iteration on relational domains. In: De Nicola, R. (ed.) ESOP 2007. LNCS, vol. 4421, pp. 237–252. Springer, Heidelberg (2007). https://doi.org/10.1007/978-3-540-71316-6_17

24. Gawlitza, T., Seidl, H.: Precise fixpoint computation through strategy iteration. In: De Nicola, R. (ed.) ESOP 2007. LNCS, vol. 4421, pp. 300–315. Springer, Heidelberg (2007). https://doi.org/10.1007/978-3-540-71316-6_21

25. Gonnord, L., Halbwachs, N.: Combining widening and acceleration in linear relation analysis. In: Yi, K. (ed.) SAS 2006. LNCS, vol. 4134, pp. 144–160. Springer, Heidelberg (2006). https://doi.org/10.1007/11823230_10

26. Gopan, D., Reps, T.: Lookahead widening. In: Ball, T., Jones, R.B. (eds.) CAV 2006. LNCS, vol. 4144, pp. 452–466. Springer, Heidelberg (2006). https://doi.org/10.1007/11817963_41

27. Gopan, D., Reps, T.: Guided static analysis. In: Nielson, H.R., Filé, G. (eds.) SAS 2007. LNCS, vol. 4634, pp. 349–365. Springer, Heidelberg (2007). https://doi.org/10.1007/978-3-540-74061-2_22

28. Gurfinkel, A., Kahsai, T., Komuravelli, A., Navas, J.A.: The SeaHorn verification framework. In: Kroening, D., Păsăreanu, C.S. (eds.) CAV 2015. LNCS, vol. 9206, pp. 343–361. Springer, Cham (2015). https://doi.org/10.1007/978-3-319-21690-4_20

29. Halbwachs, N., Henry, J.: When the decreasing sequence fails. In: Miné, A., Schmidt, D. (eds.) SAS 2012. LNCS, vol. 7460, pp. 198–213. Springer, Heidelberg (2012). https://doi.org/10.1007/978-3-642-33125-1_15

30. Halbwachs, N., Merchat, D., Gonnord, L.: Some ways to reduce the space dimension in polyhedra computations. Formal Methods Syst. Des. **29**(1), 79–95 (2006). https://doi.org/10.1007/s10703-006-0013-2

31. Halbwachs, N., Proy, Y.-E., Raymond, P.: Verification of linear hybrid systems by means of convex approximations. In: Le Charlier, B. (ed.) SAS 1994. LNCS, vol. 864, pp. 223–237. Springer, Heidelberg (1994). https://doi.org/10.1007/3-540-58485-4_43

32. Henry, J., Monniaux, D., Moy, M.: PAGAI: a path sensitive static analyser. Electron. Notes Theor. Comput. Sci. **289**, 15–25 (2012). https://doi.org/10.1016/j.entcs.2012.11.003

33. Jeannet, B., Miné, A.: APRON: a library of numerical abstract domains for static analysis. In: Bouajjani, A., Maler, O. (eds.) CAV 2009. LNCS, vol. 5643, pp. 661–667. Springer, Heidelberg (2009). https://doi.org/10.1007/978-3-642-02658-4_52

34. Mansur, M.N., Mariano, B., Christakis, M., Navas, J.A., Wüstholz, V.: Automatically tailoring abstract interpretation to custom usage scenarios. In: Silva, A., Leino, K.R.M. (eds.) CAV 2021. LNCS, vol. 12760, pp. 777–800. Springer, Cham (2021). https://doi.org/10.1007/978-3-030-81688-9_36

35. Miné, A.: The octagon abstract domain. High. Order Symb. Comput. **19**(1), 31–100 (2006). https://doi.org/10.1007/s10990-006-8609-1

36. Monniaux, D., Guen, J.L.: Stratified static analysis based on variable dependencies. Electron. Notes Theor. Comput. Sci. **288**, 61–74 (2012). https://doi.org/10.1016/j.entcs.2012.10.008

37. Nielson, F., Nielson, H., Hankin, C.: Principles of Program Analysis. Springer, Berlin (1999). https://doi.org/10.1007/978-3-662-03811-6

38. Simon, A., King, A.: Widening polyhedra with landmarks. In: Kobayashi, N. (ed.) APLAS 2006. LNCS, vol. 4279, pp. 166–182. Springer, Heidelberg (2006). https://doi.org/10.1007/11924661_11

39. Singh, G., Püschel, M., Vechev, M.: Fast polyhedra abstract domain. In: Castagna, G., Gordon, A. (eds.) Proceedings of the 44th ACM SIGPLAN Symposium on Principles of Programming Languages, POPL 2017, Paris, France, 18–20 January 2017, pp. 46–59. ACM (2017). https://doi.org/10.1145/3009837.3009885

Inferring Region Types via an Abstract Notion of Environment Transformation

Ulrich Schöpp and Chuangjie Xu(⊠)

fortiss GmbH, Guerickestraße 25, 80805 Munich, Germany
{schoepp,xu}@fortiss.org

Abstract. Region-based type systems are a powerful tool for various kinds of program analysis. We introduce a new inference algorithm for region types based on an abstract notion of environment transformation. It analyzes the code of a method only once, even when there are multiple invocations of the method of different region types in the program. Elements of such an abstract transformation are essentially constraints for equality and subtyping that capture flow information of the program. In particular, we work with access graphs in the definition of abstract transformations to guarantee the termination of the inference algorithm, because they provide a finite representation of field access paths.

Keywords: Program analysis · Region type · Type inference · Environment transformation · Type constraint · Featherweight Java

1 Introduction

Programs typically make extensive use of libraries. Analyzing a program thus often involves analysis of big libraries which can be heavy and expensive. The situation gets worse for those analyses where multiple invocations of the same library method requires to re-analyze the library. Therefore, it is significant for analyses to be *compositional*, that is, the analysis result of a program can be computed from the results of its components. Once a library has been analyzed, the result can be directly used to analyze programs that use the library. This work aims at making *region type inference* compositional.

Region-based type systems have been illustrated to be a powerful tool for e.g. memory management [7,8], pointer analysis and taint analysis [5,14,15]. The usage of regions in effect-and-type systems can improve the precision of analysis of trace properties [10,11]. The idea of these type-based analysis approaches are to infer the type of a program which allows one to verify if the program satisfies certain properties. However, the type inference algorithms for the region type systems for Featherweight Java from the previous work [5,10,11,14] are *not* compositional. The type of a method is inferred from the ones of its arguments.

Supported by the German Research Foundation (DFG) under the research grant 250888164 (GuideForce).

I. Sergey (Ed.): APLAS 2022, LNCS 13658, pp. 45–64, 2022.
https://doi.org/10.1007/978-3-031-21037-2_3

If the method is called with arguments of different types, its code is analyzed multiple times, one for each invocation.

To avoid redundant analysis, we introduce a new inference algorithm based on an abstract notion of environment transformation. The idea is to summarize the flow information of the program using an abstract transformation. Then we derive the type of a method by applying its abstract transformation to the types of its arguments. When analyzing some new code which invokes some methods that have been analyzed, we can use the abstract transformations computed in the previous round of analysis, rather than re-analyzing the code of the methods as in the previous work [5,10,11,14]. We now explain the idea in more detail.

Region Types and Typing Environments. We work with the region type system of Beringer et al. [5] for Featherweight Java [16]. But our approach can be adapted for other type systems. In our type system, *region types* represent some properties of values. For example, we consider a region $\texttt{CreatedAt}(\ell)$ for references to objects that were created in the position with label ℓ. One can think of the label ℓ as a line number in the source code. This region enables us to track where in the program an object originates. We allow *typing environments* to carry field typing. For example, the environment

$$E = (x : \texttt{CreatedAt}(\ell_1), \ \texttt{CreatedAt}(\ell_1).f : \texttt{CreatedAt}(\ell_2))$$

means that x points to an object which is created at position ℓ_1 and the field f of any object created at ℓ_1 is an object created at ℓ_2.

Environment Transformations. Inferring region types is essentially a flow analysis. The execution of a program may change the types of its variables and fields. Thus we want to assign it an *environment transformation* that captures how the types are updated in the program. For example, the program

$$\begin{aligned} y &= x.f; \\ x &= \texttt{new}^{\ell_3} \ C(); \end{aligned}$$

can be assigned the transformation

$$[y :\mapsto x.f, \ x :\mapsto \texttt{CreatedAt}(\ell_3)].$$

It updates the environment E to

$$(x : \texttt{CreatedAt}(\ell_3), \ y : \texttt{CreatedAt}(\ell_2), \ \texttt{CreatedAt}(\ell_1).f : \texttt{CreatedAt}(\ell_2)).$$

Note that the substitutions are performed simultaneously. If the program returns the variable x, then we look it up in the above updated environment and conclude that the program has return type $\texttt{CreatedAt}(\ell_3)$, meaning that it returns an object created at position ℓ_3.

Field Access Graphs. Directly using field access paths like $x.f$ in environments as above is problematic, because the lengths of access paths may be unbounded. The computation of environment transformations involving such access paths may not terminate. For example, consider a class of linked lists with a field next : Node pointing to the next node. The following method returns the last node of a list.

```
Node last() {
    if (next == null) {return this; }
    else {return next.last(); }
}
```

Its return type can be the same as the type of variable this, or the types of the paths this.next, this.next.next and so on, resulting in an infinite set of access paths. To solve this, we work with *access graphs* which provide a finite representation of access paths [18,28]. For example, the Node class has three access graphs to represent all its access paths. The return type of last is then computed via the set containing these three graphs.

Field Update and Constraints. We work with *weak update* for field typing as in [5]: If a field f of some object is assigned a value of type B, and in another occasion it is assigned a value of type C, then the field should have a type containing both B and C. Therefore, for an assignment statement like $y.f = x$, we assign it a *constraint* $y.f :\geq x$, meaning that the type of the field f of any object of the type of y should be greater than or equal to the type of x.

Abstract Transformations. With the above ingredients, we introduce a notion of abstract transformation. An *abstract transformation* consists of assignments $x :\mapsto u$ and constraints $\kappa :\geq v$. The value such as u, v is a formal disjunction of some atoms. An *atom* is a variable, a type or a field graph following a variable or a type. The key κ is a non-empty graph representing access paths. To capture how types are updated in a program, we define the following operations on abstract transformations. We *instantiate* an abstract transformation to an end-ofunction on typing environments. It computes the types of variables and fields of a program with a given initial typing. We define the *composition* of abstract transformations to model type updates in a statement followed by another. We also define the *join* of abstract transformations to tackle conditional branches.

Type Inference. Suppose we have a table T assigning an abstract transformation to each method of a program. Then we can compute an abstract transformation for any expression e of the program by induction on e. For example, when e is an invocation of a method, we lookup the table T to get the abstract transformation; and when e is a conditional expression, we join the abstract transformations of its branches. For any well-typed program, we have a fixed-point algorithm to compute such a table T for it. To infer the type of a method, we find its abstract transformation from T, feed it with the argument types, and then get the type of the return variable from the resulting typing environment.

Related Work. Constraint-based analysis is a common technique for type inference with a rich history [1–3, 21, 22, 29–31]. It may be divided into two main phases. The first phase is to generate constraints by traversing the program. To improve the efficiency of type inference, some simplification may be performed on the generated constraints. Our computation of the table T of abstract transformations corresponds to constraint generation, where constraints are simplified by the composition operation of abstract transformations. The second phase is to solve the generated constraints. There are many different constraint solvers. In our approach, we instantiate the abstract transformations in T to infer the type of the program, which corresponds to constraint solving. Therefore, our approach is essentially a constraint-based type inference algorithm. But it departs from the existing work in the following aspects. We make use of constraints to infer region information of the program rather than implementation types (i.e., sets of classes) [1, 22, 31]. Moreover, we work with access graphs for the constraint language to guarantee the termination of our inference algorithm, rather than requiring an additional termination test [29, 31].

Our approach is also closely related to the framework for Interprocedural Distributive Environments (IDE) of Sagiv et al. [25]. The main idea of the IDE framework is to reduce a program-analysis problem to a pure graph-reachability problem. A user defines a set of environment transformers, that is, endofunctions on environments describing the effect of a statement, and then uses an IDE solver such as Heros [6, 23] to compute analysis results for the entire program. In particular, IDE requires environment transformers to be distributive: transforming the join of any environments gives the same result of joining the transformed environments. We attempted to use IDE to infer region types, but the environment transformer for statement such as $x = y.f$ is not distributive, because it needs to access the input environment multiple times in order to get the type of $y.f$. This failed attempt motivated us to develop a symbolic representation of environment transformers for type inference, resulting in our notion of abstract transformation.

2   Background

We briefly recall the definitions of Featherweight Java and access graphs.

2.1   Featherweight Java

We work with a variant of Featherweight Java (FJ) using the formulation of [10]. It extends FJ [16] with field updates, and has primitive if- and let-expressions for convenience. In the presence of field updates, we omit constructors for simplicity.

The syntax of the language uses four kinds of names.

$$\text{variables: } x, y \in \textit{Var} \quad \text{classes: } C, D \in \textit{Cls}$$
$$\text{fields: } f \in \textit{Fld} \quad \text{methods: } m \in \textit{Mtd}$$

Program expressions are defined as follows:

$$Expr \ni e ::= \quad x \mid \texttt{let } x = e_1 \texttt{ in } e_2 \mid \texttt{if } x = y \texttt{ then } e_1 \texttt{ else } e_2$$
$$\mid \texttt{null} \mid \texttt{new}^\ell\, C \mid (C)\, e \mid x^C.m(\bar{y}) \mid x^C.f \mid x^C.f := y$$

The expression $\texttt{new}^\ell\, C$ creates a new object of class C with all fields initiated to $\texttt{null}$. It is annotated with a label $\ell \in Pos$. We use labels only to distinguish different occurrences of $\texttt{new}$ in a program, since our type system will track where objects were created. In a few expressions we have added type annotations and write x^C for a variable of class C. They will be needed when looking up in the class table. This is simpler than working with typed variable declarations, since we do not need to find the declarations in order to get the type of a variable. We sometimes omit annotations when they are not needed.

We assume three distinguished formal elements: $\texttt{Object}, \texttt{NullType} \in Cls$ and $\texttt{this} \in Var$. The $\texttt{NullType}$ class plays the role of the type of $\texttt{null}$ from the Java language specification [13, §4]. It may not be used in programs, i.e. we require $C \neq \texttt{NullType}$ in create expression $\texttt{new}^\ell\, C$ and casting expression $(C)\, e$. When x is not a free variable of e_2, we may write $e_1; e_2$ rather than $\texttt{let } x = e_1 \texttt{ in } e_2$.

An FJ program $(\prec, \textit{fields}, \textit{methods}, \textit{mtable})$ consists of

- a subtyping relation $\prec \in \mathcal{P}^{\text{fin}}(Cls \times Cls)$ with $C \prec D$ meaning that C is an immediate subclass of D,
- a field list $\textit{fields} : Cls \to \mathcal{P}^{\text{fin}}(Fld)$ mapping a class to its fields,
- a method list $\textit{methods} : Cls \to \mathcal{P}^{\text{fin}}(Mtd)$ mapping a class to its methods,
- a method table $\textit{mtable} : Cls \times Mtd \rightharpoonup Var^* \times Expr$ mapping a method to the pair of its formal parameters and its body.

All components are required to be well-formed. We refer the reader to e.g. [10, Section 3] for details. Let $\preceq$ be the reflexive and transitive closure of $\prec$. Then we have $C \preceq \texttt{Object}$ and $\texttt{NullType} \preceq C$ for any class $C \in Cls$.

In the standard FJ type system [16], types are simply classes. In the rest of this paper, we consider only FJ programs that are well-typed with respect to the standard FJ type system.

2.2   Access Graphs

For recursive data types such as linked lists, the lengths of access paths may be unbounded. If environment transformations are defined upon access paths, their computation may not terminate. In this paper, we choose to work with the finite representation of access paths given by access graphs [18,28] among the others [9,17,19].

An *access graph* $x.G$ consists of a local variable x, called its *base*, and a field graph G. A *field graph* is a directed graph whose nodes are fields. The empty field graph is denoted by $\mathcal{E}$. The access graph $x.\mathcal{E}$ represents the plain variable x. Thus we often omit the empty field graph $\mathcal{E}$ and simply write x. If a field graph is not empty, it has a head node $h \in Fld$ and a tail node $t \in Fld$ such that for each node $n \in Fld$ within the field graph there exists a path from h to t passing through n. Note that the head and tail can be the same. A non-empty field graph can be uniquely identified by its head h, tail t and edge set $E \subseteq Fld \times Fld$; thus, we write $\langle h, E, t \rangle$ to denote it. Each access graph $x.\langle h, E, t \rangle$ represents the set of access paths obtained by traversing the field graph from the head to the tail. We write $\mathcal{F}$ to denote the set of field graphs and use G, G' to range over field graphs in the paper.

Example 1. Consider the following access graphs for a class of nodes for linked lists. The field v is the value stored in the current node and the field n points to the next node.

In the above diagrams, each bold circle represents a tail. These access graphs represent access paths as explained below:

(1) $x.\mathcal{E}$ represents the variable x.
(2) $x.\langle v, \emptyset, v \rangle$ represents the path $x.v$.
(3) $x.\langle n, \{(n, n), (n, v)\}, v \rangle$ represents the paths $x.n.v$, $x.n.n.v$ and so on. □

Given any two field graphs G and G', we *concatenate* them and obtain a field graph $G.G' \in \mathcal{F}$ as follows:

$$G.\mathcal{E} := G$$
$$\mathcal{E}.G' := G'$$
$$\langle h, E, t \rangle.\langle h', E', t' \rangle := \langle h, E \cup \{(t, h')\} \cup E', t' \rangle.$$

Intuitively, the concatenation of a path in G with one in G' lives in $G.G'$. This operation is needed for defining composition of environment transformations.

We work with a generalization of access graphs $b.G$ where b can be either a variable or a type in order to model field typing as explained in Session 3.2.

3   A Theory of Abstract Transformations

Our idea is to type a program via environment transformations. Consider the simple example given in Fig. 1. Each statement of the program is assigned an environment transformation. They are composed into an environment transformation σ for the whole program. For any given initial typing environment *env*, we obtain the updated environment $\sigma(env)$ containing the typing information after executing the program. Lastly, we get the return type of the program from the updated typing environment $\sigma(env)$. In this section, we explain what environment transformations are and how they update typing environments.

This section is organized as follows. Section 3.1 presents the assumptions and definitions of types and typing environments. Section 3.2 introduces our abstract notion of environment transformation which is based on access graphs. Lastly, Sect. 3.3 demonstrates some operations on abstract transformations which are essential for modeling the type updates of the program.

$$env = (y : A, A.f : B)$$

```
x = y.f;        ........ [x :↦ y.f]
y = new C();    ........ [y :↦ C]
y.f = x         ........ [y.f :≥ x]
```

$$\sigma = [x :\mapsto y.f,\ y :\mapsto C,\ C.f :\geq y.f]$$

$$\sigma(env) = (x : B,\ y : C,\ A.f : B,\ C.f : B)$$

Fig. 1. An example illustrating the idea of typing via environment transformations

3.1 Types and Environments

We use abstract transformations to encode the changes of types in the program. But our approach is general and works for various type systems including those in the previous work [5,10,11,14]. We target at flow type systems in the spirit of Microsoft's TypeScript [20] and Facebook's Flow [12], rather than the standard FJ typing [16]. We leave the notion of type generic in this section. For instance, when working with classes, our approach can infer implementation types [1,22, 31]. In the next section, we work with region types to present a new algorithm for inferring region information using abstract transformations.

In this section, we assume a finite set Typ of atomic *types* and use A, B, C to range over atomic types. In addition, we assume a set $Cls(A) \subseteq Cls$ of actual classes of an object of type A. This allows us to get the set $Fld(A) \subseteq Fld$ of fields of (objects of) type A. We write $A.f$ to denote the field $f \in Fld(A)$.

We consider the field typing as a part of an environment; thus, a typing *environment* is a mapping $Var \cup Typ \times Fld \rightharpoonup \mathcal{P}(Typ)$ that assigns a variable or a field its possible types. We work with a partial order $\sqsubseteq$ on environments given by $env \sqsubseteq env'$ iff $env(\kappa) \subseteq env'(\kappa)$ for all $\kappa \in \text{dom}(env)$. Given an environment env, we write $env|_v : Var \rightharpoonup \mathcal{P}(Typ)$ and $env|_f : Typ \times Fld \rightharpoonup \mathcal{P}(Typ)$ to denote the typings of variables and fields of env respectively. Given a variable typing $V : Var \rightharpoonup \mathcal{P}(Typ)$ and a field typing $F : Typ \times Fld \rightharpoonup \mathcal{P}(Typ)$, we write (V, F) to denote the environment combining the typings from V and F. In particular, we have $env = (env|_v, env|_f)$.

We often call a set of atomic types a *type*. We simply write A to denote the singleton set $\{A\}$ and misuse the disjunction symbol $\vee$ for set unions. The set $\{A, B, C\}$ for example is thus denoted as $A \vee B \vee C$. In particular, we write $\bot$ to denote the empty set of atomic types. For instance, $(x : A,\ A.f : B \vee C)$ is an environment stating that the variable x has type A and the field f of any object of type A can have type B or C.

3.2 Abstract Transformations

Now we define our notion of abstract transformation which encodes type updates of the variables and fields of a program.

When assigning transformations to statements in the program, the interesting cases are the assignment statements. Consider a statement $x = e$ and its following possible transformations:

- If e is a constant of type A, then the resulting transformation is $[x :\mapsto A]$, meaning that the type of x is A.
- If e is a variable y whose type is unknown yet, then the resulting transformation is $[x :\mapsto y]$, meaning that x has the same type as y.
- If e is a field $y.f$ and the type of y is known to be A, then the resulting transformation is $[x :\mapsto A.f]$, meaning that x has the same type as the field f of any object of type A.
- If e is a field $y.f$ and the type of y is unknown, then the resulting transformation is $[x :\mapsto y.f]$, meaning that x has the same type as the field f of any object of the type of y.

The above cases list four *atomic* kinds of assignment values: atomic type A, variable y, fields $A.f$ and $y.f$ of a type and a variable. As discussed earlier, we work with access graphs instead of access paths to avoid non-terminating computation. All of above assignment values can be represented using a generalization $b.G$ of access graphs where the base b can also be a type. For instance, the type A is represented by $A.\mathcal{E}$ where $\mathcal{E}$ is the empty field graph, and the field $A.f$ is represented by $A.\langle f, \emptyset, f \rangle$. We consider one more possible case of e:

- If e involves some branches and thus has type $B \vee C$, then $x = e$ results in a transformation $[x :\mapsto B \vee C]$, meaning that x has type B or C.

More generally, the value v of an assignment $x :\mapsto v$ can be the 'formal disjunction' of some access graphs $b.G$. These cases bring the following definition of terms to represent assignment values.

Definition 1 (Atoms and terms). Atoms *are a generalization of access graphs whose base is either a variable or an atomic type. We write $b.G$ to denote the atom with base $b \in Var \cup Typ$ and field graph $G \in \mathcal{F}$.*

A term is simply a set (or a formal disjunction) of atoms. We write $\bot$ to denote the empty term, i.e., the empty set of atoms, and $u \vee v$ to denote the join of terms u and v, i.e., the union of the two sets u, v of atoms. Therefore, we have $u \vee \bot = u = \bot \vee u$ for any term u.

When the field graph G is empty, the atom $b.G$ represents a variable or an atomic type. Thus we often omit G and simply write b to denote the atom. If $G = \langle f, \emptyset, f \rangle$, that is, a graph consisting of only the singleton field access path f, then we may write $b.f$ rather than $b.\langle f, \emptyset, f \rangle$.

By definition, each term u has the form $\bigvee_{i=1}^{n} b_i.G_i$ where $u = \bot$ if $n = 0$. We *concatenate* a term u with a field graph G by

$$u.G = (\bigvee_{i=1}^{n} b_i.G_i).G = \bigvee_{i=1}^{n} b_i.(G_i.G)$$

where the concatenation $G_i.G$ of field graphs has been defined in Sect. 2.2.

A term is a formal expression that can be instantiated into a concrete type with a given typing environment (see Definition 6). We denote the set of terms by Tm and use u, v, w to range over terms.

Definition 2 (Assignments). *An* assignment *is a pair consists of a variable* x *and a term* u, *written as* $x :\mapsto u$. *It means that the type of variable* x *is the instantiation of the term* u *w.r.t. any typing environment. We call* x *the* key *of the assignment.*

We want a notion of environment transformation that encodes also the update of field typing. In particular, we choose to work with *weak update* for field typing as in the previous work [5,10,11,14]: If a field f of an object of type A is assigned a value of type B and f of another object of the same type A is assigned a value of type C, then the field $A.f$ of any object of type A should have a type containing both B and C. Therefore, for a statement like $y.f = x$, we cannot give it the assignment $y.f :\mapsto x$ as it expresses that $y.f$ has the same type of x. Instead, we assign it a constraint $y.f :\geq x$, meaning that the type of the field f of any object of the type of y should be greater than or equal to the type of x. If y has type A, then the constraint becomes $A.f :\geq x$. More generally, we define constraints as follows.

Definition 3 (Constraints). *A constraint is a pair consisting of a nonempty access graph* $b.G$ *and a term* u, *written as* $b.G :\geq u$. *It means that the type of any field reachable via some path of* $b.G$ *is greater than or equal to the instantiation of the term* u *w.r.t. any typing environment. We call* $b.G$ *the* key *of the constraint.*

Abstract transformations consists of assignments and/or constraints.

Definition 4 (Abstract transformations). *An* abstract transformation

$$[x_1 :\mapsto u_1, \ldots, x_n :\mapsto u_n, \kappa_1 :\geq v_1, \ldots, \kappa_m :\geq v_m]$$

is a finite set consisting of assignments $x_i :\mapsto u_i$ *and constraints* $\kappa_j :\geq v_j$ *such that all the keys are different and* $x_i \neq u_i$ *for all* $i \in \{1, \ldots, n\}$ *and* $v_j \neq \bot$ *for all* $j \in \{1, \ldots, m\}$. *Let* σ *be the above abstract transformation. We write* $\text{dom}(\sigma)$ *to denote its* domain, *that is, the set of keys* $\{x_1, \ldots, x_n, \kappa_1, \ldots, \kappa_m\}$.

Let $\mathcal{K}$ be the set of *keys*, that is, variables and nonempty access graphs. Each abstract transformation σ is a representation of a total function from $\mathcal{K}$ to Tm

$$\sigma(x) := \begin{cases} u & \text{if } (x :\mapsto u) \in \sigma \\ x & \text{if } x \notin \text{dom}(\sigma) \end{cases} \qquad \sigma(\kappa) := \begin{cases} v & \text{if } (\kappa :\geq v) \in \sigma \\ \bot & \text{if } \kappa \notin \text{dom}(\sigma). \end{cases}$$

In other words, identity assignments $x :\mapsto x$ and bottom constraints $\kappa :\geq \bot$ are omitted in abstract transformations. This is because they add no information to the transformations. For instance, if a transformation contains only identity assignments and bottom constraints, then it is instantiated into the identity function on typing environments according to Definition 7.

We write *ATrans* to denote the set of abstract transformations and use σ, θ to range over abstract transformations in the paper. The empty transformation is denoted as $[]$, and the one consisting of only bottom assignments $x :\mapsto \bot$ for all variable x is denoted as $\bot$. As will become clear, $[]$ is the identity environment transformation and $\bot$ the 'least' environment transformation.

Example 2. Consider again the example in Fig. 1. The program

$$\texttt{x = y.f; y = new C(); y.f = x}$$

results in the transformation

$$[x :\mapsto y.f,\ y :\mapsto C,\ C.f :\geq y.f].$$

For $\texttt{x = y.f}$, the type of $\texttt{y}$ is not known yet and thus it leads to the assignment $x :\mapsto y.f$. In this example, we assume that the type of $\texttt{new C()}$ is some type C which can be different from class $\texttt{C}$. Thus $\texttt{y = new C()}$ leads to $y :\mapsto C$. The last statement $\texttt{y.f = x}$ by itself results in the constraint $y.f :\geq x$. But because of $x :\mapsto y.f$ and $y :\mapsto C$, the constraint is updated to $C.f :\geq y.f$ by substituting y in the key $y.f$ by C and the constraint value x by $y.f$.   □

3.3   Operations on Abstract Transformations

Consider again the example from Fig. 1. In this section, we firstly demonstrate how the transformation $\sigma = [x :\mapsto y.f,\ y :\mapsto C,\ C.f :\geq y.f]$ updates the environment $env = (y : A,\ A.f : B)$ to $\sigma(env) = (x : B,\ y : C,\ A.f : B,\ C.f : B)$. Then we show that abstract transformations can be composed and joined so that we can construct the transformation σ for the program from those of its statements.

To begin with, we look into how the type of x is computed in $\sigma(env)$. There is an assignment $x :\mapsto y.f$ in σ, meaning that x has the same type as $y.f$. We have to instantiate the term $y.f$ using the typing information given by the input environment env. Because y has type A in env, we instantiate $y.f$ to $A.f$. And because $A.f$ has type B in env, we instantiate $y.f$ further to B. Therefore, x has type B in the updated environment $\sigma(env)$.

We have seen from the above example that we need to instantiate a term to a type according to the environment which we want to update. In particular, we consider how to instantiate an atom $A.\langle h, E, t\rangle$. For example, let us instantiate $A.f.g$ according to $(A.f : A \vee B,\ B.g : C,\ C.g : D)$. The goal is to compute the type of the field g of $A.f$. Which field in the environment should be considered, $B.g$ or $C.g$? Because $A.f$ can have type A or B, we can *reach* the field $B.g$ but not $C.g$. Therefore, we should instantiate $A.f.g$ only to C, i.e., the type of $B.g$.

In the following, we describe how to compute the *reachable fields* from a field $A.h$ via an edge set E according to the field typing in an environment env. Then, to instantiate $A.\langle h, E, t\rangle$ w.r.t. env, we simply join the types of all fields $B.t$ in env which are reachable from $A.h$.

Definition 5 (Reachable fields). *Let A be an atomic type, h a field, E an edge set and env an environment. We construct the set $\mathcal{R}(A.h, E, env) \subseteq Typ \times Fld$ of reachable fields from $A.h$ via E according to env as follows:*

(1) Let $\mathcal{R}(A.h, E, env) = \{A.h\}$.
*(2) For each $B.f \in \mathcal{R}(A.h, E, env)$, let $\mathcal{R}(A.h, E, env) = \mathcal{R}(A.h, E, env) \cup \mathcal{S}_{B.f}$,
     where $\mathcal{S}_{B.f}$ is the set of immediate successors of $B.f$ defined by*

$$\mathcal{S}_{B.f} := \{C.g \mid C \in env(B.f)\ and\ (f, g) \in E\ and\ g \in Fld(C)\}.$$

(3) Repeat (2) until $\mathcal{R}(A.h, E, env)$ cannot be updated anymore.

Any field $A.f$ is reachable from itself. To compute the other reachable fields from $A.f$, the above algorithm simply gets the immediate successors of $A.f$, and then those of the immediate successors and so on.

Example 3. Let $env = (A.f : A \vee B, B.g : C)$ and assume $Fld(A) = \{f, g\}$ and $Fld(B) = \{g\}$. By definition, we have

$$\mathcal{R}(A.f, \emptyset, env) = \{A.f\}$$

because the edge set is empty and thus f has no successors. We have

$$\mathcal{R}(A.f, \{(f, g)\}, env) = \{A.f, A.g, B.g\}$$

indicating that $A.g$ and $B.g$ are also reachable from $A.f$. That's because g is a successor of f and g is a field of both A and B. $\qquad\square$

The instantiation $(A.\langle h, E, t \rangle)[env] \subseteq Typ$ is given by the join of $env(B.t)$ for all reachable fields $B.t \in \mathcal{R}(A.h, E, env)$. With this, we can instantiate arbitrary atoms and thus terms.

Definition 6 (Instantiation of terms). *Let env be an environment. We define the* instantiation $(b.G)[env] \subseteq Typ$ *of atom $b.G$ as follows:*

$$A[env] := A$$
$$(A.\langle h, E, t \rangle)[env] := \bigvee \{env(B.t) \mid B.t \in \mathcal{R}(A.h, E, env)\}$$
$$(x.G)[env] := \bigvee \{(A.G)[env] \mid A \in env(x)\}.$$

The instantiation of a term u is the join of the instantiations of its atoms, i.e.,

$$u[env] = (\bigvee_{i=1}^{n} b_i.G_i)[env] := \bigvee_{i=1}^{n} (b_i.G_i)[env].$$

In the above definition, we assume that if $a \notin dom(env)$ then $env(a) = \bot$, that is, the empty set of types, where a is a variable x or a field $A.f$. Therefore, we have $x[env] = env(x)$ and $(A.f)[env] = env(A.f)$.

Example 4. Let $env = (A.f : A \vee B, B.g : C)$ and assume $Fld(A) = \{f, g\}$ and $Fld(B) = \{g\}$ as in Example 3. By definition, we have

$$(A.f)[env] = env(A.f) = A \vee B$$

and

$$\begin{aligned}
(A.f.g)[env] &= (A.\langle f, \{(f, g)\}, g \rangle)[env] \\
&= \bigvee \{env(X.g) \mid X.g \in \mathcal{R}(A.f, \{(f, g)\}, env)\} \\
&= env(A.g) \vee env(B.g) \\
&= \bot \vee C = C
\end{aligned}$$

because from Example 3 we know both $A.g$ and $B.g$ are reachable from $A.f$. $\qquad\square$

Lastly, we instantiate abstract transformations to endofunctions on typing environments. The type of a variable is computed by instantiated the its assigned term in the transformation, as discussed above. To compute the types of fields, we solve the constraints using a fixed-point algorithm.

Definition 7 (Instantiation of abstract transformations). *Let σ be an abstract transformation. We define an endofunction φ_σ on environments by*

$$\varphi_\sigma(env)(x) := \begin{cases} u[env] & \text{if } (x :\mapsto u) \in \sigma \\ env(x) & \text{otherwise} \end{cases}$$

$$\varphi_\sigma(env)(A.f) := env(A.f) \vee \bigvee \{u[env] \mid (b.\langle h, E, f\rangle :\geq u) \in \sigma \text{ and} \\ B \in b[env] \text{ and } A.f \in \mathcal{R}(B.h, E, env)\}.$$

Let env be an environment. We define an environment $\sigma(env)$ by

1. *Let $env' = env$.*
2. *Let $env'' = \varphi_\sigma(env|_v, env'|_f)$, where $(env|_v, env'|_f)$ is the environment obtained by combining the variable typing of env and the field typing of env'.*
3. *If $env' \neq env''$, then let $env' = env''$ and go back to Step 2. Otherwise, let $\sigma(env) = env'$.*

This procedure results in an environment transformation mapping env to $\sigma(env)$.

To instantiate an abstract transformation σ, we use the above fixed-point algorithm to solve the constraints for field typings in σ. What crucial is the function φ_σ that updates the environment in each iteration towards the fixed point. If $(x :\mapsto u) \in \sigma$, then $\varphi_\sigma(env)$ assigns x to the instantiation $u[env]$; otherwise, x is assigned the type as claimed in env. Because of weak update for field typing, $\varphi_\sigma(env)$ assigns a field $A.f$ to the join containing its previous type $env(A.f)$ given by the environment and the instantiations of constraint values from whose keys the field $A.f$ can reach.

Note that, in each iteration towards the fixed point, the input of φ_σ consists of the variable typing $env|_v$ from the original environment env and the field typing $env'|_f$ from the result env' of the previous iteration. This is because types of variables and of fields are updated in different manners. We 'accumulate' the field typing by feeding φ_σ with the field typing from the previous iteration due to weak update as explained earlier. However, variable typing is not updated in this way. For instance, consider the code x = y; y = new C(), resulting in the transformation $\sigma = [x :\mapsto y, y :\mapsto C]$, and the environment $env = (y : A)$. We have $\varphi_\sigma(env) = (x : A, y : C)$ which gives the correct type to x, because x should have the same type of y before the assignment y = new C() which is A. But applying φ_σ to the updated environment would give x type C.

By definition, the empty transformation $[]$ is identity on environments. For a more interesting example, we consider the transformation from Fig. 1.

Example 5. Recall the abstract transformation from Fig. 1:

$$\sigma = [x :\mapsto y.f, \ y :\mapsto C, \ C.f :\geq y.f].$$

Let $env = (y : A, A.f : B)$. The variables and fields that should appear in the updated environment $\sigma(env)$ consist of x, y, $A.f$ and $C.f$. By definition, we have

$$\varphi_\sigma(env)(x) = (y.f)[env] = B$$
$$\varphi_\sigma(env)(y) = C[env] = C$$
$$\varphi_\sigma(env)(A.f) = env(A.f) \vee \bot = B$$
$$\varphi_\sigma(env)(C.f) = env(C.f) \vee (y.f)[env] = \bot \vee B = B.$$

Because $\varphi_\sigma(env) = \varphi_\sigma(env|_v, \varphi_\sigma(env)|_f)$, we reach the fixed point and get the updated environment $\sigma(env) = \varphi_\sigma(env) = (x : B, y : C, A.f : B, C.f : B)$.   □

As explained in the next section, each statement of a program can be assigned a transformation indicating the assignment or constraint of the involved type. To combine them into one transformation that summarizes the type updates of the whole program, the operations of composition and join for transformations are needed. Due to the lack of space, we characterize these operations in the following theorems. Details of their (non-surprising) constructions are available in the arXiv version of the paper [26, Appendix A].

Theorem 1 (Composition of abstract transformations). *For any abstract transformations σ and θ, we can construct an abstract transformation δ such that $\sigma(\theta(env)) \sqsubseteq \delta(env)$. We write $\sigma\theta$ to denote δ and call it the composition of σ and θ. Moreover, we have $\sigma[] = \sigma = []\sigma$ for any transformation σ, where $[]$ is the empty transformation.*   □

The difficult part of the work is to come up with the right notion of abstract transformation that supports composition. But the construction of composition and its correctness are then straightforward. The idea to compose our abstract transformations is similar to the one for substitutions (see e.g. [4, §2.1]). And its correctness can be proved with a standard inductive argument on the length of the abstract transformation.

Note that we have only $\sigma(\theta(env)) \sqsubseteq (\sigma\theta)(env)$ where $\sqsubseteq$ is the ordering on environments defined pointwisely. This is because $\sigma\theta$ involves concatenation of field graphs which causes the over approximation. For instance, concatenating a singleton path f with itself does not give the path $f.f$. Instead it results in the field graph $\langle f, \{(f, f)\}, f \rangle$ which represents all the paths consisting of f with length greater than 1. However, the type inference algorithm presented in next section is still sound. It may give a less precise type to the program.

Theorem 2 (Join of abstract transformations). *For any abstract transformations σ and θ, we can construct an abstract transformation δ such that $\sigma(env) \sqcup \theta(env) \sqsubseteq \delta(env)$. We write $\sigma \vee \theta$ to denote δ and call it the join of σ and θ. Moreover, we have $\sigma \vee \theta = \theta \vee \sigma$ and $\sigma \vee \bot = \sigma$ for all σ and θ, where $\bot$ is the bottom transformation that assigns all variables to the bottom type.*   □

The join $\sigma \vee \theta$ is constructed componentwise using the join operator on terms. It does not preserve fixed points and we have only $\sigma(env) \sqcup \theta(env) \sqsubseteq (\sigma \vee \theta)(env)$. As discussed above, this causes no harm to the soundness of the type inference.

4 Type Inference via Abstract Transformations

In this section, we demonstrate how to infer the type of an FJ program using abstract transformations. The idea is to use abstract transformations to capture the flow information of a program, which leads to a more efficient type inference algorithm. As an example, we work with the region type system of Beringer et al. [5]. Our inference algorithm firstly computes an abstract transformation for each method of the program, and then uses them for the type inference rather than analyzing the method bodies.

4.1 Region Type System

We briefly recall the region type system of Beringer et al. [5].

A *region* represents a property of a value such as its provenance information. In this paper, we use the following definition of regions:

$$Reg \ni r, s ::= \texttt{Null} \mid \texttt{CreatedAt}(\ell)$$

The region $\texttt{Null}$ contains only the value *null*. The region $\texttt{CreatedAt}(\ell)$ contains all references to objects that were created by an expression of the form $\texttt{new}^\ell\ C$. This region allows us to track where in the program an object originates. One can use a richer definition of regions to capture other properties of interest such as taintedness [10]. We keep it simple here because we focus on the type inference.

Region type information is complementary to FJ type information and can be captured without repeating the FJ type system. Therefore, we directly work with region types rather than refining FJ types as in the original system [5, Section 3].

As for FJ, we need a class table to record the region types of methods and fields. This is needed to formulate typing rules for method call and field access. A *class table* (F, M) consists of

- a *field typing* $F : Cls \times Reg \times Fld \rightharpoonup \mathcal{P}(Reg)$ that assigns to each class C, region r and field $f \in fields(C)$ a set $F(C, r, f)$ of regions of the field f, and
- a *method typing* $M : Cls \times Reg \times Mtd \times Reg^* \rightharpoonup \mathcal{P}(Reg)$ that assigns to each class C, region r, method $m \in methods(C)$ and sequence $\bar{s}$ of regions of m's formal arguments a set $M(C, r, m, \bar{s})$ of regions of the method m.

The typing functions are required to be well-formed, which reflects the subtyping properties of FJ. See [11, Definition 4.2] for the details.

Typing judgments take the form $\Gamma \vdash e : R$, where $\Gamma : Var \rightharpoonup Reg$ is a typing environment for variables, $e \in Expr$ a term expression and $R \subseteq Reg$ a set of regions. The typing rules are listed in Fig. 2. For instance, the CALL rule looks up the method typing M for all possible regions where the object x and arguments $\bar{y}$ may reside and joins the matched entries as the return type of the method invocation $x.m(\bar{y})$.

An FJ program $(\prec, fields, methods, mtable)$ is *well-typed* w.r.t. a class table (F, M) if for any $(C, r, m, \bar{s})$ with $M(C, r, m, \bar{s}) = R$ and $mtable(C, m) = (\bar{x}, e)$,

$$\text{VAR} \; \frac{}{\Gamma, x\!:\!R \vdash x : R} \qquad \text{NULL} \; \frac{}{\Gamma \vdash \texttt{null} : \texttt{Null}} \qquad \text{NEW} \; \frac{}{\Gamma \vdash \texttt{new}^{\ell}\, C : \texttt{CreatedAt}(\ell)}$$

$$\text{SUB} \; \frac{\Gamma \vdash e : R \qquad R \subseteq R'}{\Gamma \vdash e : R'} \qquad \text{CAST} \; \frac{\Gamma \vdash e : R}{\Gamma \vdash (D)\, e : R}$$

$$\text{IF} \; \frac{\Gamma, x\!:\!R \cap S,\, y\!:\!R \cap S \vdash e_1 : T_1 \qquad \Gamma, x\!:\!R,\, y\!:\!S \vdash e_2 : T_2}{\Gamma,\, x\!:\!R,\, y\!:\!S \vdash \texttt{if } x = y \texttt{ then } e_1 \texttt{ else } e_2 : T_1 \cup T_2}$$

$$\text{LET} \; \frac{\Gamma \vdash e_1 : R \qquad \Gamma, x\!:\!R \vdash e_2 : T}{\Gamma \vdash \texttt{let } x = e_1 \texttt{ in } e_2 : T} \qquad \text{CALL} \; \frac{T = \bigcup \{ M(C, r, m, \bar{s}) \mid r \in R, \bar{s} \in \bar{S} \}}{\Gamma, x\!:\!R,\, \bar{y}\!:\!\bar{S} \vdash x^C.m(\bar{y}) : T}$$

$$\text{GET} \; \frac{T = \bigcup \{ F(C, r, f) \mid r \in R \}}{\Gamma, x\!:\!R \vdash x^C.f : T} \qquad \text{SET} \; \frac{\forall r \in R.\; S \subseteq F(C, r, f)}{\Gamma, x\!:\!R,\, y\!:\!S \vdash x^C.f := y : S}$$

Fig. 2. The region type system of Beringer et al. [5]

the typing judgment $\texttt{this}\!:\!r,\, \bar{x}\!:\!\bar{s} \vdash e : R$ is derivable. A soundness theorem has been proved in [5, Theorem 1], stating that, for any expression e in a well-typed FJ program with respect to a class table (F, M), if e evaluates to some value v and e has type R, then v is in some region in R.

4.2 Inferring Region Types via Abstract Transformations

Let an FJ program P be given. Now we introduce an algorithm to construct a class table (F, M) with respect to which P is well-typed. As mentioned above, our approach is based on abstract transformations. From now on, the atomic types we are working with are the regions, i.e., take $Typ = Reg$ for the development of abstract transformations.

We firstly compute an abstract transformation σ and a term t for each FJ expression e. The transformation σ encodes the type updates of the variables and fields in e, while the term t pre-calculates type of e. Once we are given a typing environment env, we update it using σ and then instantiate t with the updated environment to compute the type of e, i.e., e has type $t[\sigma(env)]$.

For this, we define the following operations on pairs of abstract transformations and terms: Let $(\sigma, s), (\theta, t) \in ATrans \times Tm$.

- *Composition*: We define $(\sigma, s)\theta := (\sigma\theta, s\theta)$, where $\sigma\theta$ is the composition of transformations, and $s\theta$ is term substitution.
- *Join*: We define $(\sigma; s) \vee (\theta, t) := (\sigma \vee \theta, s \vee t)$.

Suppose we have a function $T : Cls \times Mtd \to ATrans \times Tm$, called an *abstract method table*, that assigns an abstract transformation and a term to each method. The transformations capture the type updates for the method and the term will be instantiated to the type for the method. Then we define a pair

$[\![e]\!] : A\mathit{Trans} \times \mathit{Tm}$ by induction on the FJ expression e:

$$[\![x]\!] := ([], x)$$
$$[\![\texttt{if } x = y \texttt{ then } e_1 \texttt{ else } e_2]\!] := [\![e_1]\!] \vee [\![e_2]\!]$$
$$[\![\texttt{let } x = e_1 \texttt{ in } e_2]\!] := [\![e_2]\!]([x :\mapsto t]\theta) \quad \text{where } (\theta, t) = [\![e_1]\!]$$
$$[\![\texttt{null}]\!] := ([], \texttt{Null})$$
$$[\![\texttt{new}^\ell \; C]\!] := ([], \texttt{CreatedAt}(\ell))$$
$$[\![(D)\, e]\!] := [\![e]\!]$$
$$[\![x.f]\!] := ([], x.f)$$
$$[\![x.f := y]\!] := ([x.f :\geq y], y)$$
$$[\![x^C.m(\bar{y})]\!] := T(C, m)[\texttt{this} :\mapsto x, \mathit{args}(C, m) :\mapsto \bar{y}]$$

where $\mathit{args}(C, m)$ denotes the arguments of m, i.e., if $\mathit{mtable}(C, m) = (\bar{x}, e)$ then $\mathit{args}(C, m) = \bar{x}$.

Given an FJ program, we compute an abstract method table T as follows:

1. Initialize T with $T(C, m) = ([], \bot)$ for all $m \in \mathit{methods}(C)$, where $\bot$ is the empty term, i.e., the empty set of atoms.
2. For each method, compute an abstract transformation and a term for its body, and then update the corresponding entry in T. Specifically, for each $m \in \mathit{methods}(C)$ with $(\bar{x}, e) = \mathit{mtable}(C, m)$, let $T(C, m) = T(C, m) \vee [\![e]\!]$.
3. Close T under the subclass relation, i.e., let $T(C, m) = T(C, m) \vee T(D, m)$ if D is a subclass of C.
4. Repeat steps 2 and 3 until no more update of T is possible.

After computing the table T, we compute a class table (F, M) as follows:

(a) Initialize F and M with the least type, i.e., the empty set of regions.
(b) Use T to update the entries in F and M. Specifically, for each $C, r, m, \bar{s}$ with $(\sigma, u) = T(C, m)$, we update the environment and get $\mathit{env} = \sigma(\Gamma, F)$ where $\Gamma = \texttt{this}{:}r, \mathit{args}(C, m){:}\bar{s}$. Then we update the class table by taking $F = F \vee \mathit{env}|_f$ and $M(C, r, m, \bar{s}) = M(C, r, m, \bar{s}) \vee u[\mathit{env}]$.
(c) Ensure that (F, M) are well-formed. For instance, if D is a subclass of C, then both $F(C, r, f)$ and $F(D, r, f)$ are set to their join.
(d) Repeat steps (b) and (c) until no more update of F and M is possible.

To summarize, the inference algorithm has two steps. It firstly computes an abstract method table T. The abstract transformations in T capture the flow information of each method. This step is similar to constraint generation and preprocessing such as simplification or closure in the constraint-based type inference [29, 31]. Then it computes the class table (F, M) by instantiating the abstract transformations in T. This step solves the constraints collected in T via a least fixed-point argument.

The inference algorithm in the previous work [10, Appendix F] analyzes the same method body multiple times when the method is fed with arguments of different types at different invocations. Our algorithm instead uses the abstract transformation stored in T to infer the types of different method calls. Therefore, it can effectively enhance the efficiency of analysis especially when the analyzed program contains many method invocations with arguments of different types. The arXiv version [26, Appendix B] has an example demonstrating how to compute and use T to analyze invocations of the same method.

Lastly, the computed class table (F, M) reveals the region information of the program in the following sense.

Theorem 3 (Correctness of type inference). *Let P be an FJ program. The above algorithm gives a class table (F, M) with respect to which P is well-typed. In particular, for any $C, r, m, \bar{s}$ with $M(C, r, m, \bar{s}) = R$ and for any $x : r$ and $\bar{y} : \bar{s}$, if $x.m(\bar{y})$ evaluates to a value v, then v resides in some region in R.* $\qquad \square$

The second part of the above theorem is a corollary of the soundness result [5, Theorem 1]. It states that the type of each method computed by M is correct. We sketch the proof of the first claim that the program is well-typed with respect to the class table (F, M) given by our algorithm. Because the typings F and M are computed by the abstract transformations of the table T, we only need to prove that these abstract transformations compute types greater than the ones from typing derivation. More precisely, we need to prove

$$\text{if } \Gamma \vdash e : R \text{ then } R \subseteq \mathsf{Type}(\llbracket e \rrbracket(\Gamma))$$

where $\mathsf{Type}(\llbracket e \rrbracket(\Gamma))$ is the type of the expression e obtained by firstly applying the transformation component of $\llbracket e \rrbracket$ to Γ to obtained an updated environment and then instantiating the term component with the updated environment. The above statement can be proved by induction on the length of typing derivation as usual, because the definition of $\llbracket e \rrbracket$ reflects the typing rules.

5   Conclusion, Implementation and Discussion

In this paper, we develop a theory of abstract transformations to capture type changes in programs. The elements of an abstract transformation can be viewed as equality and subtyping constraints. In particular, we work with access graphs when defining these constraints. Access graphs provide a finite representation of field access paths and thus ensure the termination of the procedure to compute abstract transformations for the program. We instantiate abstract transformations to endofunctions on typing environments to compute the types of the program, which solves the constraints in the abstract transformations. As an example, we work with the region type system of Beringer et al. [5] to demonstrate how to use our inference algorithm based on abstract transformations to compute region information of Featherweight Java programs. The advantage is that the code of a method is analyzed only once even when it is invoked with arguments of different region types in multiple occasions of the program.

We have a prototype implementation of the type inference algorithm using the Soot framework [24]. It takes a Java bytecode program as input and computes the region types of the program. The implementation of abstract transformations and their operations follows the definitions in this paper. The function $[\![-]\!]$ computing an abstract transformation and a type term for FJ expressions becomes a forward flow analysis for the control flow graphs of the program. In particular, it has a flow-through method that computes an abstract transformation for each node in the control flow graph and then concatenates it with the one generated from the previous nodes. Then a fixed point procedure is implemented to compute an abstract transformation for each method in the program using the flow analysis. Lastly, the generated abstract transformations are instantiated to compute the types of the methods in the program. The prototype implementation is available [27].

Region types can make the analysis of trace properties more precise [10,11]. By extending region type systems with effect annotations to give information about possible event traces of the program, a method invocation $x.m(\bar{y})$ can have different effects for $x, \bar{y}$ in different regions. Our approach can be extended to reason also such region-sensitive trace effects. Our idea is to make the abstract method table T to compute also a formal expression capturing the information of traces and method calls. For example, consider the following FJ program

$$\texttt{emit}(a); \ x.f(\bar{y}); \ \texttt{emit}(b); \ x.g(\bar{z})$$

where $\texttt{emit}(a)$ is a primitive method that emits the event a. We can assign it a formal expression

$$\{a\} \cdot X_{(x,f,\bar{y})} \cdot \{b\} \cdot X_{(x,g,\bar{z})}$$

meaning that any trace generated by the program starts with the event a, followed by a trace generated by the method call $x.f(\bar{y})$ and then the event b and a trace generated by $x.g(\bar{z})$. Here $x, \bar{y}, \bar{z}$ are variables and can be instantiated to region types with a given environment; thus, the formal expression can be instantiated such that it contains only variables like $X_{(r,f,\bar{s})}$ for the effect of the method call of f for an object in region r with arguments in regions $\bar{s}$. For each method in a calling context, we use its abstract transformation to update the environment and then use the updated environment to instantiate its call expression. In this way, we obtained a set of call expressions, one for each method invocation in a calling context. Then we can use a least fixed point algorithm to compute the trace effect of each method from these call expressions. Currently we are still tackling the details to develop such a compositional algorithm for inferring region-sensitive trace effects.

Acknowledgements. We thank Fredrick Nordvall Forsberg for the fruitful discussion on this work and the anonymous reviewers for their valuable comments and suggestions on the paper and its accompanying artifact.

References

1. Agesen, O.: Constraint-based type inference and parametric polymorphism. In: Le Charlier, B. (ed.) SAS 1994. LNCS, vol. 864, pp. 78–100. Springer, Heidelberg (1994). https://doi.org/10.1007/3-540-58485-4_34

2. Fuh, Y.-C., Mishra, P.: Type inference with subtypes. In: Ganzinger, H. (ed.) ESOP 1988. LNCS, vol. 300, pp. 94–114. Springer, Heidelberg (1988). https://doi.org/10.1007/3-540-19027-9_7

3. Aiken, A., Wimmers, E.L.: Type inclusion constraints and type inference. In: Proceedings of the Conference on Functional Programming Languages and Computer Architecture (FPCA 1993), p. 31–41. Association for Computing Machinery, New York (1993). https://doi.org/10.1145/165180.165188

4. Baader, F., Snyder, W.: Unification theory. In: Robinson, J.A., Voronkov, A. (eds.) Handbook of Automated Reasoning (in 2 volumes), pp. 445–532. Elsevier and MIT Press (2001). https://doi.org/10.1016/b978-044450813-3/50010-2

5. Beringer, L., Grabowski, R., Hofmann, M.: Verifying pointer and string analyses with region type systems. Comput. Lang. Syst. Struct. **39**(2), 49–65 (2013). https://doi.org/10.1016/j.cl.2013.01.001

6. Bodden, E.: Inter-procedural data-flow analysis with IFDS/IDE and Soot. In: Proceedings of the ACM SIGPLAN International Workshop on State of the Art in Java Program Analysis (SOAP 2012), pp. 3–8. Association for Computing Machinery (2012). https://doi.org/10.1145/2259051.2259052

7. Boyapati, C., Salcianu, A., Beebee, W., Rinard, M.: Ownership types for safe region-based memory management in Real-Time Java. In: Proceedings of the ACM SIGPLAN 2003 Conference on Programming Language Design and Implementation (PLDI 2003), pp. 324–337. Association for Computing Machinery, New York (2003). https://doi.org/10.1145/781131.781168

8. Chin, W.N., Craciun, F., Qin, S., Rinard, M.: Region inference for an object-oriented language. In: Proceedings of the ACM SIGPLAN 2004 Conference on Programming Language Design and Implementation (PLDI 2004), pp. 243–254. Association for Computing Machinery, New York (2004). https://doi.org/10.1145/996841.996871

9. Deutsch, A.: Interprocedural may-alias analysis for pointers: Beyond k-limiting. In: Proceedings of the ACM SIGPLAN 1994 conference on Programming language design and implementation (PLDI 1994), vol. 29(6), pp. 230–241. Association for Computing Machinery (1994). https://doi.org/10.1145/773473.178263

10. Erbatur, S., Hofmann, M., Zălinescu, E.: Enforcing programming guidelines with region types and effects. In: Chang, B.-Y.E. (ed.) APLAS 2017. LNCS, vol. 10695, pp. 85–104. Springer, Cham (2017). https://doi.org/10.1007/978-3-319-71237-6_5

11. Erbatur, S., Schöpp, U., Xu, C.: Type-based enforcement of infinitary trace properties for Java. In: 23rd International Symposium on Principles and Practice of Declarative Programming (PPDP 2021), pp. 18:1–18:14. Association for Computing Machinery (2021). https://doi.org/10.1145/3479394.3479413

12. Facebook: Flow - A static type checker for JavaScript. https://flow.org

13. Gosling, J., Joy, B., Steele, G., Bracha, G., Buckley, A.: The Java Language Specification. Oracle America Inc., Java SE 14 edn. (2020). http://docs.oracle.com/javase/specs/jls/se14/jls14.pdf

14. Grabowski, R., Hofmann, M., Li, K.: Type-based enforcement of secure programming guidelines - code injection prevention at SAP. In: Barthe, G., Datta, A., Etalle, S. (eds.) FAST 2011. LNCS, vol. 7140, pp. 182–197. Springer, Heidelberg (2012). https://doi.org/10.1007/978-3-642-29420-4_12

15. Huang, W., Dong, Y., Milanova, A.: Type-based taint analysis for Java web applications. In: Gnesi, S., Rensink, A. (eds.) FASE 2014. LNCS, vol. 8411, pp. 140–154. Springer, Heidelberg (2014). https://doi.org/10.1007/978-3-642-54804-8_10

16. Igarashi, A., Pierce, B.C., Wadler, P.: Featherweight Java: a minimal core calculus for Java and GJ. ACM Trans. Program. Lang. Syst. **23**(3), 396–450 (2001). https://doi.org/10.1145/503502.503505

17. Jones, N.D., Muchnick, S.S.: Flow analysis and optimization of LISP-like structures. In: Proceedings of the 6th ACM SIGACT-SIGPLAN Symposium on Principles of Programming Languages (POPL 1979), pp. 244–256. Association for Computing Machinery (1979). https://doi.org/10.1145/567752.567776

18. Khedker, U.P., Sanyal, A., Karkare, A.: Heap reference analysis using access graphs. ACM Trans. Program. Lang. Syst. **30**(1), 1–41 (2007). https://doi.org/10.1145/1290520.1290521

19. Lerch, J., Späth, J., Bodden, E., Mezini, M.: Access-path abstraction: Scaling field-sensitive data-flow analysis with unbounded access paths. In: Proceedings of the 30th IEEE/ACM International Conference on Automated Software Engineering (ASE 2015), pp. 619–629. IEEE Press (2015). https://doi.org/10.1109/ASE.2015.9

20. Microsoft: TypeScript - Typed JavaScript at any scale. https://www.typescriptlang.org/

21. Odersky, M., Sulzmann, M., Wehr, M.: Type inference with constrained types. Theory Practice Object Syst. **5**(1), 35–55 (1999). https://doi.org/10.1002/(SICI)1096-9942(199901/03)5:1<35::AID-TAPO4>3.0.CO;2-4

22. Palsberg, J., Schwartzbach, M.I.: Object-oriented type inference. SIGPLAN Notices **26**(11), 146–161 (1991). https://doi.org/10.1145/118014.117965

23. Sable Group, M.U.: Heros IFDS/IDE solver. https://github.com/Sable/heros

24. Sable Group M.U: Soot - A framework for analyzing and transforming Java and Android applications. https://soot-oss.github.io/soot/

25. Sagiv, S., Reps, T.W., Horwitz, S.: Precise interprocedural dataflow analysis with applications to constant propagation. Theoret. Comput. Sci. **167**(1–2), 131–170 (1996). https://doi.org/10.1016/0304-3975(96)00072-2

26. Schöpp, U., Xu, C.: Inferring region types via an abstract notion of environment transformation (2022). arXiv:2209.02147 [cs.PL]

27. Schöpp, U., Xu, C.: Inferring Region Types via an Abstract Notion of Environment Transformation. Artifact (2022). https://doi.org/10.5281/zenodo.7009655

28. Späth, J., Do, L.N.Q., Ali, K., Bodden, E.: Boomerang: Demand-Driven Flow- and Context-Sensitive Pointer Analysis for Java. In: Krishnamurthi, S., Lerner, B.S. (eds.) 30th European Conference on Object-Oriented Programming (ECOOP 2016). Leibniz International Proceedings in Informatics (LIPIcs), vol. 56, pp. 22:1–22:26. Schloss Dagstuhl-Leibniz-Zentrum fuer Informatik, Dagstuhl, Germany (2016). https://doi.org/10.4230/LIPIcs.ECOOP.2016.22

29. Traytel, D., Berghofer, S., Nipkow, T.: Extending Hindley-Milner type inference with coercive structural subtyping. In: Yang, H. (ed.) APLAS 2011. LNCS, vol. 7078, pp. 89–104. Springer, Heidelberg (2011). https://doi.org/10.1007/978-3-642-25318-8_10

30. Wand, M., O'Keefe, P.: On the complexity of type inference with coercion. In: Proceedings of the Fourth International Conference on Functional Programming Languages and Computer Architecture (FPCA 1989), pp. 293–298. Association for Computing Machinery, New York (1989). https://doi.org/10.1145/99370.99394

31. Wang, T., Smith, S.F.: Precise constraint-based type inference for Java. In: Knudsen, J.L. (ed.) ECOOP 2001. LNCS, vol. 2072, pp. 99–117. Springer, Heidelberg (2001). https://doi.org/10.1007/3-540-45337-7_6

Testing and Verification

RHLE: Modular Deductive Verification of Relational ∀∃ Properties

Robert Dickerson$^{(\boxtimes)}$, Qianchuan Ye, Michael K. Zhang,
and Benjamin Delaware

Purdue University, West Lafayette 47907, USA
{dicker18,ye202,bendy}@purdue.edu,
michael.k.zhang@alumni.purdue.edu

Abstract. Hoare-style program logics are a popular and effective technique for software verification. Relational program logics are an instance of this approach that enables reasoning about relationships between the execution of two or more programs. Existing relational program logics have focused on verifying that *all* runs of a collection of programs do not violate a specified relational behavior. Several important relational properties, including refinement and noninterference, do not fit into this category, as they also mandate the *existence* of specific desirable executions. This paper presents RHLE, a logic for verifying these sorts of relational ∀∃ properties. Key to our approach is a novel form of function specification that employs a variant of ghost variables to ensure that valid implementations exhibit certain behaviors. We have used a program verifier based on RHLE to verify a diverse set of relational ∀∃ properties drawn from the literature.

1 Introduction

Hoare-style program logics are a popular and effective verification technique. Starting with Hoare's seminal paper [20], this approach has been adapted to cover a variety of programming languages and assertions [3, 21, 28, 32, 34]. These logics typically feature several pleasant properties: they can be declaratively specified via a set of rules over the syntax of the target programming language, they permit compositional reasoning over individual program components, and they often admit effective automated verification procedures. Most of these logics focus on proving *safety* properties of *single* programs, i.e., that executing a program in a valid initial state never results in a state violating a postcondition.

Not all program behaviors fall into this category, however. As one example, consider the common scenario where a developer decides they want to migrate a hand-rolled implementation of a function to one that uses a third-party library. Figure 1 gives a concrete example of this situation. The program on the left, sample$_1$, uses a random number generator to directly sample a subset of an array. The program on the right, sample$_2$, opts to delegate the task to an external list library which supports shuffling and constructing sublists. While sample$_1$ works *with replacement* (the same elements may be sampled multiple times), sample$_2$ works *without*

I. Sergey (Ed.): APLAS 2022, LNCS 13658, pp. 67–87, 2022.
https://doi.org/10.1007/978-3-031-21037-2_4

```
int[] sample₁(int[] arr,
              int size) {
  assert(size <= arr.length);
  int[] samp = new int[size];
  for (i in [0..size]) {
    int j = randB(arr.length);
    samp[i] = arr[j];
  }
  return samp;
}
```

```
int[] sample₂(int[] arr,
              int size) {
  assert(size <= arr.length);
  list = new List(arr);
  perm = list.permute();
  samp = perm.sublist(size);
  return samp.toArray();
}
```

Fig. 1. An example migration of a function which randomly samples a list of integers with replacement to a function which samples without replacement. The original program (sample₁) uses a function which generates random numbers, while the migrated program (sample₂) uses a list abstraction with a permute operation.

replacement (an element may be sampled at most once). In order to ensure that this change does not break things, the developer may wish to verify that sample₂ does not do anything that sample₁ could not, i.e., that the updated function *refines* the original. Notably, this refinement property relates the behavior of *multiple* programs. In addition, it does not have the form of a standard safety property. The developer does not want to enforce that sample₂ produces *every* permutation that the hand-rolled implementation does; rather, they wish to ensure it does not start returning previously impossible samples.

As another example, consider the encode function on the right which performs a simple xor cipher. This function takes a single high-security argument, msg^H, and returns a pair of high-security and low-security results,

```
int encode(int msg^H) {
  int key^H = randB(MAX_INT);
  int enc^L = msg^H xor key^H;
  return (key^H, enc^L);
}
```

key^H and enc^L, respectively. The function encodes its argument by first generating a random key (randB returns a random value between 0 and its argument), taking the xor of the key and the message, and finally returning the key along with the encoded message. The developer may wish to guarantee an attacker can learn nothing about the secret message given only the encoded message. Whether or not encode meets this *generalized noninterference* [26] property crucially depends on the behavior of randB: if the attacker knows this function *always* returns 3, for example, they can decipher any encoded message. We can again frame this behavior as a relational property between the executions of two programs (in this case calls to encode with arbitrary arguments msg_1^H and msg_2^H): every execution of encode(msg_1^H) must have a corresponding execution of encode(msg_2^H) that returns the same low-security encoded value.

In both examples, the desired behavior has the shape *for all* executions of some program, *there exists* a corresponding execution of a second program that is somehow related. Thus, we call these properties *relational* ∀∃ properties. While several *relational program logics* have been developed for reasoning about the behavior of multiple programs [8,9,36], all have focused on relational *safety* properties, i.e.,

$$n \in \mathbb{N} \quad x, y \in \mathcal{V}$$
$$f, g \in \mathcal{N} \qquad \sigma \in \mathcal{V} \to \mathbb{N}$$
$$a ::= n \mid x \mid a + a \mid a - a \mid a * a$$
$$b ::= \text{true} \mid \text{false}$$
$$\mid a = a \mid a < a \mid \neg b \mid b \wedge b$$

$$s ::= \text{skip} \mid s;\ s$$
$$\mid \text{if } b \text{ then } s \text{ else } s$$
$$\mid \text{while } b \text{ do } s \text{ end}$$
$$\mid x := a \mid x := \text{havoc} \mid x := f(\overline{a})$$
$$FD ::= \text{def } f(\overline{x})\ \{s; \text{return } a\}$$

Fig. 2. Syntax of FUNIMP.

that *all* the final states of multiple programs satisfy some relational postcondition. Unfortunately, in the presence of nondeterminism, none of these logics are capable of verifying relational ∀∃ properties such as refinement and generalized noninterference. The need to reason about nondeterminism naturally arises in the presence of external functions like permute in Fig. 1, where specifications are used to approximate the behavior of multiple possible implementations.

This paper addresses this gap by introducing RHLE, a relational program logic for reasoning about ∀∃ properties. Key to our approach is a novel form of function specifications which approximate the set of behaviors a valid implementation *must* exhibit. These specifications use a novel variant of ghost variables, which we call *choice variables*, that guarantee the existence of required behaviors. RHLE admits a modular reasoning principle, where any properties verified against a set of function specifications continue to hold whenever the program is linked to any satisfying implementation. While techniques based on Constrained Horn Clauses [38] and model checking [25] have recently been developed that are capable of reasoning about ∀∃ properties, RHLE is, to the best of our knowledge, the first Hoare-style program logic for doing so. We have used a verifier based on RHLE to verify a range of ∀∃ properties including refinement, noninterference (with and without delimited release), semantic parameter usage, and flaky tests.

We begin by defining a core imperative language with function calls (Sect. 2) equipped with semantics for both over- and under-approximating function behaviors (Sect. 3). We next present RHLE, and a corresponding verification algorithm for verifying ∀∃ properties (Sect. 5). We evaluate our approach by applying an implementation of this algorithm to verify a diverse set of relational properties (Sect. 6). We conclude with an examination of related work (Sect. 7). We have formalized the details of our approach in the Coq proof assistant; this development is available in the supplementary materials of this paper [16]. Our verification tool and benchmark suite are also publicly available [16,17].

2   The FunIMP Language

We begin with the definition of FUNIMP, a core imperative language with function calls $x := f(\overline{a})$ and nondeterministic variable assignment $x := \text{havoc}$. The full syntax of FUNIMP is presented in Fig. 2. The calculus is parameterized over disjoint sets of identifiers for program variables $\mathcal{V}$ and function names $\mathcal{N}$.

Functions have a fixed arity. Function definitions consist of a sequence of statements followed by an expression that computes the result of the function. For brevity, we denote sequences $x_1, \ldots, x_n$ as $\overline{x}$. For ease of presentation, we treat functions as returning a single value, although it is straightforward to extend FUNIMP to allow for multiple return values: $(x, y, \ldots) := f(\overline{a})$. Our verification tool, ORHLE (see Sect. 6), uses such an extension to model functions which mutate their arguments.

The semantics of FUNIMP programs are defined via a standard big-step evaluation relation from initial to final program states. States are mappings from variables to integers, and are usually notated as σ. We write $[x \mapsto a]\sigma$ to refer to state σ updated with a mapping from x to a. The evaluation rules are parameterized over an *implementation context*, a mapping $I \in \mathcal{N} \to FD$ from function names to their definitions, which is used to evaluate function calls:

$$\frac{I(f) = \mathbf{def}\ f(\overline{x})\ \{s; \mathbf{return}\ e\} \qquad I \vdash \sigma, \overline{a} \Downarrow \overline{v} \qquad I \vdash [\overline{x} \mapsto \overline{v}], s \Downarrow \sigma' \qquad I \vdash \sigma', e \Downarrow r}{I \vdash \sigma, y := f(\overline{a}) \Downarrow [y \mapsto r]\sigma} \text{ECALL}$$

We use $\Downarrow$ for the evaluation relation of both expressions and statements; $\sigma, e \Downarrow \sigma'$ holds when executing e on state σ can result in state σ'. Since programs may be nondeterministic, there may be multiple final states related to a single initial state for a given program. Note that havoc is the only source of nondeterminism when evaluating a FUNIMP program. The remaining evaluation rules for FUNIMP are standard and can be found in the extended version of the paper [15].

3   Approximating FUNIMP Behaviors

In order to modularly reason about relational ∀∃ properties, we first present semantics for capturing the possible executions of a FUNIMP program in *any* valid implementation context. In order to account for both "for all" and "there exists" behaviors of functions, we rely on two kinds of specifications. To reason about *all* possible executions of a valid implementation, i.e., a standard *safety* property, we use a *universal* specification. For guarantees about the *existence* of certain executions, we use an *existential* specification.

3.1   Universal Executions

Both kinds of specifications are parameterized over an assertion language $\mathcal{A}$ on program states and a mechanism for judging when a state satisfies an assertion. We write $\sigma \models P$ to denote that a state σ satisfies the assertion P. The universal specifications used to reason about programs on the "for all" side of ∀∃ properties are written as $FA:: = \mathsf{ax}_\forall\ f(\overline{x})\ \{P\}\{Q\}$, where $P \in \mathcal{A}$ is a precondition with free variables in $\overline{x}$ and $Q \in \mathcal{A}$ is a postcondition with free variables in $\overline{x} \cup \{\rho\}$. The postcondition uses the distinguished variable ρ to refer to the value returned by f. Universal specifications promise client programs that the valid implementations of a function will only evaluate to states satisfying the postcondition when evaluated in a starting state that satisfies the precondition.

Definition 1 ($\forall - Compatibility$). *A function definition* **def** $f(\overline{x})\{s; \text{return } r\}$ *is* $\forall$*-compatible with a universal specification* $\text{ax}_\forall \ f(\overline{x})\{P\}\{Q\}$ *if only values satisfying Q may be returned whenever f is called with arguments satisfying P:*

$$\forall \sigma, \sigma'. \ (\sigma \models P) \ \wedge \ (I \vdash \sigma, s \Downarrow \sigma') \ \wedge \ (\sigma', r \Downarrow v) \implies ([\rho \mapsto v]\sigma \models Q)$$

We say that an implementation context I is $\forall$-compatible with a context of universal specifications $S_\forall \in \mathcal{N} \to FA$ when every definition in I is $\forall$-compatible with the corresponding specification in $S_\forall$.

To characterize the set of possible behaviors of a program under any $\forall$-compatible implementation context, we define a new *overapproximate* semantics for FUNIMP, $\Downarrow_\forall$. The evaluation rules of this semantics are based on $\Downarrow$, but they use a universal specification context, $S_\forall$, instead of an implementation context, and replace ECALL with the following two evaluation rules:

$$\frac{S_\forall(f) = \text{ax}_\forall \ f(\overline{x})\{P\}\{Q\} \qquad S_\forall \vdash \sigma, \overline{a} \Downarrow_\forall \overline{v} \qquad [\overline{x} \mapsto \overline{v}] \models P \qquad [\rho \mapsto r, \overline{x} \mapsto \overline{v}] \models Q}{S_\forall \vdash \sigma, y := f(\overline{a}) \Downarrow_\forall [y \mapsto r]\sigma} \text{ECALL}_{\forall 1}$$

$$\frac{S_\forall(f) = \text{ax}_\forall \ f(\overline{x})\{P\}\{Q\} \qquad S_\forall \vdash \sigma, \overline{a} \Downarrow_\forall \overline{v} \qquad [\overline{x} \mapsto \overline{v}] \not\models P}{S_\forall \vdash \sigma, y := f(\overline{a}) \Downarrow_\forall [y \mapsto r]\sigma} \text{ECALL}_{\forall 2}$$

The first rule states that if a function is called with arguments satisfying its precondition, it will return a value satisfying its postcondition; otherwise, the second rule states that it can return *any* value. The latter case allows the overapproximate semantics to capture evaluations where a function is called with arguments that do not meet its precondition. The extended version of this paper [15] includes a complete listing of the $\Downarrow_\forall$ relation.

Any final state of a program evaluated under an implementation context I which is $\forall$-compatible with $S_\forall$ can also be produced using $\Downarrow_\forall$ and $S_\forall$. Appealing to this intuition, we call the evaluations of a FUNIMP program p using $\Downarrow_\forall$ the *overapproximate executions* of p under $S_\forall$.

Theorem 1. *When run under an implementation context I that is $\forall$-compatible with specification context $S_\forall$ and an initial state σ, a program p will either diverge or evaluate to a state σ' which is also the result of one of its overapproximate executions under $S_\forall$.*

3.2   Existential Executions

Universal specifications approximate function calls on the "for all" side of $\forall\exists$ properties by constraining what a compatible implementation *can* do. Existential specifications approximate the "there exists" executions by describing the required values a valid implementation *must* be able to return. In order to flexibly capture these behaviors, existential pre- and post-conditions are indexed by a set of *choice variables* $\overline{c} \subseteq \mathcal{V}$. Each instantiation of these variables defines

```
def randB(x) {        def randB(x) {                     def randB(x) {
   skip;                 r := havoc;                         r := havoc;
   return 0              while (x ≤ r) do r := r − x end;     return r
}                        return r }                         }
```

Fig. 3. Implementations of a function which returns an integer within a bound.

a particular behavior that an implementation has to exhibit. The syntax for writing an existential specification is: $FE::= \mathsf{ax}_\exists\ f(\overline{x})\ [\overline{c}]\ \{P\}\{Q\}$.

We write $A[x/y]$ to denote the predicate A with all free occurrences of x replaced with y. Intuitively, for any instantiation $\overline{v}$ of choice variables $\overline{c}$, an existential specification requires an implementation to produce at least one value satisfying the specialized postcondition $Q[\overline{v}/\overline{c}]$, when called with arguments that satisfy the corresponding precondition $P[\overline{v}/\overline{c}]$. This intuition is embodied in our notion of compatibility for existential specifications:

Definition 2 (∃-Compatibility). *A function definition* $\mathbf{def}\ f(\overline{x})\{s;\mathsf{return}\ r\}$ *is ∃-compatible with an existential specification* $\mathsf{ax}_\exists\ f(\overline{x})[\overline{c}]\{P\}\{Q\}$ *if, for every selection of choice variables* $\overline{v}$, *calling* f *with arguments that satisfy* $P[\overline{v}/\overline{c}]$ *can return at least one value satisfying* $Q[\overline{v}/\overline{c}]$:

$$\forall \sigma, \overline{v}.\ (\sigma \models P[\overline{v}/\overline{c}]) \implies \exists \sigma'.\ (I \vdash \sigma, s \Downarrow \sigma') \wedge (\sigma', r \Downarrow v) \wedge ([\rho \mapsto v]\sigma \models Q[\overline{v}/\overline{c}])$$

Example 1. To see how universal and existential specifications work together to describe a function's behavior, consider a function $\mathsf{randB}(\mathsf{x})$ which is intended to return some integer between 0 and its argument x. We can write a universal specification requiring all return values to be within the desired bound: $\mathsf{ax}_\forall$ $\mathsf{randB}(x)\ \{0 < x\}\ \{0 \leq \rho < x\}$. This does not, however, *guarantee* every value in this range is possible. To express this requirement, we reify the choice of the random value using an existential specification: $\mathsf{ax}_\exists\ \mathsf{randB}(x)\ [c]\ \{0 < x \wedge 0 \leq c < x\}\ \{\rho = c\}$. Figure 3 lists a variety of possible randB implementations; the first implementation is compatible with the aforementioned universal specification and the third definition is compatible with the existential specification, but only the middle one satisfies both. Note how c acts as a ghost variable which constrains the choice of the random number. Thus, when reasoning about a client of randB, we can select a concrete value for c that forces the desired result.

Equipped with a context of existential specifications $S_\exists \in \mathcal{N} \to FE$, we characterize the set of behaviors a program *must* exhibit under every ∃-compatible implementation context via an underapproximate semantics for FUNIMP programs. The judgements of this semantics are denoted as $S_\exists \vdash \sigma, p \Downarrow_\exists \Sigma$, which reads as: under context $S_\exists$ and initial state σ, the program p will produce at least one final state in the set of states Σ. The evaluation rules of this semantics are given in Fig. 4. Most of the rules in Fig. 4 adapt the FUNIMP evaluation rules to account for the fact that commands now produce *sets* of states from an

$$\frac{}{S_\exists \vdash \sigma, \mathsf{skip} \Downarrow_\exists \{\sigma\}} \; \text{ESKIP}_\exists \qquad \frac{}{S_\exists \vdash \sigma, x := \mathsf{havoc} \Downarrow_\exists \{\sigma' \mid \exists v.[x \mapsto v]\sigma'\}} \; \text{EHAVOC}_\exists$$

$$\frac{\sigma, a \Downarrow v}{S_\exists \vdash \sigma, x := a \Downarrow_\exists \{[x \mapsto v]\sigma\}} \; \text{EASSN}_\exists \qquad \frac{S_\exists \vdash \sigma, s \Downarrow_\exists \Sigma \qquad \Sigma \subseteq \Sigma'}{S_\exists \vdash \sigma, s \Downarrow_\exists \Sigma'} \; \text{ECONSQ}_\exists$$

$$\frac{S_\exists \vdash \sigma, s_1 \Downarrow_\exists \Sigma \qquad \forall \sigma' \in \Sigma. \; S_\exists \vdash \sigma', s_2 \Downarrow_\exists \Sigma'}{S_\exists \vdash \sigma, s_1; \, s_2 \Downarrow_\exists \Sigma'} \; \text{ESEQ}_\exists$$

$$\frac{\sigma, b \Downarrow \mathsf{true} \qquad S_\exists \vdash \sigma, c \Downarrow_\exists \Sigma \qquad \forall \sigma' \in \Sigma. \; S_\exists \vdash \sigma', \mathsf{while} \; b \; \mathsf{do} \; c \; \mathsf{end} \Downarrow_\exists \Sigma'}{S_\exists \vdash \sigma, \mathsf{while} \; b \; \mathsf{do} \; c \; \mathsf{end} \Downarrow_\exists \Sigma'} \; \text{ELPT}_\exists$$

$$\frac{\sigma, b \Downarrow \mathsf{false}}{S_\exists \vdash \sigma, \mathsf{while} \; b \; \mathsf{do} \; c \; \mathsf{end} \Downarrow_\exists \{\sigma\}} \; \text{ELPF}_\exists \qquad \frac{\sigma, b \Downarrow \mathsf{true} \qquad S_\exists \vdash \sigma, s_1 \Downarrow_\exists \Sigma}{S_\exists \vdash \sigma, \mathsf{if} \; b \; \mathsf{then} \; s_1 \; \mathsf{else} \; s_2 \Downarrow_\exists \Sigma} \; \text{EIFT}_\exists$$

$$\frac{\sigma, b \Downarrow \bot \qquad S_\exists \vdash \sigma, s_2 \Downarrow_\exists \Sigma}{S_\exists \vdash \sigma, \mathsf{if} \; b \; \mathsf{then} \; s_1 \; \mathsf{else} \; s_2 \Downarrow_\exists \Sigma} \; \text{EIFF}_\exists$$

$$\frac{S_\exists(f) = \mathsf{ax}_\exists \; f(\overline{x}) \, [c] \, \{P\} \, \{Q\} \qquad S_\exists \vdash \sigma, \overline{a} \Downarrow \overline{v} \qquad [\overline{x} \mapsto \overline{v}] \models P[\overline{k}/\overline{c}]}{S_\exists \vdash \sigma, y := f(\overline{a}) \Downarrow_\exists \quad \{\sigma' \mid \exists r. \, \sigma' = [y \mapsto r]\sigma \, \wedge \, [\rho \mapsto r, \overline{x} \mapsto \overline{v}] \models Q[\overline{k}/\overline{c}]\}} \; \text{ECALL}_\exists$$

Fig. 4. The existential evaluation relation.

initial state. For example, the evaluation rule for sequences, $\text{ESEQ}_\exists$, states that s_2 produces a final state corresponding to every state in the set produced by s_1. The rule for function calls, $\text{ECALL}_\exists$, is the most interesting: it *chooses* one of the behaviors guaranteed by the existential specification of a function and produces a *set* of final states for every return value consistent with that choice.

Every set of final states for a program p produced by these semantics under $S_\exists$ includes a possible final state of p when evaluated under any $\exists$-compatible implementation context. For this reason, we term the evaluations of p using $\Downarrow_\exists$ the *underapproximate executions* of p under $S_\exists$.

Theorem 2. *If there is an underapproximate evaluation of program p to a set of states Σ from an initial state σ under $S_\exists$, then p must terminate in at least one final state $\sigma' \in \Sigma$ when it is run from σ under an implementation context I that is $\exists$-compatible with $S_\exists$.*

3.3 Approximating ∀∃ Behaviors

Taken together, the over- and under-approximate semantics allow us to relate the ∀∃ behaviors of multiple client programs under every ∀- and ∃-compatible implementation context. This admits a modular reasoning principle, where if a set of clients can be shown to exhibit some behaviors using the overapproximate and underapproximate semantics, linking the client with any compatible environment will continue to exhibit those behaviors. The key challenge to ensuring these $\forall\exists$ behaviors is identifying, for every overapproximate execution, an appropriate selection of choice variables that cause the underapproximate executions to evaluate to a collection of final states satisfying a desired $\forall\exists$ property.

Example 2. Consider the second example from the introduction, and assume that randB has the universal and existential specifications from Example 1. To ensure that encode does not reveal anything about its secret input via its public output, it suffices to establish that for any universal execution of encode on a specific input, every other possible input to encode could produce the same encoded message under the existential semantics. The first execution begins with the statement **int** $\mathtt{key}_\forall^\mathtt{H}=$ randB(MAX_INT) (for convenience, we annotate program variables from the first and second executions with the subscripts $\forall$ and $\exists$, respectively). By $\mathrm{ECALL}_{\forall 1}$, this statement will update $\mathtt{key}_\forall^\mathtt{H}$ to hold a value between 0 and MAX_INT. The function then encodes the message using this key, and returns the result. In order to show this leaks nothing, we need to establish a corresponding execution of encode that returns this same result regardless of the value of its argument. In effect, this amounts to finding a strategy for instantiating the choice variable in $\mathrm{ECALL}_\exists$ to assign an appropriate value to $\mathtt{key}_\exists^\mathtt{H}$. In this case, the choice is straightforward: we need a c such that c xor $\mathtt{msg}_\exists^\mathtt{H} =\mathtt{enc}_\forall^\mathtt{L}$. Using $\mathtt{msg}_\exists^\mathtt{H}$ xor $\mathtt{enc}_\forall^\mathtt{L}$ for c in $\mathrm{ECALL}_\exists$ achieves the desired result. Using this strategy, we can construct an appropriate execution in response to *every* execution of encode. In contrast, if our existential specification were $\mathtt{ax}_\exists$ randB(x) [ ] $\{0 < x\}$ $\{0 \le \rho < x\}$, it would only guarantee the existence of a single result, and there would be no workable strategy. Indeed, the first definition of randB in Fig. 3 satisfies this specification, and encode will always leak the full message when using this implementation!

4   RHLE

We now present RHLE, a relational program logic for proving that a collection of FUNIMP programs exhibit some desired set of $\forall\exists$ behaviors. As a consequence of Theorem 1 and Theorem 2, this entails that properties established in RHLE will continue to hold when the programs are linked with any compatible implementation context.

RHLE specifications use *relational* assertions (denoted $\Phi, \Psi \in \mathcal{A}$) to relate the execution of multiple programs. As normal assertions are predicates on a single state, a relational assertion is a predicate on multiple states. Each program in a RHLE triple operates over a distinct state space. To disambiguate between variables that occur in multiple copies, shared variable names are annotated with an identifier unique to each program. Following existing convention [9,36], we use a natural number to identify which state a variable belongs to. As an example, the relational assertion $x_1 \le x_2$ is a binary predicate over (at least) two states. This assertion is satisfied by any set of two (or more) states where the value of x in the first state is less than or equal to the value of x in the second.

Table 1. Example RHLE assertions. In the second row, low_x refers to the low security state in program p_x; note the ∀∃ relationship must hold for *any* pair of initial high security values, so $high_x$ is not constrained in the precondition.

Property	RHLE Assertion
Refinement	$S_\forall, S_\exists \models \langle \overline{x_1} = \overline{x_2} \rangle \, y_1 := f(\overline{x_1}) \sim_\exists y_2 := f(\overline{x_2}) \, \langle y_1 = y_2 \rangle$
Noninterference	$S_\forall, S_\exists \models \langle low_1 = low_2 \rangle \, p_1 \sim_\exists p_2 \, \langle low_1 = low_2 \rangle$
Injectivity	$S_\forall, S_\exists \models \langle x_1 \neq x_2 \rangle \, y_1 := f(x_1) \circledast y_2 := f(x_2) \sim_\exists \mathsf{skip} \, \langle y_1 \neq y_2 \rangle$
Nondeterminism	$S_\forall, S_\exists \models \langle x_1 = x_2 \rangle \, \mathsf{skip} \sim_\exists y_1 := f(x_1) \circledast y_2 := f(x_2) \, \langle y_1 \neq y_2 \rangle$

RHLE triples have the form $S_\forall, S_\exists \models \langle \Phi \rangle \, \overline{p_\forall} \sim_\exists \overline{p_\exists} \, \langle \Psi \rangle$ and assert that *for all* universal executions of the programs $\overline{p_\forall}$, *there exist* existential executions of the programs $\overline{p_\exists}$ satisfying the relational pre- and post-condition Φ and Ψ:

$$S_\forall, S_\exists \models \langle \Phi \rangle \, \overline{p_\forall} \sim_\exists \overline{p_\exists} \, \langle \Psi \rangle \equiv \forall \overline{\sigma_\forall} \, \overline{\sigma_\exists} \, \overline{\sigma_\forall'}. \; \overline{\sigma_\forall}, \overline{\sigma_\exists} \models \Phi \wedge S_\forall \vdash \overline{\sigma_\forall}, \overline{p_\forall} \Downarrow_\forall \overline{\sigma_\forall'} \implies$$
$$\exists \Sigma. \, S_\exists \vdash \overline{\sigma_\exists}, \overline{p_\exists} \Downarrow_\exists \Sigma \wedge \forall \sigma_\exists' \in \Sigma. \, \overline{\sigma_\forall'}, \overline{\sigma_\exists'} \models \Psi$$

We use $\circledast$ to delineate different programs on the universal and existential sides of $\sim_\exists$ so that, e.g., a sequence of n programs $\overline{p}$ is also denoted as $p_1 \circledast \ldots \circledast p_n$. For example, to assert the program $x := \mathsf{havoc}$ is nondeterministic, we write a RHLE triple with two copies of the program, adding a subscript to the variable x in each for clarity: $\cdot \models \langle \top \rangle \, \mathsf{skip} \sim_\exists x_1 := \mathsf{havoc} \circledast x_2 := \mathsf{havoc} \, \langle x_1 \neq x_2 \rangle$. This triple says that, for all starting states and all executions of the trivial program skip, there exist executions of the programs $x_1 := \mathsf{havoc}$ and $x_2 := \mathsf{havoc}$ such that $x_1 \neq x_2$ after both programs have executed. Note that $\circledast$ is *not* a concatenation operator; it does nothing more than delineate multiple programs in a RHLE triple. Table 1 gives some additional examples of RHLE assertions.

$$\frac{}{S_\forall, S_\exists \vdash \langle \Phi \rangle \, \overline{\mathsf{skip}} \sim_\exists \overline{\mathsf{skip}} \, \langle \Phi \rangle} \; \text{Finish}$$
$$\frac{S_\forall, S_\exists \vdash \langle \Phi \rangle \, \overline{p_\forall; \, \mathsf{skip}} \sim_\exists \overline{p_\exists; \, \mathsf{skip}} \, \langle \Psi \rangle}{S_\forall, S_\exists \vdash \langle \Phi \rangle \, \overline{p_\forall} \sim_\exists \overline{p_\exists} \, \langle \Psi \rangle} \; \text{SkipI}$$

$$\frac{\forall \overline{\sigma} \, \overline{\sigma_\exists}. \, S_\forall \vdash \{ \Phi \mid_i \overline{\sigma}, \overline{\sigma_\exists} \} \; s_i \; \{ \Phi' \mid_i \overline{\sigma}, \overline{\sigma_\exists} \} \qquad S_\forall, S_\exists \vdash \langle \Phi' \rangle \, p_1 \circledast \ldots \circledast s_i' \circledast \ldots \circledast s_n \sim_\exists \overline{p_\exists} \, \langle \Psi \rangle}{S_\forall, S_\exists \vdash \langle \Phi \rangle \, p_1 \circledast \ldots \circledast s_i; \, s_i' \circledast \ldots \circledast p_n \sim_\exists \overline{p_\exists} \, \langle \Psi \rangle} \; \text{Step}\forall$$

$$\frac{\forall \overline{\sigma_\forall} \, \overline{\sigma}. \, S_\exists \vdash [\Phi \mid_i \overline{\sigma_\forall}, \overline{\sigma}] \; s_i \; [\Phi' \mid_i \overline{\sigma_\forall}, \overline{\sigma}]_\exists \qquad S_\forall, S_\exists \vdash \langle \Phi' \rangle \, \overline{p_\forall} \sim_\exists p_1 \circledast \ldots \circledast s_i' \circledast \ldots \circledast p_n \, \langle \Psi \rangle}{S_\forall, S_\exists \vdash \langle \Phi \rangle \, \overline{p_\forall} \sim_\exists p_1 \circledast \ldots \circledast s_i; \, s_i' \circledast \ldots \circledast p_n \, \langle \Psi \rangle} \; \text{Step}\exists$$

Fig. 5. Core RHLE proof rules.

The core logic of RHLE is given in Fig. 5. Relational proofs are built by reasoning about the topmost statement of either one of the universally quantified programs via the STEP∀ rule or one of the existentially quantified programs using the STEP∃ rule. Once all program statements have been considered, final proof obligations can be discharged using the FINISH rule. The SKIPI rule is used to ensure that all programs end with skip, so that FINISH can be applied. Both STEP rules rely on non-relational logics for reasoning about the universal $S_\forall \vdash \{P\}\ p\ \{Q\}$ and existential $S_\exists \vdash [P]\ p\ [Q]_\exists$ behaviors of single statements; we will present the details of both logics shortly. The STEP rules employ a projection operation, $\overline{\sigma}|_i \Psi$, which maps a relational assertion to a non-relational one. Given a collection of n states, $\Psi|_i\overline{\sigma}$ is satisfied by any state σ' which satisfies Ψ when inserted at the ith position:

$$\sigma' \models \Psi|_i\,\overline{\sigma} \quad \equiv \quad \sigma_1, \ldots, \sigma_{i-1}, \sigma', \sigma_{i+1}, \ldots, \sigma_n \models \Psi$$

In effect, this operation ensures the states of the other programs remain unchanged when reasoning about the ith program in the triple.

Universal Hoare Logic. The program logic for universal executions has a standard partial correctness semantics:

$$S_\forall \models \{P\}\ p\ \{Q\} \quad \equiv \quad \forall \sigma, \sigma'.\ \sigma \models P \wedge S_\forall \vdash \sigma, p \Downarrow_\forall \sigma' \implies \sigma' \models Q$$

The rules of this logic are largely standard[1], except for the rule for function calls, which uses a context of universal function specifications:

$$\frac{S_\forall(f) = \mathsf{ax}_\forall\ f(\overline{x})\{P\}\{Q\}}{S_\forall \vdash \left\{ \begin{array}{c} P[\overline{a}/\overline{x}] \quad \wedge \\ \forall v.Q[v/\rho; \overline{a}/\overline{x}] \quad \implies R[v/y] \end{array} \right\}\ y := f(\overline{a})\ \{R\}} \quad \forall\mathrm{SPEC}$$

Existential Hoare Logic. The assertions of our program logic for existential executions say that, for any state meeting the precondition, there *exists* an execution of the program ending in a set of states meeting the post-condition:

$$S_\exists \models [P]\ p\ [Q]_\exists \quad \equiv \quad \forall \sigma.\ \sigma \models P \implies \exists \Sigma.\ S_\exists \vdash \sigma, p \Downarrow_\exists \Sigma \quad \wedge \quad \forall \sigma' \in \Sigma.\ \sigma' \models Q$$

These rules are largely standard *total* Hoare logic rules[2], augmented with a rule for calls to existentially specified functions:

$$\frac{S_\exists(f) = \mathsf{ax}_\exists f(\overline{x})\ [\overline{c}]\ \{P\}\ \{Q\}}{S_\exists \vdash \left[\begin{array}{c} \exists \overline{k}.\ ([\overline{x} \mapsto \overline{a}] \models P[\overline{k}/\overline{c}] \\ \wedge \quad \exists v.[\rho \mapsto v, \overline{x} \mapsto \overline{a}] \models Q[\overline{k}/\overline{c}] \\ \wedge \quad \forall v.[\rho \mapsto v, \overline{x} \mapsto \overline{a}] \models Q[\overline{k}/\overline{c}] \\ \implies R[v/y]) \end{array} \right]\ y := f(\overline{a})\ [R]_\exists} \quad \exists\mathrm{SPEC}$$

---

[1] The extended version of this paper [15] gives a full listing of the rules of this logic.
[2] The full existential logic is presented in the extended version of this paper [15].

The precondition of this rule is quantified over instantiations $\overline{k}$ of the specification's choice variables. The first of the three conjuncts under this quantifier ensures that the statement is executed in a state satisfying the function's precondition. The next conjunct ensures that the function's post-condition is inhabited. The final conjunct requires that every possible return value satisfying the function's post-condition also satisfies the triple's post-condition.

Example 3. Given the existential specification $\mathsf{ax_\exists\ zeroOrOne()}\ [c]\ \{c = 0 \vee c = 1\}$ $\{\rho = c\}$, we can use $\exists\textsc{Spec}$ (along with the standard rule for while loops, see the extended paper [15]) to prove the existential assertion $S_\exists \vdash [k = 0]$ while $k < 4$ do $k := k + \mathsf{zeroOrOne()}$ end $[k = 4]_\exists$. This loop *could* loop forever by choosing to add 0 to k at every iteration. Nevertheless, by using measure $4 - k$ with the well-founded relation $<$ and instantiating the choice variable with 1 at each iteration, we can prove a terminating path through the program exists.

4.1 Synchronous Rules

While the rules in Fig. 5 are sufficient to reason about relational properties, it is possible to lessen the verification burden for structurally similar programs by employing *synchronous rules* which exploit structural similarities between the programs being verified [27]. Reasoning over similar control flow structures in lockstep can reduce the space of states verification must consider and simplify loop invariants. This is particularly useful when reasoning about *hyperproperties* [12], or relational properties on multiple executions of the *same* program. In order to more easily reason about structurally similar programs, RHLE also includes synchronous rules inspired by the Cartesian loop logic presented by Sousa and Dillig [36]. The extended version of this paper [15] includes a full listing of these rules.

Example 4. Consider proving that while $(x < 10)$ do $y := y + \mathsf{randB(9)}$ end refines while $(x < 10)$ do $y := y + \mathsf{randB(5)}; y := y + \mathsf{randB(6)}$ end. Intuitively, the first program refines the second because the bodies of the loops are themselves refinements. A proof using only the rules in Fig. 5 is unable to take advantage of this intuition, however. Instead, the proof requires a sufficiently strong invariant characterizing the behavior of the entire loop on the left, and then an invariant for the righthand program that accounts for the behavior of individual iterations of the lefthand loop.

The SyncLoops rule is designed for this situation:

$$\frac{S_\forall, S_\exists \vdash \langle \mathbb{I} \wedge \bigwedge_{0 \leq i \leq n} b_i \rangle\ s_0 \circledast \cdots \circledast s_k \sim_\exists s_{k+1} \circledast \cdots \circledast s_n\ \langle \mathbb{I} \rangle \quad \mathbb{I} \wedge \bigwedge_{0 \leq i \leq n} \neg b_i \implies \Psi \quad \mathbb{I} \wedge \neg \bigwedge_{0 \leq i \leq n} b_i \implies \bigwedge_{0 \leq i \leq n} \neg b_i}{S_\forall, S_\exists \vdash \langle \mathbb{I} \rangle\ \text{while } b_0 \text{ do } s_0 \text{ end} \circledast \cdots \circledast \text{while } b_k \text{ do } s_k \text{ end} \sim_\exists \text{while } b_{k+1} \text{ do } s_{k+1} \text{ end} \circledast \cdots \circledast \text{while } b_n \text{ do } s_n \text{ end}\ \langle \Psi \rangle}\ \textsc{SyncLoops}$$

The first premise of this rule says that executing all loop bodies preserves some invariant $\mathbb{I}$, the second ensures the invariant is strong enough to imply the post-condition, and the third requires all loops to end on the same iteration. Since this invariant is reestablished after the execution of every loop body; the invariant that y_1 and y_2 are equal at each iteration suffices to verify this example.

4.2   Soundness

The combination of the core and synchronous rules provide a sound methodology for reasoning about $\forall\exists$ properties:

Theorem 3 (RHLE is Sound). *Suppose* $S_\forall, S_\exists \vdash \langle\varPhi\rangle \; \overline{p_\forall} \sim_\exists \overline{p_\exists} \; \langle\varPsi\rangle$. *Then, for any function context I compatible with* $S_\forall$ *and* $S_\exists$, *any set of initial states* $\overline{\sigma_\forall}$ *and* $\overline{\sigma_\exists}$ *satisfying* $\varPhi$, *and every collection of final states* $\overline{\sigma'_\forall}$ *of* $\overline{p_\forall}$, *there must exist a collection of final states produced by* $\overline{p_\exists}$ *that, together with* $\overline{\sigma'_\forall}$, *satisfies the relational post-condition* $\varPsi$.

5   Verification

Algorithm 1: RHLEVerify

Inputs : $\varPhi$, relational precondition
$p_\forall$, universal programs
$p_\exists$, existential programs
$\varPsi$, relational postcondition
Output: $\langle\varPhi\rangle \; p_\forall \sim_\exists p_\exists \; \langle\varPsi\rangle$ validity
1 **begin**
2    $\overline{\varPsi} \leftarrow (\varnothing, \varnothing, \varPsi)$
3    $(\overline{a}, \overline{e}, \varPsi') \leftarrow$
     VCGen $(\overline{skip; p_\forall}, \overline{skip; p_\exists}, \overline{\varPsi})$
4   **return**
     Verify $(\forall\overline{a}\exists\overline{e}. \; \varPhi \implies \varPsi')$

We now turn to the relational verification algorithm based on RHLE, presented in Algorithm 1. The algorithm is implicitly parameterized over a pair of universal and existential contexts, and Verify, a decision procedure for checking validity of a formula in the underlying assertion logic. The bulk of the work is delegated to VCGen, presented in Algorithm 2, which builds a weakest relational precondition for the input RHLE triple. The algorithm then checks that the RHLE triple's precondition entails the calculated weakest precondition.

The body of VCGen builds a formula by recursively generating verification conditions for the input programs statement by statement. This loop tries to maximize opportunities to apply synchronous rules at each step, as these rules allow us to simultaneously generate proof obligations for multiple subprograms, as discussed in Sect. 4.1. After establishing there are still program statements to step over (lines 3–4), VCGen looks for and processes any trailing program statements which are not loops (lines 5–8), as such statements are not subject to synchronous rule applications. To process individual program statements, VCGen relies on a pair of verification condition generators, $VC_\forall$ and $VC_\exists$, for the non-relational program logics. These functions are largely standard weakest

---

Algorithm 2: VCGen

Inputs : $p_\forall$, a set of universal programs
$p_\exists$, a set of existential programs
$\overline{\Psi} = (Q_\forall, Q_\exists, \Psi)$, Ψ a postcondition with quantified variables $Q_\forall, Q_\exists$

Output: $(\{v_0, \dots, v_n\}, \{w_0, \dots, w_n\}, \Phi)$ such that v_i, w_i free in Φ and
$\langle \Phi \rangle \, p_\forall \sim_\exists p_\exists \, \langle\!\langle \Psi \rangle\!\rangle$ is valid if $\forall v_0, \dots, v_n \, \exists w_0, \dots w_n. \, \Phi \implies \Psi$

1 **begin**
2   **match** $p_\forall \sim_\exists p_\exists$:
3   **case** $\overline{skip} \sim_\exists \overline{skip}$ **do**
4   **return** $\overline{\Psi}$

5   **case** $\overline{p'_\forall} \circledast (s_1; s_2) \circledast \overline{p''_\forall} \sim_\exists p_\exists$ **where** s_2 *not a loop* **do**
6   VCGen $(\overline{p'_\forall} \circledast s_1 \circledast \overline{p''_\forall}, p_\exists, VC_\forall(s_2, \overline{\Psi}))$

7   **case** $p_\forall \sim_\exists \overline{p'_\exists} \circledast (s_1; s_2) \circledast \overline{p''_\exists}$ **where** s_2 *not a loop* **do**
8   VCGen $(p_\forall, \overline{p'_\exists} \circledast s_1 \circledast \overline{p''_\exists}, VC_\exists(s_2, \overline{\Psi}))$

9   **case** $\overline{p'_\forall} \circledast s_1; \textbf{if } b \textbf{ then } s_t \textbf{ else } s_e \circledast \overline{p''_\forall} \sim_\exists \overline{p'_\exists}$ **do**
10        $(Q_\forall, Q_\exists, \Psi_T) \leftarrow$ VCGen $(\overline{p'_\forall} \circledast s_1; s_t \circledast \overline{p''_\forall}, p_\exists, b \implies \Psi))$
11        $(Q'_\forall, Q'_\exists, \Psi_E) \leftarrow$ VCGen $(\overline{p'_\forall} \circledast s_1; s_e \circledast \overline{p''_\forall}, p_\exists, \neg b \implies \Psi))$
12   **return** $(Q_\forall \cup Q'_\forall, Q_\exists \cup Q_\exists, \Psi_T \wedge \Psi_E)$

13   **case** $p_0; \textbf{while } b_0 \textbf{ do } s_0 \circledast \cdots \circledast p_{i-1}; \textbf{while } b_{i-1} \textbf{ do } s_{i-1} \sim_\exists$
           $p'_i; \textbf{while } b_i \textbf{ do } s_i \circledast \cdots \circledast p'_n; \textbf{while } b_n \textbf{ do } s_n$ **do**
14        $\mathbb{I} \leftarrow$ FindInvariant $(\textbf{while } b_0 \textbf{ do } s_0 \circledast \cdots \circledast \textbf{while } b_{i-1} \textbf{ do } s_{i-1} \sim_\exists$
               $\textbf{while } b_i \textbf{ do } s_i \circledast \cdots \circledast \textbf{while } b_n \textbf{ do } s_n)$
15        $(Q'_\forall, Q'_\exists, \Psi_{body}) \leftarrow$ VCGen $(s_0 \circledast \cdots \circledast s_{i-1} \sim_\exists s_i \circledast \cdots \circledast s_n, \mathbb{I})$
16        $inductive \leftarrow \mathbb{I} \wedge \bigwedge_{0 \leq i \leq n} b_i \implies \Psi_{body}$
17        $lockstep \leftarrow \mathbb{I} \wedge \neg \bigwedge_{0 \leq i \leq n} b_i \implies \bigwedge_{0 \leq i \leq n} \neg b_i$
18        $post \leftarrow \mathbb{I} \wedge \bigwedge_{0 \leq i \leq n} \neg b_i \implies \Psi$
19        $(Q_\forall, Q_\exists, \Psi) \leftarrow \overline{\Psi}$
20   **if** Verify $(Q_\forall \cup Q'_\forall, Q_\exists \cup Q'_\exists, inductive \wedge lockstep \wedge post)$ **then**
21   VCGen $(\overline{p}, \overline{p'}, (Q_\forall, Q_\exists, \mathbb{I}))$

22   **else**
23   **next case**

24   **case** $\overline{p'_\forall} \circledast (s_1; s_2) \circledast \overline{p''_\forall} \sim_\exists p_\exists$ **do**
25   VCGen $(\overline{p'_\forall} \circledast s_1 \circledast \overline{p''_\forall}, p_\exists, vc_\forall(s_2, \overline{\Psi}))$

26   **case** $p_\forall \sim_\exists \overline{p'_\exists} \circledast (s_1; s_2) \circledast \overline{p''_\exists}$ **do**
27   VCGen $(p_\forall, \overline{p'_\exists} \circledast s_1 \circledast \overline{p''_\exists}, vc_\exists(s_2, \overline{\Psi}))$

---

precondition generators extended with support for existential function calls. The consequents of ∀SPEC and ∃SPEC immediately yield weakest precondition rules, so that if $S_\forall(f) = \mathsf{ax}_\forall \, f(\overline{x})\{P\}\{Q\}$ and $S_\exists(f) = \mathsf{ax}_\exists f(\overline{x}) \, [\overline{c}] \, \{P\} \, \{Q\}$, then:

$$\mathrm{VC}_\forall(\Psi, y := f(\overline{a})) = P[\overline{a}/\overline{x}] \wedge \forall v. Q[v/\rho; \overline{a}/\overline{x}] \implies \Psi[v/y]$$

$$\mathrm{VC}_\exists(\Psi, y := f(\overline{a})) = \exists \overline{k}. \, ([\overline{x} \mapsto \overline{a}] \models P[\overline{k}/\overline{c}] \, \wedge \, \exists v. [\rho \mapsto v, \overline{x} \mapsto \overline{a}] \models Q[\overline{k}/\overline{c}]$$

$$\wedge \, \forall v. [\rho \mapsto v, \overline{x} \mapsto \overline{a}] \models Q[\overline{k}/\overline{c}] \implies \Psi[v/y])$$

If the first three cases fail, the final statements of all the remaining programs are loops. In this case, VCGen attempts to simultaneously process the loops (lines 9–19) à la the SYNCLOOPS rule in Example 4. To be eligible for fusion, loops must execute in lockstep. This condition is checked (line 16) before returning; if loops may execute different numbers of times, the algorithm proceeds to the next match case. If no synchronized reasoning is possible, VCGen defaults to stepping over an arbitrary loop in one of the programs (lines 20–23).

VCGen is parameterized over a procedure called FindInvariant, which acts as an oracle for relational loop invariants. Our prototype implementation of Algorithm 1 currently requires loops to be annotated with their invariants; these annotations are used to implement FindInvariant. We have experimented with adapting both purely logical [18, 19] and data-driven approaches [30, 31] for invariant inference, but have yet to discover one that is effective for our larger benchmarks. Unlike traditional loop invariants, which must be re-established on every possible execution of the loop body, invariants in existentially quantified executions need only be re-established on a subset of the possible executions of the body. A robust invariant inference approach thus requires finding not only the invariant itself, but a strategy for instantiating choice variables that consistently re-establish the chosen invariant. Scalable invariant inference for existentially quantified executions is an important and interesting direction for future work.

See the extended version of this paper [15] for an example application of Algorithm 1 to RandB.

6   Implementation and Evaluation

To evaluate our approach, we have implemented ORHLE, a publicly available [16] automatic program verifier based on Algorithm 1. ORHLE is implemented in Haskell, and uses Z3 as a backend solver to fill the role of Verify. As previously mentioned, invariants are provided by the programmer via annotations in the code. Input to ORHLE consists of a collection of FUNIMP programs, a declaration of how many copies of each program should be included in the universal and existential contexts, and a collection of function specifications expressed using the SMT-LIB2 format. Functions can have both universal and existential specifications, with the latter containing declarations of choice variables. See the extended version of this paper [15] for example ORHLE input listings. ORHLE outputs a set of verification conditions along with a success or failure message. When a property fails to verify, ORHLE outputs a falsifying model.

Our evaluation addresses the following questions:

(R1) Is RHLE *expressive* enough to represent a variety of interesting properties?
(R2) Is our approach *effective*; that is, can it be used to verify or invalidate relational assertions about a diverse corpus of programs?
(R3) Is it possible to realize an *efficient* implementation of our verification approach which returns results within a reasonable time frame?

To answer these questions, we have developed a suite of 41 programs over 5 kinds of relational specifications drawn from the literature. We have also compiled an additional set of 12 benchmarks over two non-relational existentially quantified properties in order to evaluate similar questions about the non-relational existential logic from Sect. 4. Both sets of benchmarks contain a mix of valid and invalid properties. We have made these benchmarks publicly available[3] via GitHub [17].

Our benchmarks for the non-relational existential logic from Sect. 4 fall into two categories:

Winning Strategy. Programs in this category play a simplified version of the card game twenty-one. Players start with two cards valued between 1 and 10, and can then request any number of additional cards. The goal is to get a hand value as close to 21 as possible without going over. The property of interest is whether an algorithmic strategy for this game permits the *possibility* of achieving the maximum hand value of 21 given any starting hand.

Branching Time Properties. Our next set of benchmarks are taken from work by Cook and Koskinen [14] which considered verification of properties of single programs expressed in CTL. The programs in this category are adaptations of the subset of those benchmarks which assert the existence of desirable final states and are thus expressible in RHLE.

Our set of relational benchmarks cover program refinement in addition to:

Noninterference. Generalized noninterference is a possibilistic information security property which ensures that programs do not leak knowledge about high-security state via low-security outputs. Our formalization of this property is based on Mclean [26] and requires that, for any execution of a program p whose state is divided into high security p_H and low security p_L partitions, any other starting state with the same initial low partition can potentially yield the same final low partition, regardless of the high partition.

Delimited Release. Delimited release is a relaxation of generalized noninterference which allows for limited information about secure state to be released. For example, given a confidential list of employee salaries, it may be acceptable to publicize the average salary as long as no other salary information is leaked. We formulate delimited release as a noninterference property with an additional condition requiring that the programs agree on the values of the released information. For the previous example, we would add a precondition asserting the average salary across all executions is equal.

Parameter Usage. Our parameter usage benchmarks check whether a function parameter is semantically unused, in that the existence of the parameter does

---

[3] Branching time property benchmarks are adapted from a proprietary source, and are thus omitted from the publicly available benchmarks.

Property	Shape	Pos	Neg	Unk	Med(ms)	Max(ms)
Delimited Release	$\forall p_1 \exists p_2$	7	6	0	222	253
Flaky Tests	$\exists p_1 p_2$	2	0	0	231	245
Generalized Noninterference	$\forall p_1 \exists p_2$	4	6	0	222	229
Parameter Usage	$\forall p_1 \exists p_2$	4	3	0	220	245
Program Refinement	$\forall p_1 \exists p_2$	4	4	1	224	1367
Winning Strategy	$\exists p$	1	2	0	228	230
Branching Time	$\exists p$	7	2	0	226	259

Fig. 6. ORHLE verification results over a set of relational and non-relational properties. The **Shape** column gives the execution quantification pattern for the property; each property is of the form $\forall p_0 \dots p_n \exists q_o \dots q_n$, where p_i's and q_i's are (possibly empty) sets of executions. The **Pos** and **Neg** columns give the number of benchmarks over which the property holds or does not hold, respectively. The **Unk** column gives the number of benchmarks whose verification conditions could not be decided by the SMT solver. The **Med** and **Max** columns give (respectively) the median and maximum verification times in milliseconds over each set of benchmarks.

not affect the program's reachable final states. For example, the flag parameter in f(flag) = if flag then return 1 else return 1 is syntactically used in f, even affecting its control flow, but does not have any effect on f's possible outputs; we therefore consider flag to be semantically unused. For an n-ary function $f(p_1, \dots, p_n)$, we say parameter p_i is semantically unused if

$$\langle v_i \neq w_i \wedge \bigwedge_{j \neq i} v_j = w_j \rangle \ a := f(v_1, \dots, v_n) \sim_\exists b := f(w_1, \dots, w_n) \ \langle a = b \rangle$$

Flaky Tests. Tests of program behavior which can nondeterministically pass or fail pose a significant hazard as they can trigger false alarms or allow regressions to go undetected. We modeled representative nondeterministic tests in FUNIMP based on examples from The Illinois Dataset of Flaky Tests (IDoFT) [24,35], framing flakiness as a $\forall \exists$ property containing only existential executions. We consider a test verifiably flaky when there exists both a test execution that succeeds and one that fails. We model nondeterminsitic system behavior (e.g., getCurrentTimeMs() or the results of network calls) as function calls. For example, to model the imprecision of thread sleeps, we give the verifier leeway to sleep within a ±20 ms window around the requested interval: $ax_\exists$ sleep(interval, currentTime) [sleepTime] $\{0 \leq \text{sleepTime} \wedge \text{interval} - 20 \leq \text{sleepTime} \leq \text{interval} + 20\}$ $\{\rho = \text{currentTime} + \text{sleepTime}\}$.

The variety of properties we were able to represent in ORHLE provides evidence that it is sufficiently expressive (R1). To show that ORHLE is both effective and efficient (R2)-(R3), we have used it to verify and/or invalidate examples of the benchmark properties described above. All of these experiments were done using an Intel Core i7-6700K CPU with 8 4GHz cores. Figure 6 presents the results of these experiments. ORHLE yielded the expected verification result in all cases except for one refinement benchmark, where the backing SMT solver (Z3) was unable to determine the validity of the verification conditions. While most benchmarks' verification conditions fell within the theory of linear integer arithmetic, verification conditions fell in a non-decidable fragment of arithmetic in this benchmark. This undecidable instance accounts for the outlier maximum verification time in the refinement benchmarks. Overall, these results offer evidence that ORHLE is both effective and efficient for verifying a variety of existential and ∀∃ properties.

7 Related Work

Relational Program Logics. Relational program logics are a common approach to verifying relational specifications. Relational Hoare Logic [9] (RHL) was one of the first examples of these logics, and is capable of proving 2-safety properties. Relational Higher-order Logic [2] is a higher-order relational logic for reasoning about higher-order functional programs expressed in a simply-typed λ-calculus. Probabilistic RHL [8] is a logic for reasoning about probabilistic programs in order to prove security properties of cryptographic schemes. The relational logic closest to RHLE is Cartesian Hoare Logic [36] (CHL) developed by Sousa and Dillig. This logic which provides an axiomatic system for reasoning about k-safety hyperproperties along with an automatic verification algorithm. RHLE can be thought of as an extension of CHL for reasoning about the more general class of ∀∃ properties. Nagasamudram and Naumann [27] examine *alignment completeness* for relational Hoare logics, which classifies the ability of these logics to reason about programs in lockstep. Banerjee et al. [4] introduce a relational Hoare logic capable of reasoning about encapsulation and invariant hiding, but which is confined to 2-safety properties.

Underapproximate Program Logics. Several program logics have been proposed to reason about the existence of particular executions of a single program, similar to the non-relational existential logic presented in Sect. 4. Reverse Hoare Logic [39] is a program logic for reasoning about reachability over single executions of programs which have access to a nondeterministic binary choice (⊔) operator. Incorrectness Logic [29] is a recent adaptation of Reverse Hoare Logic to a more realistic programming language. While these logics express the existence of a satisfying start state for all satisfying end states ($\forall\sigma'\exists\sigma$), the existential logic presented in Sect. 4 requires there to exist a satisfying end state for all satisfying start states ($\forall\sigma\exists\sigma'$). Reverse Hoare Logic and Incorrectness Logic both reason about reachability over single executions, but properties in these logics are pure underapproximations: every state in a given postcondition must be reachable. In contrast, our reasoning over existential specifications is underapproximate *with respect to the choice variables only*. While every valid choice value must correspond to a reachable set of final states, each of these sets are still overapproximate. This feature of our existential specifications enables a natural integration with standard Hoare logics.

First-order dynamic logic [33] is a reinterpretation of Hoare logic in first-order, multi-modal logic. For a program p, the modal operators $[p]$ and $\langle p \rangle$ capture universal and existential quantification over program executions. Our universal Hoare triple $\vdash \{P\}p\{Q\}$ corresponds to $P \implies [p]Q$, and our existential Hoare triple $\vdash [P]p[Q]_\exists$ corresponds to $P \implies \langle p \rangle Q$. In contrast to RHLE, dynamic logic reasons about properties of single program executions.

Prophecy Variables. Prophecy variables were originally introduced by Abadi and Lamport [1] in order to establish refinement mappings between state machines. Choice variables in our existential specifications are similar to prophecy variables in that they capture the required value of some "future" state, although we use them as part of a program logic rather than to reason about refinement mappings between state machines. Jung et al. [22] incorporate prophecy variables into a separation Hoare logic to reason about nondeterminism in concurrent programs, but differ from our approach in that the program logic operates in a non-relational setting and is designed for interactive and not automated verification.

Relational Verification. The concept of a hyperproperty was originally introduced by Clarkson and Schneider [12], building on earlier work by Terauchi and Aiken [37]. The initial work discusses verification but it does not offer an algorithm; numerous program techniques have been subsequently proposed to verify hyperproperties. Product programs are an alternative approach to relational verification [5]. This approach can leverage existing non-relational verification tools and techniques when verifying the product program, but the large state space of product programs can make verification difficult in practice. Product programs have been used to verify k-safety properties and reason about noninterference and secure information flow [7,23]. Barthe et al. [6] have developed a set of necessary conditions for "left-product programs"; these product programs can be used to verify hyperproperties outside of k-safety, including our $\forall\exists$ properties, although the work does not address how to construct left-product programs.

Unno et al. [38] have developed a technique for verifying $\forall\exists$ properties including program refinement, generalized noninterference, and cotermination by encoding a constraint satisfaction problem expressed using a generalization of constrained Horn clauses. The approach solves constraints using a stratified CEGIS approach, and can synthesize non-trivial alignment predicates for interleaving executions of loop bodies. This work is not based on a Hoare-style program logic, but rather develops per-property embeddings of $\forall\exists$ verification problems in a novel adaptation of constrained Horn clauses.

There are several modal logics which support a style of existential reasoning similar to our existential logic. Temporal logics like HyperLTL and HyperCTL [11] can be used to reason about hyperproperties, although verification tooling [10] is focused on model checking state transition systems rather than program logics. Coenen et al. [13] examine verification and synthesis of computational models using HyperLTL formulas with alternating quantifiers. Cook et al. [14] examine existential reasoning in branching-time temporal logics by way of removing state space until universal reasoning methods can be used. Lamport and Schneider [25] examine using TLA to verify $\forall\exists$ properties including refinement and GNI. While the above approaches are capable of reasoning about the kinds of liveness properties we consider in this paper, they all focus on model checking state transition systems rather than using a Hoare-style logic to reason directly over programs as in our approach.

8 Conclusion

This paper presented RHLE, a novel relational Hoare-style program logic for reasoning about ∀∃ properties. These properties can capture a variety of interesting behaviors of multiple program executions, including program refinement and information flow properties. Key to our logic is a novel form of function specifications which constrain the set of behaviors that a valid implementation of a function *must* exhibit. We have developed an automated verification algorithm based on RHLE, and we demonstrated that an implementation of this algorithm is able to check the validity of a variety of ∀∃ properties over a benchmark suite of programs.

Acknowledgments. We would like to thank Roopsha Samanta for her valuable input on initial drafts of this work. We would also like to thank the anonymous reviewers of this and previous iterations of this paper for their much-appreciated feedback. This research was partially supported by the National Science Foundation under Grant CCF-1755880 and by a grant from the Purdue Research Foundation.

References

1. Abadi, M., Lamport, L.: The existence of refinement mappings. In: [1988] Proceedings. Third Annual Symposium on Logic in Computer Science, pp. 165–175 (1988)
2. Aguirre, A., Barthe, G., Gaboardi, M., Garg, D., Strub, P.Y.: A relational logic for higher-order programs. Proc. ACM Program. Lang. 1(ICFP), 21:1–21:29 (Aug 2017)
3. Appel, A.W.: Verified software toolchain. In: Barthe, G. (ed.) Programming Languages and Systems, vol. 6602, pp. 1–17. Springer, Berlin Heidelberg, Berlin, Heidelberg (2011). https://doi.org/10.1007/978-3-642-19718-5_1
4. Banerjee, A., Nagasamudram, R., Naumann, D.A., Nikouei, M.: A relational program logic with data abstraction and dynamic framing. arXiv preprint arXiv:1910.14560 (2019)
5. Barthe, G., Crespo, J.M., Kunz, C.: Relational Verification Using Product Programs. In: Butler, M., Schulte, W. (eds.) FM 2011. LNCS, vol. 6664, pp. 200–214. Springer, Heidelberg (2011). https://doi.org/10.1007/978-3-642-21437-0_17
6. Barthe, G., Crespo, J.M., Kunz, C.: Beyond 2-safety: asymmetric product programs for relational program verification. In: International Symposium on Logical Foundations of Computer Science, pp. 29–43. Springer (2013). https://doi.org/10.1007/978-3-642-35722-0_3
7. Barthe, G., D'Argenio, P.R., Rezk, T.: Secure information flow by self-composition. Math. Struct. Comput. Sci. 21(6), 1207–1252 (2011)
8. Barthe, G., Grégoire, B., Zanella Béguelin, S.: Formal certification of code-based cryptographic proofs. SIGPLAN Not. 44(1), 90–101 (2009)

9. Benton, N.: Simple relational correctness proofs for static analyses and program transformations. In: Proceedings of the 31st ACM SIGPLAN-SIGACT Symposium on Principles of Programming Languages, pp. 14–25. POPL '04, ACM, New York, NY, USA (2004)

10. Clarke, E., Grumberg, O., Long, D.: Verification tools for finite-state concurrent systems. In: de Bakker, J.W., de Roever, W.-P., Rozenberg, G. (eds.) REX 1993. LNCS, vol. 803, pp. 124–175. Springer, Heidelberg (1994). https://doi.org/10.1007/3-540-58043-3_19

11. Clarkson, M.R., Finkbeiner, B., Koleini, M., Micinski, K.K., Rabe, M.N., Sánchez, C.: Temporal logics for hyperproperties. In: International Conference on Principles of Security and Trust, pp. 265–284. Springer (2014). https://doi.org/10.1007/978-3-642-54792-8_15

12. Clarkson, M.R., Schneider, F.B.: Hyperproperties. J. Comput. Secur. **18**(6), 1157–1210 (2010)

13. Coenen, N., Finkbeiner, B., Sánchez, C., Tentrup, L.: Verifying hyperliveness, pp. 121–139 (07 2019)

14. Cook, B., Koskinen, E.: Reasoning about nondeterminism in programs. In: Proceedings of the 34th ACM SIGPLAN conference on Programming language design and implementation, pp. 219–230 (2013)

15. Dickerson, R., Ye, Q., Zhang, M.K., Delaware, B.: Rhle: modular deductive verification of relational ∀∃ properties (extended paper) (2020). 10.48550/ARXIV.2002.02904

16. Dickerson, R., Ye, Q., Zhang, M.K., Delaware, B.: ORHLE (2022). https://doi.org/10.5281/zenodo.7058107

17. Dickerson, R., Ye, Q., Zhang, M.K., Delaware, B.: RHLE Benchmarks (2022). https://github.com/rcdickerson/rhle-benchmarks

18. Dillig, I., Dillig, T., Li, B., McMillan, K.: Inductive invariant generation via abductive inference. In: Proceedings of the 2013 ACM SIGPLAN International Conference on Object Oriented Programming Systems Languages and Applications, pp. 443–456. OOPSLA '13, Association for Computing Machinery, New York, NY, USA (2013)

19. Flanagan, C., Leino, K.R.M.: Houdini, an Annotation Assistant for ESC/Java. In: Proceedings of the International Symposium of Formal Methods Europe on Formal Methods for Increasing Software Productivity, pp. 500–517. FME '01, Springer-Verlag, Berlin, Heidelberg (2001)

20. Hoare, C.A.R.: An axiomatic basis for computer programming. Commun. ACM **12**(10), 576–580 (1969)

21. Jung, R., Jourdan, J.H., Krebbers, R., Dreyer, D.: Rustbelt: securing the foundations of the rust programming language. Proc. ACM Program. Lang. **2**(POPL), 1–34 (dec 2017)

22. Jung, R., et al.: The future is ours: prophecy variables in separation logic. Proc. ACM Program. Lang. **4**(POPL), 1–32 (Dec 2019)

23. Kovács, M., Seidl, H., Finkbeiner, B.: Relational abstract interpretation for the verification of 2-hypersafety properties, pp. 211–222 (11 2013)

24. Lam, W., Oei, R., Shi, A., Marinov, D., Xie, T.: idflakies: a framework for detecting and partially classifying flaky tests. In: 2019 12th IEEE Conference on Software Testing, Validation and Verification (ICST), pp. 312–322 (2019)

25. Lamport, L., Schneider, F.B.: Verifying Hyperproperties with TLA. In: 2021 IEEE 34th Computer Security Foundations Symposium (CSF), pp. 1–16. iSSN: 2374-8303 (Jun 2021)

26. McLean, J.: A general theory of composition for a class of "possibilistic" properties. IEEE Trans. Softw. Eng. **22**(1), 53–67 (Jan 1996)
27. Nagasamudram, R., Naumann, D.A.: Alignment completeness for relational hoare logics. In: 2021 36th Annual ACM/IEEE Symposium on Logic in Computer Science (LICS), pp. 1–13 (2021)
28. O'Hearn, P.W.: Resources, concurrency, and local reasoning. Theor. Comput. Sci. **375**(1), 271–307 (2007), festschrift for John C. Reynolds's 70th birthday
29. O'Hearn, P.W.: Incorrectness logic. Proc. ACM Program. Lang. **4**(POPL) 1–32 (Dec 2019)
30. Padhi, S., Sharma, R., Millstein, T.: Data-driven precondition inference with learned features. ACM SIGPLAN Notices **51**(6), 42–56 (2016)
31. Padhi, S., Sharma, R., Millstein, T.: Loopinvgen: a loop invariant generator based on precondition inference (2017)
32. Poetzsch-Heffter, A., Müller, P.: A Programming Logic for Sequential Java. In: Swierstra, S.D. (ed.) Programming Languages and Systems, vol. 1576, pp. 162–176. Springer, Berlin Heidelberg, Berlin, Heidelberg (1999). https://doi.org/10.1007/3-540-49099-X_11
33. Pratt, V.R.: Semantical consideration on Floyd-Hoare logic. In: 17th Annual Symposium on Foundations of Computer Science (sfcs 1976), pp. 109–121. IEEE (1976)
34. Reynolds, J.: Separation logic: a logic for shared mutable data structures. In: Proceedings 17th Annual IEEE Symposium on Logic in Computer Science, pp. 55–74 (2002)
35. Shi, A., Gyori, A., Legunsen, O., Marinov, D.: Detecting assumptions on deterministic implementations of non-deterministic specifications. In: 2016 IEEE International Conference on Software Testing, Verification and Validation (ICST), pp. 80–90 (2016)
36. Sousa, M., Dillig, I.: Cartesian hoare logic for verifying k-safety properties. In: Proceedings of the 37th ACM SIGPLAN Conference on Programming Language Design and Implementation, pp. 57–69. PLDI '16, ACM, New York, NY, USA (2016)
37. Terauchi, T., Aiken, A.: Secure information flow as a safety problem. In: Hankin, C., Siveroni, I. (eds.) Static Analysis, vol. 3672, pp. 352–367. Springer, Berlin Heidelberg, Berlin, Heidelberg (2005). https://doi.org/10.1007/11547662_24
38. Unno, H., Terauchi, T., Koskinen, E.: Constraint-Based Relational Verification. In: Silva, A., Leino, K.R.M. (eds.) CAV 2021. LNCS, vol. 12759, pp. 742–766. Springer, Cham (2021). https://doi.org/10.1007/978-3-030-81685-8_35
39. de Vries, E., Koutavas, V.: Reverse hoare logic. In: Proceedings of the 9th International Conference on Software Engineering and Formal Methods, pp. 155–171. SEFM'11, Springer-Verlag, Berlin, Heidelberg (2011). https://doi.org/10.1007/978-3-642-24690-6_12

Automated Temporal Verification
for Algebraic Effects

Yahui Song[(✉)], Darius Foo, and Wei-Ngan Chin

School of Computing, National University of Singapore, Singapore, Singapore
{yahuis,dariusf,chinwn}@comp.nus.edu.sg

Abstract. Although effect handlers offer a versatile abstraction for user-defined effects, they produce complex and less restricted execution traces due to the composable non-local control flow mechanisms. This paper is interested in the temporal behaviors of effect sequences, such as unhandled effects, termination of the communication, safety, fairness, etc. Specifically, we propose a novel effects logic *ContEffs*, to write precise and modular specifications for programs in the presence of user-defined effect handlers and primitive effects. As a second contribution, we devise a forward verifier together with a fixpoint calculator to infer the behaviors of such programs. Lastly, our automated verification framework provides a purely algebraic *term-rewriting system* (TRS) as the back-end solver, efficiently checking the entailments between *ContEffs* assertions. To demonstrate the feasibility, we prototype a verification system where zero-shot, one-shot, and multi-shot continuations coexist; prove its correctness; present experimental results; and report on case studies.

1 Introduction

User-defined effects and effect handlers are advertised and advocated as a relatively easy-to-understand and modular approach to delimited control. They offer the ability to suspend and resume computations, allowing information to be transmitted both ways. More specifically, an effect handler resembles an exception handler, i.e., control is transferred to an enclosing handler. Unlike the exception handlers, the key difference is that effects handlers have access to a continuation. By invoking this continuation, the handler can communicate a reply to the suspended computation and resume its execution.

For example, `effect Yield : int -> unit`, declares the `Yield` effect, to be used in the *generator functions*. When it is performed, the program suspends its current execution and returns the yielded `int` value to the handler. Such usages separate the logic, e.g., iterating a list, from the effectful operations, such as "printing on the console" or "sending an element to a consumer", thereby improving code reuse and memory efficiency. Functions perform effects without needing to know how the handlers are implemented, and the computation may be enclosed by different handlers that handle the same effect differently.

Recently, effect handlers are found in several research programming languages, such as Eff [1], Frank [2], Links [3], Multicore OCaml [4], and Scala [5],

I. Sergey (Ed.): APLAS 2022, LNCS 13658, pp. 88–109, 2022.
https://doi.org/10.1007/978-3-031-21037-2_5

etc. There is a growing need for programmers and researchers to reason about the combination of primitive effects and user-defined handlers. In particular, we are interested in the techniques for inferring and verifying temporal behaviors of such non-local control flows, which have not been extensively studied. In this paper, we tackle the following verification challenges:

1. *The coexistence of zero-shot, one-shot and multi-shot continuations.* The design decisions of various implementations [4,6] and verification solutions [7,8] diverge upon the question that, should it be permitted or forbidden to invoke a captured continuation more than once? In this paper, our forward inference rules shows the generality to incorporate both one-shot and multi-shot continuations. Furthermore, it naturally supports reasoning on exceptions by treating them as *zero-shot*, i.e., that abandon the continuations completely.

2. *Non-terminating behaviors.* Figure 1 presents the so-called "recursive cow" program drawn from the benchmark [9], which looks like it is terminating but it actually cycles. Function f() performs the predefined effect Foo; then loop () handles effect Foo by resuming a closure which in turn performs Foo when applied.

With higher-order effect signatures and in the setting of deep handlers[1], the communications between the computation and handlers potentially lead to infinite traces. It is useful yet challenging to automatically infer/verify the termination of the communication. In this paper, we devise *ContEffs*, i.e., extended regular expressions with arithmetic constraints, to provide more precise

```
1  effect Foo : (unit -> unit)
2
3  let f() = perform Foo ()
4
5  let loop()
6  = match f () with
7  | _ -> () (*normal return*)
8  | effect Foo k -> continue k
9    (fun () -> perform Foo ())
```

Fig. 1. A loop.

specifications by integrating: $\star$ for finite traces; ω for infinite traces; ∞ for possibly finite or infinite traces.

3. *Linear temporal properties.* For decades monads have dominated the scene of pure functional programming with effects, and the recent popularization of algebraic effects and handlers promises to change the landscape. However, with rapid change also comes confusion. In monads, the effectful behavior is defined in *bind* and *return*, statically determining the behavior inside the *do* block. Whereas algebraic effects call effectful operations with no inherent behavior. Instead, the behavior is determined dynamically by the encompassing handler. Although this gives greater flexibility in the composition of effectful code, it requires further specifications and verification to enforce the temporal requirements.

In this work, *ContEffs* smoothly encode and go beyond the linear temporal logic (LTL). For examples: *"Effect A will never be followed by effect B"* is a fairness property, and it is expressed as: $(\_^\star \cdot A \cdot \overline{B})^\star$, where $\_$ is a wildcard matching to any events; $\star$ denotes a repeated pattern; $\overline{B}$ denotes the negation of an effect

---

[1] A deep handler is persistent: after it has handled one effect, it remains installed, as the topmost frame of the captured continuation [10,11].

B. "Function `send(int n)` *terminates when* `n` *is non-negative, otherwise it does not terminate"* is expressed as: $n \geq 0 \wedge (\_)^{\star} \vee n < 0 \wedge (\_)^{\omega}$, which is beyond LTL.

Having *ContEffs* as the specification language, we are interested in the following verification problem: Given a program $\mathcal{P}$, and a temporal property Φ', does $\Phi^{\mathcal{P}} \sqsubseteq \Phi'$ hold[2]? In a typical verification context, checking the inclusion/entailment between the program effects $\Phi^{\mathcal{P}}$ and the valid traces Φ' proves that: the program $\mathcal{P}$ will never lead to unsafe traces which violate Φ'.

To effectively check $\Phi^{\mathcal{P}} \sqsubseteq \Phi'$, we deploy a purely algebraic TRS inspired by Antimirov and Mosses' algorithm [12], which was originally designed for deciding the inequalities of regular expressions. Our TRS shows the ability to solve inclusions beyond the expressiveness of finite-state automata, also suggests that it is a better average-case algorithm than those based on automata theory.

We aim to lay the foundation for a practical verification system that is precise, concise, and modular to prove temporal properties of effectful programs. To the best of the authors' knowledge, this work is the first to provide an extensive temporal verification framework for programs with user-defined effects and handlers. We summarize our main contributions as follows:

1. **The Continuous Effect (*ContEffs*):** We define the syntax and semantics of *ContEffs*, to be the specification language, which captures the temporal behaviors of given higher-order programs with algebraic effects.
2. **Front-End Effects Inference:** Targeting a ML-like language with the presence of algebraic effects [4,13], we establish a set of forward rules, to compositionally infer the program's temporal behaviors. The inference process makes use of a fixpoint calculator and the back-end solver TRS.
3. **The Term Rewriting System (TRS):** To check the entailments (i.e., the language inclusion relation) between two *ContEffs*s, we present the rewriting rules, to prove the inferred effects against given temporal specifications.
4. **Implementation and Evaluation:** We prototype the proposed verification system based on the latest Multicore OCaml (4.12.0) implementation. We prove its correctness and present case studies investigating *ContEffs*' expressiveness and the potential for various extensions.

2   Overview

2.1   A Sense of *ContEffs* in File I/O

We define Hoare-triple style specifications, marked in `lavender`, for each program, which leads to a compositional verification strategy, where temporal reasoning can be done locally. We model an abstract form of file I/O in Fig. 2. Effects `Open` and `Close` are both declared to be *performed* with a value of type `int`, indexing the operated file.

---

[2] The inclusion notation $\sqsubseteq$ is formally defined in Definition 3.

Function open_file takes an argument n. Its precondition uses a wildcard '_' under a Kleene star, indicating that any finite number/kind of effects is allowed to have occurred *before* the call to open_file. In other words, it is always possible to open a file. Its postcondition indicates that it performs the effect Open applied with n.

The precondition of close_file states that it can only be called after such a history trace where the nth file has been requested to be Opened, and not been requested to be Closeed[3].

We use . to denote the sequential composition of effect traces, ! denotes the emission of a certain effect, and ~ denotes the negation of a certain effect label.

```
1   effect Open : int -> unit
2   effect Close: int -> unit
3
4   let open_file n
5   (*@ req _^* @*)
6   (*@ ens Open(n)! @*)
7   = perform (Open n)
8   let close_file n
9   (*@ req _^*.Open(n)!
10            .(~Close(n)!)^* @*)
11  (*@ ens Close(n)! @*)
12  = perform (Close n)
13
14  let file_9 ()
15  (*@ req emp @*)
16  (*@ ens Open(9)!.Close(9)!@*)
17  = open_file 9;
18    close_file 9
```

Fig. 2. A simple file I/O example.

The precondition of file_9: emp, stands for an empty trace, which means no history trace is *allowed* by the calling site of function file_9. We formalize this idea of *being allowed* as an entailment relation between specifications in Sec. 5. The verification fails when the real implementation violates the specifications.

2.2   Effects Inferences via a Fixpoint Calculation

We continue to examine a variant of the so-called "recursive cow" benchmark program [9] in Fig. 3., which generates an infinite trace. The handling of effects Foo and Goo are notable because their resumption carry closures back to the suspended points, which in turn perform effects when fully applied.

We argue informally that loop is non-terminating. This is because the invocation of f_g () performs Foo, which obtains the resumed closure (defined in line 16) and stores it in the variable f. Then the application to f in turn performs Goo. The performing of Goo brings us to the handler at line

```
1   effect Goo : (unit -> unit)
2
3   let f_g ()
4   (*@ req _^* @*)
5   (*@ ens Foo!.Goo!.Foo?() @*)
6   = let f = perform Foo in
7     let g = perform Goo in
8     f () (* g is abandoned *)
9
10  let loop ()
11  (*@ req _^* @*)
12  (*@ ens _^*.(Foo.Goo)^w @*)
13  = match f_g () with
14  | _ -> ()
15  | effect Foo k -> continue k
16    (fun () -> perform Goo ())
17  | effect Goo k -> continue k
18    (fun () -> perform Foo ())
```

Fig. 3. Another Loop.

---

[3] close_file's precondition prevents closing files that are not opened. The constraints can be strengthened or loosened as needed. For example, to prevent opening a file which is already opened, we need to strengthen open_file's precondition accordingly.

18, which resumes a closure that performs `Foo` when applied. The resulting post-condition, deploys the ω operator, states that `loop` *finally* performs an infinite succession of alternating `Foo` and `Goo` effects. In fact, our fixpoint calculator computes the final effects for `loop` as $Foo \cdot Goo \cdot Goo \cdot Foo \cdot (Goo \cdot Foo)^\omega$, which entails the declared postcondition (c.f. Fig. 4.).

Loops like these between handler and callee are generally caused by performing effects in the recovery closure when handling an effect, that results in a cycle back to that same (deep) handler. However, resuming with a closure, is a useful pattern for inverting control between handler and callee, does give rise to this trap. Our fixpoint analysis and specifications are aimed at capturing such situations, which have not been extensively explored.

2.3 The TRS: To Prove Effects Inclusions

The rewriting system proposed by Antimirov and Mosses [14] decides inequalities of regular expressions (REs) through an iterated process of checking the inequalities of their *partial derivatives* [15]. There are two basic rules: [DISPROVE], which infers false from trivially inconsistent inequalities; and [UNFOLD], which applies Definition 1 to generate new inequalities. In detail, given Σ is the whole set of the alphabet, $D_A(r)$ is the partial derivative of r w.r.t the event A.

Definition 1 (REs Inequality). *For REs r, s, $r \preceq s \Leftrightarrow \forall (A \in \Sigma). \ D_A(r) \preceq D_A(s)$.*

Similarly, we formally define the inclusion of *ContEffs* in Definition 3.

Next we present the effects inclusion, generated from Fig. 3, proving process for the post condition checking in Fig. 4. Termination is guaranteed because the set of derivatives to be considered is finite, and possible cycles are detected using *memorization*. We use ♠ to indicate such pairings. The rewriting rules are defined in Sec. 5. In particular, the rule [*Reoccur*] finds the syntactic identity from the internal proof tree, for the current open goal [16].

$$
\cfrac{
\cfrac{
\cfrac{
\cfrac{
\underline{Foo} \cdot Goo \cdot Goo \cdot Foo \cdot (Goo \cdot Foo)^\omega \sqsubseteq \_^* \cdot (Foo \cdot Goo)^\omega
}{
\underline{Goo} \cdot Goo \cdot Foo \cdot (Goo \cdot Foo)^\omega \sqsubseteq \_^* \cdot (Foo \cdot Goo)^\omega \vee Goo \cdot (Foo \cdot Goo)^\omega
} \ {\scriptstyle fst=Foo}
}{
\underline{Goo} \cdot Foo \cdot (Goo \cdot Foo)^\omega \sqsubseteq \_^* \cdot (Foo \cdot Goo)^\omega \vee (Foo \cdot Goo)^\omega
} \ {\scriptstyle fst=Goo}
}{
Foo \cdot (Goo \cdot Foo)^\omega \sqsubseteq \_^* \cdot (Goo \cdot Foo)^\omega \ ♠
} \ {\scriptstyle fst=Goo}
}{
\underline{Goo} \cdot Foo \cdot (Goo \cdot Foo)^\omega \sqsubseteq \_^* \cdot (Goo \cdot Foo)^\omega \vee Goo \cdot (Foo \cdot Goo)^\omega
} \ {\scriptstyle fst=Foo}
$$

$$
\cfrac{Foo \cdot (Goo \cdot Foo)^\omega \sqsubseteq \_^* \cdot (Goo \cdot Foo)^\omega \ ♠ \vee (Foo \cdot Goo)^\omega}{\cdots} \ {\scriptstyle fst=Goo}
$$

Fig. 4. Proving the postcondition of `loop` ().

3 Language and Specifications

3.1 The Target Language

Syntax. We target a minimal, ML-like (typed, higher-order, call-by-value) core pure language, defined in Fig. 5. Here, c, x and A are meta-variables ranging respectively over integer constants, variables, and labels of effects.

A program $\mathcal{P}$ comprises a list of effect declarations eff^* and a list of method definitions $meth^*$; the $*$ superscript denotes a finite, possibly empty list of items. Programs are typed according to basic types τ. Each method $meth$ has a name mn, an expression body e, and pre- and postconditions Φ_{pre} and Φ_{post} (the syntax of effect specifications Φ is given in Fig. 7). Constructs like sequencing are defined via elaboration to more primitive forms.

$$
\begin{array}{lll}
(Program) & \mathcal{P} ::= eff^* \ meth^* \\
(Effect\ Declarations) & eff ::= A : \tau \\
(Method\ Definition) & meth ::= \tau \ mn \ (\tau \ v) \ [\textbf{req}\ \Phi_{pre}\ \textbf{ens}\ \Phi_{post}] \ \{e\} \\
(Types) & \tau ::= bool \mid int \mid unit \mid \tau_1 \to \tau_2 \\
(Values) & v ::= c \mid x \mid \lambda x \Rightarrow e \\
(Handler) & h ::= (return\ x \mapsto e \mid ocs) \\
(Operation\ Cases) & ocs ::= \emptyset \mid \{effect\ A(x, \kappa) \mapsto e\} \uplus ocs \\
(Expressions) & e ::= v \mid v_1\ v_2 \mid let\ x{=}v\ in\ e \mid if\ v\ then\ e_1\ else\ e_2 \mid \\
& \qquad perform\ A(v, \lambda x \Rightarrow e) \mid match\ e\ with\ h \mid resume\ v
\end{array}
$$

$(Selected\ Elaborations)$

$$
\begin{array}{c}
e_1; e_2 \implies let\ ()=e_1\ in\ e_2 \\
e_1\ e_2 \implies let\ f=e_1\ in\ let\ x=e_2\ in\ (f\ x) \\
perform\ A(e_1, \lambda y \Rightarrow e_2) \implies let\ x=e_1\ in\ perform\ A(x, \lambda y \Rightarrow e_2) \\
let\ x=perform\ A(v, \lambda y \Rightarrow e_1)\ in\ e_2 \implies perform\ A(v, \lambda y \Rightarrow let\ x=e_1\ in\ e_2) \\
perform\ A(v) \implies perform\ A(v, \lambda x \Rightarrow x)
\end{array}
$$

$c \in \mathbb{Z} \cup \mathbb{B} \cup \textbf{unit}$ \qquad\qquad $x, y, mn, \kappa \in \textbf{var}$ \qquad\qquad $A \in \Sigma$

Fig. 5. Syntax of expressions.

$(Evaluation\ contexts)$ \quad $E ::= \square \mid let\ x{=}E\ in\ e \mid match\ E\ with\ h$

$(Reduction\ rules)$
$$
\begin{array}{rl}
E[e_1] \longrightarrow & E[e_2]\ if\ e_1 \longrightarrow e_2 \\
let\ x{=}v\ in\ e \longrightarrow & e[v/x] \\
(\lambda x \Rightarrow e)\ v \longrightarrow & e[v/x] \\
if\ true\ then\ e_1\ else\ e_2 \longrightarrow & e_1 \\
if\ false\ then\ e_1\ else\ e_2 \longrightarrow & e_2 \\
match\ v\ with\ h \longrightarrow & e[v/x]\ if\ (return\ x \mapsto e) \in h \\
match\ (perform\ A(v, \lambda y \Rightarrow e_1))\ with\ h \longrightarrow & e_2[v/x][(\lambda y \Rightarrow match\ e_1\ with\ h)/\kappa] \\
& if\ (effect\ A(x, \kappa) \mapsto e_2) \in h \\
match\ (perform\ A(v, \lambda y \Rightarrow e_1))\ with\ h \longrightarrow & perform\ A(v, \lambda y \Rightarrow match\ e_1\ with\ h) \\
& if\ A \notin h
\end{array}
$$

Fig. 6. Evaluation contexts and reduction rules

Operational Semantics. The reduction rules up to those for $match$ are standard. Matching on a pure value results in the body of the always-present $return$ handler being executed, with x bound to the value. The next two cases define how effects are performed and handled, but before covering them, we first explain how the expression *perform* $A(v, \lambda x \Rightarrow e)$ works informally: it performs the effect A (e.g. a shared-memory read) with argument v (e.g. the memory location to be read). The result value of the effect (e.g. the contents of the memory location) is then bound to x and evaluation resumes with the continuation e. Note that how exactly the read is *implemented* is defined by handlers which enclose the *perform*.

With that in mind, there are two cases when matching on an effectful expression. If the effect A is handled by an appropriate case in an enclosing handler, both value and continuation are substituted into the body of the case – note that the continuation contains an identical handler (making the enclosing handler *deep*). Otherwise, if the effect is unhandled, reduction proceeds with the current *match* "pushed" into the continuation, to handle subsequent *performs*.

3.2 The Specification Language

Syntax. We enrich a Hoare-style verification system with effect specifications, using the notation $\{$req Φ_{pre} ens $\Phi_{post}\}$ for function pre- and postconditions. As defined in Fig. 7, Φ is a set of disjunctive tuples including a pure formula π, an event sequence θ, and a return value v.

(ContEffs)	Φ ::=	$\bigvee(\pi, \theta, v)$
(Parameterized Label)	l ::=	$\Sigma(v)$
(Event Sequences)	θ ::=	$\bot \mid \epsilon \mid ev \mid Q \mid \theta_1 \cdot \theta_2 \mid \theta_1 \vee \theta_2 \mid \theta^* \mid \theta^\infty \mid \theta^\omega$
(Single Events)	ev ::=	$\_ \mid l \mid \bar{l}$
(Placeholders)	Q ::=	$l! \mid l?(v)$
(Pure formulae)	π ::=	$True \mid False \mid R(t_1, t_2) \mid \pi_1 \wedge \pi_2 \mid \pi_1 \vee \pi_2 \mid \neg \pi \mid \pi_1 \Rightarrow \pi_2$
(Terms)	t ::=	$n \mid x \mid t_1 + t_2 \mid t_1 - t_2$

$x \in \mathbf{var}$ *(Finite Kleene Star)* $\star$ *(Finite/Infinite)* ∞ *(Infinite)* ω

Fig. 7. Syntax of *ContEffs*.

A is an effect label drawn from Σ, a finite set of user-defined effect labels. A *parameterized label* is an effect label together with a value argument v. An *event* ev is an assertion about the (non-)occurrence of an individual, *handled* effect.

Placeholders Q stand for *traces* (sequences of events). The two kinds of placeholders are *unhandled* effects $l!$, which may give rise to further effects upon being handled, and $l?(v)$, which describes the trace that results when l is resumed with a higher-order function, and this function is applied to v. Placeholders enable modular verification, allowing higher-order *perform* sites to be described independently of any particular handler. They are only instantiated while verifying handlers, using the fixed-point reasoning (Sect. 4.2).

Effect sequences θ can be constructed by *false* ($\bot$); the empty trace ϵ; a single event ev; a placeholder Q; a sequence concatenation $\theta_1 \cdot \theta_2$; and sequence disjunction $\theta_1 \vee \theta_2$. Effect sequences can be also constructed by $\star$, representing finite (zero or more) repetition of a trace; by ω, representing an infinite repetition of a trace; or by ∞, representing an overapproximation of both finite and infinite possibilities [17]. Although $\theta^\star$ and θ^ω are subsumed by θ^∞, integrating all of the operators makes the specification language more flexible and precise. It also makes the logic conveniently fuse traditional linear temporal logics.

Pure formulae π are Presburger arithmetic formulae. $R(t_1, t_2)$ is a binary relation ($R \in \{=, >, <, \geq, \leq\}$). Terms are constant integer values n, integer variables x, and additions and subtractions of terms.

Semantic Model of Effect Sequences. To define the model, var is the set of program variables, val is the set of primitive values, α is the set of concrete events drawn from single events l or placeholders Q. Let $\mathcal{E}, \varphi \models \Phi$ denote the *models* relation, i.e., the context $\mathcal{E}$ and linear temporal events φ satisfy the effect specification Φ, where $\mathcal{E}$ records the stack status and the bindings from variables to placeholders, $\mathcal{E} \triangleq var \rightarrow (val \cup Q)$; and φ is a list of events, $\varphi \triangleq [\alpha]$.

Since the return value in effect specifications is irrelevant to the semantic model, we define $\mathcal{E}, \varphi \models (\pi, \theta)$ to be $\mathcal{E}, \varphi \models (\pi, \theta, v)$ for some return value v.

The semantics of effect sequences is defined in Fig. 8. [] is an empty sequence; $[l]$ is the sequence that contains one parameterized label l; ++ is the append operation of two effect sequences; and $\bigvee j$ is a disjunction of parameterized labels j. Comparisons between labels use simple lexical equivalence.

$\mathcal{E}, \varphi \models \Phi$	*iff*	$\exists (\pi, \theta, v) \in \Phi.\ \mathcal{E}, \varphi \models (\pi, \theta, v)$
$\mathcal{E}, \varphi \models (\pi, \epsilon)$	*iff*	$[\![\pi]\!]_\mathcal{E} = True$ and $\varphi = []$
$\mathcal{E}, \varphi \models (\pi, \_)$	*iff*	$[\![\pi]\!]_\mathcal{E} = True$ and $\exists l \in \Sigma(v),\ \varphi = [l]$
$\mathcal{E}, \varphi \models (\pi, l)$	*iff*	$[\![\pi]\!]_\mathcal{E} = True$ and $\varphi = [l]$
$\mathcal{E}, \varphi \models (\pi, \bar{l})$	*iff*	$[\![\pi]\!]_\mathcal{E} = True$ and $\mathcal{E}, \varphi \models \bigvee j$ where $j \in \Sigma(v)$ and $j \neq l$
$\mathcal{E}, \varphi \models (\pi, Q)$	*iff*	$[\![\pi]\!]_\mathcal{E} = True$ and $\varphi = [Q]$
$\mathcal{E}, \varphi \models (\pi, \theta_1 \cdot \theta_2)$	*iff*	$\exists \varphi_1, \varphi_2.\ \varphi = \varphi_1 ++ \varphi_2$ and $\mathcal{E}, \varphi_1 \models (\pi, \theta_1)$ and $\mathcal{E}, \varphi_2 \models (\pi, \theta_2)$
$\mathcal{E}, \varphi \models (\pi, \theta_1 \vee \theta_2)$	*iff*	$\mathcal{E}, \varphi \models (\pi, \theta_1)$ or $\mathcal{E}, \varphi \models (\pi, \theta_2)$
$\mathcal{E}, \varphi \models (\pi, \theta^\star)$	*iff*	$\mathcal{E}, \varphi \models (\pi, \epsilon)$ or $\mathcal{E}, \varphi \models (\pi, \theta \cdot \theta^\star)$
$\mathcal{E}, \varphi \models (\pi, \theta^\infty)$	*iff*	$\mathcal{E}, \varphi \models (\pi, \theta^\star)$ or $\mathcal{E}, \varphi \models (\pi, \theta^\omega)$
$\mathcal{E}, \varphi \models (\pi, \theta^\omega)$	*iff*	$\mathcal{E}, \varphi \models (\pi, \theta \cdot \theta^\omega)$
$\mathcal{E}, \varphi \models (False, \bot)$	*iff*	*false*

Fig. 8. Semantics of effect sequences.

3.3   Instrumented Semantics

To facilitate the soundness proof in Theorem 1 for the verification rules presented in Sect. 4, we also define an instrumented reduction relation $\xrightarrow{i}$, which operates on program states of the form $\lceil e, \mathcal{E}, \varphi \rceil$, where an expression is associated with a context and the trace of effects performed in the course of its execution. $\xrightarrow{i}{}^*$ denotes its reflexive, transitive closure. Here, given $e \longrightarrow e'$ and a most general high-order effects signature $(A : \tau_1 {\to} (\tau_2 {\to} \tau_3)) \in \mathcal{P}$:

$$\frac{e = v_1\ v_2 \qquad \mathcal{E}(v_1) = A(v)?}{\lceil e, \mathcal{E}, \varphi \rceil \xrightarrow{i} \lceil e', \mathcal{E}, \varphi \text{++} [A(v)?(v_2)] \rceil}[Inst\text{-}App] \qquad \frac{e = let\ x {=} v\ in\ e_1}{\lceil e, \mathcal{E}, \varphi \rceil \xrightarrow{i} \lceil e', (x {\mapsto} v) {::} \mathcal{E}, \varphi \rceil}[Inst\text{-}Bind]$$

$$\frac{e = match\ perform\ A(v, \lambda x {\Rightarrow} e_1)\ with\ h \qquad A \notin h}{\lceil e, \mathcal{E}, \varphi \rceil \xrightarrow{i} \lceil e', (x {\mapsto} A(v)?) {::} \mathcal{E}, \varphi \text{++} [A(v)!] \rceil}[Inst\text{-}Escape]$$

$$\frac{e = match\ perform\ A(v, \lambda x {\Rightarrow} e_1)\ with\ h \qquad A \in h}{\lceil e, \mathcal{E}, \varphi \rceil \xrightarrow{i} \lceil e', \mathcal{E}, \varphi \text{++} [A(v)] \rceil}[Inst\text{-}Caught]$$

4   Forward Verification

An overview of our automated verification system is given in Fig. 9. It consists of a Hoare-style forward verifier and a TRS. The input of the forward verifier is a target program annotated with temporal specifications written in *ContEffs*.

The input of the TRS is a pair of effects LHS and RHS, referring to the inclusion LHS $\sqsubseteq$ RHS to be checked *(LHS for left-hand-side trace, and RHS for right-hand-side trace)*. The verifier calls the TRS to prove produced inclusions.

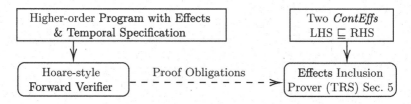

Fig. 9. System overview. Rounded boxes are the main procedures. Rectangular boxes describe the inputs to the procedures. The verification relies on the TRS (dash line).

We formalize a set of syntax-directed forward verification rules for the core language. $\mathcal{P}$ denotes the program being checked. With pre/postconditions declared for each method in $\mathcal{P}$, we apply modular verification to a method's body using Hoare-style triples $\mathcal{E} \vdash \{\Phi\}\ e\ \{\Phi'\}$ where $\mathcal{E}$ is the context; if Φ describes the effects which have been performed since the beginning of $\mathcal{P}$, if e terminates, Φ' describes the effects that will have been performed after.

4.1   Forward Verification Rules

In [*FV-Meth*], the rule computes the final effects Φ from the method body, and checks the inclusion between Φ and the declared specifications. Note that for succinctness, the user-provided Φ_{post} only denotes the *extension* of the effects from executing the method body. Formally, $\mathcal{E} \vdash \{\Phi_{pre}\} \, e \, \{\Phi_{pre} \cdot \Phi_{post}\}$ is a valid triple.

$$\frac{\mathcal{E} \vdash \{\Phi_{pre}\} \, e \, \{\Phi\} \qquad \Phi \sqsubseteq \Phi_{pre} \cdot \Phi_{post}}{\vdash \tau \; mn \; (\tau \; v) \; [\textbf{req} \; \Phi_{pre} \; \textbf{ens} \; \Phi_{post}] \; \{e\}} \; [FV\text{-}Meth]$$

Definition 2 (*ContEffs* Concatenation). *Given two* ContEffs *Φ_1 and Φ_2,*
$$\Phi_1 \cdot \Phi_2 = \{(\pi_1 \wedge \pi_2, \theta_1 \cdot \theta_2, v_2) \mid (\pi_1, \theta_1, v_1) \in \Phi_1, (\pi_2, \theta_2, v_2) \in \Phi_2\}$$

[*FV-Perform*] concatenates a placeholder to the current effects, where $\Phi \cdot A(v)!$ $\equiv \{(\pi, \theta \cdot A(v)!, v) \mid (\pi, \theta, v) \in \Phi\}$, then extends the environment by binding x to $A(v)?$, referring to the resumed value of performing $A(v)$.

$$\frac{\Phi' = \Phi \cdot A(v)! \qquad (x \mapsto A(v)?) :: \mathcal{E} \vdash \{\Phi'\} \, e \, \{\Phi''\}}{\mathcal{E} \vdash \{\Phi\} \, perform \; A(v, \lambda x \Rightarrow e) \; \{\Phi''\}} \; [FV\text{-}Perform]$$

For applications $v_1 v_2$, if v_1 is a function definition with annotated specifications, [*FV-Call*] checks whether the instantiated precondition of callee, $\Phi_{pre}[v_2/v]$, is satisfied by the current effects state, then it obtains the next effects state by concatenating the instantiated postcondition, $\Phi_{post}[v_2/v]$, to the current effects state; if v_1 maps to $l?$, [*FV-App*] concatenates $l?(v_2)$ into the current effect state, referring to the effects generated by applying v_2 to the value resumed from performing l. [*FV-Value*] updates the current return value.

$$\frac{\mathcal{E}(v_1) = \tau \; mn \; (\tau \; v) \; [\textbf{req} \; \Phi_{pre} \; \textbf{ens} \; \Phi_{post}] \; \{e\} \qquad \Phi \sqsubseteq \Phi_{pre}[v_2/v]}{\mathcal{E} \vdash \{\Phi\} \, v_1 v_2 \; \{\Phi \cdot \Phi_{post}[v_2/v]\}} \; [FV\text{-}Call]$$

$$\frac{\mathcal{E}(v_1) = l? \qquad \theta' = l?(v_2)}{\mathcal{E} \vdash \{\Phi\} \, v_1 v_2 \; \{\Phi \cdot \theta'\}} \; [FV\text{-}App] \qquad \frac{\Phi' = \{(\pi, \theta, v') \mid (\pi, \theta, v) \in \Phi\}}{\mathcal{E} \vdash \{\Phi\} \, v' \; \{\Phi'\}} \; [FV\text{-}Value]$$

[*FV-If-Else*] unions the effects from both branches, where $\Phi \wedge \pi' \equiv \{(\pi \wedge \pi', \theta, v) \mid (\pi, \theta, v) \in \Phi\}$. [*FV-Let*] extends $\mathcal{E}$ with x binding to v.

$$\frac{\mathcal{E} \vdash \{\Phi \wedge (v = true)\} \, e_1 \, \{\Phi_1\} \qquad \mathcal{E} \vdash \{\Phi \wedge (v = false)\} \, e_2 \, \{\Phi_2\}}{\mathcal{E} \vdash \{\Phi\} \, if \; v \; then \; e_1 \; else \; e_2 \; \{\Phi_1\} \cup \{\Phi_2\}} \; [FV\text{-}If\text{-}Else]$$

$$\frac{(x \mapsto v) :: \mathcal{E} \vdash \{\Phi\} \, e \, \{\Phi'\}}{\mathcal{E} \vdash \{\Phi\} \, let \; x = v \; in \; e \; \{\Phi'\}} \; [FV\text{-}Let]$$

[*FV-Match*] computes the effects of e using the initial state $\{(\textit{True}, \epsilon, ())\}$, then deploys the fixpoint algorithm to compute the final effects after been handled by h. The notion $\heartsuit$ is a special event marking the end of the traces, which is essential when distinguishing the zero/one/multi-shots continuations.

$$\frac{\mathcal{E} \vdash \{(\textit{True}, \epsilon, ())\}\ e\ \{\Phi'\} \qquad \Phi'' = \{(\pi, \theta \cdot \heartsuit, v) \mid (\pi, \theta, v) \in \Phi'\}}{\mathcal{E} \vdash \{\Phi\}\ \textit{match}\ e\ \textit{with}\ h\ \{\Phi \cdot \Phi_{\textit{fix}}\}} \quad [\textit{FV-Match}]$$
$$\mathcal{E}, h \vdash_{\textit{fix}} \Phi'' \rightsquigarrow \Phi_{\textit{fix}} \quad (\text{cf. Sec. 4.2})$$

4.2 Fixpoint Computation

Given any effect Φ and fixed environment $\mathcal{E}$ and handler $\mathcal{H}$, the relation $\mathcal{E}, \mathcal{H} \vdash_{\textit{fix}} \Phi \rightsquigarrow \Phi_{\textit{fix}}$ concludes the fixpoint effects $\Phi_{\textit{fix}}$ via the following rule, where

$$\frac{\forall (\pi, \theta, v) \in \Phi.\ \|\mathcal{E}, \epsilon, \mathcal{H}\| \vdash_{\textit{fix}} (\pi, \theta, v) \rightsquigarrow \Phi'}{\mathcal{E}, \mathcal{H} \vdash_{\textit{fix}} \Phi \rightsquigarrow \bigcup \Phi'} [\textit{Fix-Disj}]$$

for all execution tuples (π, θ, v) from Φ, given $\mathcal{E}$ and $\mathcal{H}$, it is reduced to Φ'. Their relation is captured by: $\|\mathcal{E}, \theta_{his}, \mathcal{H}\| \vdash_{\textit{fix}} (\pi, \theta, v) \rightsquigarrow \Phi'$, where θ_{his} is the history trace and initialized by ϵ. The final result $\Phi_{\textit{fix}}$ is a union set of all the Φ'.

Rule [*Fix-Normal*] is applied when the trace is reduced to the ending mark $\heartsuit$, which indicates that the execution of the handled program is finished. In this case, the resulting state Φ' is achieved by computing the strongest post condition of $e_{ret}[v/x]$ from the starting state $\{(\pi, \theta_{his}, v)\}$.

$$\frac{(\textit{return}\ x \mapsto e_{ret}) \in \mathcal{H} \qquad ([x \mapsto v])::\mathcal{E} \vdash \{(\pi, \theta_{his}, v)\}\ e_{ret}\ \{\Phi'\}}{\|\mathcal{E}, \theta_{his}, \mathcal{H}\| \vdash_{\textit{fix}} (\pi, \heartsuit, v) \rightsquigarrow \Phi'} [\textit{Fix-Normal}]$$

Rule [*Fix-Unfold-Skip*] is applied when the starting events α are handled effects ev, or placeholders corresponding to the effects cannot be handled by the current handler. In this case, the rule simple achieves α into the history context θ_{his} and continues to reason about the tail of the trace, i.e., θ.

$$\frac{\alpha \in \{ev, l!, l?(v')\}\ (l \notin \mathcal{H}) \qquad \|\mathcal{E}, \theta_{his} \cdot \alpha, \mathcal{H}\| \vdash_{\textit{fix}} (\pi, \theta, v) \rightsquigarrow \Phi'}{\|\mathcal{E}, \theta_{his}, \mathcal{H}\| \vdash_{\textit{fix}} (\pi, \alpha \cdot \theta, v) \rightsquigarrow \Phi'} [\textit{Fix-Unfold-Skip}]$$

Rule [*Fix-Unfold-Handle*] is applied when the starting events α are unhandled effects $l!$ which can be handled by the current handler. In this case, the rule uses the relation $\mathcal{E}', \mathcal{H}, \mathcal{D} \vdash_h \langle \Phi \rangle\ e\ \langle \Phi' \rangle$ to reason about the handling code e, where $\mathcal{E}'$ extends $\mathcal{E}$ with $x \mapsto v$. Note that, here the rule achieves l into the history context, indicating that the emission $l!$ is handled.

$$\frac{\begin{array}{cccc} \alpha \in \{l!\} & (\textit{effect } A(x,\kappa) \mapsto e) \in \mathcal{H} & (l{=}A(v')) \\ \mathcal{E}'{=}(x{\mapsto}v)::\mathcal{E} & \mathcal{E}',\mathcal{H},\theta \vdash_h \langle(\pi,\theta_{his}\cdot l,v)\rangle \; e \; \langle\Phi'\rangle \; (\textit{cf. Sec. 4.3}) \end{array}}{\|\mathcal{E},\theta_{his},\mathcal{H}\| \vdash_{\textit{fix}} (\pi,\alpha\cdot\theta,v) \rightsquigarrow \Phi'} [\textit{Fix-Unfold-Handle}]$$

4.3   Reasoning in the Handling Program

Rules for $\mathcal{E},\mathcal{H},\mathcal{D} \vdash_h \langle\Phi\rangle \; e \; \langle\Phi'\rangle$ (where $\mathcal{D}$ stands for the not-yet-handled continuation, of the type θ) are mostly similar to the top-level forward relation $\mathcal{E} \vdash \{\Phi\} \; e \; \{\Phi'\}$, except for the rules:

$$\frac{\begin{array}{cc} \forall(\pi,\theta,v) \in \Phi & \|\mathcal{E},\theta,\mathcal{H}\| \vdash_{\textit{fix}} (\pi,\mathcal{D}[v'/l?],v) \rightsquigarrow \Phi' \\ & \mathcal{E},\mathcal{H},\mathcal{D} \vdash_h \langle\Phi'\rangle \; e \; \langle\Phi''\rangle \end{array}}{\mathcal{E},\mathcal{H},\mathcal{D} \vdash_h \langle\Phi\rangle \; \textit{let } x{=}\kappa \; v' \; \textit{in } e \; \langle\Phi''\rangle} [\textit{Handle-Resume}]$$

$$\frac{\Phi'{=}\{(\pi,\theta,v') \mid (\pi,\theta,v) \in \Phi\}}{\mathcal{E},\mathcal{H},\mathcal{D} \vdash_h \langle\Phi\rangle \; v' \; \langle\Phi'\rangle} [\textit{Handle-Value}]$$

In [*Handle-Resume*], all the placeholders l? shown in the continuation $\mathcal{D}$ can be finally instantiated by κ's argument value, v'. Possible loops are also captured in this step, when $\mathcal{D}[v'/l?]$ produces the effects' emissions which has already been handled. The final result Φ'' is achieved by reasoning e after handling the rest continuation. Note that if the handling program directly returns a single value, the rule [*Handle-Value*] abandons the continuation $\mathcal{D}$ completely, which is intuitively why we are able to handle exceptions (zero-shot continuations). The rest of the rules and a demonstration example are presented in Appendix A.

Lemma 1 (Soundness of the Fixpoint Computation). *Given an effect Φ, with the environment $\mathcal{E}$ and handler $\mathcal{H}$. $\Phi_{\textit{fix}}$ is the updated version of Φ, where all Φ's placeholders – which can be handled by $\mathcal{H}$ – are handled as $\mathcal{H}$ defines.*

Formally, $\forall\mathcal{E}, \forall\mathcal{H}, \forall\Phi, \textit{if } \mathcal{E},\mathcal{H} \vdash_{\textit{fix}} \Phi \rightsquigarrow \Phi_{\textit{fix}} \textit{ is valid, then:}$

when Φ is a set, $\Phi_{\textit{fix}}{=}\{\|\mathcal{E},\epsilon,\mathcal{H}\| \vdash_{\textit{fix}} (\pi,\theta,v) \rightsquigarrow \Phi' \mid (\pi,\theta,v) \in \Phi\};$ (1)

when $\Phi{=}(\pi,\theta,v), \alpha{=}\textit{fst}(\theta), \theta_{his}$ *is the handled trace,*

   if $\alpha{=}\heartsuit : ([x{\mapsto}v])::\mathcal{E} \vdash \{(\pi,\theta_{his},v)\}e_{ret}\{\Phi'\}$ *is valid, given* $(\textit{return } x{\mapsto}e_{ret}){\in}\mathcal{H};$ (2)

   if $\alpha{\in}\{ev, l!, l?(v')\} \; (l{\notin}\mathcal{H}) : \|\mathcal{E},\theta_{his}\cdot\alpha,\mathcal{H}\| \vdash_{\textit{fix}} (\pi,\mathcal{D}_\alpha(\theta),v) \rightsquigarrow \Phi'$ *is valid;* (3)

   if $\alpha{\in}\{l!\} \; (l{\in}\mathcal{H}) : (x{\mapsto}v)::\mathcal{E},\mathcal{H},\mathcal{D}_\alpha(\theta) \vdash_h \langle(\pi,\theta_{his}\cdot l,v)\rangle \; e \; \langle\Phi'\rangle$ *is valid, given*

                                                    $(\textit{effect } A(x,\kappa) \mapsto e){\in}\mathcal{H}.$ (4)

Proof. See Appendix B.

Theorem 1 (Soundness of Verification Rules). *Given an expression e, the linear effect trace produced by the real execution of e satisfies the effect specification derived via the forward verification rules.*

Formally, $\forall e, \forall \mathcal{E}, \forall \varphi, \forall \Phi$ *given* $\left\lceil e, \mathcal{E}, \varphi \right\rceil \xrightarrow{i}{}^{*} \left\lceil v, \mathcal{E}', \varphi' \right\rceil$ *and* $\mathcal{E} \vdash \{\Phi\}\ e\ \{\Phi'\}$,
if $\mathcal{E}, \varphi \models \Phi$ *then* $\mathcal{E}', \varphi' \models \Phi'$.

Proof. See Appendix B.

5   Temporal Verification via a TRS

A TRS checks inclusions among logical terms, via an iterated process of checking the inclusions of their *partial derivatives* [15]. It is triggered i) prior to function calls for the precondition checking; and ii) at the end of verifying a function for postcondition checking. Given two effects Φ_1 and Φ_2, the TRS decides if the inclusion $\Phi_1 \sqsubseteq \Phi_2$ is valid. During the rewriting process, the inclusions are of the form $\Omega \vdash \Phi_1 \sqsubseteq^{\theta} \Phi_2$, a shorthand for: $\Omega \vdash \theta \cdot \Phi_1 \sqsubseteq \theta \cdot \Phi_2$. To prove such inclusions amounts to checking whether all the possible traces in the antecedent Φ_1 are legitimately allowed in the possible traces from the consequent Φ_2. Ω is the proof context, i.e., a set of effect inclusion hypotheses, and θ is the history of effects from the antecedent that have been used to match the effects from the consequent. The inclusion checking is initially invoked with $\Omega = \{\}$ and $\theta = \epsilon$.

Effect Disjunction. An inclusion with a disjunctive antecedent succeeds if both disjunctions entail the consequent. An inclusion with a disjunctive consequent succeeds if the antecedent entails any of the disjunctions. Note that the event sequences' entailment checking is irrelevant to the returning values.

$$
\frac{\Omega \vdash (\pi, \theta) \sqsubseteq \Phi' \text{ and } \Omega \vdash \Phi \sqsubseteq \Phi'}{\Omega \vdash (\pi, \theta, v) :: \Phi \sqsubseteq \Phi'} \quad [LHS\text{-}OR]
$$

$$
\frac{\Omega \vdash (\pi, \theta) \sqsubseteq (\pi', \theta') \text{ or } (\pi, \theta) \sqsubseteq \Phi'}{\Omega \vdash (\pi, \theta) \sqsubseteq (\pi', \theta', v') :: \Phi'} \quad [RHS\text{-}OR]
$$

Definition 3 (*ContEffs* Inclusion). *For effects* (π_1, θ_1) *and* (π_2, θ_2),
$(\pi_1, \theta_1) \sqsubseteq (\pi_2, \theta_2) \Leftrightarrow \pi_1 \Rightarrow \pi_2$ *and* $(\forall \alpha \in \Sigma).\ \mathcal{D}_\alpha(\theta_1) \sqsubseteq \mathcal{D}_\alpha(\theta_2)$.

Next we provide the definitions and implementations of auxiliary functions[4] *Nullable*(δ), *Infinitable*($\varkappa$), *First*(*fst*) and *Derivative*($\mathcal{D}$) respectively. Intuitively, the Nullable function $\delta(\Phi)$ returns a boolean value indicating whether θ contains the empty trace; the Infinitable function $\varkappa(\theta)$ returns a boolean value indicating whether θ is possibly infinite; the First function *fst*(θ) computes possible initial elements of θ; and the Derivative function $\mathcal{D}_\alpha(\theta)$ eliminates an event α^5 from the head of θ and returns what remains.

---

[4] The definitions are extended from [15], to be able to deal with placeholders and infinite traces, proposed in this work.

[5] α could be a single label l, a negated label $\bar{l}$, a wildcard _, or a placeholder Q.

Definition 4 (Nullable). *Given any sequence θ, we recursively define $\delta(\theta)$[6]*

$$\delta(\epsilon)=\delta(\theta^\star)=\delta(\theta^\infty)=true \quad \delta(\theta_1 \cdot \theta_2)=\delta(\theta_1)\wedge\delta(\theta_2) \quad \delta(\theta_1 \vee \theta_2)=\delta(\theta_1)\vee\delta(\theta_2)$$

Definition 5 (Infinitable). *Given any sequence θ, we recursively define $\varkappa(\theta)$[7]*

$$\varkappa(\theta^\infty)=\varkappa(\theta^\omega)=true \quad \varkappa(\theta_1 \cdot \theta_2)=\varkappa(\theta_1)\vee\varkappa(\theta_2) \quad \varkappa(\theta_1 \vee \theta_2)=\varkappa(\theta_1)\vee\varkappa(\theta_2)$$

Definition 6 (First). *Let $fst(\theta)$ be the set of initial elements derivable from sequence represents all the traces contained in θ.*

$$fst(\bot)=fst(\epsilon)=\{\} \quad fst(ev)=\{ev\} \quad fst(Q)=\{Q\} \quad fst(\theta_1 \vee \theta_2)=fst(es_1) \cup fst(es_2)$$

$$fst(\theta_1 \cdot \theta_2)=\begin{cases} fst(es_1) \cup fst(es_2) & if\ \delta(\theta_1)=true \\ fst(\theta_1) & if\ \delta(\theta_1)=false \end{cases} \quad fst(\theta^\star)=fst(\theta^\infty)=fst(\theta^\omega)=fst(\theta)$$

Definition 7 (Partial Derivative). *The partial derivative $\mathcal{D}_\alpha(\theta)$ of effects θ w.r.t. an element α computes the effects for the left quotient, $\alpha^{-1}[\![\theta]\!]$[8].*

$$\mathcal{D}_\alpha(\bot)=\bot \quad \mathcal{D}_\alpha(\epsilon)=\bot \quad \mathcal{D}_\alpha(\theta_1 \vee \theta_2)=\mathcal{D}_\alpha(\theta_1) \vee \mathcal{D}_\alpha(\theta_2) \quad \mathcal{D}_\alpha(\theta^\star)=\mathcal{D}_\alpha(\theta) \cdot \theta^\star$$

$$\mathcal{D}_\alpha(ev)=\begin{cases} \epsilon & if\ \alpha \subseteq ev \\ \bot & else \end{cases} \quad \mathcal{D}_\alpha(Q)=\begin{cases} \epsilon & if\ \alpha=Q \\ \bot & else \end{cases} \quad \mathcal{D}_\alpha(\theta^\infty)=\mathcal{D}_\alpha(\theta) \cdot \theta^\infty$$

$$\mathcal{D}_\alpha(\theta_1 \cdot \theta_2)=\begin{cases} (\mathcal{D}_\alpha(\theta_1) \cdot \theta_2) \vee \mathcal{D}_\alpha(\theta_2) & if\ \delta(\theta_1)=true \\ \mathcal{D}_\alpha(\theta_1) \cdot \theta_2 & if\ \delta(\theta_1)=false \end{cases} \quad \mathcal{D}_\alpha(\theta^\omega)=\mathcal{D}_\alpha(\theta) \cdot \theta^\omega$$

5.1 Rewriting Rules

1. **Axioms.** Analogous to the standard propositional logic, $\bot$ (referring to *false*) entails any effects, while no *non-false* effects entails $\bot$.

$$\frac{\pi_1 \Rightarrow \pi_2}{\Omega \vdash (\pi_1, \bot) \sqsubseteq (\pi_2, \theta)}\ [Bot\text{-}LHS] \qquad \frac{\theta \neq \bot}{\Omega \vdash (\pi_1, \theta) \not\sqsubseteq (\pi_2, \bot)}\ [Bot\text{-}RHS]$$

2. **Disprove (Heuristic Refutation).** These rules are used to disprove the inclusions when the antecedent obviously contains more traces than the consequent. Here *nullable* and *infinitable* witness the empty trace and infinite traces respectively.

$$\frac{\delta(\theta_1) \wedge \neg\delta(\theta_2)}{\Omega \vdash (\pi_1, \theta_1) \not\sqsubseteq (\pi_2, \theta_2)}\ [Dis\text{-}Nullable] \qquad \frac{\varkappa(\theta_1) \wedge \neg\varkappa(\theta_2)}{\Omega \vdash (\pi_1, \theta_1) \not\sqsubseteq (\pi_2, \theta_2)}\ [Dis\text{-}Infinitable]$$

---

[6] *false* for unmentioned constructs.

[7] *false* for unmentioned constructs.

[8] $[\![\theta]\!]$ represents all the traces contained in θ.

3. **Prove.** We use the rule [*Reoccur*] to prove an inclusion when there exist inclusion hypotheses in the proof context Ω, which are able to soundly prove the current goal. One of the special cases of this rule is when the identical inclusion is shown in the proof context, we then prove it valid.

$$\frac{(\pi_1,\theta_1)\sqsubseteq(\pi_3,\theta_3) \in \Omega \quad (\pi_3,\theta_3)\sqsubseteq(\pi_4,\theta_4) \in \Omega \quad (\pi_4,\theta_4)\sqsubseteq(\pi_2,\theta_2) \in \Omega}{\Omega \vdash (\pi_1,\theta_1) \sqsubseteq (\pi_2,\theta_2)} \ [Reoccur]$$

4. **Unfolding (Induction).** This is the inductive step of unfolding the inclusions. Firstly, we make use of the auxiliary function *fst* to get a set of effects F, which are all the possible initial elements from the antecedent. Secondly, we obtain a new proof context Ω' by adding the current inclusion, as an inductive hypothesis, into the current proof context Ω. Thirdly, we iterate each element $\alpha \in F$, and compute the partial derivatives (*next-state* effects) of both the antecedent and consequent w.r.t α. The proof of the original inclusion succeeds if all the derivative inclusions succeed.

$$\frac{F = fst(\theta_1) \quad \pi_1 \Rightarrow \pi_2 \quad \forall \alpha \in F. \ (\theta_1 \sqsubseteq \theta_2) :: \Omega \vdash D_\alpha(\theta_1) \sqsubseteq D_\alpha(\theta_2)}{\Omega \vdash (\pi_1,\theta_1) \sqsubseteq (\pi_2,\theta_2)} \ [Unfold]$$

Theorem 2 (TRS-Termination). *The rewriting system TRS is terminating.*

Proof. See Appendix C.

Theorem 3 (TRS-Soundness). *Given an inclusion $\Phi_1 \sqsubseteq \Phi_2$, if the TRS returns TRUE when proving $\Phi_1 \sqsubseteq \Phi_2$, then $\Phi_1 \sqsubseteq \Phi_2$ is valid.*

Proof. See Appendix D.

6   Implementation and Evaluation

To show the feasibility of our approach, we have prototyped our automated verification system using OCaml (See Zenodo [18]). The proof obligations generated by the verifier are discharged using Z3 [19]. We prove termination and soundness of the TRS. We validate the front-end forward verifier against the latest Multicore OCaml (4.12.0) implementation for conformance.

Table 1 presents the evaluation results of a microbenchmark, to demonstrate how verification scales with program size. We annotate 12 synthetic test programs with temporal specifications, half of which fail to verify. The experiments were done on a MacBook Pro with a 2.6 GHz 6-Core Intel Core i7 processor. The table records: **No.**, the index of the program; **LOC**, lines of code; **Infer(ms)**, effects inference time; **#Prop(✓)**, number of valid properties; **Avg-Prove(ms)**, average proving time for the valid properties; **#Prop(✗)**, number of invalid properties; and **Avg-Dis(ms)**, average disproving time for the invalid properties.

Table 1. Experimental results.

No.	LOC	Infer(ms)	#Prop(✓)	Avg-Prove(ms)	#Prop(✗)	Avg-Dis(ms)
1	32	14.128	5	7.7786	5	6.2852
2	48	14.307	5	7.969	5	6.5982
3	71	15.029	5	7.922	5	6.4344
4	98	14.889	5	18.457	5	7.9562
5	156	14.677	7	10.080	7	4.819
6	197	15.471	7	8.3127	7	6.8101
7	240	18.798	7	18.559	7	7.468
8	285	20.406	7	23.3934	7	9.9086
9	343	26.514	9	16.5666	9	13.9667
10	401	26.893	9	18.3899	9	10.2169
11	583	49.931	14	17.203	15	10.4443
12	808	75.707	25	21.6795	24	16.9064

Discussion: Generally, inference and proving time increase linearly with program length. Furthermore, we notice that disproving times for invalid properties are consistently lower than those for proved properties, regardless of program complexity. This finding echos the insights from prior TRS-based works [14, 20–23], which suggest that TRS is a better average-case algorithm than those based on the comparison of automata.

A summary: A TRS is efficient because *it only constructs automata as far as it needs*, which makes it more efficient when disproving incorrect specifications, as we can disprove it earlier without constructing the whole automata. In other words, the more invalid inclusions are, the more efficient our solver is.

6.1   Case Studies

I. Encoding LTL. Classical LTL uses the temporal operators $\mathcal{G}$ ("globally") and $\mathcal{F}$ ("in the future"), which we also write $\square$ and $\lozenge$, respectively; and introduced the concept of fairness, which places additional constraints on infinite paths. LTL was subsequently extended to include the $\mathcal{U}$ ("until") operator and the $\mathcal{X}$ ("next time") operator. As shown in Fig. 2, we encode these basic operators into our effects, making the specification more intuitive and readable, mainly when nested operators occur. Furthermore, by putting the effects in the precondition, our approach naturally subsumes *past-time LTL* along the way[9].

---

[9] Our implementation supports specifications written in LTL formulae, by providing a translator from LTL to *ContEffs*. The translation schema is taken from [17].

Table 2. Examples for converting LTL formulae into Effects. (l, j are labels.)

$\Box l \equiv l^{\infty}$	$\Diamond l \equiv \_^* \cdot l$	$l \, \mathcal{U} \, j \equiv l^* \cdot j$	$l \to \Diamond j \equiv \neg l \vee \_^* \cdot j$
$\mathcal{X} l \equiv \_ \cdot l$	$\Box \Diamond l \equiv (\_^* \cdot l)^{\infty}$	$\Diamond \Box l \equiv \_^* \cdot l^{\infty}$	$\Diamond l \vee \Diamond j \equiv \_^* \cdot l \vee \_^* \cdot j$

II. Encoding Exceptions. Exceptions are a special case of algebraic effects which never resume, and Fig. 10 demonstrates how our framework soundly reasons about exceptions together with other kinds of effects. Here `raise()` performs `Exc` first, then does some other operations afterwards, represented by performing effect `Other`.

The handler on line 15 discharges `Exc` and returns, leaving the continuation `k` completely unused. Our fixpoint calculator computes the final trace of `excHandler` as simply `Exc`. We observe that the handler defined in the normal return (line 14) will be completely abandoned – because execution flow does not go back to `raise()` after handling `Exc`. The verified postcondition of `excHandler` matches how we would intuitively expect exceptions to work[10].

```
1   effect Exc: unit
2   effect Other: unit
3
4   let raise ()
5   (*@ req _^*    @*)
6   (*@ ens Exc!.Other!  @*)
7   = perform Exc;
8     perform Other
9
10  let excHandler
11  (*@ req _^*  @*)
12  (*@ ens Exc @*)
13  = match raise () with
14  | _ -> (* Abandoned *)
15  | effect Exc k -> ()
```

Fig. 10. Encoding Exceptions.

7   Related Work

Verification Framework: This work is a significant extension of [20,25], which deploys the verification framework, i.e., a forward verifier with a TRS. However, the goal of this paper is to reason about algebraic effects, which are octagonal and have different features from the sequential programs targeted in [20,25]. More specifically, our proposal handles coexistence of zero/one/multi-shot continuations; detects non-terminating behaviors; enforces static temporal properties of algebraic effects. None of these challenges has been tackled before.

Temporal Verification: One of the leading communities of temporal verification is automata-based model checking, mainly for finite-state systems. Various model checkers are based on some temporal logic specifications, such as LTL and CTL. Such tools extract the logic design from the program using modeling languages and verify specific assertions to guarantee various properties. Meanwhile,

---

[10] In general, each procedure has a set of circumstances for which it will terminate *normally*. An exception breaks the normal flow (these circumstances) of execution and executes a pre-registered exception handler instead [24].

to conduct temporal reasoning locally and for higher-order program, there is a sub-community whose aim is to support temporal specifications in the form of *effects* via the type-and-effect system. The inspiration from this approach is that it leads to a modular and compositional verification strategy, where temporal reasoning can be combined together to reason about the overall program [13,26,27]. However, the temporal effects in prior work tend to coarsely over-approximate the behaviors either via ω-regular expressions [26] or Büchi automata [27]. The conventional effects [13] have the form (Φ_u, Φ_v), which separates the finite and infinite effects. In this work, by integrating finite, infinite, and possibly both into a single disjunctive form, our effects eliminate the finiteness distinction, and enable an expressive modular temporal verification.

Type-and-effect Systems: Many languages with algebraic effects are equipped with type-and-effect systems – which enrich existing types with information about effects – to allow the effect-related behaviors of functions to be specified and checked. A common method of doing this is row-polymorphic effect types, used by languages such as Koka [6,28], Helium [29,30], Frank [31], and Links [32]. An effect *row* specifies a multiset of effects a function may perform, and is popular for its simplicity, expressiveness (naturally enabling *effect polymorphism*), and support for inference of principal effects [6]. There are numerous extensions to this model, including *presence types* attached to effect labels, allowing one to express the *absence* of an effect [32], existential and local effects for modularity [29], and linearity [33]. Other choices include sets of (instances of) effects [30], and structural subtyping constraints [34]. We consider finer-grained specifications of program behavior outside the realm of effect systems and discuss them separately.

Trace-based Effect Systems: Combining program events with a temporal program logic for asserting properties of event traces yields a powerful and general engine for enforcing program properties. Several works [35–37] have demonstrated that static approximations of program event traces can be generated by type and effect analyses [38,39], in a form amenable to existing model-checking techniques for verification. Trace-based analyses have been shown capable of statically enforcing flow-sensitive security properties such as safe locking behavior [40]; resource usage policies such as file usage protocols and memory management [37]; and enforcement of secure service composition [41].

More related to our work, prior research has been extending Hoare logic with event traces. Malecha et al. [42] focuses on finite traces (terminating) for web applications, leaving the divergent computation, which indicates *false*, verified for every specification. Nakata et al. [43] focuses on infinite traces (non-terminating) by providing coinductive trace definitions. Moreover, this paper draws similarities to *contextual effects* [44], which computes the effects that have already occurred as the prior effects. The effects of the computation yet to take place as the future effects. Besides, prior work [45] proposes an annotated type and effect system and infers behaviors from Concurrent ML [46] programs for channel-based communications, though it did not provide any inclusion solving process.

8   Conclusion

This work is mainly motivated by *how to modularly specify and verify programs in the presence of both user-defined primitive effects and effect handlers.*
To provide a practical proposal to verify such higher-order programs with crucial temporal constraints, we present a novel effects logic, *ContEffs*, to specify user-defined effects and effect handlers. This logic enjoys two key benefits that enable modular reasoning: the placeholder operator and the disjunction of finite and infinite traces. We demonstrate several small but non-trivial case studies to show *ContEffs*' feasibility. Our code and specification are particularly compact and generic; furthermore, as far as we know, this is the first temporal specification and proof of correctness of control inversion with the presence of algebraic effects.

Acknowledgement. We would like to thank the referees of APLAS 2022 for their helpful advice. This work is supported by grants NSOE-TSS2019-06 and MoE Tier-1 251RES1822.

References

1. Bauer, A., Pretnar, M.: Programming with algebraic effects and handlers. J. Log. Algebraic Methods Program. **84**(1), 108–123 (2015). https://doi.org/10.1016/j.jlamp.2014.02.001
2. Convent, L., Lindley, S., McBride, C., McLaughlin, C.: Doo bee doo bee doo. J. Funct. Program. **30**, e9 (2020). https://doi.org/10.1017/S0956796820000039
3. Hillerström, D., Lindley, S., Atkey, R.: Effect handlers via generalised continuations. J. Funct. Program. 30, e5 (2020). https://doi.org/10.1017/S0956796820000040
4. Sivaramakrishnan, K.C., Dolan, S., White, L., Kelly, T., Jaffer, S., Madhavapeddy, A.: Retrofitting effect handlers onto OCaml. In: PLDI '21: 42nd ACM SIGPLAN International Conference on Programming Language Design and Implementation, Virtual Event, Canada, June 20–25, 2021, S. N. Freund and E. Yahav, Eds. ACM, pp. 206–221 (2021). https://doi.org/10.1145/3453483.3454039
5. Brachthäuser, J.I., Schuster, P., Ostermann, K.: Effekt: capability-passing style for type-and effect-safe, extensible effect handlers in scala. J. Funct. Programm. **30**, 1–46 (2020)
6. Leijen, D.: Koka: programming with row polymorphic effect types. In: Proceedings 5th Workshop on Mathematically Structured Functional Programming, MSFP@ETAPS 2014, Grenoble, France, 12 April 2014, ser. EPTCS, P. B. Levy and N. Krishnaswami, Eds., vol. 153, pp. 100–126 (2014). https://doi.org/10.4204/EPTCS.153.8
7. Landin, P.J.: A generalization of jumps and labels. Higher-Order Symbolic Comput. **11**(2), 125–143 (1998). https://doi.org/10.1023/A:1010068630801
8. De Vilhena, P.E., Pottier, F.: A separation logic for effect handlers. Proc. ACM Program. Lang. **5**, 1–28 (2021). https://doi.org/10.1145/3434314

9. Recursive cow. https://github.com/effect-handlers/effects-rosetta-stone/tree/master/examples/recursive-cow

10. Hillerström, D., Lindley, S.: Shallow effect handlers. In: Ryu, S. (ed.) APLAS 2018. LNCS, vol. 11275, pp. 415–435. Springer, Cham (2018). https://doi.org/10.1007/978-3-030-02768-1_22

11. Kammar, O., Lindley, S., Oury, N.: Handlers in action. ACM SIGPLAN Notices **48**(9), 145–158 (2013)

12. Antimirov, V.: Rewriting regular inequalities. In: Reichel, H. (ed.) FCT 1995. LNCS, vol. 965, pp. 116–125. Springer, Heidelberg (1995). https://doi.org/10.1007/3-540-60249-6_44

13. Nanjo, Y., Unno, H., Koskinen, E., Terauchi, T.: A fixpoint logic and dependent effects for temporal property verification. In: Proceedings of the 33rd Annual ACM/IEEE Symposium on Logic in Computer Science, ACM, pp. 759–768 (2018)

14. Antimirov, V.M., Mosses, P.D.: Rewriting extended regular expressions. Theor. Comput. Sci. **143**(1), 51–72 (1995). https://doi.org/10.1016/0304-3975(95)80024-4

15. Antimirov, V.: Partial derivatives of regular expressions and finite automata constructions. In: Mayr, E.W., Puech, C. (eds.) STACS 1995. LNCS, vol. 900, pp. 455–466. Springer, Heidelberg (1995). https://doi.org/10.1007/3-540-59042-0_96

16. Brotherston, J.: Cyclic proofs for first-order logic with inductive definitions. In: Beckert, B. (ed.) TABLEAUX 2005. LNCS (LNAI), vol. 3702, pp. 78–92. Springer, Heidelberg (2005). https://doi.org/10.1007/11554554_8

17. Leucker, M., Sánchez, C.: Regular linear temporal logic. In: Jones, C.B., Liu, Z., Woodcock, J. (eds.) ICTAC 2007. LNCS, vol. 4711, pp. 291–305. Springer, Heidelberg (2007). https://doi.org/10.1007/978-3-540-75292-9_20

18. Zenodo. https://zenodo.org/record/7009799#.Yw-yyuxBwRS

19. de Moura, L., Bjørner, N.: Z3: an efficient SMT solver. In: Ramakrishnan, C.R., Rehof, J. (eds.) TACAS 2008. LNCS, vol. 4963, pp. 337–340. Springer, Heidelberg (2008). https://doi.org/10.1007/978-3-540-78800-3_24

20. Song, Y., Chin, W.-N.: Automated temporal verification of integrated dependent effects. In: Lin, S.-W., Hou, Z., Mahony, B. (eds.) ICFEM 2020. LNCS, vol. 12531, pp. 73–90. Springer, Cham (2020). https://doi.org/10.1007/978-3-030-63406-3_5

21. Almeida, M., Moreira, N., Reis, R.: Antimirov and Mosses's rewrite system revisited. Int. J. Found. Comput. Sci. **20**(4), 669–684 (2009). https://doi.org/10.1142/S0129054109006802

22. Keil, M., Thiemann, P.: Symbolic solving of extended regular expression inequalities. In: 34th International Conference on Foundation of Software Technology and Theoretical Computer Science, FSTTCS 2014, December 15–17, 2014, New Delhi, India, ser. LIPIcs, V. Raman and S. P. Suresh, Eds., vol. 29. Schloss Dagstuhl - Leibniz-Zentrum für Informatik, pp. 175–186 (2014). https://doi.org/10.4230/LIPIcs.FSTTCS.2014.175

23. Hovland, D.: The inclusion problem for regular expressions. J. Comput. Syst. Sci. **78**(6), 1795–1813 (2012). https://doi.org/10.1016/j.jcss.2011.12.003

24. Exception WiKi. https://en.wikipedia.org/wiki/Exception_handling

25. Song, Y., Chin, W.-N.: A synchronous effects logic for temporal verification of pure esterel. In: Henglein, F., Shoham, S., Vizel, Y. (eds.) VMCAI 2021. LNCS, vol. 12597, pp. 417–440. Springer, Cham (2021). https://doi.org/10.1007/978-3-030-67067-2_19

26. Hofmann, M., Chen, W.: Abstract interpretation from büchi automata. In: Proceedings of the Joint Meeting of the Twenty-Third EACSL Annual Conference on Computer Science Logic (CSL) and the Twenty-Ninth Annual ACM/IEEE Symposium on Logic in Computer Science (LICS), p. 51. ACM (2014)

27. Koskinen, E., Terauchi, T.: Local temporal reasoning. In: Proceedings of the Joint Meeting of the Twenty-Third EACSL Annual Conference on Computer Science Logic (CSL) and the Twenty-Ninth Annual ACM/IEEE Symposium on Logic in Computer Science (LICS), p. 59. ACM (2014)

28. Daan, L.: Type directed compilation of row-typed algebraic effects. In: Proceedings of the 44th ACM SIGPLAN Symposium on Principles of Programming Languages, pp. 486–499 (2017)

29. Biernacki, D., Piróg, M., Polesiuk, P., Sieczkowski, F.: Abstracting algebraic effects. In: Proceedings of the ACM on Programming Languages, vol. 3, no. POPL, pp. 1–28 (2019)

30. Dariusz, B., Maciej, P., Piotr, P., Filip, S.: Binders by day, labels by night: effect instances via lexically scoped handlers. In: Proceedings of the ACM on Programming Languages, vol. 4, no. POPL, pp. 1–29 (2019)

31. Lindley, S., McBride, C., McLaughlin, C.: Do be do be do. CoRR, vol. abs/1611.09259, (2016). http://arxiv.org/abs/1611.09259

32. Lindley, S., Cheney, J.: Row-based effect types for database integration. In: Proceedings of the 8th ACM SIGPLAN Workshop on Types in Language Design and Implementation, pp. 91–102 (2012)

33. Leijen, D.: Algebraic effect handlers with resources and deep finalization. Technical Report MSR-TR-2018-10. Tech. Rep, Microsoft Research (2018)

34. Pretnar, M.: Inferring algebraic effects. arXiv preprint arXiv:1312.2334 (2013)

35. Skalka, C., Smith, S., Van Horn, D.: Types and trace effects of higher order programs. J. Funct. Programm. 18(2), 179–249 (2008)

36. Skalka, C., Smith, S.: History effects and verification. In: Chin, W.-N. (ed.) APLAS 2004. LNCS, vol. 3302, pp. 107–128. Springer, Heidelberg (2004). https://doi.org/10.1007/978-3-540-30477-7_8

37. Marriott, K., Stuckey, P.J., Sulzmann, M.: Resource usage verification. In: Ohori, A. (ed.) APLAS 2003. LNCS, vol. 2895, pp. 212–229. Springer, Heidelberg (2003). https://doi.org/10.1007/978-3-540-40018-9_15

38. Talpin, J.-P., Jouvelot, P.: The type and effect discipline. Inf. Comput. 111(2), 245–296 (1994)

39. Amtoft, T., Nielson, H.R., Nielson, F.: Type and effect systems: behaviours for concurrency. World Sci. (1999)

40. Foster, J.S., Terauchi, T., Aiken, A.: Flow-sensitive type qualifiers. In: Proceedings of the ACM SIGPLAN 2002 Conference on Programming language design and implementation, pp. 1–12 (2002)

41. Bartoletti, M., Degano, P., Ferrari, G.L.: Enforcing secure service composition. In: 18th IEEE Computer Security Foundations Workshop (CSFW'05). IEEE, pp. 211–223 (2005)

42. Malecha, G., Morrisett, G., Wisnesky, R.: Trace-based verification of imperative programs with i/o. J. Symbolic Comput. 46(2), 95–118 (2011)

43. Nakata, K., Uustalu, T.: A Hoare logic for the coinductive trace-based big-step semantics of while. In: Gordon, A.D. (ed.) ESOP 2010. LNCS, vol. 6012, pp. 488–506. Springer, Heidelberg (2010). https://doi.org/10.1007/978-3-642-11957-6_26

44. Neamtiu, I., Hicks, M., Foster, J.S., Pratikakis, P.: Contextual effects for version-consistent dynamic software updating and safe concurrent programming. In: Proceedings of the 35th Annual ACM SIGPLAN-SIGACT Symposium on Principles of Programming Languages, pp. 37–49 (2008)
45. Nielson, H.R., Amtoft, T., Nielson, F.: Behaviour analysis and safety conditions: a case study in CML. In: Astesiano, E. (ed.) FASE 1998. LNCS, vol. 1382, pp. 255–269. Springer, Heidelberg (1998). https://doi.org/10.1007/BFb0053595
46. Reppy, J.H.: Concurrent ML: design, application and semantics. In: Lauer, P.E. (ed.) Functional Programming, Concurrency, Simulation and Automated Reasoning. LNCS, vol. 693, pp. 165–198. Springer, Heidelberg (1993). https://doi.org/10.1007/3-540-56883-2_10

Model-Based Fault Classification
for Automotive Software

Mike Becker[1], Roland Meyer[1], Tobias Runge[1,2], Ina Schaefer[1,2],
Sören van der Wall[1], and Sebastian Wolff[3(✉)]

[1] TU Braunschweig, Braunschweig, Germany
{mike.becker,roland.meyer,s.van-der-wall}@tu-bs.de
[2] KIT Karlsruhe, Karlsruhe, Germany
{tobias.runge,ina.schaefer}@kit.edu
[3] New York University, New York, USA
sebastian.wolff@nyu.edu

Abstract. Intensive testing using model-based approaches is the standard way of demonstrating the correctness of automotive software. Unfortunately, state-of-the-art techniques leave a crucial and labor intensive task to the test engineer: identifying bugs in failing tests. Our contribution is a model-based classification algorithm for failing tests that assists the engineer when identifying bugs. It consists of three steps. (i) Fault localization replays the test on the model to identify the moment when the two diverge. (ii) Fault explanation then computes the reason for the divergence. The reason is a subset of messages from the test that is sufficient for divergence. (iii) Fault classification groups together tests that fail for similar reasons. Our approach relies on machinery from formal methods: (i) symbolic execution, (ii) Hoare logic and a new relationship between the intermediary assertions constructed for a test, and (iii) a new relationship among Hoare proofs. A crucial aspect in automotive software are timing requirements, for which we develop appropriate Hoare logic theory. We also briefly report on our prototype implementation for the CAN bus *Unified Diagnostic Services* in an industrial project.

Keywords: Fault explanation · Fault classification · Hoare proofs

1 Introduction

Intensive testing is the de-facto standard way of demonstrating the correctness of automotive software, and the more tests the higher the confidence we have in a system [42]. Model-based approaches have been instrumental in pushing the number of tests that can be evaluated, by increasing the degree of automation for the testing process. Indeed, all of the following steps are fully automated today: determining the test cases including the expected outcome, running them on the system, and comparing the outcome to the expectation [45]. Yet, there is a manual processing step left that, so far, has resisted automation. If the outcome of the test and the expectation do not match, the bug has to be identified. This

© The Author(s), under exclusive license to Springer Nature Switzerland AG 2022
I. Sergey (Ed.): APLAS 2022, LNCS 13658, pp. 110–131, 2022.
https://doi.org/10.1007/978-3-031-21037-2_6

```
Test-1                    Ⓐ   Test-2                    Ⓐ   Test-3                    Ⓑ
[   5ms]   req CTR set 5       [   0ms]   req CTR set 5       [   4ms]   req CTR set 5
[   2ms] ● res CTR ack 5       [   5ms] ● res CTR ack 5       [   3ms]   res CTR ack 5
                         ～     [● 12ms]   req CTR log <data>   [   2ms]   req CTR log <data>
                              [● 11ms]   res CTR done          [  12ms]   res CTR done
[● 14ms] ● req CTR get         [   1ms] ● req CTR get          [● 56ms] ● req CTR get
[●  4ms] ✳ res CTR ret 0       [   3ms] ✳ res CTR ret 0        [●  4ms] ✳ res CTR ret 5
```

Fig. 1. Traces of an ECU CTR with operations set, get, and log. Faults are marked with ✳, relevant events with ●. Labels Ⓐ and Ⓑ indicate distinct causes for the faults.

is the moment the test engineer comes into play, and also the moment when automation strikes back. The bug will not only show up in one, but rather in a large number of test cases, and the engineer has to go through all of them to make sure not to miss a mistake. This is the problem we address: assist the test engineer when searching for bugs among a large number of failing tests.

Though our ideas may apply more broadly, we develop them in the context of hardware-in-the-loop testing for embedded controllers (ECUs) in the automotive industry [5]. The final ECU with its software is given to the test engineer as a black box. During testing, the ECU interacts with a (partly simulated) physical environment. This interaction is driven by a test suite derived from a test model. There are several characteristics that make hardware-in-the-loop testing substantially different from the earlier steps in the continuous integration and testing process (model/software/processor-in-the-loop testing). The first is the importance of timing requirements [2]. Second, the ECU with its software is a black-box. Indeed, in our setting it is provided by a supplier and the testing unit does not have access to the development model. Third, there is a test model capturing the product requirements document (PRD). It is a complex artifact that specifies the intended system behavior at a fine level of detail, including logical states, transitions, timing requirements, and message payloads. Indeed, *"testing automotive systems often requires test scenarios with a very precise sequence of time-sensitive actions"* [5]. As is good practice [5,42,45], the test model is different from the development model (it is even developed by a different company). Lastly, there are hundreds to thousands of tests, which is not surprising as it is known that real-time requirements *"are notoriously hard to test"* [45].

Example 1. Figure 1 illustrates the task at hand (ignore the ● marks for now). The figure shows three traces derived from the *Unified Diagnostic Services* [25]. A trace is a recording of the requests and responses resulting from executing a test case (pre-defined request sequence) on the ECU under test. Each line of the trace contains one message, carrying: (i) a time stamp indicating the time since the last message resp. the start, (ii) the type of message, req for requests and res for responses, (iii) an ECU identifier, the recipient for requests and the sender for responses, (iv) the name of an operation, e.g., set, and (v) optional payload.

In the first trace, the ECU with identifier CTR is requested to perform the set operation with value 5. The ECU acknowledges that the operation was executed successfully, repeating value 5. Subsequently, CTR receives a get request to which it responds with (returns) value 0. The second trace additionally requests a log operation between set and get. In the third trace, get returns 5 instead of 0.

The get responses in all traces are marked with 🌟 because they are faulty. Our example PRD requires get to return the value of the latest set, unless more than 50 ms have passed since the latest (response to) set, in which case 0 has to be returned. Assume the PRD does not specify any influence of log on set/get, and vice versa. The first two traces expose the same fault, indicated by Ⓐ: the set appears to have been ignored. The last trace exposes a different fault, indicated by Ⓑ: CTR appears to have ignored that 50 ms have passed.   □

Our contribution is an algorithm that classifies failing test cases according to their causes. The algorithm expects as input the same information that is available to the test engineer: the test model and the traces of the failing tests. It consists of three steps: fault localization, fault explanation, and fault classification. The fault localization can be understood as replaying a trace on the model to identify the moment when the two diverge. In Example 1, this yields the 🌟 marks. The fault explanation then computes the reason for the divergence. The reason can be understood as a small set of messages in the trace that is sufficient for the divergence. In the example, this set is marked with ●. Even when removing the remaining messages, we would still have a bug. The fault classification groups together traces that are faulty for similar reasons. In the example, labels Ⓐ and Ⓑ.

Our approach relies on machinery from formal methods, following the slogan in [5]: *"more formal semantics are needed for test automation"*. Behind the fault localization is a symbolic execution [14,29]. The challenge here is to summarize loops in which time passes but no visible events are issued. We solve the problem with a widening approach from abstract interpretation [7]. Our fault explanation [3,18–20,28,40,52] is based on Hoare logic [6,44]. The challenge is to identify messages as irrelevant (for making the test fail), if they only let time pass but their effect is dominated by earlier parts of the test. We achieve this using a new relationship between the assertions in the Hoare proof that is constructed for the test at hand. The fault classification [50,51] equates Hoare proofs [38]. The challenge is again related to timing: the precise moments in which messages arrive will be different from test to test. We propose a notion of proof template that allows us to equate Hoare proofs only based on timing constraints satisfied by the underlying tests. The precise timing does not matter.

We implemented the classification in a project with the automotive industry, targeting the CAN bus *Unified Diagnostic Services*. The test model has all the features mentioned above: real time, messages, and numerical payloads. It is derived from a PRD with 350 pages of natural language and has 12k states and 70k transitions. Our approach is practical: in 24 min we process test suites of up to 1000 tests with an average of 40 and outliers of up to 2500 messages in length.

One may wonder why we classify tests at all. Since they are derived from a test model, why not group them by the functionality they test or coverage they achieve? The point is that functionality and coverage are only means of exposing faults [50]. The faults are what matters for the test engineer, and the same fault will show up in tests for different functions. Our experiments confirm this: we discover previously undetected faults in tests that targeted functions different from the failing one. We are particularly successful with faults involving timing, which are largely function independent and therefore admit a high degree of non-determinism. Taking a step back, tests are designed by functionality or coverage, because it is hard to anticipate or even formulate possible faults in advance [45, 47, 50, 51]. Our explanation step makes the notion of a fault precise, and allows us to obtain the classification that the engineer needs for writing a test report.

Another question is whether we approach the problem from the wrong side. There is a large body of work on test suite minimization [36, 50]. So why classify tests a posteriori when we could have executed fewer tests in the first place? The answer is that test suite minimization techniques are known to reduce the fault detection effectiveness, as demonstrated in the famous WHLM [48], WHMP [49], and Siemens [41] studies. This is unacceptable in the automotive sector.

A companion technical report containing missing details is available as [4].

2   Formal Model

We introduce a class of automata enriched by memory and clocks to model PRDs. A so-called *PRD automaton* is a tuple $\mathcal{A} = (Q, \rightarrow, S, E, V, C)$ with a finite set of states Q, a finite transition relation $\rightarrow$ among states, initial states $S \subseteq Q$, a finite set of events E, a finite set of memory variables V, and a finite set of clocks C. Variables and clocks are disjoint, $V \cap C = \varnothing$. Transitions take the form $p \xrightarrow{e, g, up} q$ with states $p, q \in Q$, event $e \in E$, guard g, and update up. Additionally, there are transitions $p \xrightarrow{\Delta, g, up} q$ that react on time progression, denoted by the special symbol $\Delta \notin E$. *Guards* are Boolean formulas over (in)equalities of memory variables, clocks, and constants. We assume a strict typing and forbid (in)equalities among memory variables and clocks. *Updates* are partial functions that may give new values to variables v, $up(v) \in \mathbb{Z}$, or reset clocks c, $up(c) = 0$. Lifting variable updates from values to terms (over variables) is straightforward.

The runtime behavior of PRD automata is defined in terms of labeled transitions between configurations. A *configuration* of $\mathcal{A}$ is a tuple $cf = (p, \varphi)$ consisting of a state $p \in Q$ and a total valuation $\varphi : V \rightarrow \mathbb{Z} \cup C \rightarrow \mathbb{R}_{\geq 0}$ of variables and clocks. The configuration is initial if $p \in S$ is initial (no constraints on φ).

Valuations φ are affected by the progression of time t and updates up. Progressing φ by t yields a new valuation $\varphi + t$, coinciding with φ on all variables v and advancing all clocks c by t, $(\varphi + t)(c) = \varphi(c) + t$. To apply up to φ, we introduce the *transformer* $[\![up]\!]$. It yields a new valuation $[\![up]\!](\varphi) = \varphi'$ such that

$$\varphi'(v) \ = \ up(v) \neq \bot \ ? \ up(v) : \varphi(v) \quad \text{and} \quad \varphi'(c) \ = \ up(c) \neq \bot \ ? \ 0 : \varphi(c) \ .$$

PRD automata $\mathcal{A}$ process finite traces $w = s_1 \ldots s_n$ of events and time progressions, $s_i \in E \cup \mathbb{R}_{\geq 0}$. Events are instantaneous and time progressions make explicit the passing of time. A *basic run* $(p_1, \varphi_1) \xrightarrow{s_1} \cdots \xrightarrow{s_n} (p_{n+1}, \varphi_{n+1})$ of $\mathcal{A}$ on w is a sequence of steps where (p_1, φ_1) is initial. Steps $(p, \varphi) \xrightarrow{e} (q, \varphi')$ for events $e \in E$ are due to transitions in $\mathcal{A}$, so they satisfy the following two conditions:

(i) There is a transition $p \xrightarrow{e,\, g,\, up} q$ such that g is enabled. Enabledness means that φ is a model of g, written $\varphi \models g$.

(ii) The valuation φ' is induced by the transformer for up, $\varphi' = \llbracket up \rrbracket(\varphi)$.

Similarly, steps $(p, \varphi) \xrightarrow{t} (q, \varphi')$ taking time $t \in \mathbb{R}_{\geq 0}$ require:

(i) There is a Δ-transition $p \xrightarrow{\Delta,\, g,\, up} q$ enabled after waiting t time, $\varphi + t \models g$.

(ii) Valuation φ' is induced by clock progression plus up, $\varphi' = \llbracket up \rrbracket(\varphi + t)$.

Finally, there are stuttering steps $(p, \varphi) \xrightarrow{0} (p, \varphi)$ which have no requirements.

Next, we lift basic runs to allow for multiple Δ-transitions during a single time progression t in w. This is needed to support complex behavior while waiting, as seen in Example 1. We rewrite w by splitting and merging time progressions. More precisely, we rewrite w into w' along these equivalences:

$$w_1.w_2 \equiv w_1.0.w_2 \quad \text{and} \quad w_1.t.w_2 \equiv w_1.t_1.t_2.w_2 \text{ if } t = t_1 + t_2 \ . \quad \text{(TEQ)}$$

Then, we say that $\mathcal{A}$ *has a run on* w if there is w' with $w' \equiv w$ so that $\mathcal{A}$ has a basic run on w'. The specification $\mathcal{L}(\mathcal{A})$ induced by $\mathcal{A}$ is the set of all traces w on which $\mathcal{A}$ has a run. Readers familiar with hybrid systems will observe that our rewriting produces finite decompositions only, thus excludes zeno behavior [1].

To simplify the exposition, we hereafter implicitly assume that traces w are normalized in the sense that every event is preceded and succeeded by exactly one time progression. This normalization is justified by the (TEQ) equivalences.

In practice, models have many transitions between two states in order to capture state changes that ignore parts of the event or accept a large number of possible values. To avoid PRD automata growing unnecessarily large, we use regular expressions instead of single events as transition labels. The automaton model presented so far naturally extends to such a lift. Our implementation integrates this optimization, see Sect. 7. For simplicity, we stick to vanilla automata hereafter.

Example 2. The automata $\mathcal{A}_E, \mathcal{A}_\Delta$ from Fig. 2 specify CTR from Example 1. Automaton $\mathcal{A}_E$ addresses get, log, and set. The set request takes an arbitrary value <val> as a parameter. As discussed above, we use <val> as shorthand which can be translated on-the-fly into vanilla automata. The set request is always enabled and does not lead to updates. It may be followed by an ack, indicating success, or a fail response. If successful, variable ctx is updated to <val>. The reset of ctx after 50 ms is implemented by $\mathcal{A}_\Delta$. Operations get and log are similar.

Automaton $\mathcal{A}_E$ does not specify any timing behavior, all its states have an always-enabled Δ-self-loop without updates. The timing behavior is specified by automaton $\mathcal{A}_\Delta$. It uses ack responses as a trigger to reset the timer clk and then waits until clk holds a value of at least 50. Once the threshold is reached, the Δ-transition from p_4 to p_5 setting ctx to 0 becomes enabled. Here, $\mathcal{A}_\Delta$ allows for slack: the reset must happen within 5 ms once 50 ms have passed. Within these 5 ms, $\mathcal{A}_\Delta$ may choose to cycle in p_4 without resetting or move to p_5 while

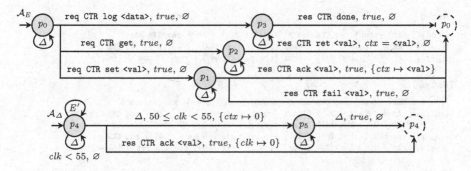

Fig. 2. Model $\mathcal{A}_E \times \mathcal{A}_\Delta$ for the ECU CTR from Example 1. Automaton $\mathcal{A}_E$ specifies operations **log**, **get**, and **set**. Automaton $\mathcal{A}_\Delta$ specifies how variable ctx is reset. We omit the guards $true$ and updates $\varnothing$ on Δ-loops. We use $E' \triangleq E \backslash \{\text{res CTR ack <val>}\}$.

resetting ctx. In practice, this kind of slack is common to account for the inability of hardware to execute after exactly 50 ms, as a guard like $clk \leq 50$ would require.

The overall specification of our example is the composition $\mathcal{A}_E \times \mathcal{A}_\Delta$. The cross-product is standard: a step can be taken only if both $\mathcal{A}_E$ and $\mathcal{A}_\Delta$ can take the step. We do not go into the details of operations over automata.   □

3   Fault Localization

We propose a method for localizing faults in traces w. Intuitively, we do so by letting $\mathcal{A}$ run on w. If for some prefix $w'.s$ of w there is no step to continue the run, i.e., $w' \in \mathcal{L}(\mathcal{A})$ but $w'.s \notin \mathcal{L}(\mathcal{A})$, then s is a fault and $w'.s$ is its *witness*. Witnesses play an integral role in our approach: a Hoare proof for a witness yields a formal reason for the fault. In Sect. 4, we will refine this reason by extracting a concise explanation for the fault. This explanation then allows us to classify faults in Sect. 5.

Technically, identifying faults s in w is more involved. Establishing $w' \in \mathcal{L}(\mathcal{A})$ requires us to find $w'' \equiv w'$ and a basic run of $\mathcal{A}$ on w''. Establishing $w'.s \notin \mathcal{L}(\mathcal{A})$, however, requires us to show that there exists no basic run of $\mathcal{A}$ on $w'.s$ at all. It is not sufficient to show that the single basic run witnessing $w' \in \mathcal{L}(\mathcal{A})$ cannot be extended to $w'.s$. We have to reason over all $\tilde{w} \equiv w'.s$ and over all basic runs on them. To cope with this, we encode symbolically all such basic runs of $\mathcal{A}$ as a Hoare proof. The Hoare proof can be thought of as a certificate for the fault.

Interestingly, our techniques for fault localization (Sect. 3), explanation (Sect. 4), and classification (Sect. 5) do not rely on the exact form of Hoare proofs or how they are obtained—any valid proof will do. Hence, we prefer to stay on the *semantic level*. We discuss how to efficiently generate the necessary proofs in Sect. 6. Note that the timing aspect of our model requires us to develop novel Hoare theory in Sect. 6.

Symbolic Encoding. We introduce a symbolic encoding to capture infinitely many configurations in a finite and concise manner.

Test-1   (A)

{*true*} [5ms] {*true*} req CTR set 5 {*true*} [2ms] {*true*} res CTR ack 5
{(p_0, p_4 : *ctx* $\neq 0 \wedge$ *clk* < 32)} [14ms] {(p_0, p_4 : *ctx* $\neq 0 \wedge$ *clk* < 46)} req CTR get
{(p_2, p_4 : *ctx* $\neq 0 \wedge$ *clk* < 46)} [4ms] {(p_2, p_4 : *ctx* $\neq 0$)} res CTR ret 0 {*false*}

Test-2   (A)

{*true*} [0ms] {*true*} req CTR set 5 {*true*} [5ms] {*true*} res CTR ack 5
{(p_0, p_4 : *ctx* $\neq 0 \wedge$ *clk* < 23)} [12ms] {(p_0, p_4 : *ctx* $\neq 0 \wedge$ *clk* < 35)} req CTR log <data>
{(p_3, p_4 : *ctx* $\neq 0 \wedge$ *clk* < 35)} [11ms] {(p_3, p_4 : *ctx* $\neq 0 \wedge$ *clk* < 46)} res CTR done
{(p_0, p_4 : *ctx* $\neq 0 \wedge$ *clk* < 46)} [1ms] {(p_0, p_4 : *ctx* $\neq 0 \wedge$ *clk* < 47)} req CTR get
{(p_2, p_4 : *ctx* $\neq 0 \wedge$ *clk* < 47)} [3ms] {(p_2, p_4 : *ctx* $\neq 0$)} res CTR ret 0 {*false*}

Fig. 3. Hoare proofs for Test-1 and Test-2.

A *symbolic configuration* is a pair $cf_\sharp = (p, F)$ where p is a state and F is a first-order formula. We use F to encode potentially infinitely many variable/clock valuations φ. We say F denotes φ if φ is a model for F, written $\varphi \models F$.

A *condition* P is a finite set of symbolic configurations. We write $(p, \varphi) \models P$ if there is $(p, F) \in P$ with $\varphi \models F$. We also write $P \sqsubseteq R$ if $cf \models P$ implies $cf \models R$ for all cf. If $P \sqsubseteq R$ and $R \sqsubseteq P$, we simply write $P = R$. The initial condition is $Init \triangleq \{ (p, true) \mid p \in S \}$ and the empty condition is $false = \varnothing$. For simplicity, we assume that conditions contain exactly one symbolic configuration per state, as justified by the next lemma. With that assumption, checking $P \sqsubseteq R$ can be encoded as an SMT query and discharged by an off-the-shelf solver like Z3 [35].

Lemma 1. $P \cup \{(p, F), (p, G)\} = P \cup \{(p, F \vee G)\}$ *and* $P \cup \{(p, false)\} = P$.

Later, we will use conditions P below quantifiers $\exists \overline{x}.P$ and in the standard Boolean connectives $G \oplus P$ with formulas G. We lift those operations to conditions by pushing them into the symbolic configurations of P as follows:

$$\exists \overline{x}.\ P \triangleq \{(p, \exists \overline{x}.\ F) \mid (p, F) \in P\} \quad \text{and} \quad G \oplus P \triangleq \{(p, G \oplus F) \mid (p, F) \in P\}.$$

Finding Faults. We localize faults in traces $w = s_1 \dots s_n$. This means we check whether or not $\mathcal{A}$ has a run on w. To do so, we rely on a Hoare proof for w which takes the form

$$\{ P_0 \}\ s_1\ \cdots\ \{ P_{i-1} \}\ s_i\ \{ P_i \}\ \cdots\ s_n\ \{ P_n \}\ ,$$

where every triple $\{ P_i \}\ s_i\ \{ P_{i+1} \}$ is a Hoare triple. Intuitively, the Hoare triple means: every step for s_i starting in a configuration from P_i leads to a configuration in P_{i+1}. Hoare triples are defined to be insensitive to trace equivalence:

$$\models \{P\}\, s\, \{R\}\ :\Longleftrightarrow\ \forall cf, cf', w'.\ cf \models P \wedge s \equiv w' \wedge cf \xrightarrow{w'} cf' \implies cf' \models R.$$

If the condition is satisfied, we call the Hoare triple *valid*. For brevity, we write $\{ P \}\, w'.s\, \{ S \}$ if there is R so that $\{ P \}\, w'\, \{ R \}$ and $\{ R \}\, s\, \{ S \}$ are both valid. Strengthening resp. weakening the precondition P resp. postcondition R preserves validity: $P' \sqsubseteq P$ and $\models \{ P \}\, s\, \{ R \}$ and $R \sqsubseteq R'$ implies $\models \{ P' \}\, s\, \{ R' \}$.

Now, finding faults boils down to checking the validity of Hoare triples. It is easy to see that $\mathcal{A}$ has no run on $w'.s$ if and only if $\models \{ \mathit{Init} \} \, w'.s \, \{ \mathit{false} \}$.

Lemma 2. *If* $\models \{ \mathit{Init} \} \, w' \, \{ P \} \, s \, \{ \mathit{false} \}$ *and* $P \neq \mathit{false}$, *then* $w'.s$ *witnesses fault* s.

Example 3. Figure 3 gives proofs that perform fault localization in Test-1 and Test-2 from Fig. 1. The beginning of both traces is irrelevant for the fault, so *true* is used as precondition. Then, the conditions track the amount of time that passes in the form of an upper bound on clock *clk*. Since *clk* stays below 50 ms, variable *ctx* is never reset by $\mathcal{A}_\Delta$. Hence, get must not return 0. But because get does return 0 in the trace, we arrive at *false*—the response is a fault. □

The Hoare proof certifying witness $w'.s$ is input to the fault explanation and classification in the next sections. As stated earlier, we defer the generation of Hoare proofs (by means of strongest postconditions and weakest preconditions) to Sect. 6, as it is orthogonal to fault explanation and classification.

4   Fault Explanation

We analyze the Hoare proof generated in Sect. 3 which certifies the fault in a witness. Our goal is to extract the events that contribute to the fault and dispose of those that are irrelevant. The result will be another valid Hoare proof that concisely explains the fault. On the one hand, the explanation will help the test engineer understand the fault and ultimately prepare the test report alluded to in Sect. 1. On the other hand, explanations of distinct test cases may be similar in terms of our classification approach from Sect. 5 while the original test cases are not, thus improving the effectiveness of the classification.

To determine a concise explanation, assume the Hoare proof certifying the fault can be partitioned into $\{ \mathit{Init} \} \, w_1 \, \{ P \} \, w_2 \, \{ R \} \, w_3 \, \{ P_k \}$. If P denotes fewer configurations than R, $P \sqsubseteq R$, we say that w_2 is irrelevant (the events therein). To see this, consider some configuration $cf \models P$. Executing w_2 from cf leads to some $cf' \models R$ which in turn leads to the fault by executing w_3. However, $cf \models R$ already holds. So, we can just execute w_3 from cf to exhibit the fault— w_2 is irrelevant indeed.

When timing plays a role in the fault, one might not be able to establish the simple inclusion $P \sqsubseteq R$ because removing w_2 altogether also removes the time that passes in it. However, it might be this passing of time, rather than the events, that leads to the fault. Therefore, we also check if the events (and the events only) in w_2 are irrelevant. This is the case if waiting has the same effect as performing full w_2. Technically, we check the validity of the triple $\{ P \} \, w_2|_{\mathbb{R}_{\geq 0}} \, \{ R \}$. The projection $w_2|_{\mathbb{R}_{\geq 0}}$ removes all events E from w_2: $e|_{\mathbb{R}_{\geq 0}} = \epsilon$ and $t|_{\mathbb{R}_{\geq 0}} = t$. The validity of the triple captures our intuition: any configuration $cf \models P$ can simply wait (taking Δ-transitions) for the same amount as w_2 and arrive in $cf' \models R$ from which w_3 and the fault are executable—the removed events $w_2|_E$ are irrelevant.

We apply the above reasoning—both $P \sqsubseteq R$ as well as $\models \{ P \} \, w_2|_{\mathbb{R}_{\geq 0}} \, \{ R \}$— to all partitionings of the given proof to identify the irrelevant sequences. The remaining events and time progressions all contribute to the fault. The result is the most concise explanation of the fault.

Unfortunately, our pruning rules are not confluent, meaning that different sequences of *irrelevance checks* may lead to different explanations. A witness may have more than one explanation if two irrelevant sequences partially overlap. To see this, consider the following (special case) partitioning of the witness' proof

$$\{ \mathit{Init} \}\ w_1\ \{ P \}\ w_2\ \{ R \}\ w_3\ \{ P \}\ w_4\ \{ R \}\ w_5\ \{ \mathit{false} \}\ .$$

Here, we deem irrelevant $w_2.w_3$ and $w_3.w_4$. However, we cannot remove $w_2.w_3.w_4$ entirely because the resulting proof might not be valid, which requires $P \sqsubseteq R$. Even removing the intersection w_3 of the irrelevant sequences may not produce a valid proof as $R \sqsubseteq P$ might not hold either. The same problems arise if only $(w_2.w_3)|_E$ and/or $(w_3.w_4)|_E$ is irrelevant. We argue that this is desired: the witness is, in fact, a witness for two different faults, explained by $w_1.w_4.w_5$ resp. $w_1.w_2.w_5$. Overall, we compute all explanations in case there are overlapping irrelevant sequences. While this gives exponentially many explanations in theory, we rarely find overlaps in practice.

Example 4. We give the fault explanation for the proof of `Test-2` from Fig. 3. As expected, both events `req CTR log <data>` and `res CTR done` are irrelevant. The condition $P = \{ (p_0, p_4 : \mathit{ctx} \neq 0 \wedge \mathit{clk} < 23) \}$ before the `log` request reaches condition $R = \{ (p_0, p_4 : \mathit{ctx} \neq 0 \wedge \mathit{clk} < 47) \}$ after the `log` response. This remains true after removing both events. Indeed, $\{ P \}$ `[12ms][11ms][ 1ms]` $\{ R \}$ is a valid Hoare triple and thus justifies removing the events.   □

5   Fault Classification

We propose a classification technique that groups together witnesses exhibiting the same or a similar fault. Grouping together similar faults significantly reduces the workload of test engineers when preparing a test report for a large number of failing tests since only one (representative) test case per group needs to be inspected. The input to our classification is a set W of witness explanations as constructed in Sect. 4. The result of the classification is a partitioning of W into disjoint classes $W = W_1 \uplus \cdots \uplus W_m$. The partitioning is obtained by factorizing W along an equivalence $\sim$ that relates witness explanations which have similar faults. If $\sim$ is effectively computable, so is the factorization. We focus on $\sim$.

Intuitively, two explanations are similar, and thus related by $\sim$, if comprised of the same sequence of Hoare triples, that is, the same sequence of events and intermediary assertions. This strict equality, however, does not work well when timing is involved. Repeatedly executing the same sequence of events is expected to observe a difference in timing due to fluctuations in the underlying hardware. Moreover, explanations have already been stripped by irrelevant sequences the events and duration of which might differ across explanations.

To make up for these discrepancies, we relate explanations that are equal up to *similar clocks*. Consider an (in)equality F over clocks C. We can think of F, more concretely its solutions, as a polytope $M \subseteq \mathbb{R}^{|C|}$. Then, two clock assignments $\varphi, \varphi' \in \mathbb{R}^{|C|}$ are similar if they agree on the membership in M. That is, φ and φ' are similar if $\varphi, \varphi' \in M$ or $\varphi, \varphi' \notin M$. The polytope M we consider will stem from the transition guards in $\mathcal{A}$. Similarity thus means that $\mathcal{A}$ cannot distinguish the two clock assignments—they fail for the same reason.

Clock similarity naturally extends to sets of polytopes. The set of polytopes along which we differentiate clock assignments is taken from a *proof template*. A proof template for a trace is a unique Hoare proof where placeholders are used instead of actual time progressions. Hence, the explanations under consideration are instances of the template, i.e., can be obtained by replacing the placeholders with the appropriate time progressions. More importantly, the template gives rise to a set of *atomic constraints* from which all polytopes appearing in the explanations can be constructed (using Boolean connectives). Overall, this means that two explanations are similar if the clocks they allow for are similar wrt. the polytopes of the associated proof template, meaning that $\mathcal{A}$ cannot distinguish them and thus fails for the same reason.

A proof template for events $e_1 \ldots e_k$ is a Hoare proof of the form

$$\{ \textit{Init} \}\, u_0 \, \cdots \, \{ P_{2i-1} \}\, e_i\, \{ P_{2i} \}\, u_i\, \{ P_{2i+1} \} \, \cdots \, u_k\, \{ \textit{false} \} \ .$$

This proof is a template because $\overline{u} = u_0, \ldots, u_k$ are symbolic time progressions, i.e., they can be thought of as variables rather than actual values from $\mathbb{R}_{\geq 0}$. An instance of the template is a valid Hoare proof

$$\{ \textit{Init} \}\, t_0 \, \cdots \, \{ R_{2i-1} \}\, e_i\, \{ R_{2i} \}\, t_i\, \{ R_{2i+1} \} \, \cdots \, t_k\, \{ \textit{false} \}$$

with actual time progressions $\overline{t} = t_0, \ldots, t_k$ such that the P_i subsume the R_i for the given choice of symbolic time progressions, $R_i \sqsubseteq P_i[\overline{u} \mapsto \overline{t}]$.

For the classification to work, we require the following properties of templates:

(C1) the template is uniquely defined by the sequence $u_0.e_1 \ldots e_k.u_k$, and
(C2) the symbolic configurations appearing in the P_i are quantifier-free.

The former property associates a unique template to every trace. This is necessary for a meaningful classification via templates. The latter property ensures that the atomic constraints we extract from the template (see below) will contain only clocks from C. This is necessary for equisatisfiability to be meaningful. In Sect. 6 we show that weakest preconditions generate appropriate templates.

An atomic clock constraint is an (in)equality over symbolic time progressions and ordinary clocks (from C). We write $acc(P)$ for all such constraints syntactically occurring in P. For P_i from the above proof template, $acc(P_i)$ is a set of building blocks from which the R_i of *all* instantiations can be constructed. Moreover, $\mathcal{A}$ cannot distinguish time progression beyond $acc(P_i)$, making them ideal candidates for judging similarity.

We turn to the definition of the equivalence relation $\sim$. To that end, consider two explanations α, β of the following form

$$\alpha: \quad \{\,Init\,\} \cdots \{\,R_{2i-1}\,\}\, e_i \,\{\,R_{2i}\,\}\, t_i \,\{\,R_{2i+1}\,\} \cdots \{\,false\,\}$$
$$\beta: \quad \{\,Init\,\} \cdots \{\,R'_{2i-1}\,\}\, e_i \,\{\,R'_{2i}\,\}\, t'_i \,\{\,R'_{2i+1}\,\} \cdots \{\,false\,\}\,.$$

The events $e_1, \ldots, e_k$ match in both explanations, but the time progressions $\overline{t}$ and $\overline{t'}$ may differ. (Explanations with distinct event sequences are never related by $\sim$.) Both explanations are instances of the same proof template σ,

$$\sigma: \quad \{\,Init\,\} \cdots \{\,P_{2i-1}\,\}\, e_i \,\{\,P_{2i}\,\}\, u_i \,\{\,P_{2i+1}\,\} \cdots \{\,false\,\}\,.$$

Now, for α and β to be similar, $\alpha \sim \beta$, we require the R_i and R'_i to satisfy the exact same atomic clock constraints appearing in P_i relative to the appropriate instantiation of the symbolic clock values. It is worth stressing that we require satisfiability, not logical equivalence, because we want the clocks to be similar, not equal. We write $\mathrm{SAT}(F)$ if F is satisfiable, that is, if there is an assignment φ to the free variables in F such that $\varphi \models F$. Formally then, we have:

$$\alpha \sim \beta \qquad \text{iff} \qquad \forall i \ \forall F \in acc(P_i).\ \mathrm{SAT}(F[\overline{u} \mapsto \overline{t}]) \iff \mathrm{SAT}(F[\overline{u} \mapsto \overline{t'}])\,.$$

It is readily checked that $\sim$ is an equivalence relation, that is, is reflexive, symmetric, and transitive, as alluded to in the beginning. Transitivity, in particular, is desirable in our use case. First, it means that all explanations from a class W_i of W are pairwise similar, that is, exhibit the same fault. Second, the partitions are guaranteed to be disjoint. Finally, it allows for the partitioning of W to be computed efficiently (by tabulating the result of the SAT queries), provided the SAT queries are efficient for the type of (in)equalities used.

Lemma 3. *Relation $\sim$ is an equivalence relation.*

Example 5. We classify the explanations of `Test-1` and `Test-2`, which correspond to the proofs from Fig. 3 with the `log` events removed (cf. Example 4). Both explanations agree on the sequence of events. Figure 4 gives their common template. The atomic clock constraints are $u_1 + u_2 < 50$, $clk + u_1 < 50$, and $clk + u_1 + u_2 < 50$. `Test-1` and `Test-2` are similar because each clock constraint is satisfiable after instantiating the symbolic time progressions with the values in the respective trace. Hence, our classification groups these explanations together, `Test-1` $\sim$ `Test-2`.   □

```
Template<Test-1, Test-2>   Ⓐ

{(p₁, p₄ : u₁ + u₂ < 50)}
res CTR ack 5
{(p₀, p₄ : ctx ≠ 0 ∧ clk + u₁ + u₂ < 50)}
[ u₂ms]
{(p₀, p₄ : ctx ≠ 0 ∧ clk + u₁ < 50)}
req CTR get
{(p₂, p₄ : ctx ≠ 0 ∧ clk + u₁ < 50)}
[ u₁ms]
{(p₂, p₄ : ctx ≠ 0)}
res CTR ret 0
{false}
```

Fig. 4. Proof template for the explanations of `Test-1` and `Test-2`.

6   Hoare Proofs with Timing

For the techniques presented so far to be useful, it remains to construct Hoare proofs for traces w. Strongest postconditions and weakest preconditions are the standard way of doing so. The former yields efficient fault localization (Sect. 3). The latter satisfies the requirements for templates (Sect. 5). Moreover, interpolation between the two produces concise proofs beneficial for fault explanations (Sect. 4).

It is worth pointing out that the aforementioned concepts are well-understood for programs and ordinary automata. However, they have not been generalized to a setting like ours where timing plays a role. Indeed, works like [21, 23, 24, 43] involve timing, but do not develop the Hoare theory required here.

Strongest Postconditions. We compute the *post image*, that is, make precise how $\mathcal{A}$ takes steps from symbolic configurations. A step from a symbolic configuration (p, F) due to transition $p \xrightarrow{\Delta, g, up} q$ on time progression t can be taken if the guard is enabled after waiting for t time. After waiting, all clocks c are $c' = c + t$. This means before waiting we have $c = c' - t$. However, clocks are always non-negative, $c' - t \geq 0$. Overall, we replace in F all clocks by their old versions and enforce non-negativity, $F' = F[C \mapsto C - t] \wedge C \geq t$. It remains to check guard g and apply update up. It is easy to see that the set of valuations in F' satisfying g is precisely $G = F' \wedge g$. To perform a singleton update $\{x \mapsto y\}$, we capture the new valuation of x by the equality $x = y$. To avoid an influence of the update of x on other variables/clocks, we have to rewrite G to not contain x. This is needed as G might use x to correlate other variables/clocks—we want to preserve these correlations without affecting them. We use an existential abstraction that results in $G' = \exists z.\ G[x \mapsto z] \wedge x = y$. Then, the post image is (q, G'). For stuttering steps, we add the original configuration (p, F) to the post image. Steps due to events from E are similar.

We define a symbolic transformer that implements the above update of the symbolic encoding F to G' in the general case:

$$\llbracket g | \{\overline{x} \mapsto \overline{y}\} \rrbracket_t^\sharp (F) \triangleq \exists \overline{z}.\ (F[C \mapsto C - t] \wedge C \geq t \wedge g)[\overline{x} \mapsto \overline{z}] \wedge \overline{x} = \overline{y}\ ,$$

where $\overline{x}$ is short for a sequence $x_1, \ldots, x_m$ of variables/clocks. We arrive at:

$$post_t^\sharp(P) \triangleq \{\, (q, \llbracket g | up \rrbracket_t^\sharp(F)) \mid (p, F) \in P \wedge p \xrightarrow{\Delta, g, up} q \,\} \cup \left(t = 0\ ?\ P\ :\ \varnothing\right)$$

$$post_e^\sharp(P) \triangleq \{\, (q, \llbracket g | up \rrbracket_0^\sharp(F)) \mid (p, F) \in P \wedge p \xrightarrow{e, g, up} q \,\}\ .$$

The post image is sound and precise in the sense that it captures accurately the steps the configurations denoted by P can take. The lemma makes this precise.

Lemma 4. $cf' \models post_s^\sharp(P)$ *iff there is* $cf \models P$ *with* $cf \xrightarrow{s} cf'$.

Example 6. We apply $post^\sharp$ to $P = \{(p_4, 49 \leq clk \leq 52)\}$ for $\mathcal{A}_\Delta$ from Fig. 2. Recall that $\mathcal{A}_\Delta$ resets variable ctx within 5 ms after clk has reached the 50 ms mark. Indeed, $post_1^\sharp(P)$ for 1 ms contains both the resetting and the non-resetting case: $(p_5, 50 \leq clk \leq 53 \wedge ctx = 0)$ and $(p_4, 50 \leq clk \leq 53)$.

The post image still lacks a way to commute with the (TEQ) congruences. While $post_5^\sharp(post_1^\sharp(P))$ witnesses the reset via condition $55 \leq clk \leq 58 \wedge ctx = 0$ for both p_4 and p_5, it is not equivalent to $post_6^\sharp(P)$, which is *false* since all transitions in p_4 are disabled for a full 6 ms wait. $\qquad\square$

While the post image captures the individual steps of basic runs on traces w, we have to consider the basic runs of all traces $w' \equiv w$ to generate a Hoare proof for w. Basically, the (TEQ) equivalences state that the time progressions between events can be split/merged arbitrarily. To that end, we define the strongest postcondition sp which inspects all basic runs simultaneously, intuitively, by rewriting according to the (TEQ) equivalences on-the-fly. (Note that normalization according to Sect. 2 avoids the merging case of (TEQ).) Then, for events e the strongest postcondition merely applies the post image to e. For time progressions t, the strongest postcondition considers all decompositions of t into fragments $t_1, \ldots, t_k$ that add up to t and applies the post image iteratively to all the t_i. This includes stuttering where 0 is rewritten to $0 \ldots 0$. If there are loops in $\mathcal{A}$, the strongest postcondition might need to consider infinitely many decompositions. We address this problem by enumerating decompositions of increasing length and applying to each decomposition a widening ∇ with the following properties: (i) the result of the widening is $\sqsubseteq$-weaker than its input, $P_i \sqsubseteq \nabla(P_1, \cdots, P_k)$ for all i, and (ii) the widening stabilizes after finitely many iterations for $\sqsubseteq$-increasing sequences, $P_1 \sqsubseteq P_2 \sqsubseteq \cdots$ implies that there is k so that $\nabla(P_1, \cdots, P_i) = \nabla(P_1, \cdots, P_{i+1})$ for all $i \geq k$. We write $\nabla(P_i)_{i \in \mathbb{N}}$ and mean the stabilized $\nabla(P_1, \cdots, P_k)$. Given a widening, the strongest postcondition is:

$$sp_t(P) \triangleq \nabla \left(\exists t_1, \cdots, t_i.\ t = t_1 + \cdots + t_i\ \wedge\ post^\sharp_{t_i} \circ \cdots \circ post^\sharp_{t_1}(P) \right)_{i \in \mathbb{N}}$$

$$sp_e(P) \triangleq post^\sharp_e(P) \qquad sp_{s.w}(P) \triangleq sp_w \circ sp_s(P) \qquad sp(P, w) \triangleq sp_w(P)$$

where the $t_1, \ldots, t_i$ are fresh. Observe that the sequence of post images in sp_t is $\sqsubseteq$-increasing: one can always extend the decomposition by additionally waiting for 0 time, $post^\sharp_{t_i}(P) \sqsubseteq post^\sharp_0 \circ post^\sharp_{t_i}(P)$. The strongest postcondition considers all basic runs and ∇ overapproximates the reachable configurations. It is sound.

Lemma 5. *If $sp(P, w) \sqsubseteq R$, then $\models \{ P \} w \{ R \}$.*

For the lemma to be useful, an appropriate widening ∇ is required. In general, finding such a widening is challenging—after all, it resembles finding loop invariants—and for doing so we refer to existing works, like [8,12,13], to name a few. In practice, a widening may be obtained more easily. In case $\mathcal{A}$ is free from Δ-cycles, stabilization is guaranteed after k iterations, where k is the length of the longest simple Δ-path. If there are Δ-cycles, stabilization is still guaranteed after k iterations if all Δ-cycles are *idempotent*. A Δ-cycle is idempotent if repeated executions of the cycle produce only configurations that already a single execution of the cycle produces. Interestingly, idempotency can be checked while computing the widening: if the $(k+1)$st iteration produces new configurations, idempotency does not hold. In our setting, idempotency was always satisfied. For the remainder of this paper, we assume an appropriate widening is given.

Weakest Preconditions. We also compute weakest preconditions, the time-reversed dual of strongest postconditions. Our definition will satisfy the template requirements (C1) and (C2) from Sect. 5.

The *pre image* is the set of symbolic configurations that reach a given configuration in automaton $\mathcal{A}$. Consider some (q, G) and $p \xrightarrow{\Delta, g, up} q$. The pre image first rewinds updates $up = \{\overline{x} \mapsto \overline{y}\}$ by replacing $\overline{x}$ with $\overline{y}$. Then, it adds a disjunct $H = G[\overline{x} \mapsto \overline{y}] \vee \neg g$. Adding the disjunct makes the pre image weaker; it does not affect soundness in Lemma 6 which ignores the *stuck* configurations denoted by $(p, \neg g)$. Finally, we rewind the clock progression t by replacing all clocks c in H with $c + t$. We arrive at the pre image $F = H[C \mapsto C + t]$. Transitions due to events are similar. We define a symbolic transformer to apply the above process:

$$\overline{[\![g|\{\overline{x} \mapsto \overline{y}\}]\!]}_t^{\sharp}(G) \triangleq (G[\overline{x} \mapsto \overline{y}] \vee \neg g)[C \mapsto C + t] \ .$$

To account for other transitions leaving p that are enabled in H, we compute the meet $\sqcap$ of the per-transition pre images. Intuitively, this intersects symbolic configurations on a per-state basis, ensuring that any configuration from the pre image either gets stuck or steps to one of the configurations we computed the pre image for. Technically, the meet $\sqcap$ for sets M of symbolic configurations is:

$$\bigsqcap M \triangleq \{ (p, \bigwedge_{(p,F) \in M} F) \mid p \in Q \} \ .$$

Notably, when considering the meet of M, we cannot understand M as a condition. This is because conditions treat symbolic configurations disjunctively and can be normalized by Lemma 1. However, the meet is not preserved under these transformations. We write $M_1 \sqcap M_2$ to mean $\bigsqcap (M_1 \cup M_2)$.

The discussion yields the following definition of the pre image:

$$pre_t^{\sharp}(P) \triangleq \bigsqcap \{(p, \overline{[\![g|up]\!]}_t^{\sharp}(G)) \mid (q, G) \in P \wedge p \xrightarrow{\Delta, g, up} q\} \sqcap (t = 0 \ ? \ P \ : \ \varnothing)$$

$$pre_e^{\sharp}(P) \triangleq \bigsqcap \{(p, \overline{[\![g|up]\!]}_0^{\sharp}(G)) \mid (q, G) \in P \wedge p \xrightarrow{e, g, up} q\} \ ,$$

capturing precisely the forced reachability in $\mathcal{A}$, as stated by the next lemma.

Lemma 6. $cf \models pre_s^{\sharp}(P)$ *iff for all* cf', $cf \xrightarrow{s} cf'$ *implies* $cf' \models P$.

Example 7. We apply $pre^{\sharp}$ to $P = \{(p_4, 49 \leq clk \leq 52)\}$ for $\mathcal{A}_\Delta$ from Fig. 2. Computing $pre_1^{\sharp}(P)$ highlights the need for the meet. The Δ-loop on p_4 does not give $(p_4, 48 \leq clk \leq 51)$ as precondition. Instead, it is $(p_4, 48 \leq clk < 49)$ which is the result of $\{(p_4, 48 \leq clk \leq 51)\} \sqcap \{(p_4, clk \geq 54 \vee clk < 49)\}$. Indeed, $\mathcal{A}_\Delta$ reaches a non-P configuration via the resetting transition to p_5 if $clk = 49$. $\quad\square$

The weakest precondition $wp(s, R)$ denotes all configurations that either step to R under s or have no step at all. Technically, the weakest precondition repeatedly applies the pre image for all decompositions of time progressions. For termination, we again rely on the widening ∇. Since the pre image sequence is $\sqsubseteq$-decreasing, we turn it into an increasing sequence by taking complements. More precisely, we use the widening $\overline{\nabla}(P_1, \cdots, P_m) \triangleq \neg\nabla(\neg P_1, \cdots, \neg P_m)$. The weakest precondition is defined by:

$$wp_t(P) \triangleq \overline{\nabla}\left(\forall t_1, \cdots, t_i.\ t = t_1 + \cdots + t_i \implies pre_{t_1}^\sharp \circ \cdots \circ pre_{t_i}^\sharp(P)\right)_{i \in \mathbb{N}}$$

$$wp_e(P) \triangleq pre_e^\sharp(P) \qquad wp_{w.s}(P) \triangleq wp_w \circ wp_s(P) \qquad wp(w, P) \triangleq wp_w(P) .$$

Note that wp_t applies to ordinary time progressions t as well as symbolic time progressions u appearing in proof templates. The weakest precondition is sound.

Lemma 7. *If $P \sqsubseteq wp(w, R)$, then $\models \{P\}\, w\, \{R\}$.*

Concise Hoare Proofs. The developed theory allows for an efficient way to produce concise Hoare proofs. We first apply strongest postconditions to generate an initial proof. Then, starting from the back, we apply weakest preconditions and interpolation [9] to simplify the initial proof. We make this precise.

Combining Lemmas 2 and 5 gives an effective way of finding faults in traces $w = s_1 \ldots s_n$ and extracting a witness: iteratively compute the strongest postcondition for increasing prefixes of w and check if the result is unsatisfiable. That is, compute $P = sp(s_1. \cdots .s_k, Init)$ and check if $P = false$. If so, then $\widehat{w} = s_1 \ldots s_k$ is a witness for fault s_k. Otherwise, continue with the prefix $s_1 \ldots s_k.s_{k+1}$ which can reuse the previously computed P: $sp(s_1 \ldots s_k.s_{k+1}, Init) = sp(s_{k+1}, P)$. As per Lemma 5, the approach gives rise to the valid Hoare proof

$$\{Init\}\, s_1\ \cdots\ \{P_i\}\, s_{i+1}\, \{P_{i+1}\}\ \cdots\ s_k\, \{false\} \quad \text{with} \quad P_{i+1} = sp(P_i, s_{i+1}) .$$

It is well-known that strongest postconditions produce unnecessarily complex proofs [34]. To alleviate this weakness, we use interpolation [9]. For two formulas F and G with $F \implies G$, an interpolant is a formula I with $F \implies I$ and $I \implies G$. The interpolant for conditions P and R with $P \sqsubseteq R$, denoted $I(P, R)$, results from interpolating the symbolic configurations in P with the corresponding ones in R. Interpolants exist in first-order predicate logic [9,32].

From the above sp- generated proof we construct an interpolated proof

$$\{Init\}\, s_1\ \cdots\ \{I(P_i, R_i)\}\, s_{i+1}\, \{I(P_{i+1}, R_{i+1})\}\ \cdots\ s_k\, \{false\}$$

using wp as follows. Assume we already constructed, starting from the back, the interpolants $I(P_k, R_k)$ through $I(P_{i+1}, R_{i+1})$. Now, the goal is to obtain an interpolant I so that $\{I\}\, s_{i+1}\, \{I(P_{i+1}, R_{i+1})\}$ is valid. The weakest precondition for the latest interpolant yields $R_i = wp(s_i, I(P_{i+1}, R_{i+1}))$. This gives a valid Hoare triple $\models \{R_i\}\, s_{i+1}\, \{I(P_{i+1}, R_{i+1})\}$. Our goal is to interpolate P_i and R_i. If $P_i \sqsubseteq R_i$, we can interpolate P_i and R_i to obtain $I = I(P_i, R_i)$.[1] Otherwise, we simply choose $I = R_i$. By Lemma 7 together with $I \sqsubseteq R_i$, we know that $\models \{I\}\, s_{i+1}\, \{I(P_{i+1}, R_{i+1})\}$ is valid. Overall, this constructs a valid proof.

---

[1] One can show that the inclusion $P_i \sqsubseteq R_i$ is always satisfied in our setting where Δ-cycles are idempotent and the widenings ∇ and $\overline{\nabla}$ simply enumerate all necessary decompositions of time progressions. Refer to [4] for a more general property.

7 Application in Automotive Software

We implemented and tested our approach on benchmarks provided by our project partner from the automotive industry. The implementation parses, classifies, and annotates traces of ECUs running the Unified Diagnostic Services (UDS). We turned a PRD with 350 pages of natural language specifying 23 services into a PRD automaton of 12.5k states and 70k transitions. We evaluated our tool on 1000 traces which are processed within 24 minutes. Our tool is implemented in C# and processes traces in the three stages explained below. It naturally supports multi-threading for the localization, explanation, and classification since they are agnostic to the (set of) other traces being analyzed.

Preprocessing Stage. The first stage parses trace files and brings them into a shape similar to Fig. 1. UDS specify a request-response protocol for ECUs communicating over a CAN bus. The traces are a recording of all messages seen on the bus during a test run. We found the preprocessing more difficult than expected, because the trace files have a non-standard format. These problems stem from the fact that our industrial partner creates tests partly manually and inserts natural language annotations. A useful type of annotation that we could extract are the positions deemed erroneous by the test environment.

Modeling Stage. The second stage creates the test model, a PRD automaton as defined in Sect. 2. Modeling a natural language PRD is a non-trivial and time-consuming process. To translate the PRD into an automaton, we developed an API capable of programmatically describing services and their communication requirements. The API supports a declarative formulation of the communication requirements which it compiles down into an automaton. The compilation is controlled by a set of parameters because the PRD prescribes different behavior depending on the ECU version (and related static parameters). There are further high-level modeling constructs such as regular expressions, as alluded to in Sect. 2 and seen in Fig. 2.

Unfortunately, not all requirements from the PRD are restricted to the trace: they may refer to events internal to the ECU that are not contained in the trace files. While our API and PRD automata are capable of expressing these requirements, the test environment is unable to detect them. To circumvent the problem of missing information, we over-approximated our model using non-determinism. That is, we simply allow our model to do any of the specified behaviors for unobservable internal events. A downside of this is that errors dependent on these events cannot be found during fault localization.

Analysis Stage. The last stage performs fault localization (Sect. 3), explanation (Sect. 4), and classification (Sect. 5). We carefully inspected 86 traces curated by our industrial partner. The tests targeted one of the 23 services, yet they contain requests and responses to a multitude of services responsible for setting up the ECU configuration. The annotations of the test environment marked 100 faults, 95 of which are also found by our fault localization. Our tool finds and explains another 10 undetected faults, which totals to 105 fault explanations. The five faults missed by our localization are actually incorrect annotations by the test environment, which we will explain in a moment.

Figure 5 gives the lengths of the found witnesses and the average lengths of their explanations. The explanation lengths are closely tied to the kinds of faults in the test set. In our set, long witnesses tend to have a long prefix unimportant to the fault. This is reflected in the partitioning found by our classification.

The classification divides the faults into six partitions. We found that each partition belongs to one of the following three error types: (i) ECU responds too late (1+8); (ii) ECU fails to reset a variable upon restart (2); (iii) ECU responds when it should not (2+1+91). Here, 1+8 means we have two partitions and one with a single witness, one with eight equivalent witnesses. Each error type consists of at most two relevant events. Unrelated events in-between those two events are dropped by fault explanation. The relevant events are: (i) the request and the late response, (ii) the response event which revealed that the variable has not been reset, and (iii) the request and the incorrectly given response.

There are two partitions with error type (i). This is because the late response is given by another service and thus leads to different control flow in the automaton. Indeed, there might be distinct root causes: different services are likely controlled by different pieces of code. A similar reason produces three partitions of error type (iii). Interestingly, the singleton partition for (i) is completely missed by the test environment (no fault was marked). This supports our claim that the test environment only detects faults targeted by the tests and ignores other faults. The other partition of (i) was detected by the test environment by accident: in some traces, the ECU response is so late that the test environment incorrectly marks the response as missing. These incorrect marks represent no faults and are not considered by our localization. Instead, our localization actually detects the late responses and marks them correctly.

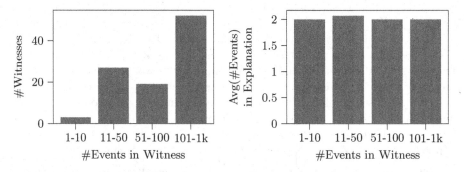

Fig. 5. Statistics on witnesses: number (left) and average explanation length (right).

Our tool provides a partitioning file with direct links to the trace files. It also modifies the trace files to highlight the events related to the fault (cf. Sect. 4) and provides an intuitive explanation of the fault. As for the latter, the user is informed about the difference between the observed and the automaton-expected behavior. Our manual inspection showed no incorrect classification. That is, our tool has never grouped together traces which test engineers would deem caused by distinct faults. This is promising feedback because incorrect classification is dreaded: a single missed flaw of an ECU can cause large costs. Overall, we reduced the workload of manually inspecting 86 traces with 100 fault marks to inspecting six representative faults that expose more misbehavior than marked by the test environment.

8   Related Work

Fault Explanation. Our work on fault explanation is related to minimizing unit tests in [30]: tests are pruned by removing the commands that are not contained in a backward slice from a failing instruction. With timing constraints, slicing does not work (every command is relevant), which is why we have developed our approach based on Hoare logic. The assertions provided by a Hoare proof have the additional advantage of being able to prune even dependent commands inside a slice (based on the relationship between intermediary assertions), which leads to higher reduction rates. Similar to our approach is the fault localization and explanation from [6,44]. That work also makes use of interpolation [33] and is able to strip infixes from a trace despite dependencies. Our fault localization can be understood as a generalization to a timed setting where every command contributes to the progression of time and therefore is delicate to remove.

A popular fault explanation approach that can be found in several variants in the literature [3,18–20,28,40,52] is Delta debugging: starting from a failing test, produce a similar but passing test, and take the difference in commands as an explanation of the fault. In [18–20,40,52], the passing test is found by repeatedly testing the concrete system [19], which is impossible in our in-vitro setting. In [3,18,28], a model checker resp. a solver is queried for a passing test resp. a satisfiable subset of clauses. Our Hoare proof can be understood as building up an alternative and valid execution. Different from a mere execution, however, intermediary assertions provide valuable information about the program state that we rely on when classifying tests.

The explanation from [26] divides a computation into fated and free segments, the former being deterministic reactions to inputs and the latter being inputs that, if controlled appropriately, avoid the fault and hence should be considered responsible for it. The segments are computed via rather heavy game-theoretic techniques, which would be difficult to generalize to timed systems. A more practical variant can be found in [46,53]. These works modify tests in a way that changes the evaluation of conditionals. Neither can we re-run tests in an in-vitro setting, nor would we be able to influence the timing behavior.

There is a body of literatur on statistical approaches to finding program points that are particularly prone to errors, see the surveys [47,50]. We need to pinpoint the precise as possible cause of a bug, instead.

Fault Classification. Previous works on test case classification follow the same underlying principle [10,11,15–17,27,31,37,39]: devise a distance metric on test cases that is used to group them. The metrics are based on properties like the commonality/frequency of words in comments and variables in the code [11] or the correlation of tests failing/passing in previous test runs [15]. Symbolic execution has been used to derive more semantic properties based on the source code location of faults [31] and the longest prefix a failing trace shares with some passing trace [37]. The problem is that the suggested metrics are at best vague surrogates for the underlying faults. Using a model-based approach, we compare traces not against each other but against a ground truth (the PRD automaton).

Another related line of work is test case prioritization, test case selection, and test suite minimization [50]. Although formulated differently, these problems share the task of choosing tests from a predefined pool. Experiments have shown that manually chosen test suites outperform automatically selected ones in their ability to expose bugs [51]. To increase the number of tests that can be evaluated manually by an expert, the literature has proposed the use of clustering algorithms to group together tests with similar characteristics (so that the expert only has to evaluate clusters). The clustering is computed from syntactic information (a bitwise comparison of test executions). As argued before, we use semantic information and compute the classification wrt. a ground truth.

On the automatic side, [38] suggests the use of Hoare proofs to classify error traces. Our approach follows this idea and goes beyond it with the proposal of proof templates. Proof templates seem to be precisely the information needed to classify tests that are subject to real-time constraints. Harder et al. suggest to minimize test suites based on likely program invariants inferred from sample values obtained in test runs [22]. Hoare triples are more precise than invariants, even more so as we work with a ground truth rather than sample values.

Acknowledgements. The results were obtained in the projects *"Virtual Test Analyzer I – III"*, conducted in collaboration with *IAV GmbH*. The last author is supported by a Junior Fellowship from the Simons Foundation (855328, SW).

References

1. Abadi, M., Lamport, L.: An old-fashioned recipe for real time. In: de Bakker, J.W., Huizing, C., de Roever, W.P., Rozenberg, G. (eds.) REX 1991. LNCS, vol. 600, pp. 1–27. Springer, Heidelberg (1992). https://doi.org/10.1007/BFb0031985
2. Alur, R., Dill, D.L.: A theory of timed automata. TCS **126**(2), 183–235 (1994)
3. Ball, T., Naik, M., Rajamani, S.K.: From symptom to cause: localizing errors in counterexample traces. In: POPL, pp. 97–105. ACM (2003)
4. Becker, M., Meyer, R., Runge, T., Schaefer, I., van der Wall, S., Wolff, S.: Model-based fault classification for automotive software. CoRR abs/2208.14290 (2022)
5. Bringmann, E., Krämer, A.: Model-based testing of automotive systems. In: ICST, pp. 485–493. IEEE (2008)

6. Christ, J., Ermis, E., Schäf, M., Wies, T.: Flow-sensitive fault localization. In: Giacobazzi, R., Berdine, J., Mastroeni, I. (eds.) VMCAI 2013. LNCS, vol. 7737, pp. 189–208. Springer, Heidelberg (2013). https://doi.org/10.1007/978-3-642-35873-9_13

7. Cousot, P., Cousot, R.: Abstract interpretation: a unified lattice model for static analysis of programs by construction or approximation of fixpoints. In: POPL, pp. 238–252. ACM (1977)

8. Cousot, P., Halbwachs, N.: Automatic discovery of linear restraints among variables of a program. In: POPL, pp. 84–96. ACM Press (1978)

9. Craig, W.: Linear reasoning. A new form of the Herbrand-Gentzen theorem. J. Symb. Log. **22**(3), 250–268 (1957)

10. Dickinson, W., Leon, D., Podgurski, A.: Finding failures by cluster analysis of execution profiles. In: ICSE, pp. 339–348. IEEE (2001)

11. DiGiuseppe, N., Jones, J.A.: Concept-based failure clustering. In: SIGSOFT FSE, p. 29. ACM (2012)

12. Dillig, I., Dillig, T., Li, B., McMillan, K.L.: Inductive invariant generation via abductive inference. In: OOPSLA, pp. 443–456. ACM (2013)

13. Flanagan, C., Leino, K.R.M.: Houdini, an annotation assistant for ESC/Java. In: Oliveira, J.N., Zave, P. (eds.) FME 2001. LNCS, vol. 2021, pp. 500–517. Springer, Heidelberg (2001). https://doi.org/10.1007/3-540-45251-6_29

14. Godefroid, P., Klarlund, N., Sen, K.: DART: directed automated random testing. In: PLDI, pp. 213–223. ACM (2005)

15. Golagha, M., Lehnhoff, C., Pretschner, A., Ilmberger, H.: Failure clustering without coverage. In: ISSTA, pp. 134–145. ACM (2019)

16. Golagha, M., Pretschner, A., Fisch, D., Nagy, R.: Reducing failure analysis time: an industrial evaluation. In: ICSE-SEIP, pp. 293–302. IEEE (2017)

17. Golagha, M., Raisuddin, A.M., Mittag, L., Hellhake, D., Pretschner, A.: Aletheia: a failure diagnosis toolchain. In: ICSE (Companion Volume), pp. 13–16. ACM (2018)

18. Groce, A.: Error explanation with distance metrics. In: Jensen, K., Podelski, A. (eds.) TACAS 2004. LNCS, vol. 2988, pp. 108–122. Springer, Heidelberg (2004). https://doi.org/10.1007/978-3-540-24730-2_8

19. Groce, A., Visser, W.: What went wrong: explaining counterexamples. In: Ball, T., Rajamani, S.K. (eds.) SPIN 2003. LNCS, vol. 2648, pp. 121–136. Springer, Heidelberg (2003). https://doi.org/10.1007/3-540-44829-2_8

20. Guo, L., Roychoudhury, A., Wang, T.: Accurately choosing execution runs for software fault localization. In: Mycroft, A., Zeller, A. (eds.) CC 2006. LNCS, vol. 3923, pp. 80–95. Springer, Heidelberg (2006). https://doi.org/10.1007/11688839_7

21. Haase, V.: Real-time behavior of programs. IEEE Trans. Softw. Eng. SE. **7**(5), 494–501 (1981)

22. Harder, M., Mellen, J., Ernst, M.D.: Improving test suites via operational abstraction. In: ICSE, pp. 60–73. IEEE (2003)

23. Haslbeck, M.P.L., Nipkow, T.: Hoare logics for time bounds. In: Beyer, D., Huisman, M. (eds.) TACAS 2018. LNCS, vol. 10805, pp. 155–171. Springer, Cham (2018). https://doi.org/10.1007/978-3-319-89960-2_9

24. Hooman, J.: Extending Hoare logic to real-time. Formal Aspects Comput. **6**(1), 801–825 (1994). https://doi.org/10.1007/BF01213604

25. ISO: ISO 14229–1:2020 Road vehicles – Unified diagnostic services (UDS) – Part 1: Application layer. Standard ISO 14229–1:2020, International Organization for Standardization, Geneva, CH (2020)

26. Jin, H.S., Ravi, K., Somenzi, F.: Fate and free will in error traces. In: Katoen, J.-P., Stevens, P. (eds.) TACAS 2002. LNCS, vol. 2280, pp. 445–459. Springer, Heidelberg (2002). https://doi.org/10.1007/3-540-46002-0_31

27. Jordan, C.V., Hauer, F., Foth, P., Pretschner, A.: Time-series-based clustering for failure analysis in hardware-in-the-loop setups: an automotive case study. In: ISSRE Workshops, pp. 67–72. IEEE (2020)

28. Jose, M., Majumdar, R.: Cause clue clauses: error localization using maximum satisfiability. In: PLDI, pp. 437–446. ACM (2011)

29. King, J.C.: Symbolic execution and program testing. CACM **19**(7), 385–394 (1976)

30. Leitner, A., Oriol, M., Zeller, A., Ciupa, I., Meyer, B.: Efficient unit test case minimization. In: ASE, pp. 417–420. ACM (2007)

31. Liu, C., Han, J.: Failure proximity: a fault localization-based approach. In: SIG-SOFT FSE, pp. 46–56. ACM (2006)

32. Lyndon, R.: An interpolation theorem in the predicate calculus. Pac. J. Math. **9**, 129–142 (1959)

33. McMillan, K.L.: Interpolation and SAT-based model checking. In: Hunt, W.A., Somenzi, F. (eds.) CAV 2003. LNCS, vol. 2725, pp. 1–13. Springer, Heidelberg (2003). https://doi.org/10.1007/978-3-540-45069-6_1

34. McMillan, K.L.: Interpolation and Model Checking. In: Clarke, E., Henzinger, T., Veith, H., Bloem, R. (eds) Handbook of Model Checking, pp. 421–446. Springer, Cham (2018). https://doi.org/10.1007/978-3-319-10575-8_14

35. de Moura, L., Bjørner, N.: Z3: an efficient SMT solver. In: Ramakrishnan, C.R., Rehof, J. (eds.) TACAS 2008. LNCS, vol. 4963, pp. 337–340. Springer, Heidelberg (2008). https://doi.org/10.1007/978-3-540-78800-3_24

36. Pan, R., Bagherzadeh, M., Ghaleb, T.A., Briand, L.C.: Test case selection and prioritization using machine learning: a systematic literature review. Empir. Softw. Eng. **27**(2), 29 (2022)

37. Pham, V.-T., Khurana, S., Roy, S., Roychoudhury, A.: Bucketing failing tests via symbolic analysis. In: Huisman, M., Rubin, J. (eds.) FASE 2017. LNCS, vol. 10202, pp. 43–59. Springer, Heidelberg (2017). https://doi.org/10.1007/978-3-662-54494-5_3

38. Podelski, A., Schäf, M., Wies, T.: Classifying bugs with interpolants. In: Aichernig, B.K.K., Furia, C.A.A. (eds.) TAP 2016. LNCS, vol. 9762, pp. 151–168. Springer, Cham (2016). https://doi.org/10.1007/978-3-319-41135-4_9

39. Podgurski, A., et al.: Automated support for classifying software failure reports. In: ICSE, pp. 465–477. IEEE (2003)

40. Renieris, M., Reiss, S.P.: Fault localization with nearest neighbor queries. In: ASE, pp. 30–39. IEEE (2003)

41. Rothermel, G., Harrold, M.J., Ostrin, J., Hong, C.: An empirical study of the effects of minimization on the fault detection capabilities of test suites. In: ICSM, pp. 34–43. IEEE (1998)

42. Schäuffele, J., Zurawka, T.: Automotive Software Engineering - Grundlagen, Prozesse, Methoden und Werkzeuge effizient einsetzen (6. Aufl.). Vieweg (2016)

43. Schneider, F.B., Bloom, B., Marzullo, K.: Putting time into proof outlines. In: de Bakker, J.W., Huizing, C., de Roever, W.P., Rozenberg, G. (eds.) REX 1991. LNCS, vol. 600, pp. 618–639. Springer, Heidelberg (1992). https://doi.org/10.1007/BFb0032010

44. Schwartz-Narbonne, D., Oh, C., Schäf, M., Wies, T.: VERMEER: a tool for tracing and explaining faulty C programs. In: ICSE, vol. 2, pp. 737–740. IEEE (2015)

45. Utting, M., Pretschner, A., Legeard, B.: A taxonomy of model-based testing approaches. Softw. Test. Verif. Reliab. **22**(5), 297–312 (2012)

46. Wang, T., Roychoudhury, A.: Automated path generation for software fault local-ization. In: ASE, pp. 347–351. ACM (2005)
47. Wong, W.E., Gao, R., Li, Y., Abreu, R., Wotawa, F.: A survey on software fault localization. IEEE Trans. Softw. Eng. **42**(8), 707–740 (2016)
48. Wong, W.E., Horgan, J.R., London, S., Mathur, A.P.: Effect of test set minimiza-tion on fault detection effectiveness. Softw. Pract. Exp. **28**(4), 347–369 (1998)
49. Wong, W.E., Horgan, J.R., Mathur, A.P., Pasquini, A.: Test set size minimization and fault detection effectiveness: a case study in a space application. J. Syst. Softw. **48**(2), 79–89 (1999)
50. Yoo, S., Harman, M.: Regression testing minimization, selection and prioritization: a survey. Softw. Test. Verification Reliab. **22**(2), 67–120 (2012)
51. Yoo, S., Harman, M., Tonella, P., Susi, A.: Clustering test cases to achieve effective and scalable prioritisation incorporating expert knowledge. In: ISSTA, pp. 201–212. ACM (2009)
52. Zeller, A.: Isolating cause-effect chains from computer programs. In: SIGSOFT FSE, pp. 1–10. ACM (2002)
53. Zhang, X., Gupta, N., Gupta, R.: Locating faults through automated predicate switching. In: ICSE, pp. 272–281. ACM (2006)

Types

Characterizing Functions Mappable over GADTs

Patricia Johann[(✉)] and Pierre Cagne

Appalachian State University, Boone, NC 28608, USA
{johannp,cagnep}@appstate.edu

Abstract. It is well-known that GADTs do not admit standard map functions of the kind supported by ADTs and nested types. In addition, standard map functions are insufficient to distribute their data-changing argument functions over all of the structure present in elements of deep GADTs, even just deep ADTs or nested types. This paper develops an algorithm that characterizes those functions on a (deep) GADT's type arguments that are mappable over its elements. The algorithm takes as input a term t whose type is an instance of a (deep) GADT G, and returns a set of constraints a function must satisfy to be mappable over t. This algorithm, and thus this paper, can in some sense be read as *defining* what it means for a function to be mappable over t: f is mappable over an element t of G precisely when it satisfies the constraints returned when our algorithm is run on t and G. This is significant: to our knowledge, there is no existing definition or other characterization of the intuitive notion of mappability for functions over GADTs.

Keywords: GADTs · Map functions · Initial algebra semantics

1 Introduction

Initial algebra semantics [5] is one of the cornerstones of the modern theory of data types. It has long been known to deliver practical programming tools—such as pattern matching, induction rules, and structured recursion operators—as well as principled reasoning techniques—like relational parametricity [15]—for algebraic data types (ADTs). Initial algebra semantics has also been developed for the syntactic generalization of ADTs known as nested types [6], and it has been shown to deliver analogous tools and techniques for them as well [11]. Generalized algebraic data types (GADTs) [14,16,17] generalize nested types—and thus further generalize ADTs—syntactically:

$$\boxed{\text{ADTs}} \xrightarrow[\text{generalized by}]{\text{syntactically}} \boxed{\text{nested types}} \xrightarrow[\text{generalized by}]{\text{syntactically}} \boxed{\text{GADTs}} \quad (1)$$

Given their ubiquity in modern functional programming, an important open question is whether or not an initial algebra semantics can be defined for GADTs in such a way that a semantic analogue of (1) holds as well.

I. Sergey (Ed.): APLAS 2022, LNCS 13658, pp. 135–154, 2022.
https://doi.org/10.1007/978-3-031-21037-2_7

The standard initial algebra semantics of ADTs provides a functor $D : Set \rightarrow Set$ interpreting each such data type D, where Set is the category of sets and functions between them interpreting types [4]. The construction of D is sufficiently uniform in its set argument to ensure not only that the data constructors of D are interpreted as natural transformations, but also that the standard map function[1]

$$\text{map}_D : \forall A\, B \rightarrow (A \rightarrow B) \rightarrow (D\, A \rightarrow D\, B)$$

for D is interpreted by D's functorial action. The naturality of the interpretations of D's constructors, which captures their polymorphic behavior, is reflected in syntax by the pattern-matching clauses defining map_D on data constructed using them.

As a concrete example, consider the standard data type

$$
\begin{aligned}
&\text{data List : Set} \rightarrow \text{Set where} \\
&\quad \text{nil} \quad : \forall A \rightarrow \text{List A} \\
&\quad \text{cons} : \forall A \rightarrow A \rightarrow \text{List A} \rightarrow \text{List A}
\end{aligned}
\tag{2}
$$

The data type List is interpreted as a functor $List : Set \rightarrow Set$ mapping each set A to the set of finite sequences of elements of A. The data constructor nil is interpreted as the natural transformation whose component at a set A is the function of type $1 \rightarrow List\, A$ mapping the single element of the singleton set 1 to the empty sequence, and the data constructor cons is interpreted as the natural transformation whose component at a set A is the function of type $A \times List\, A \rightarrow List\, A$ mapping the pair $(a, (a_1, \ldots, a_n))$ to $(a, a_1, \ldots, a_n)$. The functorial action of $List$ on a function $f : A \rightarrow B$ is the function of type $List\, A \rightarrow List\, B$ taking a sequence $(a_1, \ldots, a_n)$ to the sequence $(f\, a_1, \ldots, f\, a_n)$. This functorial action indeed interprets the standard map function for lists, defined by pattern matching as follows:

$$
\begin{aligned}
&\text{map}_{List} : \forall A\, B \rightarrow (A \rightarrow B) \rightarrow (List\, A \rightarrow List\, B) \\
&\text{map}_{List}\, f\, \text{nil} = \text{nil} \\
&\text{map}_{List}\, f\, (\text{cons}\, a\, l) = \text{cons}\, (f\, a)\, (\text{map}_{List}\, f\, l)
\end{aligned}
$$

Nested types generalize ADTs by allowing their constructors to take as arguments data whose types involve instances of the nested type other than the one being defined. The return type of each of its data constructors must still be precisely the instance being defined, though. This is illustrated by the following definitions of the nested types PTree of perfect trees and Bush of bushes:

$$
\begin{aligned}
&\text{data PTree : Set} \rightarrow \text{Set where} \\
&\quad \text{pleaf} \quad : \forall A \rightarrow A \rightarrow \text{PTree A} \\
&\quad \text{pnode} : \forall A \rightarrow \text{PTree}\, (A \times A) \rightarrow \text{PTree A}
\end{aligned}
$$

---

[1] Although our results apply to GADTs in any programming language, we use Agda syntax for code in this paper. But while Agda allows type parameters to be implicit, we always write all type parameters explicitly. Throughout, we use sans serif font for code snippets and *italic* font for mathematics (specifically, for meta-variables).

```
data Bush : Set → Set where
  bnil   : ∀ A → Bush A
  bcons  : ∀ A → A → Bush (Bush A) → Bush A
```

A nested type N with at least one data constructor at least one of whose argument types involves an instance of N that itself involves an instance of N is called a *truly nested type*. The type of the data constructor bcons thus witnesses that Bush is a truly nested type. Because the recursive calls to a nested type's type constructor can be at instances of the type other than the one being defined, a nested type thus defines an entire family of types that must be constructed simultaneously. That is, a nested type defines an *inductive family of types*. By contrast, an ADT is usually understood as a *family of inductive types*, one for each choice of its type arguments. This is because every recursive call to an ADT's type constructor must be at the very same instance as the one being defined.

The initial algebra semantics of nested types given in [11] provides a semantic analogue of the first inclusion in (1). Every nested type N has a map function $map_N : ∀ A B → (A → B) → (N A → N B)$, and map_N coincides with the standard map function when N is an ADT. If we think of each element of a nested type N as a "container" for data arranged at various "positions" in the underlying "shape" determined by the data constructors of N used to build it, then, given a function f of type $A → B$, the function $map_N f$ is the expected shape-preserving-but-possibly-data-changing function that transforms an element of N with shape S containing data of type A into another element of N also of shape S but containing data of type B by applying f to each of its elements. The function map_N is interpreted by the functorial action of the functor $N : Set → Set$ interpreting N whose existence is guaranteed by [11]. Like map_N itself, this functor specializes as expected when N is an ADT.

Since GADTs, like nested types, can also be regarded as containers in which data can be stored, we might expect every GADT G to support a shape-preserving-but-possibly-data-changing map function

$$map_G : ∀ A B → (A → B) → (G A → G B) \tag{3}$$

We might also expect to have initial algebra semantics interpreting G's constructors as natural transformations and map_G as the functorial action of the functor interpreting G. But this exception is perhaps too ambitious; see Sect. 5 for a discussion. In particular, a *proper* GADT—i.e., a GADT that is not a nested type (and thus is not an ADT)—need not support a map function as in (3). For example, the GADT[2]

---

[2] The type of Seq is actually $Set → Set_1$, but to aid readability we elide the explicit tracking of Agda universe levels in this paper. The data type Seq may be familiar to Haskell programmers as a fragment of the GADT Term introduced in [14] to represent terms in a simply-typed language. This fragment of Term is enough for the purposes of our discussion.

```
data Seq : Set → Set where
     const : ∀A → A → Seq A
     pair  : ∀A B → Seq A → Seq B → Seq (A × B)
```

of sequences does not. If it did, then the clause of $\mathsf{map_{Seq}}$ for an element of Seq of the form $\mathsf{pair}\,x\,y$ for $x : \mathsf{Seq}\,A$ and $y : \mathsf{Seq}\,B$ would be such that if $f : (A \times B) \to C$ then $\mathsf{map_{Seq}}\,f\,(\mathsf{pair}\,x\,y) = \mathsf{pair}\,u\,v' : \mathsf{Seq}\,C$ for some appropriately typed u and v. But there is no way to achieve this unless C is of the form $A' \times B'$ for some A' and B', $u : \mathsf{Seq}\,A'$ and $v : \mathsf{Seq}\,B'$, and $f = f_1 \times f_2$ for some $f_1 : A \to A'$ and $f_2 : B \to B'$. The non-uniformity in the type-indexing of proper GADTs—which is the very reason a GADT programmer is likely to use GADTs in the first place—thus turns out to be precisely what prevents them from supporting standard map functions.

Although not every function on a proper GADT's type arguments is mappable over its elements, it is nevertheless reasonable to ask: which functions *can* be mapped over an element of a proper GADT in a shape-preserving-but-possibly-data-changing way? To answer this question we first rewrite the type of $\mathsf{map_G}$ in (3) as $\forall A\,B \to G\,A \to (A \to B) \to G\,B$. This rewriting mirrors our observation above that those functions that are mappable over an element of a GADT can *depend* on that element. More precisely, it suggests that the type of the map function for G should actually be

$$\mathsf{map_G} : \forall A\,B \to (e : G\,A) \to (A \to_e B) \to G\,B \qquad (4)$$

where $A \to_e B$ is a type, dependent on an element $e : G\,A$, containing exactly those functions from A to B that can be successfully mapped over e.

In this paper we develop an algorithm characterizing those functions that should be in the type $A \to_e B$. Our algorithm takes as input a term t whose type is (an instance of) a GADT G at type A, and returns a set of constraints a function must satisfy in order to be mappable over t. Our algorithm, and thus this paper, can in some sense be read as *defining* what it means for a function to be mappable over t. This is significant: to our knowledge, there is no existing definition or other characterization of the intuitive notion of mappability for functions over GADTs.

The crux of our algorithm is its ability to separate t's "essential structure" as an element of G—i.e., the part of t that is essential for it to have the shape of an element of G—from its "incidental structure" as an element of G—i.e., the part of t that is simply data in the positions of this shape. The algorithm then ensures that the constraints that must be met in order for f to be mappable come only from t's essential structure as an element of G. The separation of a term into essential and incidental structure is far from trivial, however. In particular, it is considerably more involved than simply inspecting the return types of G's constructors. As for ADTs and other nested types, a subterm built using one of G's data constructors can be an input term to another one (or to itself again). But if G is a proper GADT then such a dependency between constructor inputs and outputs can force structure to be essential in the overall term even though it would be incidental in the subterm if the subterm were considered in isolation, and this can impose constraints on the functions mappable over it. This is illustrated in Examples 2 and 3 below, both of which involve a GADT G whose data constructor pairing can construct a term suitable as input to projpair.

Our algorithm is actually far more flexible than just described. Rather than simply considering t to be an element of the top-level GADT in its type, the algorithm instead takes as an additional argument a *specification*—i.e., a type expression over designated variables—one of whose instances t should be considered an element of. The specification D can either be a "shallow" data type of the form $G\,\beta$ (with designated variable β) indicating that t is to be considered an element of a simple variable instance of G, or a deep[3] data type such as $G\,(G\,\beta)$ (with designated variable β) indicating that t should be considered an element of a more complex instance of G. The algorithm then returns a set of constraints a function must satisfy in order to be mappable over t relative to that given specification. We emphasize that the separation of essential and incidental structure in terms can become quite complicated when D is a deep data type. For example, if D is $G\,(G\,\beta)$ then those functions that are mappable over its relevant subterms relative to $G\,\beta$ must be computed before those that are mappable over the term itself relative to $G\,(G\,\beta)$ can be computed. Runs of our algorithm on deep specifications are given in Examples 5 and 10 below, as well as in our accompanying artifact [7].

Although we use Agda syntax in this paper for convenience, the overarching setting for this work is not intended to be dependent type theory, but rather a language akin to a small pure fragment of Haskell. We deliberately remain language-agnostic, but the intended type system should be an impredicative extension of System F containing a fixpoint operator data_ where as described in (5) and (6) below.

This paper is organized as follows. Motivating examples highlighting the delicacies of the problem our algorithm solves are given in Sect. 2. Our algorithm is given in Sect. 3, and fully worked out sample runs of it are given in Sect. 4. Our conclusions, related work, and some directions for future work are discussed in Sect. 5. An Agda implementation of our algorithm is available at [7], along with a collection of examples on which it has been run. This includes examples involving deep specifications and mutually recursively defined GADTs, as well as other examples that go beyond just the illustrative ones appearing in this paper.

2   The Problem and Its Solution: An Overview

In this section we use well-chosen example instances of the mapping problem for GADTs and deep data structures both to highlight its subtlety and to illustrate the key ideas underlying our algorithm that solves it. For each example considering a function f to be mapped over a term t relative to the essential structure specified by D we explain, intuitively, how to obtain the decomposition of t into

---

[3] An ADT/nested type/GADT is *deep* if it is (possibly mutually inductively) defined in terms of other ADTs/nested types/GADTs (including, possibly, itself). For example, List (List ℕ) is a deep ADT, Bush (List (PTree A)) is a deep nested type, and Seq (PTree A), and List (Seq A) are deep GADTs.

the essential and incidental structure specified by D and what the constraints are that ensure that f is mappable over t relative to it. Example 1 illustrates the fundamental challenge that arises when mapping functions over GADTs. Example 2 and Example 3 highlight the difference between a term's essential structure and its incidental structure. Example 4 and Example 5 show why the specification is an important input to the algorithm. By design, we handle the examples only informally in this section to allow the reader to build intuition. The results obtained by running our algorithm on their formal representations are given in Sect. 4.

Our algorithm will treat all GADTs in the class $\mathcal{G}$, whose elements have the following general form when written in Agda:

$$
\begin{aligned}
&\textsf{data G : Set}^k \to \textsf{Set where}\\
&\quad \textsf{c}_1 : \textsf{t}_1\\
&\qquad \vdots\\
&\quad \textsf{c}_m : \textsf{t}_m
\end{aligned}
\tag{5}
$$

Here, k and m can be any natural numbers, including 0. Writing $\overline{v}$ for a tuple $(v_1, ..., v_l)$ whose length l is clear from context, and identifying a tuple (a) with the element a, each data constructor $\textsf{c}_i$, $i \in \{1, ..., m\}$, has type $\textsf{t}_i$ of the form

$$
\forall \overline{\alpha} \to F_1^{c_i}\overline{\alpha} \to ... \to F_{n_i}^{c_i}\overline{\alpha} \to \textsf{G}\,(K_1^{c_i}\overline{\alpha}, ..., K_k^{c_i}\overline{\alpha})
\tag{6}
$$

Here, for each $j \in \{1, ..., n_i\}$, $F_j^{c_i}\overline{\alpha}$ is either a closed type, or is α_d for some $d \in \{1, ..., |\overline{\alpha}|\}$, or is $\textsf{D}_j^{c_i}\,(\overline{\phi_j^{c_i}\overline{\alpha}})$ for some user-defined data type constructor $\textsf{D}_j^{c_i}$ and tuple $\overline{\phi_j^{c_i}\overline{\alpha}}$ of type expressions at least one of which is not closed. The types $F_j^{c_i}\overline{\alpha}$ must not involve any arrow types. However, each $\textsf{D}_j^{c_i}$ can be any GADT in $\mathcal{G}$, including G itself, and each of the type expressions in $\overline{\phi_j^{c_i}\overline{\alpha}}$ can involve such GADTs as well. On the other hand, for each $\ell \in \{1, ..., k\}$, $K_\ell^{c_i}\overline{\alpha}$ is a type expression whose free variables come from $\overline{\alpha}$, and that involves neither G itself nor any proper GADTs.[4] When $|\overline{\alpha}| = 0$ we suppress the initial quantification over types in (6). All of the GADTs appearing in this paper are in the class $\mathcal{G}$; this class is implemented in the accompanying code [7] as part of type-expr, with formation constraints as described immediately following the definition of _‖_⊢_. All GADTs we are aware of from the literature whose constructors' argument types do not involve arrow types are also in $\mathcal{G}$. Our algorithm is easily extended to GADTs without this restriction provided all arrow types involved are strictly positive.

Our first example picks up the discussion for Seq on page 3. Because the types of the inputs of const and pair are not deep, it is entirely straightforward.

---

[4] Formally, a GADT is a *proper* GADT if it has at least one *restricted data constructor*, i.e., at least one data constructor $\textsf{c}_i$ with type as in (6) for which $K_\ell^{c_i}\overline{\alpha} \neq \overline{\alpha}$ for at least one $\ell \in \{1, ..., k\}$.

Example 1. The functions f mappable over

$$t = \mathsf{pair}\,(\mathsf{pair}\,(\mathsf{const\,tt})\,(\mathsf{const\,2}))\,(\mathsf{const\,5}) : \mathsf{Seq}\,(\,(\mathsf{Bool} \times \mathsf{Int}) \times \mathsf{Int}) \qquad (7)$$

relative to the specification $\mathsf{Seq}\,\beta$ are exactly those of the form $(f_1 \times f_2) \times f_3$ for some $f_1 : \mathsf{Bool} \to X_1$, $f_2 : \mathsf{Int} \to X_2$, and $f_1 : \mathsf{Int} \to X_3$, and some types X_1, X_2, and X_3. Intuitively, this follows from two analyses similar to that on page 3, one for each occurrence of pair in t. Writing the part of a term comprising its essential structure relative to the given specification in blue and the parts of the term comprising its incidental structure in black, our algorithm also deduces the following essential structure for t:

$$\mathsf{pair}\,(\mathsf{pair}\,(\mathsf{const\,tt})\,(\mathsf{const\,2}))\,(\mathsf{const\,5}) : \mathsf{Seq}\,(\,(\mathsf{Bool} \times \mathsf{Int}) \times \mathsf{Int})$$

The next two examples are more involved: G has purposely been crafted so that its data constructor $\mathsf{pairing}$ can construct a term suitable as the second component of a pair whose image by inj can be input to $\mathsf{projpair}$.

Example 2. Consider the GADT

```
data G  :  Set → Set where
   const    : G ℕ
   flat     : ∀ A → List (G A) → G (List A)
   inj      : ∀ A → A → G A
   pairing  : ∀ A B → G A → G B → G (A × B)
   projpair : ∀ A B → G (G A × G (B × B)) → G (A × B)
```

The functions mappable over

$$t = \mathsf{projpair}\,(\ \mathsf{inj}\ (\mathsf{inj}\,(\mathsf{cons\,2\,nil}),\ \mathsf{pairing}\,(\mathsf{inj\,2})\,\mathsf{const})\ ) : \mathsf{G}\,(\mathsf{List\,ℕ} \times \mathsf{ℕ})$$

relative to the specification $\mathsf{G}\,\beta$ are exactly those of the form $f_1 \times \mathsf{id}_ℕ$ for some type X and function $f_1 : \mathsf{List\,ℕ} \to X$. This makes sense intuitively: The call to $\mathsf{projpair}$ requires that a mappable function f must at top level be a product $f_1 \times f_2$ for some f_1 and f_2, and the outermost call to inj imposes no constraints on $f_1 \times f_2$. In addition, the call to inj in the first component of the pair argument to the outermost call to inj imposes no constraints on f_1, and neither does the call to cons or its arguments. On the other hand, the call to $\mathsf{pairing}$ in the second component of the pair argument to the second call to inj must produce a term of type $\mathsf{G}\,(ℕ \times ℕ)$, so the argument 2 to the rightmost call to inj and the call to const require that f_2 is $\mathsf{id}_ℕ$. Critically, it is the naturality of the constructor const that forces f_2 to be $\mathsf{id}_ℕ$ and not just any function of type $ℕ \to ℕ$ here. Our algorithm also deduces the following essential structure for t:

$$\mathsf{projpair}\,(\ \mathsf{inj}\ (\mathsf{inj}\,(\mathsf{cons\,2\,nil}),\ \mathsf{pairing}\,(\mathsf{inj\,2})\,\mathsf{const})\ ) : \mathsf{G}\,(\mathsf{List\,ℕ} \times \mathsf{ℕ}) \qquad (8)$$

Note that, although the argument to projpair decomposes into essential structure and incidental structure as inj (inj (cons 2 nil), pairing (inj 2) const) when considered as a standalone term relative to the specification $G\beta$, the fact that the output of pairing can be an input for projpair ensures that t has the decomposition in (8) relative to $G\beta$ when this argument is considered in the context of projpair. Similar comments apply throughout this paper.

Example 3. The functions f mappable over

$$t = \text{projpair} \; (\; \text{inj} \; (\text{flat} \; (\text{cons const nil}), \; \text{pairing} \; (\text{inj} \; 2) \; \text{const}) \;) : G \; (\text{List} \; \mathbb{N} \; \times \; \mathbb{N})$$

relative to the specification $G\beta$ for G as in Example 2 are exactly those of the form $\text{map}_{\text{List}} \; \text{id}_{\mathbb{N}} \times \text{id}_{\mathbb{N}}$. This makes sense intuitively: The call to projpair requires that a mappable function f must at top level be a product $f_1 \times f_2$ for some f_1 and f_2, and the outermost call to inj imposes no constraints on $f_1 \times f_2$. In addition, the call to flat in the first component of the pair argument to inj requires that f_1 is $\text{map}_{\text{List}} \; f_3$ for some f_3, and the call to cons in flat's argument imposes no constraints on f_3, but the call to const as cons's first argument requires that f_3 is $\text{id}_{\mathbb{N}}$. On the other hand, by the same analysis as in Example 2, the call to pairing in the second component of the pair argument to inj requires that f_2 is $\text{id}_{\mathbb{N}}$. Our algorithm also deduces the following essential structure for t:

$$\text{projpair} \; (\; \text{inj} \; (\text{flat} \; (\text{cons const nil}), \; \text{pairing} \; (\text{inj} \; 2) \; \text{const}) \;) : G \; (\text{List} \; \mathbb{N} \; \times \; \mathbb{N})$$

Again, the fact that the output of pairing can be a input for projpair in the previous two examples highlights the importance of the specification relative to which a term is considered. But this can already be seen for ADTs, which feature no such loops. This is illustrated in Examples 4 and 5 below.

Example 4. The functions f mappable over

$$t = \text{cons} \; (\text{cons} \; 1 \; (\text{cons} \; 2 \; \text{nil})) \; (\text{cons} \; (\text{cons} \; 3 \; \text{nil}) \; \text{nil}) : \text{List} \; (\text{List} \; \mathbb{N})$$

relative to the specification $\text{List} \; \beta$ are exactly those of the form $f : \text{List} \; \mathbb{N} \to X$ for some type X. This makes sense intuitively since any function from the element type of a list to another type is mappable over that list. The function need not satisfy any particular structural constraints. Our algorithm also deduces the following essential structure for t:

$$\text{cons} \; (\text{cons} \; 1 \; (\text{cons} \; 2 \; \text{nil})) \; (\text{cons} \; (\text{cons} \; 3 \; \text{nil}) \; \text{nil})$$

Example 5. The functions f mappable over

$$t = \text{cons} \; (\text{cons} \; 1 \; (\text{cons} \; 2 \; \text{nil})) \; (\text{cons} \; (\text{cons} \; 3 \; \text{nil}) \; \text{nil}) : \text{List} \; (\text{List} \; \mathbb{N})$$

relative to the specification $\mathsf{List}\,(\mathsf{List}\,\beta)$ are exactly those of the form $\mathsf{map}_{\mathsf{List}}\,f'$ for some type X' and function $f' : \mathbb{N} \to X'$. This makes sense intuitively: The fact that any function from the element type of a list to another type is mappable over that list requires that $f : \mathsf{List}\,\mathbb{N} \to X$ for some type X as in Example 4. But if the internal list structure of t is also to be preserved when f is mapped over it, as indicated by the essential structure $\mathsf{List}\,(\mathsf{List}\,\beta)$, then X must itself be of the form $\mathsf{List}\,X'$ for some type X'. This, in turn, entails that f is $\mathsf{map}_{\mathsf{List}}\,f'$ for some $f' : \mathbb{N} \to X'$. Our algorithm also deduces the following essential structure for t:

$$\mathsf{cons}\,(\mathsf{cons}\,1\,(\mathsf{cons}\,2\,\mathsf{nil}))\,(\mathsf{cons}\,(\mathsf{cons}\,3\,\mathsf{nil})\,\mathsf{nil}) : \mathsf{List}\,(\mathsf{List}\,\mathbb{N})$$

The specification $\mathsf{List}\,(\mathsf{List}\,\beta)$ determining the essential structure in Example 5 is deep *by instantiation*, rather than *by definition*. That is, inner occurrence of List in this specification is not forced by the definition of the data type List that specifies its top-level structure. The quintessential example of a data type that is deep by definition is the ADT

$$\begin{aligned}
\mathsf{data}\ \mathsf{Rose}\ &:\ \mathsf{Set} \to \mathsf{Set}\ \mathsf{where}\\
\mathsf{rnil}\ &:\ \forall A \to \mathsf{Rose}\,A\\
\mathsf{rnode}\ &:\ \forall A \to A \to \mathsf{List}\,(\mathsf{Rose}\,A) \to \mathsf{Rose}\,A
\end{aligned}$$

of rose trees, whose data constructor rnode takes as input an element of Rose at an instance of another ADT. Reasoning analogous to that in the examples above suggests that no structural constraints should be required to map appropriately typed functions over terms whose specifications are given by nested types that are deep by definition. We will see in Example 9 that, although the runs of our algorithm are not trivial on such input terms, this is indeed the case.

With more tedious algorithmic bookkeeping, results similar to those of the above examples can be obtained for data types—e.g., $\mathsf{Bush}\,(\mathsf{List}\,(\mathsf{PTree}\,A))$, $\mathsf{Seq}\,(\mathsf{PTree}\,A)$, and $\mathsf{List}\,(\mathsf{Seq}\,A)$—that are deep by instantiation [7].

3   The Algorithm

In this section we give our algorithm characterizing the functions that are mappable over GADTs. The algorithm adm takes as input a data structure t, a tuple of type expressions $\overline{f}$ representing functions to be mapped over t, and a specification Φ. Recall from the introduction that a *specification* is a type expression over designated variables in the ambient type calculus. It recursively traverses the term t recording the set C of constraints $\overline{f}$ must satisfy in order to be mappable over t viewed as an element of an instance of Φ. The elements of C are ordered pairs of the form $\langle\_,\_\rangle$, whose components are compatible in the sense made precise in the paragraphs immediately following the algorithm. A call

$$\mathsf{adm}\ t\ \overline{f}\ \Phi$$

is made only if there exists a tuple $(\Sigma_1\overline{\beta}, ..., \Sigma_k\overline{\beta})$ of type expressions such that

- $\Phi = \mathsf{G}(\Sigma_1\overline{\beta}, ..., \Sigma_k\overline{\beta})$ for some data type constructor $\mathsf{G} \in \mathcal{G} \cup \{\times, +\}$ and some type expressions $\Sigma_\ell\overline{\beta}$, for $\ell \in \{1, ..., k\}$

and

- if $\Phi = \times(\Sigma_1\overline{\beta}, \Sigma_2\overline{\beta})$, then $t = (t_1, t_2)$, and $k = 2$, $\overline{f} = (f_1, f_2)$
- if $\Phi = +(\Sigma_1\overline{\beta}, \Sigma_2\overline{\beta})$ and $t = \mathsf{inl}\, t_1$, then $k = 2$, $\overline{f} = (f_1, f_2)$
- if $\Phi = +(\Sigma_1\overline{\beta}, \Sigma_2\overline{\beta})$ and $t = \mathsf{inr}\, t_2$, then $k = 2$, $\overline{f} = (f_1, f_2)$
- if $\Phi = \mathsf{G}(\Sigma_1\overline{\beta}, ..., \Sigma_k\overline{\beta})$ for some $\mathsf{G} \in \mathcal{G}$ then
    1) $t = \mathsf{c}\, t_1...t_n$ for some appropriately typed terms $t_1, ..., t_n$ and some data constructor c for G with type of the form in (6),
    2) $t : \mathsf{G}(K_1^{\mathsf{c}}\overline{w}, ..., K_k^{\mathsf{c}}\overline{w})$ for some tuple $\overline{w} = (w_1, ..., w_{|\overline{\alpha}|})$ of type expressions, and $\mathsf{G}(K_1^{\mathsf{c}}\overline{w}, ..., K_k^{\mathsf{c}}\overline{w})$ is exactly $\mathsf{G}(\Sigma_1\overline{s}, ..., \Sigma_k\overline{s})$ for some tuple $\overline{s} = (s_1, ..., s_{|\overline{\beta}|})$ of types, and
    3) for each $\ell \in \{1, ..., k\}$, f_ℓ has domain $K_\ell^{\mathsf{c}}\overline{w}$

These invariants will be preserved by each recursive call to adm below.

The free variables in the type expressions $\Sigma_\ell\overline{\beta}$ for $\ell \in \{1, ..., k\}$ can be taken to be *among* the variables in $\overline{\beta}$, since the calls adm t $\overline{f}$ $\mathsf{G}(\Sigma_1\overline{\beta}, ..., \Sigma_k\overline{\beta})$ and adm t $\overline{f}$ $\mathsf{G}(\Sigma_1\overline{\beta^+}, ..., \Sigma_k\overline{\beta^+})$ return the same set C (up to renaming) whenever $\overline{\beta}$ is a subtuple of the tuple $\overline{\beta^+}$. We can therefore take $\overline{\beta}$ to have minimal length.

The algorithm is given as follows by enumerating each of its legal calls. Each call begins by initializing a set C of constraints to $\emptyset$.

A. adm (t_1, t_2) (f_1, f_2) $\times(\Sigma_1\overline{\beta}, \Sigma_2\overline{\beta})$
    1. Introduce a tuple $\overline{g} = g_1, ..., g_{|\overline{\beta}|}$ of fresh variables, and add the constraints $\langle \Sigma_1\overline{g}, f_1 \rangle$ and $\langle \Sigma_2\overline{g}, f_2 \rangle$ to C.
    2. For $j \in \{1, 2\}$, if $\Sigma_j\overline{\beta} = \beta_i$ for some i then do nothing and go to the next j if there is one. Otherwise, $\Sigma_j\overline{\beta} = \mathsf{D}(\zeta_1\overline{\beta}, ..., \zeta_r\overline{\beta})$, where D is a data type constructor in $\mathcal{G} \cup \{\times, +\}$ of arity r, so make the recursive call adm t_j $(\zeta_1\overline{g}, ..., \zeta_r\overline{g})$ $\mathsf{D}(\zeta_1\overline{\beta}, ..., \zeta_r\overline{\beta})$ and add the resulting constraints to C.
    3. Return C.
B. adm $(\mathsf{inl}\, t)$ (f_1, f_2) $+(\Sigma_1\overline{\beta}, \Sigma_2\overline{\beta})$
    1. Introduce a tuple $\overline{g} = (g_1, ..., g_{|\overline{\beta}|})$ of fresh variables, and add the constraints $\langle \Sigma_1\overline{g}, f_1 \rangle$ and $\langle \Sigma_2\overline{g}, f_2 \rangle$ to C.
    2. If $\Sigma_1\overline{\beta} = \beta_i$ for some i then do nothing. Otherwise, $\Sigma_1\overline{\beta} = \mathsf{D}(\zeta_1\overline{\beta}, ..., \zeta_r\overline{\beta})$, where D is a data type constructor in $\mathcal{G} \cup \{\times, +\}$ of arity r, so make the recursive call adm t $(\zeta_1\overline{g}, ..., \zeta_r\overline{g})$ $\mathsf{D}(\zeta_1\overline{\beta}, ..., \zeta_r\overline{\beta})$ and add the resulting constraints to C.
    3. Return C.
C. adm $(\mathsf{inr}\, t)$ (f_1, f_2) $+(\Sigma_1\overline{\beta}, \Sigma_2\overline{\beta})$
    1. Introduce a tuple $\overline{g} = (g_1, ..., g_{|\overline{\beta}|})$ of fresh variables, and add the constraints $\langle \Sigma_1\overline{g}, f_1 \rangle$ and $\langle \Sigma_2\overline{g}, f_2 \rangle$ to C.
    2. If $\Sigma_2\overline{\beta} = \beta_i$ for some i then do nothing. Otherwise, $\Sigma_2\overline{\beta} = \mathsf{D}(\zeta_1\overline{\beta}, ..., \zeta_r\overline{\beta})$, where D is a data type constructor in $\mathcal{G} \cup \{\times, +\}$ of arity r, so make the recursive call adm t $(\zeta_1\overline{g}, ..., \zeta_r\overline{g})$ $\mathsf{D}(\zeta_1\overline{\beta}, ..., \zeta_r\overline{\beta})$ and add the resulting constraints to C.

3. Return C.

D. $\mathsf{adm}\,(c\,t_1,...,t_n)\,(f_1,...,f_k)\,\mathsf{G}\,(\Sigma_1\overline{\beta},...,\Sigma_k\overline{\beta})$

1. Introduce a tuple $\overline{g} = (g_1,...,g_{|\overline{\beta}|})$ of fresh variables and add the constraints $\langle \Sigma_\ell \overline{g}, f_\ell \rangle$ to C for each $\ell \in \{1,...,k\}$.

2. If $c\,t_1,...,t_n : \mathsf{G}\,(K_1^c\overline{w},...,K_k^c\overline{w})$ for some tuple $\overline{w} = (w_1,...,w_{|\overline{\alpha}|})$ of types, let $\overline{\gamma} = (\gamma_1,...,\gamma_{|\overline{\alpha}|})$ be a tuple of fresh type variables and solve the system of matching problems

$$\Sigma_1\overline{\beta} \equiv K_1^c\overline{\gamma}$$
$$\Sigma_2\overline{\beta} \equiv K_2^c\overline{\gamma}$$
$$\vdots$$
$$\Sigma_k\overline{\beta} \equiv K_k^c\overline{\gamma}$$

to get a set of assignments, each of the form $\beta \equiv \psi\overline{\gamma}$ or $\sigma\overline{\beta} \equiv \gamma$ for some type expression ψ or σ. This yields a (possibly empty) tuple of assignments $\overline{\beta_i \equiv \psi_i\overline{\gamma}}$ for each $i \in \{1,...,|\overline{\beta}|\}$, and a (possibly empty) tuple of assignments $\overline{\sigma_{i'}\overline{\beta} \equiv \gamma_{i'}}$ for each $i' \in \{1,...,|\overline{\gamma}|\}$. Write $\beta_i \equiv \psi_{i,p}\overline{\gamma}$ for the pth component of the former and $\sigma_{i',q}\overline{\beta} \equiv \gamma_{i'}$ for the qth component of the latter. An assignment $\beta_i \equiv \gamma_{i'}$ can be seen as having form $\beta_i \equiv \psi\overline{\gamma}_{i'}$ or form $\sigma\overline{\beta}_i \equiv \gamma_{i'}$, but always choose the latter representation. (This is justified because adm would return an equivalent set of assignments— i.e., a set of assignments yielding the same requirements on $\overline{f}$—were the former chosen. The latter is chosen because it may decrease the number of recursive calls to adm.)

3. For each $i' \in \{1,\ldots,|\overline{\gamma}|\}$, define $\tau_{i'}\overline{\beta}\overline{\gamma}$ to be either $\sigma_{i',1}\overline{\beta}$ if this exists, or $\gamma_{i'}$ otherwise.

4. Introduce a tuple $\overline{h} = (h_1,...,h_{|\overline{\gamma}|})$ of fresh variables for $i' \in \{1,...,|\overline{\gamma}|\}$.

5. For each $i \in \{1,\ldots,|\overline{\beta}|\}$ and each constraint $\beta_i \equiv \psi_{i,p}\overline{\gamma}$, add the constraint $\langle \psi_{i,p}\overline{h}, g_i \rangle$ to C.

6. For each $i' \in \{1,\ldots,|\overline{\gamma}|\}$ and each constraint $\sigma_{i',q}\overline{\beta} \equiv \gamma_{i'}$ with $q > 1$, add the constraint $\langle \sigma_{i',q}\overline{g}, \sigma_{i',1}\overline{g} \rangle$ to C.

7. For each $j \in \{1,\ldots,n\}$, let $R_j = F_j^c(\tau_1\overline{\beta}\overline{\gamma},...,\tau_{|\overline{\gamma}|}\overline{\beta}\overline{\gamma})$.
   - if R_j is a closed type, then do nothing and go to the next j if there is one.
   - if $R_j = \beta_i$ for some i or $R_j = \gamma_{i'}$ for some i', then do nothing and go to the next j if there is one.
   - otherwise $R_j = \mathsf{D}\,(\zeta_{j,1}\overline{\beta}\overline{\gamma},...,\zeta_{j,r}\overline{\beta}\overline{\gamma})$, where D is a type constructor in $\mathcal{G} \cup \{\times,+\}$ of arity r, so make the recursive call

$$\mathsf{adm}\,t_j\,(\zeta_{j,1}\overline{g}\overline{h},...,\zeta_{j,r}\overline{g}\overline{h})\,R_j$$

and add the resulting constraints to C.

8. Return C.

We note that the matching problems in Step D.2 above do indeed lead to a set of assignments of the specified form. Indeed, since invariant 2) on page 10 ensures that $\mathsf{G}\,(K_1^c\overline{w}, ..., K_k^c\overline{w})$ is exactly $\mathsf{G}\,(\Sigma_1\overline{s}, ..., \Sigma_k\overline{s})$, each matching problem $\Sigma_\ell\overline{\beta} \equiv K_\ell\overline{\gamma}$ whose left- or right-hand side is not already just one of the βs or one of the γs must necessarily have left- and right-hand sides that are *top-unifiable* [8], i.e., have identical symbols at every position that is a non-variable position in both terms. These symbols can be simultaneously peeled away from the left- and right-hand sides to decompose each matching problem into a unifiable set of assignments of one of the two forms specified in Step D.2. We emphasize that the set of assignments is not itself unified in the course of running adm.

It is only once adm is run that the set of constraints it returns is to be solved. Each such constraint must be either of the form $\langle\Sigma_\ell\overline{g}, f_\ell\rangle$, of the form $\langle\psi_{i,p}\overline{h}, g_i\rangle$, or of the form $\langle\sigma_{i',q}\overline{g}, \sigma_{i',1}\overline{g}\rangle$. Each constraint of the first form must have top-unifiable left- and right-hand components by virtue of invariant 2) on page 10. It can therefore be decomposed in a manner similar to that described in the preceding paragraph to arrive at a unifiable set of constraints. Each constraint of the second form simply assigns a replacement expression $\psi_{i,p}\overline{h}$ to each newly introduced variable g_i. Each constraint of the third form must again have top-unifiable left- and right-hand components. Once again, invariant 2) on page 10 ensures that these constraints are decomposable into a unifiable set of constraints specifying replacements for the gs.

Performing first-order unification on the entire system of constraints resulting from the decompositions specified above, and choosing to replace more recently introduced gs and hs with ones introduced later whenever possible, yields a *solved system* comprising exactly one binding for each of the fs in terms of those later-occurring variables. These bindings actually determine the collection of functions mappable over the input term to adm relative to the specification Φ. It is not hard to see that our algorithm delivers the expected results for ADTs and nested types (when Φ is the type itself), namely, that all appropriately typed functions are mappable over each elements of such types. (See Theorem 1 below.) But since there is no already *existing* understanding of which functions should be mappable over the elements of GADTs, we actually regard the solved system's bindings for the fs as *defining* the class of functions mappable over a given element of a GADT relative to a specification Φ.

Theorem 1. *Let* N *be a nested type of arity* k *in* $\mathcal{G}$, *let* $\overline{w} = (w_1, \ldots, w_k)$ *comprise instances of nested types in* $\mathcal{G}$, *let* $t : \mathsf{N}\,\overline{w}$ *where* $\mathsf{N}\,\overline{w}$ *contains* n *free type variables, let* $\overline{\beta} = (\beta_1, \ldots, \beta_n)$, *and let* $\mathsf{N}\,(\Sigma_1\overline{\beta}, \ldots, \Sigma_k\overline{\beta})$ *be in* $\mathcal{G}$. *The solved system resulting from the call*

$$\mathsf{adm}\ t\ (\Sigma_1\overline{f}, \ldots, \Sigma_k\overline{f})\ \mathsf{N}\,(\Sigma_1\overline{\beta}, \ldots, \Sigma_k\overline{\beta})$$

for $\overline{f} = (f_1, \ldots, f_n)$ *has the form* $\bigcup_{i=1}^n\{\langle g_{i,1}, f_i\rangle, \langle g_{i,2}, g_{i,1}\rangle, \ldots, \langle g_{i,r_i-1}, g_{i,r_i}\rangle\}$, *where each* $r_i \in \mathbb{N}$ *and the* $g_{i,j}$ *are pairwise distinct variables. It thus imposes no constraints on the functions mappable over elements of nested types.*

Proof. The proof is by cases on the form of the given call to adm. The constraints added to $\mathcal{C}$ if this call is of the form A, B, or C are all of the form $\langle \Sigma_j \overline{g}, \Sigma_j \overline{f} \rangle$ for $j = 1, 2$, and the recursive calls made are all of the form adm t' $(\zeta_1 \overline{g}, ..., \zeta_r \overline{g})$ D$(\zeta_1 \overline{\beta}, ..., \zeta_r \overline{\beta})$ for some t', some $(\zeta_1, ..., \zeta_r)$, and some nested type D. Now suppose the given call is of the form D. Then Step D.1 adds the constraints $\langle \Sigma_i \overline{g}, \Sigma_i \overline{f} \rangle$ for $i = 1, ..., k$ to $\mathcal{C}$. In Step D.2, $|\overline{\alpha}| = k$, and $K_i^c \overline{w} = w_i$ for $i = 1, ..., k$ for every data constructor c for every nested type, so that the matching problems to be solved are $\Sigma_i \overline{\beta} \equiv \gamma_i$ for $i = 1, ..., k$. In Step D.3 we therefore have $\tau_i \overline{\beta \gamma} = \Sigma_i \overline{\beta}$ for $i = 1, ..., k$. No constraints involving the variables $\overline{h}$ introduced in Step D.4 are added to $\mathcal{C}$ in Step D.5, and no constraints are added to $\mathcal{C}$ in Step D.6 since the γs are all fresh and therefore pairwise distinct. For each R_j that is of the form D$(\zeta_{j,1} \overline{\beta \gamma}, ..., \zeta_{j,r} \overline{\beta \gamma})$, where D is a nested type, the recursive call added to $\mathcal{C}$ in Step D.7 is of the form adm t_j $(\zeta_{j,1} \overline{gh}, ..., \zeta_{j,r} \overline{gh})$ D$(\zeta_{j,1} \overline{\beta \gamma}, ..., \zeta_{j,r} \overline{\beta \gamma})$, which is again of the same form as in the statement of the theorem. For R_js not of this form there are no recursive calls, so nothing is added to $\mathcal{C}$. Hence, by induction on the first argument to adm, all of the constraints added to $\mathcal{C}$ are of the form $\langle \Psi \overline{\phi}, \Psi \overline{\psi} \rangle$ for some type expression Ψ and some ϕs and ψs, where the ϕs and ψs are all pairwise distinct from one another.

Each constraint of the form $\langle \Psi \overline{\phi}, \Psi \overline{\psi} \rangle$ is top-unifiable and thus leads to a sequence of assignments of the form $\langle \phi_i, \psi_i \rangle$. Moreover, the fact that $\tau_i \overline{\beta \gamma} = \Sigma_i \overline{\beta}$ in Step D.3 ensures that no hs appear in any $\zeta_{j,i} \overline{gh}$, so the solved constraints introduced by each recursive call can have as their right-hand sides only gs introduced in the call from which they spawned. It is not hard to see that the entire solved system resulting from the original call must comprise the assignments $\langle g_{1,1}, f_1 \rangle, ..., \langle g_{1,n}, f_n \rangle$ from the top-level call, as well as the assignments $\langle g_{j_i+1,1}, g_{j_i,1} \rangle, ..., \langle g_{j_i+1,n}, g_{j_i,n} \rangle$, for $j_i = 0, ..., m_i - 1$ and $i = 1, ..., n$, where m_i is determined by the subtree of recursive calls spawned by f_i. Re-grouping this "breadth-first" collection of assignments "depth-first" by the trace of each f_i for $i = 1, ..., n$, we get a solved system of the desired form.

4   Examples

Example 6. For t as in Example 1, the call   adm t f Seq β_1 results in the sequence of calls:

call 1	adm	t	f	Seq β_1
call 2.1	adm	pair (const tt) (const 2)	h_1^1	Seq γ_1^1
call 2.2	adm	const 5	h_2^1	Seq γ_2^1
call 2.1.1	adm	const tt	$h_1^{2.1}$	Seq $\gamma_1^{2.1}$
call 2.1.2	adm	const 2	$h_2^{2.1}$	Seq $\gamma_2^{2.1}$

The steps of adm corresponding to these calls are given in the table below, with the most important components of these steps listed explicitly:

Step no.	Matching problems	$\bar{\tau}$	$\bar{R}$	ζ	Constraints added to C
1	$\beta_1 \equiv \gamma_1^1 \times \gamma_2^1$	$\tau_1\beta_1\gamma_1^1\gamma_2^1 = \gamma_1^1$ $\tau_2\beta_1\gamma_1^1\gamma_2^1 = \gamma_2^1$	$R_1 = \text{Seq}\,\gamma_1^1$ $R_2 = \text{Seq}\,\gamma_2^1$	$\zeta_{1,1}\beta_1\gamma_1^1\gamma_2^1 = \gamma_1^1$ $\zeta_{2,1}\beta_1\gamma_1^1\gamma_2^1 = \gamma_2^1$	$\langle g_1^1, f\rangle$ $\langle h_1^1 \times h_2^1, g_1^1\rangle$
2.1	$\gamma_1^1 \equiv \gamma_1^{2.1} \times \gamma_2^{2.1}$	$\tau_1\gamma_1^1\gamma_1^{2.1}\gamma_2^{2.1} = \gamma_1^{2.1}$ $\tau_2\gamma_1^1\gamma_1^{2.1}\gamma_2^{2.1} = \gamma_2^{2.1}$	$R_1 = \text{Seq}\,\gamma_1^{2.1}$ $R_2 = \text{Seq}\,\gamma_2^{2.1}$	$\zeta_{1,1}\gamma_1^1\gamma_1^{2.1}\gamma_2^{2.1} = \gamma_4^{2.1}$ $\zeta_{2,1}\gamma_1^1\gamma_1^{2.1}\gamma_2^{2.1} = \gamma_2^{2.1}$	$\langle g_1^{2.1}, h_1^1\rangle$ $\langle h_2^{2.1} \times h_2^{2.1}, g_1^{2.1}\rangle$
2.2	$\gamma_1^2 \equiv \gamma_1^{2.2}$	$\tau_1\gamma_2^1\gamma_1^{2.2} = \gamma_2^1$	$R_1 = \gamma_2^1$		$\langle g_1^{2.2}, h_2^1\rangle$
2.1.1	$\gamma_1^{2.1} \equiv \gamma_1^{2.1.1}$	$\tau_1\gamma_1^{2.1}\gamma_1^{2.1.1} = \gamma_1^{2.1}$	$R_1 = \gamma_1^{2.1}$		$\langle g_1^{2.1.1}, h_1^{2.1}\rangle$
2.1.2	$\gamma_2^{2.1} \equiv \gamma_1^{2.1.2}$	$\tau_1\gamma_2^{2.1}\gamma_1^{2.1.2} = \gamma_2^{2.1}$	$R_1 = \gamma_2^{2.1}$		$\langle g_1^{2.1.2}, h_2^{2.1}\rangle$

Since the solution to the generated set of constraints requires that f has the form $(g_1^{2.1.1} \times g_1^{1.2.1}) \times g_1^{2.2}$, we conclude that the most general functions mappable over t relative to the specification $\text{Seq}\,\beta_1$ are those of the form $(f_1 \times f_2) \times f_3$ for some types X_1, X_2, and X_3 and functions $f_1 : \text{Bool} \to X_1$, $f_2 : \text{Int} \to X_2$, and $f_3 : \text{Int} \to X_3$. This is precisely the result obtained informally in Example 1.

Example 7. For G and t as in Example 2 the call $\;\text{adm}\;t\;\;f\;\;\text{G}\,\beta_1\;$ results in the sequence of calls:

call 1	adm	t	f	$\text{G}\beta_1$
call 2	adm	t_2	$\text{G}h_1^1 \times \text{G}(h_2^1 \times h_2^1)$	$\text{G}(\text{G}\gamma_1^1 \times \text{G}(\gamma_2^1 \times \gamma_2^1))$
call 3	adm	t_3	$(\text{G}g_1^2, \text{G}(g_2^2 \times g_2^2))$	$\text{G}\gamma_1^1 \times \text{G}(\gamma_2^1 \times \gamma_2^1)$
call 4.1	adm	inj (cons 2 nil)	g_1^3	$\text{G}\gamma_1^2$
call 4.2	adm	pairing (inj 2) const	$g_2^3 \times g_2^3$	$\text{G}(\gamma_2^2 \times \gamma_2^2)$
call 4.2.1	adm	inj 2	$g_1^{4.2}$	$\text{G}\gamma_2^2$
call 4.2.2	adm	const	$g_1^{4.2}$	$\text{G}\gamma_2^2$

where
$$t = \text{projpair } (\text{ inj } (\text{ inj } (\text{cons 2 nil}), \text{ pairing } (\text{inj} 2)\text{ const }))$$
$$t_2 = \text{inj } (\text{ inj } (\text{cons 2 nil}), \text{ pairing } (\text{inj} 2)\text{ const })$$
$$t_3 = (\text{ inj } (\text{cons 2 nil}), \text{ pairing } (\text{inj} 2)\text{ const })$$

The steps of adm corresponding to these calls are given in Table 1, with the most important components of these steps listed explicitly. Since the solution to the generated set of constraints requires that f has the form $g_1^{4.1} \times \mathbb{N}$, we conclude that the most general functions mappable over t relative to the specification $\text{G}\,\beta_1$ are those of the form $f' \times \text{id}_\mathbb{N}$ for some type X and some function $f' : \text{List}\,\mathbb{N} \to X$. This is precisely the result obtained intuitively in Example 2.

Example 8. For G and t as in Example 3 we have
$$\begin{aligned} K^{\text{const}} &= \mathbb{N} \\ K^{\text{flat}}\,\alpha &= \text{List}\,\alpha \\ K^{\text{inj}}\,\alpha &= \alpha \\ K^{\text{pairing}}\,\alpha_1\,\alpha_2 &= \alpha_1 \times \alpha_2 \\ K^{\text{projpair}}\,\alpha_1\,\alpha_2 &= \alpha_1 \times \alpha_2 \end{aligned}$$

Table 1. Calls for Example 7

call no.	matching problems	$\bar{\tau}$	$\bar{R}$	ζ	constraints added to C
1	$\beta_1 \equiv \gamma_1^1 \times \gamma_1^1$	$\tau_1\beta_1\gamma_1^1\gamma_2^1 = \gamma_1^1$ $\tau_2\beta_1\gamma_1^1\gamma_2^1 = \gamma_2^1$	$R_1 = G(G\gamma_1^1 \times G(\gamma_2^1 \times \gamma_2^1))$	$\zeta_{1,1}\beta_1\gamma_1^1\gamma_2 = G\gamma_1^1 \times G(\gamma_2^1 \times \gamma_2^1)$	$\langle g_1^1, f \rangle$ $\langle h_1^1 \times h_2, g_1^1 \rangle$
2	$G\gamma_1^1 \times G(\gamma_2^1 \times \gamma_2^1) \equiv \gamma_1^1$	$\tau_1\gamma_1^1\gamma_2^1\gamma_1^2 = G\gamma_1^1$ $\tau_1\gamma_1^1\gamma_2^1\gamma_1^2 = G(\gamma_2^1 \times \gamma_2^1)$	$R_1 = G\gamma_1^1 \times G(\gamma_2^1 \times \gamma_2^1)$	$\zeta_{1,1}\gamma_1^1\gamma_2^1\gamma_1^2 = G\gamma_1^1$ $\zeta_{1,2}\gamma_1^1\gamma_2^1\gamma_1^2 = G(\gamma_2^1 \times \gamma_2^1)$	$\langle Gg_1^2 \times G(g_2^2 \times g_2^2), Gh_1^1 \times G(h_2^1 \times h_2) \rangle$
3				$\zeta_1\gamma_1^2\gamma_2^2 = \gamma_1^2$ $\zeta_2\gamma_1^2\gamma_2^2 = \gamma_2^2 \times \gamma_2^2$	$\langle Gg_1^3, Gg_1^2 \rangle$ $\langle G(g_2^3 \times g_2^3), G(g_2^2 \times g_2^2) \rangle$
4.1	$\gamma_1^2 \equiv \gamma_1^{4.1}$	$\tau_1\gamma_1^2\gamma_1^{4.1} = \gamma_1^1$	$R_1 = \gamma_1^2$		$\langle g_1^{2.1}, g_1^1 \rangle$
4.2	$\gamma_2^2 \equiv \gamma_1^{4.2} \times \gamma_2^{4.2}$	$\tau_1\gamma_2^2\gamma_1^{4.2}\gamma_2^{4.2} = \gamma_1^2$ $\tau_2\gamma_2^2\gamma_1^{4.2}\gamma_2^{4.2} = \gamma_2^2$	$R_1 = G\gamma_1^2$ $R_2 = G\gamma_2^2$	$\zeta_{1,1}\gamma_1^2\gamma_2^2{}^{4.2} = \gamma_2^2$ $\zeta_{2,1}\gamma_1^2\gamma_2^2{}^{4.2} = \gamma_2^2$	$\langle g_1^{4.2}, g_1^1, g_2^3 \times g_2^3 \rangle$
4.2.1	$\gamma_2^2 \equiv \gamma_1^{4.2.1}$	$\tau_1\gamma_2^2\gamma_1^{4.2.1} = \gamma_2^2$	$R_1 = \gamma_2^2$		$\langle g_1^{4.2.1}, g_1^{4.2} \rangle$
4.2.2	$\gamma_2^2 \equiv N$		$R_1 = 1$		$\langle g_1^{4.2.2}, g_1^{4.2} \rangle$ $\langle N, g_1^{4.2.2} \rangle$

Table 2. Calls for Example 8

call no.	matching problems	$\bar{\tau}$	$\bar{R}$	ζ	constraints added to C
1	$\beta_1 \equiv \gamma_1^1 \times \gamma_1^1$	$\tau_1\beta_1\gamma_1^1\gamma_2^1 = \gamma_1^1$ $\tau_2\beta_1\gamma_1^1\gamma_2^1 = \gamma_2^1$	$R_1 = G(G\gamma_1^1 \times G(\gamma_2^1 \times \gamma_2^1))$	$\zeta_{1,1}\beta_1\gamma_1^1\gamma_2 = G\gamma_1^1 \times G(\gamma_2^1 \times \gamma_2^1)$	$\langle g_1^1, f \rangle$ $\langle h_1^1 \times h_2, g_1^1 \rangle$
2	$G\gamma_1^1 \times G(\gamma_2^1 \times \gamma_2^1) \equiv \gamma_1^1$	$\tau_1\gamma_1^1\gamma_2^1\gamma_1^2 = G\gamma_1^1$ $\tau_1\gamma_1^1\gamma_2^1\gamma_1^2 = G(\gamma_2^1 \times \gamma_2^1)$	$R_1 = G\gamma_1^1 \times G(\gamma_2^1 \times \gamma_2^1)$	$\zeta_{1,1}\gamma_1^1\gamma_2^1\gamma_1^2 = G\gamma_1^1$ $\zeta_{1,2}\gamma_1^1\gamma_2^1\gamma_1^2 = G(\gamma_2^1 \times \gamma_2^1)$	$\langle Gg_1^2 \times G(g_2^2 \times g_2^2), Gh_1^1 \times G(h_2^1 \times h_2) \rangle$
3				$\zeta_1\gamma_1^2\gamma_2^2 = \gamma_1^2$ $\zeta_2\gamma_1^2\gamma_2^2 = \gamma_2^2 \times \gamma_2^2$	$\langle Gg_1^3, Gg_1^2 \rangle$ $\langle G(g_2^3 \times g_2^3), G(g_2^2 \times g_2^2) \rangle$
4.1	$\gamma_1^2 \equiv \mathsf{List}\,\gamma_1^{4.1}$	$\tau_1\gamma_1^2\gamma_1^{4.1} = \gamma_1^1$	$R_1 = \mathsf{List}(G\gamma_1^{4.1})$	$\zeta_{1,1}\gamma_1^2\gamma_1^{4.1} = G\gamma_1^{4.1}$	$\langle g_1^{2.1}, g_1^1 \rangle$ $\langle \mathsf{List}\,h_1^{4.1}, g_1^{4.1} \rangle$
4.2	$\gamma_2^2 \times \gamma_2^2 = \gamma_1^{4.2} \times \gamma_2^{4.2}$	$\tau_1\gamma_2^2\gamma_1^{4.2}\gamma_2^{4.2} = \gamma_2^2$ $\tau_2\gamma_2^2\gamma_1^{4.2}\gamma_2^{4.2} = \gamma_2^2$	$R_1 = G\gamma_2^2$ $R_2 = G\gamma_2^2$	$\zeta_{1,1}\gamma_1^2\gamma_2^2{}^{4.2} = \gamma_2^2$ $\zeta_{2,1}\gamma_1^2\gamma_2^2{}^{4.2} = \gamma_2^2$	$\langle g_1^{4.2} \times g_1^{4.2}, g_2^3 \times g_2^3 \rangle$
4.1.1	$G\gamma_1^{4.1} \equiv \gamma_1^{4.1.1}$	$\tau_1\gamma_1^{4.1}\gamma_1^{4.1.1} = \gamma_1^{4.1}$	$R_1 = G\gamma_1^{4.1}$	$\zeta_{1,1}\gamma_1^{4.1}\gamma_1^{4.1.1} = \gamma_1^{4.1.1}{}^{4.1}$ $G\gamma_1^{4.1.1} = G\gamma_1^{4.1}$	$\langle Gg_1^{4.1.1}, Gh_1^{4.1} \rangle$
4.2.1	$\gamma_2^2 \equiv \gamma_1^{4.2.1}$	$\tau_1\gamma_2^2\gamma_1^{4.2.1} = \gamma_2^2$	$R_1 = \gamma_2^2$		$\langle g_1^{4.2.1}, g_1^{4.2} \rangle$
4.2.2	$\gamma_2^2 \equiv N$		$R_1 = 1$		$\langle g_1^{4.2.2}, g_1^{4.2} \rangle$ $\langle N, g_1^{4.2.2} \rangle$
4.1.1.1	$\gamma_1^{4.1} \equiv N$		$R_1 = 1$		$\langle g_1^{4.1.1.1}, g_1^{4.1.1} \rangle$ $\langle N, g_1^{4.1.1.1} \rangle$
4.1.1.2	$G\gamma_1^{4.1} \equiv \gamma_1^{4.1.1.2}$	$\tau_1\gamma_1^{4.1}\gamma_1^{4.1.1.2} = G\gamma_1^{4.1}$			$\langle Gg_1^{4.1.1.2}, Gg_1^{4.1.1} \rangle$

The call adm t f $\mathsf{G}\beta_1$ results in the sequence of calls:

call 1	adm	t	f	$\mathsf{G}\beta_1$
call 2	adm	t_2	$\mathsf{G}h_1^1 \times \mathsf{G}(h_2^1 \times h_2^1)$	$\mathsf{G}(\mathsf{G}\gamma_1^1 \times \mathsf{G}(\gamma_2^1 \times \gamma_2^1))$
call 3	adm	t_3	$(\mathsf{G}g_1^2, \mathsf{G}(g_2^2 \times g_2^2))$	$\mathsf{G}\gamma_1^1 \times \mathsf{G}(\gamma_2^1 \times \gamma_2^1)$
call 4.1	adm	flat (cons const nil)	g_1^3	$\mathsf{G}\gamma_1^2$
call 4.2	adm	pairing (inj 2) const	$g_2^3 \times g_2^3$	$\mathsf{G}(\gamma_2^2 \times \gamma_2^2)$
call 4.1.1	adm	cons const nil	$\mathsf{G}h_1^{4.1}$	List $(\mathsf{G}\gamma_1^{4.1})$
call 4.2.1	adm	inj 2	$g_1^{4.2}$	$\mathsf{G}\gamma_2^2$
call 4.2.2	adm	const	$g_1^{4.2}$	$\mathsf{G}\gamma_2^2$
call 4.1.1.1	adm	const	$g_1^{4.1.1}$	$\mathsf{G}\gamma_1^{4.1}$
call 4.1.1.2	adm	nil	$\mathsf{G}g_1^{4.1.1}$	List $(\mathsf{G}\gamma_1^{4.1})$

where

$$t = \mathsf{projpair}\ (\ \mathsf{inj}\ (\ \mathsf{flat}\ (\mathsf{cons}\ \mathsf{const}\ \mathsf{nil}),\ \mathsf{pairing}\ (\mathsf{inj}\ 2)\ \mathsf{const}\ )\ )$$
$$t_2 = \mathsf{inj}\ (\ \mathsf{flat}\ (\mathsf{cons}\ \mathsf{const}\ \mathsf{nil}),\ \mathsf{pairing}\ (\mathsf{inj}\ 2)\ \mathsf{const}\ )$$
$$t_3 = (\ \mathsf{flat}\ (\mathsf{cons}\ \mathsf{const}\ \mathsf{nil}),\ \mathsf{pairing}\ (\mathsf{inj}\ 2)\ \mathsf{const}\ )$$

The steps of adm corresponding to these call are given in Table 2, with the most important components of these steps listed explicitly. Since the solution to the generated set of constraints requires that f has the form List $\mathsf{N} \times \mathsf{N}$, we conclude that the only function mappable over t relative to the specification $\mathsf{G}\beta_1$ is $\mathsf{id}_{\mathsf{List}\,\mathsf{N}} \times \mathsf{id}_{\mathsf{N}}$. This is precisely the result obtained informally in Example 3.

Example 9. For t as in Example 4 the call adm t f List β_1 results in the sequence of calls:

call 1	adm	t	f	List β_1
call 2	adm	cons (cons 3 nil) nil)	g_1^1	List β_1
call 2.1	adm	nil	g_1^2	List β_1

The steps of adm corresponding to these call are given in the table below, with the most important components of these steps listed explicitly:

Step no.	Matching problems	$\bar{\tau}$	$\bar{R}$	$\bar{\zeta}$	Constraints added to C
1	$\beta_1 \equiv \gamma_1^1$	$\tau_1\beta_1\gamma_1^1 = \beta_1$	$R_1 = \beta_1$ $R_2 = \text{List }\beta_1$	$\zeta_{2,1}\beta_1\gamma_1^1 = \beta_1$	$\langle g_1^1, f\rangle$
2	$\beta_1 \equiv \gamma_1^2$	$\tau_1\beta_1\gamma_1^2 = \beta_1$	$R_1 = \beta_1$ $R_2 = \text{List }\beta_1$	$\zeta_{2,1}\beta_1\gamma_1^2 = \beta_1$	$\langle g_1^2, g_1^1\rangle$
2.1	$\beta_1 \equiv \gamma_1^{2.1}$	$\tau_1\beta_1\gamma_1^{2.1} = \beta_1$	$R_1 = 1$		$\langle g_1^{2.1}, g_1^2\rangle$

Since the solution to the generated set of constraints requries that f has the form $g_1^{2.1}$, we conclude that any function of type $\text{List }\mathbb{N} \to X$ (for some type X) is mappable over t relative to the specification $\text{List }\beta_1$.

Example 10. For t as in Example 5 the call $\text{adm }\ t\ \ f\ \ \text{List}\,(\text{List }\beta_1)$ results in the following sequence of calls:

call 1	adm	t	f	$\text{List }\beta_1$
call 2.1	adm	$\text{cons }1\,(\text{cons }2\,\text{nil})$	g_1^1	$\text{List }\beta_1$
call 2.2	adm	$\text{cons }(\text{cons }3\,\text{nil})\,\text{nil}$	$\text{List }g_1^1$	$\text{List }(\text{List }\beta_1)$
call 2.1.1	adm	$\text{cons }2\,\text{nil}$	$g_1^{2.1}$	$\text{List }\beta_1$
call 2.2.1	adm	$\text{cons }3\,\text{nil}$	$g_1^{2.2}$	$\text{List }\beta_1$
call 2.2.2	adm	nil	$\text{List }g_1^{2.2}$	$\text{List }(\text{List }\beta_1)$
call 2.1.1.1	adm	nil	$g_1^{2.1.1}$	$\text{List }\beta_1$
call 2.2.1.1	adm	nil	$g_1^{2.2.1}$	$\text{List }\beta_1$

The steps of adm corresponding to these calls are given in the table below, with the most important components of these steps listed explicitly:

Step no.	Matching problems	$\bar{\tau}$	$\bar{R}$	$\bar{\zeta}$	Constraints added to C
1	$\text{List }\beta_1 \equiv \gamma_1^1$	$\tau_1\beta_1\gamma_1^1 = \text{List }\beta_1$	$R_1 = \text{List }\beta_1$ $R_2 = \text{List }(\text{List }\beta_1)$	$\zeta_{1,1}\beta_1\gamma_1^1 = \beta_1$ $\zeta_{2,1}\beta_1\gamma_1^1 = \text{List }\beta_1$	$\langle \text{List }g_1^1, f\rangle$
2.1	$\beta_1 \equiv \gamma_1^{2.1}$	$\tau_1\beta_1\gamma_1^{2.1} = \beta_1$	$R_1 = \beta_1$ $R_2 = \text{List }\beta_1$	$\zeta_{2,2}\beta_1\gamma_1^{2.1} = \beta_1$	$\langle g_1^{2.1}, g_1^1\rangle$
2.2	$\text{List }\beta_1 \equiv \gamma_1^{2.2}$	$\tau_1\beta_1\gamma_1^{2.2} = \text{List }\beta_1$	$R_1 = \text{List }\beta_1$ $R_2 = \text{List }(\text{List }\beta_1)$	$\zeta_{1,1}\beta_1\gamma_1^{2.2} = \beta_1$ $\zeta_{2,1}\beta_1\gamma_1^{2.2} = \text{List }\beta_1$	$\langle \text{List }g_1^{2.2}, \text{List }g_1^1\rangle$
2.1.1	$\beta_1 \equiv \gamma_1^{2.1.1}$	$\tau_1\beta_1\gamma_1^{2.1.1} = \beta_1$	$R_1 = \beta_1$ $R_2 = \text{List }\beta_1$	$\zeta_{2,2}\beta_1\gamma_1^{2.1.1} = \beta_1$	$\langle g_1^{2.1.1}, g_1^{2.1}\rangle$
2.2.1	$\beta_1 \equiv \gamma_1^{2.2.1}$	$\tau_1\beta_1\gamma_1^{2.2.1} = \beta_1$	$R_1 = \beta_1$ $R_2 = \text{List }\beta_1$	$\zeta_{2,2}\beta_1\gamma_1^{2.2.1} = \beta_1$	$\langle g_1^{2.2.1}, g_1^{2.2}\rangle$
2.2.2	$\text{List }\beta_1 \equiv \gamma_1^{2.2.2}$	$\tau_1\beta_1\gamma_1^{2.2.2} = \text{List }\beta_1$	$R_1 = 1$		$\langle \text{List }g_1^{2.2.2}, \text{List }g_1^{2.2}\rangle$
2.1.1.1	$\beta_1 \equiv \gamma_1^{2.1.1.1}$	$\tau_1\beta_1\gamma_1^{2.1.1.1} = \beta_1$	$R_1 = 1$		$\langle g_1^{2.1.1.1}, g_1^{2.1.1}\rangle$
2.2.1.1	$\beta_1 \equiv \gamma_1^{2.2.1.1}$	$\tau_1\beta_1\gamma_1^{2.2.1.1} = \beta_1$	$R_1 = 1$		$\langle g_1^{2.2.1.1}, g_1^{2.2.1}\rangle$

Since the solution to the generated set of constraints requires that f has the form $\text{List }g_1^{2.2.1.1}$, we conclude that the most general functions mappable over t

relative to the specification $\mathsf{List}\,(\mathsf{List}\,\beta_1)$ are those of the form $\mathsf{map}_{\mathsf{List}}\,f'$ for some type X and function $f' : \mathbb{N} \to X$.

5   Conclusion, Related Work, and Future Directions

This paper develops an algorithm for characterizing those functions on a deep GADT's type arguments that are mappable over its elements. This algorithm, and thus this paper, can in some sense be read as *defining* what it means for a function to be mappable over t. It thus makes a fundamental contribution to the study of GADTs since there is to our knowledge, no already existing definition of characterization of the intuitive notion of mappability for functions over them. More generally, we know of no other careful study of mappability for GADTs.

The work reported here is part of a larger effort to develop a single, unified categorical theory of data types: understanding mappability for GADTs can be seen as a first step toward an initial algebra semantics for them that specializes to the standard one for nested types (which itself subsumes the standard such semantics for ADTs) whenever the GADTs in question is a nested type (or ADT).

Initial algebra semantics for GADTs have been studied in [10] and [12]. Both of these works interpret GADTs as *discrete* functors; as a result, the functorial action of the functor interpreting a GADT G cannot correctly interpret applications of G's map function to non-identity functions. In addition, [10] cannot handle truly nested data types such as Bush or the GADT G from Example 2. These discrete initial algebra semantics for GADTs thus do not recover the usual initial algebra semantics of nested types when instantiated to them.

The functorial completion semantics of [13], by contrast, does interpret GADTs as non-discrete functors. However, this is achieved at the cost of adding "junk" elements, unreachable in syntax but interpreting elements in the "map closure" of its syntax, to the interpretation of every proper GADT. Functorial completion for Seq, e.g., adds interpretations of elements of the form $\mathsf{map}_{\mathsf{Seq}}\,f\,(\mathsf{pair}\,x\,y)$ even though these may not be of the form $\mathsf{pair}\,u\,v$ for any terms u and v. Importantly, functorial completion adds no junk to interpretations of nested types or ADTs, so unlike the semantics of [12], that of [13] does extend the usual initial algebra semantics for them. But since the interpretations of [13] are bigger than expected for proper GADTs, this semantics, too, is unacceptable.

A similar attempt to recover functoriality is made in [9] to salvage the method from [10]. The overall idea is to relax the discreteness of the functors interpreting GADTs by replacing the dependent products and sums in the development of [10] with left and right Kan extensions, respectively. Unfortunately, this entails that the domains of the functors interpreting GADTs must be the category of all interpretations of types and all morphisms between them, which again leads to the inclusion of unwanted junk elements in the GADT's interpretation.

Containers [1, 2] provide an entirely different approach to describing the functorial action of an ADT or nested type. In this approach an element of such a data type is described first by its structure, and then by the data that structure contains. That is, a ADT or nested type D is seen as comprising a set of *shapes* and, for each shape S, a set of *positions* in S. The functorial action of the functor D interpreting D action does indeed interpret map_D: given a shape and a labeling of its position by elements of A, we get automatically a data structure of the same shape whose positions are labeled by elements of B as soon as we have a function $f : A \rightarrow B$ to translate elements of A to elements of B.

GADTs that go beyond ADTs and nested types have been studied from the container point of view as *indexed containers*, both in [3] and again in [10]. The authors of [3] propose encoding strictly positive indexed data types in terms of some syntactic combinators they consider "categorically inspired". But as far as we understand their claim, map functions and their interpretations as functorial actions are not worked out for indexed containers. The encoding in [3] is nevertheless essential to understanding GADTs and other inductive families as "structures containing data". With respect to it, our algorithm actually discovers the shape of its input element, and thus can be understood as determining how "containery" a given GADT is.

Acknowledgements. This research was supported in part by NSF award CCR-1906388. It was performed while visiting Aarhus University's Logic and Semantics group, which provided additional support via Villum Investigator grant no. 25804, Center for Basic Research in Program Verification.

References

1. Abbott, M., Altenkirch, T., Ghani, N.: Categories of containers. In: Foundations of Software Science and Computation Structures, pp. 23–38 (2003). https://doi.org/10.1007/3-540-36576-1_2
2. Abbott, M., Altenkirch, T., Ghani, N.: Containers - constructing strictly positive types. Theoret. Comput. Sci. **342**, 3–27 (2005). https://doi.org/10.1016/j.tcs.2005.06.002
3. Altenkirch, T., Ghani, N., Hancock, P., McBride, C., Morris, P.: Indexed containers. J. Funct. Program. **25**(e5) (2015). https://doi.org/10.1017/S095679681500009X
4. Arbib, M., Manes, E.: Algebraic Approaches to Program Semantics. Springer, New York (1986). https://doi.org/10.1007/978-1-4612-4962-7
5. Bird, R., de Moor, O.: Algebra of Programming. Prentice-Hall, London (1997)
6. Bird, R., Meertens, L.: Nested datatypes. In: Mathematics of Program Construction, pp. 52–67 (1998). https://doi.org/10.1007/BFb0054285
7. Cagne, P., Johann, P.: Accepted Artifact (APLAS 2022) supporting "Characterizing Functions Mappable Over GADTs". https://doi.org/10.5281/zenodo.7004589
8. Dougherty, D., Johann, P.: An improved general E-unification method. J. Symb. Comput. **14**, 303–320 (1992). https://doi.org/10.1016/0747-7171(92)90010-2
9. Fiore, M.: Discrete generalised polynomial functors. In: Automata, Languages, and Programming, pp. 214–226 (2012). https://doi.org/10.1007/978-3-642-31585-5_22
10. Hamana, M., Fiore, M.: A foundation for GADTs and inductive families: dependent polynomial functor approach. In: Workshop on Generic Programming, pp. 59–70 (2011). https://doi.org/10.1145/2036918.2036927

11. Johann, P., Ghani, N.: Initial algebra semantics is enough! In: Typed Lambda Calculus and Applications, pp. 207–222 (2007). https://doi.org/10.1007/978-3-540-73228-0_16

12. Johann, P., Ghani, N.: Foundations for structured programming with GADTs. In: Principles of Programming Languages, pp. 297–308 (2008). https://doi.org/10.1145/1328897.1328475

13. Johann, P., Polonsky, A.: Higher-kinded data types: syntax and semantics. In: Logic in Computer Science, pp. 1–13 (2019). https://doi.org/10.1109/LICS.2019.8785657

14. Peyton Jones, S., Vytiniotis, D., Weirich, S., Washburn, G.: Simple unification-based type inference for GADTs. In: International Conference on Functional Programming, pp. 50–61 (2006). https://doi.org/10.1145/1160074.1159811

15. Reynolds, J.C.: Types, abstraction, and parametric polymorphism. Inf. Process. **83**(1), 513–523 (1983)

16. Sheard, T., Pasalic, E.: Meta-programming with built-in type equality. In: Workshop on Logical Frameworks and Meta-languages, pp. 49–65 (2008). https://doi.org/10.1016/j.entcs.2007.11.012

17. Xi, H., Chen, C., Chen, G.: Guarded recursive datatype constructors. In: Principles of Programming Languages, pp. 224–235 (2003). https://doi.org/10.1145/604131.604150

Applicative Intersection Types

Xu Xue[1](✉), Bruno C. d. S. Oliveira[1], and Ningning Xie[2]

[1] University of Hong Kong, Hong Kong, China
xuxue@connect.hku.hk
[2] University of Cambridge, Cambridge, UK

Abstract. Calculi with intersection types have been used over the years to model various features, including: *overloading, extensible records* and, more recently, *nested composition* and *return type overloading*. Nevertheless no previous calculus supports all those features at once. In this paper we study expressive calculi with intersection types and a merge operator. Our first calculus supports an unrestricted merge operator, which is able to support all the features, and is proven to be type sound. However, the semantics is non-deterministic. In the second calculus we employ a previously proposed disjointness restriction, to make the semantics deterministic. Some forms of overloading are forbidden, but all other features are supported. The main challenge in the design is related to the semantics of applications and record projections. We propose an applicative subtyping relation that enables the inference of result types for applications and projections. Correspondingly, there is an applicative dispatching relation that is used for the dynamic semantics. The two calculi and their proofs are formalized in the Coq theorem prover.

1 Introduction

Calculi with *intersection types* [3,7,19,22] have a long history in programming languages. Reynolds [21] was the first to promote the use of intersection types in practical programming. He introduced a *merge operator* that enables building values with multiple types, where the multiple types are modelled as intersection types. Dunfield [9] refined the merge operator, to add significant additional expressive power over the original formulation by Reynolds. Over the years there have been several calculi with intersection types equipped with a merge operator, and enabling different features: *overloaded functions* [6,9], *return type overloading* [16], *extensible records* [9,21] and *nested composition* [4,14].

Nevertheless, no previous calculus supports all four features together. Some calculi enable function overloading [6], but preclude return type overloading and nested composition. On the other hand, calculi with disjoint intersection types [4,14] support return type overloading and nested composition, but disallow conventional functional overloading. Dunfield's calculus [9] supports the first three features, but not nested composition. Those features are not completely orthogonal and the interactions between them are interesting, allowing for new applications. However, the interactions also pose new technical challenges.

This paper studies expressive calculi with intersection types and a merge operator. Our goal is to design calculi that deal with all four features at once, and

I. Sergey (Ed.): APLAS 2022, LNCS 13658, pp. 155–174, 2022.
https://doi.org/10.1007/978-3-031-21037-2_8

study the interaction between these features. Our two main focuses are on type inference for *applications* and *record projection*, and the design of the operational semantics for such calculi. To enable all the features we introduce a specialized form of subtyping, called *applicative subtyping*, to deal with the flexible forms of applications and record projection allowed by the calculi. Correspondingly, there is an applicative dispatching relation that is used for the dynamic semantics. In addition, we explore the interactions between features. In particular, overloading and nested composition enable curried overloaded functions, while most previous work [5,6,9,15] only considers uncurried overloaded functions.

Our first calculus supports an unrestricted merge operator. This calculus is able to support all four features, and is proven to be type sound. However, the semantics is non-deterministic. In practice, in an implementation of this calculus we can employ a *biased* or *asymmetric* merge operator, which gives a (biased) preference to values on the left or right side of merges. This approach is similar to the approach taken by Dunfield in her calculus [9], and asymmetric merge (or concatenation) operators are also adopted in several calculi with extensible records [20,27]. In the second calculus we employ a previously proposed disjointness restriction [17], to make the semantics deterministic. Disjointness enables a *symmetric* merge operator, since conflicts in a merge are statically rejected rather than resolved with a biased semantics. In the second calculus some forms of overloading are forbidden, but all other features are supported. The two calculi and their proofs are formalized in the Coq theorem prover.

In summary, the contributions of this paper are:

- **Calculi supporting overloading, extensible records and nested composition.** We propose calculi with intersection types and a merge operator, which can support various features together, unlike previous calculi where only some features were supported.
- **Applicative subtyping and dispatching.** We develop a specialized applicative subtyping relation to deal with the problem of inferring result types for applications and record projections. In addition, the dynamic semantics supports a corresponding applicative dispatching relation.
- **First-class, curried overloading:** We show that the interaction between overloading and nested composition enables overloaded functions to be first-class, which allows the definition of curried overloaded functions.
- **Mechanical formalization and implementation:** All the calculi and proofs are formalized in the Coq theorem prover. The formalization is available in the artifact [1] and a prototype implementation can be found at:

https://github.com/juniorxxue/applicative-intersection

2   Overview

This section gives an overview of our work and introduces the key technical ideas. We then illustrate some problems, challenges and solutions when designing type systems for such calculi and features.

2.1   Background

Intersection Types and Merge Operator. Intersection types describe expressions that can have multiple types. The intersection type A & B is inhabited by terms that have both type A and type B. The merge operator (denoted as ,,) has been introduced by Reynolds [21], and later refined by Dunfield [9], to create terms with intersection types at the term level. An important feature of Dunfield's calculus is that it contains a completely unrestricted merge operator, which enables most of the applications that we will discuss in this paper, except for nested composition. However, this expressive power comes at a cost. The semantics of the calculus is ambiguous. For example, 1,,2 : Int can elaborate to both 1 and 2. Note that intersection types in the presence of the merge operator have a different interpretation from the original meaning [7], where type intersections A & B are *only* inhabited by the intersection of the sets of values of A and B. In general, with the merge operator, we can always find a term for any intersection type, even when the two types in the intersection are disjoint (i.e. when the sets of values denoted by the two types are disjoint). For example, 1,,true has the type Int & Bool. In many classical intersection type systems without the merge operator, such type would not be inhabited [19]. Thus, the use of the term "intersection" is merely a historical legacy. The merge operator adds expressive power to calculi with intersection types. As we shall see, this added expressive power is useful to model several features of practical interest for programming languages.

Disjoint Intersection Types. Oliveira et al. [17] solved the ambiguity problem by imposing a disjointness restriction on merges. Only types that are disjoint can be merged. For example, Int and Bool are disjoint, so the type Int & Bool is well-formed and 1,,true is a valid term. Huang et al. [14] improved this calculus by introducing a type-directed operational semantics where types are used to assist reduction and proved its type soundness and determinism. Unfortunately, the restriction to disjoint intersection types, while allowing many of the original applications, rules out traditional function overloading (see Sect. 5 for more details).

2.2   Applications of the Merge Operator

To show that the merge operator is useful, we now cover four applications of the merge operator that have appeared in the literature: records and record projections, function overloading, return type function overloading and nested composition. All applications can be encoded by our calculus in Sect. 4.

Records and Record Projections. The idea of using the merge operator to model record concatenation firstly appears in Reynold's work [23]. Records in our calculi are modelled as merges of multiple single-field records. Multi-field records can be viewed as syntactic sugar and {x="hello", y="world"} is simply {x = "hello"},,{y = "world"}. The behaviour of record projection is mostly standard in our calculi. After being projected by a label, the merged records will return the associated terms. For instance ($\hookrightarrow$ denotes reduce to).

```
({x = "hello"},,{y = "world"}).x ↪ "hello"
```

Function Overloading. Function overloading is a form of polymorphism where the implementation of functions can vary depending on different types of arguments that are applied by functions. There are many ways to represent types of overloaded functions. For example, suppose `show` is an overloaded function that can be applied to either integers or booleans. Haskell utilises type classes [25] to assign the type `Show a ⇒ a → String` to `show` with instances defined.

With intersection types, we can employ the merge operator [6,21] to define a simplified version of the overloaded `show` function. For instance, the `show` function below has type `(Int → String) & (Bool → String)`.

```
show : (Int → String) & (Bool → String) = showInt,,showBool
```

The behaviour of `show` is standard, acting as a normal function: it can be applied to arguments and the correct implementation is selected based on types.

```
show 1 ↪ "1"                    show true ↪ "true"
```

Return Type Overloading. One common example of return type overloading is the `read :: Read a ⇒ String → a` function in Haskell, which is the reverse operation of `show` and parses a string into some other form of data. Like `show`, we can define a simplified version of `read` using the merge operator:

```
read : (String → Int) & (String → Bool) = readInt,,readBool
```

In Haskell, because the return type `a` cannot be determined by the argument, `read` either requires programmers to give an explicit type annotation, or needs to automatically infer the return type from the context. Our calculi work in a similar manner. Suppose that `succ` is the successor function on integers and `not` is the negation function on booleans, then we can write:

```
succ (read "1") ↪ 2              not (read "true") ↪ false
```

Nested Composition. Simply stated, nested composition reflects distributivity properties of intersection types at the term level. When eliminating terms created by the merge operator (usually functions and records), the results extracted from nested terms will be composed. In the context of records, the distributive subtyping rule enabling this behaviour is $\{l : A\} \& \{l : B\} <: \{l : A \& B\}$. With this rule we can have the following expression:

```
({x = "hello"},,{x = 1}).x ↪ "hello",,1
```

Note that here we *allow* repeated fields with the same name. One may worry about ambiguities but, with a disjointness restriction, we can only accept fields with the same labels if the types of the fields are disjoint. Nested composition is a key feature in *compositional programming* [29], which uses it to solve challenging modularity problems such as the Expression Problem [26], and to model forms of *family polymorphism* [11]. We refer interested readers to the work of Zhang et al. [29] for details.

Nested composition can also occur with functional intersections, using the subtyping rule $(A \rightarrow B) \,\&\, (A \rightarrow C) <: A \rightarrow (B \,\&\, C)$. With this rule, we can, for example, write the following program:

```
(succ,,intToDigit) 5 ↪ 6,,'5'
```

which applies two functions to the integer 5. Note that here `intToDigit` takes an integer and returns a corresponding character. We will also see that nested composition enables overloaded functions to be curried.

2.3   Challenges in the Design of the Semantics

The goal of this work is to design an automatic type inference algorithm for applications and record projection and the corresponding dynamic semantics, so that the system supports all applications presented in the previous section. Unfortunately, designing the semantics of the merge operator poses significant challenges, which we explain in the rest of this section.

Inference of Projections and Applications. In traditional type systems, in applications $e_1\ e_2$ or projections $e.l$, e_1 is expected to have an arrow type and e is expected to have a record type. Such convention, however, cannot apply to our system because certain forms of intersection types can also play the role of arrow or record types. In particular, such use cases of intersection types are helpful for modelling overloaded functions and multi-field records. For example, we know that `showInt` is one branch of `show` with the subtyping statement:

```
(Int → String) & (Bool → String) <: Int → String
```

From this example we can see that the dynamic semantics must somehow be type-dependent. In our work we follow the *type-directed operational semantics* (TDOS) [14] approach, which chooses between merged functions according to type information during runtime. However, existing TDOS approaches do not support overloading for two reasons. Firstly, TDOS requires merged functions to be disjoint with each other, but in this case the merged functions are not disjoint (i.e., `Int → String` is not disjoint with `Bool → String` because of the common return type `String`). Secondly, even if we would simply ignore the disjointness restriction, we would still need to put an explicit type annotation `Int → String` and write the program as (`show : Int → String`) 1 to select the correct implementation to apply from the overloaded `show` function. This is because previous TDOS calculi have restricted application rules that cannot accommodate traditional overloading. Clearly, in a setting with overloading, having to write such explicit annotations would be unsatisfying. Therefore we wish to have an approach where we can write overloaded functions naturally.

A similar problem occurs using record projections in existing TDOS calculi. For instance, the type system of λ_{i+} [14] requires explicit annotations for projections of multi-field records with distinct labels, such as (`{x = 1},,{y = true} : {x : Int}`).`x`. This is of course, quite unnatural to write. Although source languages targetting the TDOS calculi can eliminate the explicit use of such annotations at the source level, it would be better to address this problem directly in the TDOS.

Dynamic Semantics. Giving a direct semantics to overloaded applications is a non-trivial problem. Thanks to the merge operator and the call-by-value strategy, our overloaded functions are expected to be in the form of nested merges according to the structure of types. So we can reason about the dynamic semantics as we deal with the types. Unfortunately, the distributivity of subtyping complicates the story. The challenge comes from the fact that in our setting overloaded functions are first-class. That is, they can be taken as arguments or returned as results. For instance, we can have:

```
pshow : Unit → (Int → String) & (Bool → String)
pshow = λx. show
```

In this situation, an overloaded function is wrapped with a lambda abstraction, while it should also be viewed as an overloaded function. For example, we expect the following to hold:

```
pshow unit 1 ↪ "1"                    pshow unit true ↪ "true"
```

In the last two cases, with a traditional approach to applications, `pshow` is expected to have type `Unit → Int → String` and `Unit → Bool → String` respectively. From the perspective of intersection overloading, `pshow` should be of type `(Unit → Int → String) & (Unit → Bool → String)`, which, however, is different from the given type annotation. This alternative view of types and functions poses challenges to the design of the static as well as the dynamic semantics.

Ambiguities on the Input Types. In languages like C++ and Java, overloading cannot be defined on return types, and ambiguities are detected when the input types of overloaded functions overlap. This is also a reason why many works model the inputs of overloaded functions as product types [6,9,15]. The advantages are obvious: it is easier to resolve the correct branch by only comparing the product types and types of arguments. The drawback of this model is that product types will prevent overloaded functions to be curried. This is because overloaded functions based on product types expect a tuple containing all the arguments and reject partial applications. The challenge of modelling overloaded curried functions is that partial applications may be insufficient to fully determine the implementation to take from the overloaded function. These pains can be alleviated using intersection types, the merge operator and the feature of nested composition.

```
f : Int → Int → Int                    g : Int → Bool → Bool
```

For example, with `f,,g`, we can simply reason that the result of `(f,,g) 1 true` is `g 1 true`. The problem occurs in the partially applied term `(f,,g) 1`, for which there are two possible design choices. The first choice is to reject this application term since we cannot select between overloads, thus forbidding many use cases like this. Another choice is to apply `f` and `g` in parallel to `1`, resulting in `(f 1),,(g 1)`, which has the type `(Int → Int) & (Bool → Bool)`.

2.4   Key Ideas and Results

Applicative Subtyping. To help with the inference of the result types for applications and projections, we propose a new specialized subtyping algorithm for applications and projections. Specifically, conventional subtyping algorithms take two types as inputs, and return a boolean indicating whether two types are in a subtyping relation or not. We present an *applicative subtyping* algorithm, whose intuition is simple: given a functional type A (which may be an intersection of functions), and the type of an argument B, it tells whether this function can be applied to this argument and, if yes, it computes the output type. Similarly, given a record type A, and a label l, applicative subtyping tells whether this record can be projected by this label, and if yes, it computes the result type associated with this label. Basically, we try to solve the problem in the following subtyping form (denoted as <:), where we infer the type ? given the argument type Int:

```
(Int → String) & (Bool → String) <: Int → ?
```

This problem can be split into two steps: first, check whether the application is well-typed, and if so, determine its output type. For the above example, ? is expected to be String, as Int is an argument to Int → String. Record projection works similarly. String & Int should be derived as the result type for projection ({x = "hello"},,{x = 1}).x.

```
{x : String} & {x : Int} <: {x : ?}
```

Applicative subtyping is used when typing applications and projections. Our algorithm adopts the notion of selectors S that abstract the arguments (as a type for applications, or a label for projections). The behaviour of applicative subtyping for intersection types is captured by a simple composition operator ⊙ which isolates particular design choices. In applicative subtyping, a possible result is that the application fails. We denote failure with a . symbol. We illustrate the results of applicative subtyping (denoted as ≪) for the above examples next. ïž£

```
(Int → String) & (Bool → String) ≪ Int    = String ⊙ .
(String → Int) & (String → Bool) ≪ String = Int    ⊙ Bool
{x : String) & {y : String)      ≪ x       = String ⊙ .
{x : String) & {x :Int)          ≪ x       = String ⊙ Int
```

There are two important things to notice here. Firstly, as discussed above, the second argument of ≪ is just the function argument type or a label, instead of the complete type that would be normally used in a subtyping comparison. Secondly, the results are given in terms of the composition operator ⊙. The composition operator abstracts behaviour that is specific to particular subtyping relations. When designing applicative subtyping, a desirable property is that it should be sound and complete with respect to subtyping. The soundness and completeness properties can be stated as follows (here we show the case for functions):

Lemma 1 (Soundness). *If* A ≪ B = C, *then* A <: B → C.

Lemma 2 (Completeness). *If* A <: B → C, *then* ∃D, A ≪ B = D ∧ D <: C.

$$
\begin{aligned}
.\;\odot\;. &= . \\
A_1\;\odot\;. &= A_1 \\
.\;\odot\;A_2 &= A_2 \\
A_1\;\odot\;A_2 &= A_1 \;\&\; A_2
\end{aligned}
\qquad\qquad
\begin{aligned}
.\;\odot\;. &= . \\
A_1\;\odot\;. &= A_1 \\
.\;\odot\;A_2 &= A_2 \\
Amb\;\odot\;O &= Amb \\
O\;\odot\;Amb &= Amb \\
A_1\;\odot\;A_2 &= Amb
\end{aligned}
$$

(a) Nested composition semantics.   (b) Overloading semantics.

Fig. 1. Two possible composition operators, for calculi with distributive subtyping (on the left), and without distributive subtyping (on the right). The notation Amb denotes ambiguity, which represents a type-error, while the meta-variable O denotes any output type (i.e. either a type, failure or ambiguity).

Depending on the expressive power of the subtyping relation we need different implementations of $\odot$ to satisfy soundness/completeness. In particular, whether or not the subtyping relation includes distributive subtyping rules affects the definition of $\odot$. Figure 1 illustrates this difference. In a relation with distributive subtyping rules (such as $(A \to B) \;\&\; (A \to C) <: A \to (B \;\&\; C)$), the composition operator on the left (a) leads to a sound and complete definition of applicative subtyping. This operator, which is quite simple, allows combining results that arise from multiple branches. We say that this composition operator implements a *nested composition semantics*, since it allows combining multiple results. For instance, Int $\odot$ Bool simply denotes Int & Bool, meaning that an applicative subtyping statement (String $\to$ Int) & (String $\to$ Bool) $\ll$ String succeeds, computing the output type Int & Bool. Without the distributive subtyping rule the composition operator on the left (a) is not sound with respect to subtyping. Instead we should use the implementation on the right (b), which will reject cases like Int $\odot$ Bool, since such cases denote a form of ambiguity. We say that the composition operator on the right implements an *overloading semantics*, since if multiple implementations in an overloaded definition match with an argument (or a label), we reject the application. This is similar to traditional overloading mechanisms, which reject such cases as a form of ambiguity. In other words, in the overloading semantics, only one implementation can be selected from an overloaded definition. Note that the overloading semantics implementation can also be used in a calculus with distributivity, but this would lose the completeness property. One counter example is (Int $\to$ String) & (Int $\to$ Int) <: Int $\to$ (String & Int), which holds according to the distributivity rule, but the applicative subtyping based on the overloading semantics will derive an ambiguity Amb error.

TDOS for Overloading. For the semantics, we follow up the idea of typed-directed operational semantics [14] and define a new judgment that performs *applicative dispatching* to support overloading. At a high level, applicative dispatch reflects applicative subtyping in the dynamic semantics. As we analyzed above, distributivity forbids overloaded functions to be exact nested merges, thus a canonical form of overloaded function should be settled. To solve this problem we use an explicit merge with extra annotations that play a role of "runtime types", which are used by applicative dispatching to select the correct branch during runtime.

Two Calculi. We present two calculi to demonstrate the applicative subtyping and applicative dispatching. Both calculi utilize the composition operator (Fig. 1a) since we want to allow nested composition, and explore curried and first-class overloaded functions. The first calculus embraces a simple design and adopts an unrestricted merge operator. All features mentioned above can be encoded in this calculus, but the calculus will have a non-deterministic semantics due to ambiguities. For ambiguities, we present a second calculus, which adopts a restricted merge operator: only terms with disjoint types can be merged. This calculus is deterministic but excludes certain forms of overloading, like the show function. Since $Int \to String$ is not disjoint with $Bool \to String$, such merges will be rejected.

3   Applicative Subtyping

In this section, we first present the normal subtyping algorithm for intersection types and then present applicative subtyping.

3.1   Types and Subtyping

The types that we consider in this work are:

Types	$A, B ::= Int \mid Top \mid A \to B \mid A \& B \mid \{l : A\}$
Ordinary Types	$A^\circ, B^\circ ::= Int \mid Top \mid A \to B^\circ \mid \{l : A^\circ\}$

A and B are metavariables which range over types. Int and Top are base types and Top is the supertype of all types. Compound types are function types $A \to B$, intersection types $A \& B$, and record types $\{l : A\}$. Ordinary types [8,14] are essentially types without intersection types, except for functions where intersection types can appear in argument types.

Algorithmic BCD Subtyping. Subtyping relations for intersection types can vary in whether distributivity rules are included or not. For calculi with intersection types, a common rule allows the intersection of arrow types to distribute over arrows. One well-known subtyping relation with such distributivity rule is BCD subtyping [3]. Huang et al. [14] provide a sound and complete algorithm for BCD subtyping by eliminating the transitivity rule, and employing the notions of ordinary types and splittable types. We present that subtyping relation in Fig. 2. Splittable types describe that types can be split into two simpler types and ordinary types are those which cannot be split. Rule SUB-AND is the most interesting rule as it captures the distributivity of intersection types over function types and record types. This rule splits the type B into two types B_1 and B_2 and proceeds by testing whether A is a subtype of both B_1 and B_2.

$\boxed{A_1 \lhd A \rhd A_2}$ *(Splittable Types)*

$$\text{SP-AND} \quad \frac{}{A \lhd A \& B \rhd B}$$

$$\text{SP-ARR} \quad \frac{B_1 \lhd B \rhd B_2}{A \rightarrow B_1 \lhd A \rightarrow B \rhd A \rightarrow B_2}$$

$$\text{SP-RCD} \quad \frac{A_1 \lhd A \rhd A_2}{\{l : A_1\} \lhd \{l : A\} \rhd \{l : A_2\}}$$

$\boxed{A <: B}$ *(Subtyping)*

$$\text{SUB-INT} \quad \frac{}{\text{Int} <: \text{Int}}$$

$$\text{SUB-TOP} \quad \frac{}{A <: \text{Top}}$$

$$\text{SUB-ARR} \quad \frac{C <: A \quad B <: D^\circ}{A \rightarrow B <: C \rightarrow D^\circ}$$

$$\text{SUB-RCD} \quad \frac{A <: B^\circ}{\{l : A\} <: \{l : B^\circ\}}$$

$$\text{SUB-AND} \quad \frac{B_1 \lhd B \rhd B_2 \quad A <: B_1 \quad A <: B_2}{A <: B}$$

$$\text{SUB-AND-L} \quad \frac{A <: C^\circ}{A \& B <: C^\circ}$$

$$\text{SUB-AND-R} \quad \frac{B <: C^\circ}{A \& B <: C^\circ}$$

Fig. 2. Splittable Types and Algorithmic Subtyping

$$A_1 \rightarrow A_2 \ll B = A_2 \qquad \text{when } B <: A_1 \tag{1}$$
$$A_1 \rightarrow A_2 \ll B = . \qquad \text{when } \neg(B <: A_1) \tag{2}$$
$$\{l = A\} \ll l = A \tag{3}$$
$$\{l_1 = A\} \ll l_2 = . \qquad \text{when } l_1 \neq l_2 \tag{4}$$
$$A_1 \& A_2 \ll S = (A_1 \ll S) \circledcirc (A_2 \ll S) \tag{5}$$
$$A \ll S = . \qquad \text{otherwise} \tag{6}$$

Fig. 3. Applicative subtyping

3.2   Applicative Subtyping

Applicative subtyping utilises the notion of *selectors* to find the correct output type from applicable types. We consider applicable types to be function or record types. This relation enables the type system to infer the type of applications and record projections, as shown in Sect. 4. We model the types of arguments and labels of record projections as selectors, and the outputs as being either a type or nothing (denoting the failure to find a suitable output type).

$$\text{Selectors} \quad S ::= A \mid l \qquad \text{Outputs} \quad O ::= . \mid A$$

The definition of applicative subtyping is given in Fig. 3. Selectors are used as the second parameter and propagate through the subtyping checks, until we reach arrow or record types. For arrow types, in rules (1) (2), we check the contravariant subtyping between input type A_1 and argument B. If successful, the output type A_2 is returned, otherwise we fail. For record types (3) (4), we check the equality between labels. If the labels are equal, we return the output type A, otherwise we fail. For the case of the intersection types $A_1 \& A_2$ (5), we introduce a composition operator $\circledcirc$ to combine two results which are derived from applying A_1 and A_2 with the same selector B. Rule (6) covers a number of missing cases (such as $\text{Int} \ll S$) which will all fail. For simplicity of presentation we write those rules as a single rule (6).

The composition operator accepts output results and returns a new output result. For systems with BCD subtyping, which include distributivity rules, we use the composition operator implementing the nested composition semantics in Fig. 1a.

3.3 Metatheory

We proved the soundness and completeness of our applicative subtyping with respect to the normal subtyping. The decidability of applicative subtyping is straightforward since it is modelled as a structurally recursive function. We have two versions of soundness and completeness lemmas. The first version applies to the case where the supertype is a function:

Lemma 3 (Soundness (Function)). *If* $A \ll B = C$, *then* $A <: B \rightarrow C$.

Lemma 4 (Completeness (Function)). *If* $A <: B \rightarrow C$, *then* $\exists D, A \ll B = D \wedge D <: C$.

The soundness lemma is intuitive. If the result of checking applicative subtyping with a subtype A and input type B computes a type C then it should be the case that $A <: B \rightarrow C$. For completeness we wish to show that if A is a subtype of a function type $B \rightarrow C$ then applicative subtyping will always be able to find some output type D which is a subtype of C.

The second version of the lemma, which applies to the case where the supertype is a record, is defined in a similar manner.

Lemma 5 (Soundness (Record)). *If* $A \ll l = B$, *then* $A <: \{l : B\}$.

Lemma 6 (Completeness (Record)). *If* $A <: \{l : B\}$, *then* $\exists C, A \ll l = C \wedge C <: B$.

Remark. Note that, if we would drop the distributivity of intersections over other constructs by removing the rules SP-ARR and SP-RCD, then to have soundness and completeness we need to employ the composition operator implementing the overloading semantics to the right of Fig. 1. When using that composition operator, the soundness lemmas remain the same, but we need to adjust the completeness lemmas to consider the ambiguous cases. For instance, the completeness for the case of a function supertype would become:

Lemma 7 (Completeness). *If* $A <: B \rightarrow C$, *then* $(\exists D, A \ll B = D \wedge D <: C) \vee A \ll B = Amb$.

4   A Calculus with an Unrestricted Merge Operator

This section presents a type sound calculus that supports both intersection types and a merge operator. This calculus can be viewed as a variant of Dunfield's calculus (without union types) [9]. Our calculus employs a type-directed operational semantics [14] instead of using elaboration semantics as proposed by Dunfield and adopts applicative subtyping and distributive subtyping.

$$\boxed{\Gamma \vdash e \Leftrightarrow A} \qquad\qquad\qquad\qquad\qquad \textit{(Bidirectional Typing)}$$

T-LIT
$$\frac{}{\Gamma \vdash i \Rightarrow \mathsf{Int}}$$

T-VAR
$$\frac{x : A \in \Gamma}{\Gamma \vdash x \Rightarrow A}$$

T-LAM
$$\frac{\Gamma, x : A \vdash e \Leftarrow B}{\Gamma \vdash \lambda x.\, e : A \to B \Rightarrow A \to B}$$

T-RCD
$$\frac{\Gamma \vdash e \Rightarrow A}{\Gamma \vdash \{l = e\} \Rightarrow \{l : A\}}$$

T-APP
$$\frac{\Gamma \vdash e_1 \Rightarrow A \quad \Gamma \vdash e_2 \Rightarrow B \quad A \ll B = C}{\Gamma \vdash e_1\, e_2 \Rightarrow C}$$

T-PROJ
$$\frac{\Gamma \vdash e \Rightarrow A \quad A \ll l = B}{\Gamma \vdash e.l \Rightarrow B}$$

T-MRG
$$\frac{\Gamma \vdash e_1 \Rightarrow A \quad \Gamma \vdash e_2 \Rightarrow B}{\Gamma \vdash e_1,,\, e_2 \Rightarrow A \& B}$$

T-ANN
$$\frac{\Gamma \vdash e \Leftarrow A}{\Gamma \vdash e : A \Rightarrow A}$$

T-SUB
$$\frac{\Gamma \vdash e \Rightarrow A \quad A <: B}{\Gamma \vdash e \Leftarrow B}$$

Fig. 4. Bi-directional typing. The bidirectional mode syntax is $\Leftrightarrow \; ::= \; \Leftarrow | \Rightarrow$.

4.1 Syntax

The syntax of this calculus is:

Expressions $\quad e ::= x \mid i \mid e : A \mid e_1\, e_2 \mid \lambda x.e : A \to B \mid e_1,,e_2 \mid \{l = e\} \mid e.l$

Raw Values $\quad p ::= i \mid \lambda x.e : A \to B$

Values $\qquad\quad v ::= p : A^o \mid v_1,,v_2 \mid \{l = v\}$

Contexts $\qquad \Gamma ::= \cdot \mid \Gamma, x : A$

Most expressions are standard. Lambda expressions $\lambda x.\, e : A \to B$ are fully annotated because the operational semantics is type-directed. The expression $e_1,,e_2$ creates a merge of two expressions e_1 and e_2. The expression $\{l = e\}$ denotes a single-field record with label l and field e. The projection of records is represented by $e.l$. Raw values include integers and lambdas, and values are defined on raw values annotated with ordinary types, merges of values and records whose fields are values. We stratify raw values and values because we need to utilise annotations to adopt dispatching in the semantics. The ordinary restriction on values enforces a canonical form for overloaded functions. Overloaded functions will be reduced to explicit nested merges, even in settings with distribuivity.

4.2 Typing

Figure 4 shows our bi-directional type system. Most of the rules are adapted from traditional bi-directional typing [10]. The novel rules are rules T-APP and T-PROJ, whose inferred type is derived from applicative subtyping.

Typing of Application and Projection. Our approach to type applications [28] is to infer the type of functions and arguments at the same time, pass their types into applicative subtyping (A and B in rule T-APP), and assign the computed result C to applications. This is because we allow intersection types to distribute over arrow types, thus the type of the function can be an arrow type or an intersection type. We cannot simply extract the input type of a function. Since multi-field records are also intersection types in our system, the typing for projections (rule T-PROJ) uses a similar idea to applications.

Examples. We show an example of how the rule T-APP works. Suppose that we have $\Gamma = f : I \to I \to I, g : I \to B \to B$. (I and B stand for Int and Bool)

$$\frac{\dfrac{\Gamma \vdash (f,,g) \Rightarrow (I \to I \to I) \,\&\, (I \to B \to B) \qquad \Gamma \vdash 2 \Rightarrow I}{\Gamma \vdash (f,,g)\, 2 \Rightarrow (I \to I) \,\&\, (B \to B)} \text{ T-APP} \qquad \Gamma \vdash \text{true} \Rightarrow B}{\Gamma \vdash (f,,g)\, 2 \text{ true} \Rightarrow B} \text{ T-APP} \cdot$$

Note that for space reasons we omit the applicative subtyping derivations here, which are straightforward. To infer the type of $(f,,g)\, 2$ true, we first infer both the type of $(f,,g)\, 2$ and true. The type of $(f,,g)\, 2$ is $(\text{Int} \to \text{Int}) \,\&\, (\text{Bool} \to \text{Bool})$. This result is computed from applicative subtyping with two inputs: type of function merges $f,,g$ and type of 2. Later we use the computed result of $(f,,g)\, 2$ to derive our final type Bool.

4.3   Semantics

This calculus adopts a type-directed operational semantics [14], where type annotations are used to cast terms instead of being erased after type checking.

Casting. We introduce the casting judgment in Fig. 5. Judgment $v \longmapsto_A v'$ describes that value v is cast to value v' by type A, thus forcing the value to match the type structure of A. The casting rules are essentially the same as the rules proposed by Huang et al. [14]. Rules CT-MRG-L and CT-MRG-R state that merges will be cast to one result by ordinary types. For example, show will be cast to showInt by type Int $\to$ String.

Applicative Dispatching. We introduce a new judgement called applicative dispatching (Fig. 5), which extends Huang et al.'s [14] *parallel application* judgement. In contrast to parallel application, we must also deal with overloading. Judgment $(v \bullet vl) \hookrightarrow e$ describes that value v is applied to value or label vl (i.e. $vl ::= v \mid l$) and then reduced to a term e. Rule APP-LAM performs beta-reduction and appends an extra annotation D to enforce the output type of the application. Rule APP-PROJ simply extracts the value from the single record field. The interesting part is the remaining three rules for merges. The function $\langle vl \rangle$ simply extracts out the type of a value, to provide the types to be compared with applicative subtyping. To deal with overloading we need to introduce rules APP-MRG-L and APP-MRG-R, which allows a merge to be applied when only one of the values is applicable. The last rule, rule APP-MRG-P deals with the parallel application, where both values in the merge can be applied.

$$\boxed{v \longmapsto_A v'} \hspace{8cm} \textit{(Casting)}$$

CT-INT

$$\overline{i : A \longmapsto_{\mathsf{Int}} i : \mathsf{Int}}$$

CT-TOP

$$\overline{v \longmapsto_{\mathsf{Top}} \top : \mathsf{Top}}$$

CT-RCD

$$\frac{v \longmapsto_{A^\circ} v'}{\{l = v\} \longmapsto_{\{l : A^\circ\}} \{l = v'\}}$$

CT-ARR

$$\frac{E <: C \to D^\circ}{(\lambda x.\, e : A \to B) : E \longmapsto_{(C \to D^\circ)} (\lambda x.\, e : A \to D^\circ) : (C \to D^\circ)}$$

CT-MRG-L

$$\frac{v_1 \longmapsto_{A^\circ} v_1'}{v_1 ,, v_2 \longmapsto_{A^\circ} v_1'}$$

CT-MRG-R

$$\frac{v_2 \longmapsto_{A^\circ} v_2'}{v_1 ,, v_2 \longmapsto_{A^\circ} v_2'}$$

CT-AND

$$\frac{A_1 \lhd A \rhd A_2 \hspace{1cm} v \longmapsto_{A_1} v_1 \hspace{1cm} v \longmapsto_{A_2} v_2}{v \longmapsto_A v_1 ,, v_2}$$

$$\boxed{(v \bullet vl) \hookrightarrow e} \hspace{6cm} \textit{(Applicative Dispatching)}$$

APP-LAM

$$\frac{v \longmapsto_A v'}{((\lambda x.\, e : A \to B) : C \to D \bullet v) \hookrightarrow e[x \mapsto v'] : D}$$

APP-PROJ

$$\overline{(\{l = v\} \bullet l) \hookrightarrow v}$$

APP-MRG-L

$$\frac{\langle v_2 \rangle \ll \langle vl \rangle = . \hspace{1cm} (v_1 \bullet vl) \hookrightarrow e}{((v_1 ,, v_2) \bullet vl) \hookrightarrow e}$$

APP-MRG-R

$$\frac{\langle v_1 \rangle \ll \langle vl \rangle = . \hspace{1cm} (v_2 \bullet vl) \hookrightarrow e}{((v_1 ,, v_2) \bullet vl) \hookrightarrow e}$$

APP-MRG-P

$$\frac{\langle v_1 \rangle \ll \langle vl \rangle \neq . \hspace{0.5cm} \langle v_2 \rangle \ll \langle vl \rangle \neq . \hspace{0.5cm} (v_1 \bullet vl) \hookrightarrow e_1 \hspace{0.5cm} (v_2 \bullet vl) \hookrightarrow e_2}{((v_1 ,, v_2) \bullet vl) \hookrightarrow e_1 ,, e_2}$$

Fig. 5. Casting and applicative dispatching

Operational Semantics. We present our small-step reduction rules in Fig. 6. Rules STEP-INT-ANN and STEP-ARR-ANN append extra annotations to the partial value, in order to preserve the precise types at runtime. Rule STEP-PV-SPLIT will split terms according to splittable types, forcing the type of each branch in merges to be ordinary. Rule STEP-APP,STEP-PRJ directly call applicative dispatching. Rule STEP-VAL-ANN triggers casting: v is cast to v' by type A. Rule STEP-ANN is a congruence rule with a restriction that e cannot be a raw value p. The remaining rules are normal congruence rules.

4.4 Type Soundness

For type soundness, we employ a proof technique similar to the one by Fan et al. [12]. First we need a number of results about the auxiliary relations used in reduction. We show some of the more interesting lemmas next:

Lemma 8 (Preservation (Applications and Projections)).

- If $\cdot \vdash v_1\, v_2 \Rightarrow A$ and $v_1 \bullet v_2 \hookrightarrow e$, then $\cdot \vdash e \Leftarrow A$.
- If $\cdot \vdash v.l \Rightarrow A$ and $v \bullet l \hookrightarrow e$, then $\cdot \vdash e \Leftarrow A$.

$$\boxed{e \longmapsto e'}$$ *(Small-Step Reduction)*

STEP-INT-ANN

$$\frac{}{i \longmapsto i : \mathsf{Int}}$$

STEP-ARR-ANN

$$\frac{}{\lambda x.\, e : A \to B \longmapsto (\lambda x.\, e : A \to B) : A \to B}$$

STEP-APP

$$\frac{(v_1 \bullet v_2) \hookrightarrow e}{v_1\, v_2 \longmapsto e}$$

STEP-PV-SPLIT

$$\frac{A_1 \vartriangleleft A \vartriangleright A_2}{p : A \longmapsto p : A_1 \,,\, p : A_2}$$

STEP-PRJ

$$\frac{(v \bullet l) \hookrightarrow v'}{v.l \longmapsto v'}$$

STEP-ANN

$$\frac{\neg e \in p \quad e \longmapsto e'}{e : A \longmapsto e' : A}$$

STEP-VAL-ANN

$$\frac{v \longmapsto_A v'}{v : A \longmapsto v'}$$

STEP-APP-L

$$\frac{e_1 \longmapsto e_1'}{e_1\, e_2 \longmapsto e_1'\, e_2}$$

STEP-APP-R

$$\frac{e_2 \longmapsto e_2'}{v_1\, e_2 \longmapsto v_1\, e_2'}$$

STEP-MRG-L

$$\frac{e_1 \longmapsto e_1'}{e_1 \,,\, e_2 \longmapsto e_1' \,,\, e_2}$$

STEP-MRG-R

$$\frac{e_2 \longmapsto e_2'}{v_1 \,,\, e_2 \longmapsto v_1 \,,\, e_2'}$$

STEP-RCD-R

$$\frac{e \longmapsto e'}{\{l = e\} \longmapsto \{l = e'\}}$$

STEP-PRJ-L

$$\frac{e \longmapsto e'}{e.l \longmapsto e'.l}$$

Fig. 6. Operational Semantics

Lemma 9 (Progress (Applications and Projections)).

- *If* $\cdot \vdash v_1\, v_2 \Rightarrow A$, *then* $\exists e, v_1 \bullet v_2 \hookrightarrow e$.
- *If* $\cdot \vdash v.l \Rightarrow A$, *then* $\exists e, v \bullet l \hookrightarrow e$.

Type soundness is proven via standard preservation and progress theorems.

Theorem 1 (Preservation). *If* $\cdot \vdash e \Leftrightarrow A$ *and* $e \longmapsto e'$, *then* $\cdot \vdash e' \Leftarrow A$.

Theorem 2 (Progress). *If* $\cdot \vdash e \Leftrightarrow A$, *then* e *is a value or* $\exists e', e \longmapsto e'$.

5   A Calculus with a Disjoint Merge Operator

This section presents a second calculus with a disjointness restriction on merges [17] to recover determinism. This calculus forbids some cases of conventional overloading, but still supports the other features. We focus on the key differences to the previous calculus, since most rules and relations are the same. Compared to previous calculi with disjoint intersection types, the main novelty is the use of the applicative subtyping and dispatching relations, which enables support for record projections and a restricted form of overloading naturally (without redundant type annotations).

5.1   Disjointness

We employ the definition of disjointness proposed by Oliveira et al. [17]. Informally, if all common supertypes of two types are *top-like* types, we can conclude that the two types are disjoint. Top-like types are those who are supertypes of all types (e.g., Top, $\mathsf{Top} \,\&\, \mathsf{Top}$) and defined as:

Top-like types $\rceil A \lceil \ ::= \ \mathsf{Top} \ | \ \rceil A \lceil \,\&\, \rceil B \lceil \ | \ A \to \rceil B \lceil \ | \ \{l :\rceil A \lceil\}$

Note that the including of such types into top-like types is also part of the classical BCD subtyping relation [3]. A formal specification of disjointness is given below. There is a sound and complete set of algorithmic disjointness rules that conform to this specification. The interested reader can check existing work for the algorithmic rules [14,17]. For space reasons we omit them here.

Definition 1 (Disjointness). $A * B \triangleq \forall C \ if \ A <: C \wedge B <: C, \ then \ C \ is \ top\text{-}like.$

In our calculus we allow merges of disjoint functions. Thus, types such as $\mathsf{Int} \to \mathsf{Int}$ or $\mathsf{Int} \to \mathsf{Bool}$ are disjoint. To include function types into our disjointness, types like $\mathsf{Int} \to \mathsf{Top}$ should be top-like and supertypes of all types, since otherwise $\mathsf{Int} \to \mathsf{Int}$ and $\mathsf{Int} \to \mathsf{Bool}$ cannot be disjoint according to our definition. However, this disjointness definition prevents some forms of overloading. For example, the type of show is $(\mathsf{Int} \to \mathsf{String})$ & $(\mathsf{Bool} \to \mathsf{String})$, which will be rejected by the disjointness condition since $\mathsf{Int} \to \mathsf{String}$ is not disjoint with $\mathsf{Bool} \to \mathsf{String}$. For those two types we can find a common supertype Int & $\mathsf{Bool} \to \mathsf{String}$, which is not top-like. To see why we should prevent such merges assume that show is allowed, then $\mathsf{show} \ (1,,\mathsf{true}) : \mathsf{String}$ is ambiguous since the result can be either "1" or "true". Note that some forms of overloading are still possible. For instance $\mathsf{succ},,\mathsf{not}$ will be accepted since $\mathsf{Int} \to \mathsf{Int}$ is disjoint with $\mathsf{Bool} \to \mathsf{Bool}$.

We follow previous work on disjoint intersection types [4] and generalize our subtyping rule for S-TOP to be $A <: \rceil B \lceil$ where $\rceil B \lceil$ means that B is a top-like type. Disjointness has important properties, which are helpful for the metatheory of the calculus. In particular, if two types are disjoint, their applicative subtyping results under the same partial types are also disjoint.

Lemma 10 (Applicative Subtyping and Disjointness). *If* $A * B$, $A \ll S = C_1$ *and* $B \ll S = C_2$, *then* $C_1 * C_2$.

Soundness and Completeness of Applicative Subtyping. With the more general subtyping rule for top-like types, applicative subtyping remains sound (with Lemmas 3, 5 in Sect. 3) with respect to subtyping. However, the completeness of our applicative subtyping needs to be slightly adapted.

Lemma 11 (Completeness of Applicative Subtyping). *If* $A <: B \to C$, *then* $(\exists D, A \ll B = D \wedge D <: C) \vee \mathsf{Top} <: C$.

In other words, applicative subtyping is complete except for the case where the output type is top-like. In such case applicative subtyping fails. Note though that this failure prevents strange programs from being type-checked. For example, subtyping has instances $\mathsf{Top} <: A \to \mathsf{Top}$, allowing $(1 : \mathsf{Top})\ 2$ to be well-typed, which would require special treatment in the typing rules. We reject such cases, making the typing rules simpler, and avoiding type-checking such programs.

5.2 Typing and Semantics

The main change in typing is that we add a disjoint premise in rule T-MRG.

$$\frac{\Gamma \vdash e_1 \Rightarrow A \qquad \Gamma \vdash e_2 \Rightarrow B \qquad A * B}{\Gamma \vdash e_1,,e_2 \Rightarrow A \,\&\, B}\;\text{T-MRG}$$

Most changes in the dynamic semantics are related to top-like types. Basically we need some extra conditions in the rules testing whether or not types are top-like? However, apart from these minor changes, the rules remain essentially the same. For space reasons we omit the detailed rules here.

5.3 Type Soundness and Determinism

All properties, including subject reduction and type soundness shown in the first calculus, also hold in this calculus. We only focus on determinism here, which is the most interesting property of the calculus with disjointness.

Theorem 3 (Determinism). *If* $\cdot \vdash e \Leftrightarrow A$, $e \longmapsto e_1$ *and* $e \longmapsto e_2$, *then* $e_1 = e_2$.

6 Related Work

Intersection Types, Merges and Overloading. Forsythe, introduced by Reynolds [21] has a restricted merge operator and its coherent semantics is formally proven. However, it does not account for overloaded functions since multiple functions are forbidden by merges. Pierce [18] introduced a `glue` construct in his calculus $F_\wedge$ as a language extension to support user-defined overloading and the types of overloaded functions are also modelled as intersection types. However his glue operator is unrestricted, leading to a non-deterministic semantics. Castagna et al. [6] gave a formalization to calculus for overloaded functions with subtyping. In his calculus, overloaded functions are defined as &-terms and their types are a finite list of arrow types with a consistency restriction. In overloaded applications, the "best-match" branch will be selected. The semantics is type-dependent, and overloaded applications rely on the runtime types, which is similar to our TDOS approach. Differently to our approach, nested composition is not supported in his calculus. Moreover, only one branch can be selected in the overloaded application, thus terms like `succ,,intToDigit` are rejected, forbidding currying on overloaded functions. In their work, records are encoded by lambda functions and multi-field records are overloaded functions.

Dunfield's calculus [9] is powerful enough to encode overloaded functions and record projection. Unlike our calculi, it does not support distributivity and nested composition. This means that overloaded functions do not interact nicely with currying. For example, to program `pshow unit 1` in her calculus, we should write `((pshow unit) : Int → Bool) 1`. As acknowledged by Dunfield, the semantics is not deterministic. This is similar to our first calculus in Sect. 4. To restrict the power of the merge operator and enable determinism, a disjoint-ness restriction on merges has been proposed [17]. Closest to our work is the λ_i^+ calculus [14], which is a deterministic calculus with intersection types and a disjoint merge operator. There are two major differences between our work and λ_i^+. (1) Our first calculus utilizes an unrestricted merge operator, which allows *any* functions and records to be merged. (2) Our second calculus can be viewed as a variant of λ_i^+ that employs applicative subtyping and thus avoids many unnecessary annotations that are required in λ_i^+ since function overloading and record projection are not directly supported in λ_i^+. In λ_i^+, we would need a term with an explicit type annotation instead: ((succ,,not) : Int $\rightarrow$ Int) 1. The rigid form of applications and projections in λ_i^+ prevents expressions such as (succ,,not) 1, which are not well-typed in λ_i^+.

In recent work, Rioux et al. [24] proposed a calculus with a disjoint merge operator that deals with union types and overloading. This is achieved with two more fine-grained disjointness relations called *mergeability* and *distinguishability*. Similarly to our calculus, they consider an expressive type-level dispatch relation that plays the same role as applicative subtyping in our calculus. Such dispatching relation supports union types, unlike our calculus. In terms of the operational semantics, there are significant differences between our work and Rioux et al.'s work. While their semantics still employs types at runtime, there is no casting relation. Instead there are patterns and co-patterns, which enforce runtime coercions via η-expansion. While overloading is supported, the disjointness relations are still not flexible enough to support return type overloading.

Semantic Subtyping. Semantic subtyping [13] takes a different direction to type overloaded functions with intersection types and union types. In semantic subtyping the semantics of types is set-theoretic and subtyping relations are derived from the semantics. The type system features intersection types, union types and negation types. Overloaded functions are defined by a *typecase* primitive which is similar to the elimination of union types. For example, the type of show is Int | Bool $\rightarrow$ String (| denotes union types). The approach to semantic subtyping of overloaded functions is different from ours, since in our calculi (1) only intersection types are used to represent types of overloaded functions; and (2) overloaded functions can be introduced by simply merging functions.

7   Conclusion and Future Work

In this paper, we proposed applicative subtyping, a novel subtyping algorithm to infer the return types of application and projection. We also designed its corresponding judgment applicative dispatching in the dynamic semantics. Together these features enable expressive calculi with a merge operator. We present a type sound calculus that supports all features, but is non-deterministic, and a second deterministic calculus with a disjointness restriction supporting all features except for overloading. Future work includes finding a design that enables overloading, while preserving determinism. Furthermore we are interested in extending the calculus with disjoint polymorphism [2].

Acknowledgement. We thank the anonymous reviewers for their helpful comments and our colleagues of HKU Programming Languages Group for their discussions to understand this work better. We thank Chen Cui for his valuable feedback on the draft. This work has been sponsored by Hong Kong Research Grant Council projects number 17209519, 17209520 and 17209821.

References

1. Applicative Intersection Types (Artifact). Zenodo, August 2022. https://doi.org/10.5281/zenodo.7004695
2. Alpuim, J., Oliveira, B.C.d.S., Shi, Z.: Disjoint polymorphism. In: European Symposium on Programming. pp. 1–28. Springer (2017)
3. Barendregt, H., Coppo, M., Dezani-Ciancaglini, M.: A filter lambda model and the completeness of type assignment1. The journal of symbolic logic **48**(4), 931–940 (1983)
4. Bi, X., Oliveira, B.C.D.S., Schrijvers, T.: The essence of nested composition. In: 32nd European Conference on Object-Oriented Programming (ECOOP 2018). Schloss Dagstuhl-Leibniz-Zentrum fuer Informatik (2018)
5. Bobrow, D.G., DeMichiel, L.G., Gabriel, R.P., Keene, S.E., Kiczales, G., Moon, D.A.: Common lisp object system specification. ACM SIGPLAN Not. **23**(SI), 1–142 (1988)
6. Castagna, G., Ghelli, G., Longo, G.: A calculus for overloaded functions with subtyping. Information and Computation 117(1), 115–135 (1995)
7. Coppo, M., Dezani-Ciancaglini, M., Venneri, B.: Functional characters of solvable terms. Mathematical Logic Quarterly 27(2–6), 45–58 (1981)
8. Davies, R., Pfenning, F.: Intersection types and computational effects. In: Proceedings of the Fifth ACM SIGPLAN International Conference on Functional Programming, pp. 198–208 (2000)
9. Dunfield, J.: Elaborating intersection and union types. Journal of Functional Programming 24(2–3), 133–165 (2014)
10. Dunfield, J., Krishnaswami, N.: Bidirectional typing. ACM Computing Surveys (CSUR) **54**(5), 1–38 (2021)
11. Ernst, E.: Family polymorphism. In: European Conference on Object-Oriented Programming. pp. 303–326. Springer (2001)
12. Fan, A., Huang, X., Xu, H., Sun, Y., Oliveira, B.C.D.S.: Direct foundations for compositional programming. In: 36th European Conference on Object-Oriented Programming, ECOOP 2022, 6–10 June 2022, Berlin, Germany. LIPIcs, vol. 222, pp. 18:1–18:28. Schloss Dagstuhl - Leibniz-Zentrum für Informatik (2022)
13. Frisch, A., Castagna, G., Benzaken, V.: Semantic subtyping: Dealing set-theoretically with function, union, intersection, and negation types. Journal of the ACM (JACM) **55**(4), 1–64 (2008)
14. Huang, X., Zhao, J., Oliveira, B.C.: Taming the merge operator. J. Funct. Programm. **31** (2021)
15. Kaes, S.: Parametric overloading in polymorphic programming languages. In: European Symposium on Programming. pp. 131–144. Springer (1988)

16. Marntirosian, K., Schrijvers, T., Oliveira, B.C.D.S., Karachalias, G.: Resolution as intersection subtyping via modus ponens. Proc. ACM Program. Lang. 4(OOPSLA) (2020)

17. Oliveira, B.C.D.S., Shi, Z., Alpuim, J.: Disjoint intersection types. In: Proceedings of the 21st ACM SIGPLAN International Conference on Functional Programming, pp. 364–377 (2016)

18. Pierce, B.C.: Programming with intersection types and bounded polymorphism. Ph.D. thesis. Citeseer (1991)

19. Pottinger, G.: A type assignment for the strongly normalizable λ-terms. In: To HB Curry: Essays on Combinatory Logic, Lambda Calculus and Formalism, pp. 561–577 (1980)

20. Rémy, D.: Type checking records and variants in a natural extension of ML. In: Proceedings of the 16th ACM SIGPLAN-SIGACT Symposium on Principles of Programming Languages, pp. 77–88 (1989)

21. Reynolds, J.C.: Preliminary design of the programming language Forsythe (1988)

22. Reynolds, J.C.: The coherence of languages with intersection types. In: International Symposium on Theoretical Aspects of Computer Software. pp. 675–700. Springer (1991)

23. Reynolds, J.C.: Design of the programming language forsythe. In: O'Hearn, P.W., Tennent, R.D. (eds.) ALGOL-Like Languages, pp. 173–233. Springer, Boston (1997). https://doi.org/10.1007/978-1-4612-4118-8_9

24. Rioux, N., Huang, X., Oliveira, B.C.D.S.: Zdancewic: a bowtie for a beast. Technical report, MS-CIS-22-02, Department of Computer and Information Science, University of Pennsylvania (2022)

25. Wadler, P., Blott, S.: How to make ad-hoc polymorphism less ad hoc. In: Proceedings of the 16th ACM SIGPLAN-SIGACT Symposium on Principles of Programming Languages, pp. 60–76 (1989)

26. Wadler, P., et al.: The expression problem. Posted on the Java Genericity mailing list (1998)

27. Wand, M.: Type inference for record concatenation and multiple inheritance. Information and Computation 93(1), 1–15 (1991)

28. Xie, N., Oliveira, B.C.d.S.: Let arguments go first. In: European Symposium on Programming. pp. 272–299. Springer (2018)

29. Zhang, W., Sun, Y., Oliveira, B.C.: Compositional programming. ACM Trans. Program. Lang. Syst. (TOPLAS) 43(3), 1–61 (2021)

A Calculus with Recursive Types, Record Concatenation and Subtyping

Yaoda Zhou[1]([✉]), Bruno C. d. S. Oliveira[1], and Andong Fan[2]

[1] The University of Hong Kong, Hong Kong, Hong Kong SAR, China
{ydzhou,bruno}@cs.hku.hk
[2] Zhejiang University, Hangzhou, China
afan2018@zju.edu.cn

Abstract. Calculi with subtyping, a form of record concatenation and recursive types are useful to model objects with multiple inheritance. Surprisingly, almost no existing calculi supports the three features together, partly because the combination of subtyping and record concatenation is already known to be troublesome. Recently, a line of work on *disjoint intersection types* with a *merge operator* has emerged as a new approach to deal with the interaction between subtyping and record concatenation. However, the addition of recursive types has not been studied.

In this paper we present a calculus that combines *iso-recursive types* with disjoint intersection types and a merge operator. The merge operator generalizes symmetric record concatenation, and the calculus supports subtyping as well as recursive types. We build on recent developments on the theory of iso-recursive subtyping using the so-called *nominal unfolding* rules to add iso-recursive types to a calculus with disjoint intersection types and a merge operator. The main challenge lies in the disjointness definition with iso-recursive subtyping. We show the type soundness of the calculus, decidability of subtyping, as well as the soundness and completeness of our disjointness definition. All the proofs are mechanized in the Coq theorem prover.

1 Introduction

Record calculi with a concatenation operator have attracted the attention of researchers due to their ability to give the semantics of object-oriented languages with multiple inheritance [14,15,19]. The foundational work by Cook and Palsberg [19], and Cardelli [14] work on the semantics of the Obliq language are prime examples of the usefulness of untyped record calculi with record concatenation to model the semantics of OOP with inheritance.

Unfortunately, typed calculi with record concatenation and subtyping have proven to be quite challenging to model. An important problem, identified by Cardelli and Mitchell [15], is that subtyping can hide static type information that is needed to correctly model (common forms of) record concatenation. Cardelli and Mitchell illustrate the problem with a simple example:

```
let f2 (r:{x:Int}) (s:{y:Bool}) : {x:Int} & {y:Bool} = r,,s
in f2 ({x=3, y=4}) ({y=true, x=false})
```

© The Author(s), under exclusive license to Springer Nature Switzerland AG 2022
I. Sergey (Ed.): APLAS 2022, LNCS 13658, pp. 175–195, 2022.
https://doi.org/10.1007/978-3-031-21037-2_9

Here f2 is a function that takes two records (r and s) as arguments, and returns a new record that concatenates the two records (r ,, s). For the return type of f2 we use record type concatenation (here denoted as R & S). Because of subtyping it is possible to invoke f2 with records that have *more* fields than the fields expected by the static types of the arguments of f2. For instance, while the static type of the first argument of f2 is : Intx : Int, the record that is actually provided at the application (= 3, y = 4x = 3, y = 4) also has an extra field y.

The program above is fine from a typing point of view, but what should the program evaluate to? There are a few common options for the semantics of record concatenation. Record concatenation can be *symmetric*, only allowing the concatenation of records without conflicts; or it can be *asymmetric*, implementing an overriding semantics where, in case of conflicts, fields on the left (or the right) record are given preference. Choosing a naive form of asymmetric concatenation does not work. For instance, with left-biased concatenation, the example above would evaluate to = 3, y = 4x = 3, y = 4, which has the *wrong type*! Therefore, Cardelli and Mitchell [15] state that:

> we should now feel compelled to define R & S only when R and S are **disjoint**: that is when any field present in an element of R is absent from every element of S, and vice versa.

hinting for an approach with symmetric concatenation, based on disjointness. But a naive symmetric concatenation operation would result in a record = 3, y = 4, y = true, x = falsex = 3, y = 4, y = true, x = false with conflicts, which should not be allowed! Thus, such a naive form of symmetric concatenation does not work either.

Recent work on calculi with *disjoint intersection types* [33] and a *merge operator* offers a solution to the Cardelli and Mitchell's problem for concatenation. For instance, the λ_i calculus [33] adopts disjointness and restricts subsumption to address the challenges of *symmetric* concatenation/merge. Most importantly, λ_i has a type-directed semantics to ensure proper information hiding and the preservation of the expected modular type invariants. The application of the f2 function in λ_i results in = 3, y = truex = 3, y = true, which has *no conflicts* and is of the *right type*. Types are used at runtime to ensure that fields hidden by subtyping are dropped from the record. This is enforced, for example, during beta-reduction, which uses the type of the argument to filter any hidden fields/-values from records/merges. Thus, before substitution, the first argument of f2, for instance, is first filtered using the type : Intx : Int. The actual record that is substituted in the body of f2 is = 3x = 3 (and not = 3, y = 4x = 3, y = 4).

An important limitation of existing calculi with disjoint intersection types is that they lack recursive types. For typed model of objects, supporting recursive types is important, since many object encodings require recursive types [10]. Without recursive types *binary methods* [9] and other types of methods, that refer to the current object type cannot be easily modelled. For example, it is hard to support an equality method in an object. In addition, recursive structures, such as lists or trees, require recursive types as well.

This paper studies subtyping relations combining *iso-recursive subtyping* with disjoint intersection types and a merge operator. Our calculus λ_i^μ, extends λ_i with recursive types. With λ_i^μ we can use a standard encoding of objects using recursive types [10,11,18,19] in λ_i^μ to model objects with recursive types. For instance, we can define an interface for arithmetic expressions Exp using a recursive type:

$$\text{Exp} := \mu\ \text{Exp. \{eval : nat, dbl : Exp, eq : Exp} \rightarrow \text{bool\}}$$

In Exp there are 3 methods: an evaluation method that returns the value of evaluating the expression; a dbl method that doubles all the natural numbers in (the AST of) an expression; and an equality method that compares the expression with another expression. In λ_i it is only possible to express the type of eval. However, in λ_i^μ we can also express dbl and eq. Importantly, in λ_i^μ the record type {eval : nat, dbl : Exp, eq : Exp $\rightarrow$ bool} is syntactic sugar for *intersections of single field records* [22,40]. In other words, to define the type Exp we need both intersection types and recursive types.

To add iso-recursive subtyping to λ_i^μ, we employ a recent formulation of iso-recursive subtyping based on the so-called *nominal unfolding* rules [47]. The nominal unfolding rules have equivalent expressive power to the iso-recursive Amber rules [12], but they are easier to work with formally. We prove various important properties for λ_i^μ, including *transitivity* of algorithmic subtyping, *decidability* as well as the *unfolding lemma*. A key technical challenge is how to define disjointness for iso-recursive types, which turns out to be non-trivial. By employing the notion of a *lower common supertype*, we show that it is possible to obtain a sound and complete formulation of algorithmic disjointness. All the calculi and lemmas presented in this paper have been mechanically formalized in the Coq theorem prover [42]. In summary, the contributions of this paper are:

- **Iso-recursive subtyping with intersection types:** We show the applicability of nominal unfoldings to a subtyping relation that includes intersection types. The subtyping relation is *transitive*, *decidable* and supports the *unfolding lemma*.
- **The λ_i^μ calculus,** which adds iso-recursive types to an existing calculus with record types, disjoint intersection types and a merge/concatenation operator.
- **Algorithmic disjointness for iso-recursive types.** The algorithmic formulation of disjointness for iso-recursive types is non-trivial. We introduce an approach based on *lower common supertypes*, enabling a *sound* and *complete* algorithm for disjointness.
- **Mechanical formalization:** Finally, we provide a mechanical formalization and proofs for all the calculi and proofs in the Coq theorem prover [42]. The proofs are available in the supplementary material of this submission [46].

2   Overview

2.1   Background: Disjoint Intersection Types

λ_i and other calculi with disjoint intersection types [2,6,33] have been shown to provide flexible forms of *dynamic* multiple inheritance [5,45]. Moreover, they enable a highly modular and compositional programming style that addresses the Expression Problem [43] naturally. For space reasons, here we only illustrate briefly the ability of such calculi to model *first-class traits* and a very dynamic form of inheritance [5]:

```
addId(super:Trait[Person], idNumber:Int):Trait[Student]=
    trait inherits super => { def id : Int = idNumber }
```

In this code, written in the SEDEL language [5], there are two noteworthy points. Firstly, unlike statically typed mainstream OOP languages, traits (which are similar to OOP classes) are first class. They can be passed as arguments (such as super), or returned as a result as above. Secondly, the code uses a highly dynamic form of inheritance. The trait that is inherited (super) is a parameter of the function. In contrast, in languages like Java, for class A extends B, the class B must be statically known. We refer the interested reader to the work by [5,45] for a much more extensive discussion on the applications of calculi with disjoint intersection types, as well as how to encode source language features, such as first-class traits.

2.2 λ_i^μ: Adding Recursive Types to λ_i

An important limitation of existing calculi with disjoint intersection types is that they lack recursive types, preventing *binary methods* [9] and other types of methods. As we have discussed in Sect. 1, without recursive types we cannot write object interfaces such as:

$$\mathsf{Exp} := \mu \; \mathsf{Exp}. \; \{\mathsf{eval} : \mathsf{nat}, \; \mathsf{dbl} : \mathsf{Exp}, \; \mathsf{eq} : \mathsf{Exp} \to \mathsf{bool}\}$$

where some method signatures refer to the type being defined. In λ_i^μ we add recursive types, therefore it becomes possible to define the object interface Exp. Using a standard object encoding based on records and recursive types [10,18], we can then model objects. To implement Exp we first need a few auxiliary functions (eval$'$: $\mathsf{Exp} \to \mathsf{nat}$, dbl$'$: $\mathsf{Exp} \to \mathsf{Exp}$ and eq$'$: $\mathsf{Exp} \to \mathsf{Exp} \to \mathsf{bool}$) that unfold the recursive type[1]. Then we define two recursive functions lit : $\mathsf{nat} \to \mathsf{Exp}$ and add : $\mathsf{Exp} \to \mathsf{Exp} \to \mathsf{Exp}$:

$$
\begin{aligned}
\mathsf{eval}' \; e \;\; &= (\mathsf{unfold} \; [\mathsf{Exp}] \; e).\mathsf{eval} \\
\mathsf{dbl}' \; e \;\; &= (\mathsf{unfold} \; [\mathsf{Exp}] \; e).\mathsf{dbl} \\
\mathsf{eq}' \; e_1 \; e_2 &= (\mathsf{unfold} \; [\mathsf{Exp}] \; e_1).\mathsf{eq} \; e_2 \\
\mathsf{lit} \; n \;\; &= \mathsf{fold} \; [\mathsf{Exp}]\{\mathsf{eval} = n, \; \mathsf{dbl} = \mathsf{lit}(n * 2), \\
&\qquad\qquad \mathsf{eq} = \lambda e'. \; (\mathsf{eval}' \; e' == n) : \mathsf{Exp} \to \mathsf{bool}\} \\
\mathsf{add} \; e_1 \; e_2 &= \mathsf{fold} \; [\mathsf{Exp}]\{\mathsf{eval} = \mathsf{eval}' \; e_1 + \mathsf{eval}' \; e_2, \; \mathsf{dbl} = \mathsf{add} \; (\mathsf{dbl}' \; e_1) \; (\mathsf{dbl}' \; e_2), \\
&\qquad\qquad \mathsf{eq} = \lambda e'. \; (\mathsf{eval}' \; e' == \mathsf{eval}' \; e_1 + \mathsf{eval}' \; e_2) : \mathsf{Exp} \to \mathsf{bool}\}
\end{aligned}
$$

In this example the functions lit and add act as encodings of classes or traits. The function lit is basic: it stores the literal, a double function and equality functions.

---

[1] We assume the presence of recursive functions, and that records are lazy in the example.

In add, operations such as eval′ have to be called for subexpressions. To check if $2 * 7 = 2 * (3 + 4)$, we can define e_1 : Exp = lit 7 and e_2 : Exp = add (lit 3) (lit 4). Then, we check if eq′ (dbl′ e_1) (dbl′ e_2) is satisfied.

2.3   Disjointness for Recursive Types

The disjointness restriction is an essential feature in calculi with disjoint intersection types. Such restriction ensures that certain merges of values, that could lead to ambiguity, are forbidden. For instance, in the example above merges are used to encode records. A record $\{x = 1, y = true\}$ is encoded as the merge of two single field records $\{x = 1\}, , \{y = true\}$. Here the operator , , is the merge operator [22, 40], which can be viewed as a generalization of record concatenation. Ambiguity can arise with the merge operator if the two values in the merge overlap. For instance, with records, we would like to forbid $r = \{x = 1, x = 2\}$ (a record with two fields with the same name and type), since $r.x$ would be ambiguous. With the merge operator we can merge not only records, but also arbitrary values. Thus, we need to forbid merges such as $1, , 2$ which provides two values of type Int. The disjointness restriction is employed when type-checking merges to ensure that the types being merged do not overlap. A standard specification of disjointness [29, 33] is:

Definition 1 (Specification of disjointness). $\Gamma \vdash A *_s B \equiv \forall C, (\Gamma \vdash A \le C \wedge \Gamma \vdash B \le C) \Rightarrow \rceil C \lceil$

The intuition is that two types are disjoint when all their supertypes are (isomorphic to) $\top$. The notation $\rceil \cdot \lceil$ represents toplike types, which are both supertypes and subtypes of $\top$. In essence ambiguity arises from upcasts on values. For instance if we cast $1, , 2$ under type Int there can be two possible results. Disjointness prevents merges with values having common supertypes (with the exception of $\top$). Therefore, when such disjoint merges are upcast we can ensure that only one value will be extracted for any given (non toplike) type.

One of the challenges in the design of λ_i^μ is to find an algorithmic rule to check whether two recursive types are disjoint and prove that it is complete with respect to the specification. As part of the completeness proof we must be able to find common supertypes of two types, but this is non-trivial for recursive types due to contravariance. For example, assume that we have two recursive types $\mu\alpha. ((nat \rightarrow \alpha) \rightarrow nat)$ and $\mu\alpha. ((\top \rightarrow \alpha) \rightarrow nat)$, then $\mu\alpha. ((nat \rightarrow \alpha) \& (\top \rightarrow \alpha) \rightarrow nat)$ is not a valid common supertype because α is contravariant. In contrast, for covariant recursive types and non-recursive types, finding a common supertype is simpler. For instance, for the recursive types $\mu\alpha. (String \rightarrow \alpha)$ and $\mu\alpha. (nat \rightarrow \alpha)$, the intersection of the two inputs types of the function in the recursive type gives us a common supertype $\mu\alpha. (String \& nat \rightarrow \alpha)$.

In Sect. 4, we will show that the disjoint rules for recursive types are quite simple: we only need to check if their one-time finite unfoldings are disjoint or not. Furthermore, we can address the challenge of finding supertypes using a *lower common supertype* definition, which gives a common supertype even for contravariant recursive types. This plays a crucial role in the completeness proof for disjointness.

3 Static Semantics of λ_i^μ

This section presents the static semantics of λ_i^μ, covering syntax, subtyping, disjointness and typing rules. The main novelty over λ_i is the addition of iso-recursive types, which requires novel proof techniques to deal with disjointness. Our subtyping relation supports intersection types and iso-recursive types using the nominal unfolding rule [47]. Among others, we prove *transitivity* of sub-typing, the *unfolding lemma* and *decidability* of subtyping. We note that this subtyping relation is quite general and, while it is used by our specific application in Sect. 4, it can be easily adapted to many other calculi with recursive types and intersection types.

3.1 Syntax and Subtyping

Syntax The syntax of our calculus is:

Types $A, B ::= \mathsf{nat} \mid \top \mid \bot \mid A_1 \to A_2 \mid \{\alpha : A\} \mid \alpha \mid \mu\alpha.\ A \mid A_1 \& A_2$

Expressions $e ::= i \mid \top \mid x \mid \lambda x.\ e : A \to B \mid e_1\ e_2 \mid \mathsf{fix}\ x : A.\ e \mid e : A$
$\qquad\qquad\quad \mid \mathsf{unfold}\ [A]\ e \mid \mathsf{fold}\ [A]\ e \mid \{\alpha = e\} \mid e_1,, e_2 \mid e.\alpha$

Values $v ::= i \mid \top \mid \lambda x\ .e : A \to B \mid \mathsf{fold}\ [A]\ v \mid v_1,, v_2 \mid \{\alpha = v\}$

Contexts $\Gamma ::= \cdot \mid \Gamma,\ \alpha \mid \Gamma,\ x : A$

Modes $\Leftrightarrow ::= \Leftarrow\ \mid\ \Rightarrow$

Meta-variables A, B range over types. Types are mostly standard and consist of: natural numbers (nat), the top type ($\top$), the bottom type ($\bot$), function types ($A \to B$), type variables (α), and recursive types ($\mu\alpha.\ A$). The most interesting feature is the presence of *labelled types* $\{\alpha : A\}$. Labelled types can be viewed as a simple form of nominal types. They are essentially a pair that contains a name (or type variable) α and a type. We use labelled types in two different ways: 1) we use them with the nominal unfolding rules for iso-recursive subtyping; and 2) we also use them to model records and records types in combination with intersection types and the merge operator.

Expressions, which are denoted as e, include: a top value ($\top$), lambda expressions ($\lambda x.\ e : A \to B$) and fixpoints ($\mathsf{fix}\ x : A.\ e$). Note that for lambda expressions, we annotate both input and output types, since the output types are necessary in a Type-Directed Operational Semantics (TDOS) during reduction, which will be described in Sect. 4.

Values include a canonical top value ($\top$), lambda expressions ($\lambda x.e : A \to B$), merges of values ($v_1,, v_2$) and record values ($\{\alpha = v\}$). For proving type-safety, the contexts also store the types of variables used in the program. We employ bi-directional type checking in the system, thus $\Leftarrow/\Rightarrow$ represent the checking mode and synthesis mode, respectively.

$$\boxed{\vdash \Gamma} \hspace{5cm} \textit{(Well-Formed Environment)}$$

$$
\begin{array}{ccc}
\text{WFE-NIL} & \dfrac{\vdash \Gamma \quad \text{fresh } \alpha}{\vdash \Gamma, \alpha} & \dfrac{\vdash \Gamma \quad \text{fresh } x \quad \Gamma \vdash A}{\vdash \Gamma, x : A} \\[2mm]
\dfrac{}{\vdash \cdot} & \text{WFE-SUB} & \text{WFE-TYP}
\end{array}
$$

$$\boxed{\Gamma \vdash A} \hspace{5cm} \textit{(Well-Formed Type)}$$

$$
\begin{array}{ccccc}
\text{WFT-NAT} & \text{WFT-TOP} & \text{WFT-BOT} & \text{WFT-VAR} & \text{WFT-ARR} \\[1mm]
\dfrac{\vdash \Gamma}{\Gamma \vdash \mathbf{nat}} & \dfrac{\vdash \Gamma}{\Gamma \vdash \top} & \dfrac{\vdash \Gamma}{\Gamma \vdash \bot} & \dfrac{\alpha \in \Gamma}{\Gamma \vdash \alpha} & \dfrac{\Gamma \vdash A \quad \Gamma \vdash B}{\Gamma \vdash A \to B}
\end{array}
$$

$$
\begin{array}{ccc}
\text{WFT-RCD} & \text{WFT-REC} & \text{WFT-AND} \\[1mm]
\dfrac{\Gamma \vdash A}{\Gamma \vdash \{\alpha : A\}} & \dfrac{\Gamma, \alpha \vdash A}{\Gamma \vdash \mu\alpha.\ A} & \dfrac{\Gamma \vdash A \quad \Gamma \vdash B}{\Gamma \vdash A \& B}
\end{array}
$$

Fig. 1. Well-formedness.

The syntactic sugar for record types and records is also shown below, illustrates the standard encoding [22, 40] in terms of intersection types, labelled types and merges.

$$\{\alpha_1 : A_1, \ldots, \alpha_n : A_n\} \equiv \{\alpha_1 : A_1\}\ \&\ \ldots\ \&\ \{\alpha_n : A_n\}$$
$$\{\alpha_1 = e_1, \ldots, \alpha_n = e_n\} \equiv \{\alpha_1 = e_1\}\ ,,\ \ldots\ ,,\ \{\alpha_n = e_n\}$$

Well-Formedness. The definition of well-formed types is mostly standard, as Fig. 1 shows. An environment is well-formed if all the variables are distinct.

Subtyping. Figure 2 shows the subtyping relation. Rule S-BOT states that any well-formed type A is a supertype of the $\bot$ type. Rule S-FVAR is a standard rule for type variables: variable α is a subtype of itself. The rule for function types (rule S-ARROW) and intersection types are standard. Rule S-RCD states that a labelled type is a subtype of another labelled type if the two types are labelled with the same name and $A \leq B$.

Rule S-REC, the nominal unfolding rule, is the most interesting one. In this rule, the body of the recursive type is unfolded twice. However, for the innermost unfolding, the type that we substitute is not the recursive type. Instead, we use a labelled type, where the label is a fresh name that serves as a unique identifier for the recursive types being compared. The label is associated to the bodies of both recursive types. In other words, we substitute the recursive variable by the labelled type in the recursive type body A: $[\alpha \mapsto \{\beta : A\}]\ A$. The label is useful to identify types that arise from recursive unfolding substitutions and to give distinct identities to recursive types. We should note that Zhou et al. [47] present the rule in a slightly different way, by reusing the recursive type variable

$$\boxed{\,]A\lceil\,}$$ *(Toplike Type)*

TOP-BASE
$$\dfrac{}{\,]\top\lceil\,}$$

TOP-AND
$$\dfrac{\,]A\lceil \quad]B\lceil\,}{\,]A\&B\lceil\,}$$

TOP-ARROW
$$\dfrac{\,]B\lceil \quad \Gamma \vdash A\,}{\,]A \to B\lceil\,}$$

TOP-REC
$$\dfrac{\,]A\lceil\,}{\,]\mu\alpha.\,A\lceil\,}$$

TOP-RCD
$$\dfrac{\,]A\lceil\,}{\,]\{\alpha : A\}\lceil\,}$$

$$\boxed{\,\Gamma \vdash A \leq B\,}$$ *(Subtyping)*

S-NAT
$$\dfrac{\vdash \Gamma}{\Gamma \vdash \mathbf{nat} \leq \mathbf{nat}}$$

S-TOP
$$\dfrac{\vdash \Gamma \quad]B\lceil}{\Gamma \vdash A \leq B}$$

S-BOT
$$\dfrac{\vdash \Gamma \quad \Gamma \vdash A}{\Gamma \vdash \bot \leq A}$$

S-RCD
$$\dfrac{\Gamma \vdash A \leq B}{\Gamma \vdash \{\alpha : A\} \leq \{\alpha : B\}}$$

S-ARROW
$$\dfrac{\Gamma \vdash B_1 \leq A_1 \quad \Gamma \vdash A_2 \leq B_2}{\Gamma \vdash A_1 \to A_2 \leq B_1 \to B_2}$$

S-AND
$$\dfrac{\Gamma \vdash A \leq B_1 \quad \Gamma \vdash A \leq B_2}{\Gamma \vdash A \leq B_1 \& B_2}$$

S-FVAR
$$\dfrac{\vdash \Gamma \quad \alpha \in \Gamma}{\Gamma \vdash \alpha \leq \alpha}$$

S-ANDR
$$\dfrac{\Gamma \vdash A_1 \quad \Gamma \vdash A_2 \leq B}{\Gamma \vdash A_1 \& A_2 \leq B}$$

S-ANDL
$$\dfrac{\Gamma \vdash A_2 \quad \Gamma \vdash A_1 \leq B}{\Gamma \vdash A_1 \& A_2 \leq B}$$

S-REC
$$\dfrac{\Gamma, \alpha \vdash [\alpha \mapsto \{\beta : A\}]\,A \leq [\alpha \mapsto \{\beta : B\}]\,B \quad \text{fresh } \beta}{\Gamma \vdash \mu\alpha.\,A \leq \mu\alpha.\,B}$$

Fig. 2. Subtyping rules.

as a label:

S-OLDREC
$$\dfrac{\Gamma, \alpha \vdash [\alpha \mapsto \{\alpha : A\}]A \leq [\alpha \mapsto \{\alpha : B\}]\,B}{\Gamma \vdash \mu\alpha.\,A \leq \mu\alpha.\,B}$$

The two presentations are equivalent, but the original presentation implicitly assumes that bound variables and free variables are distinct. Thus, the α that is bound by the recursive type $\mu\alpha.\,A$ and the α used in the label should be considered distinct (and the α used in the label should be distinct from other free variables as well). To avoid confusion we make such implicit assumptions explicit in the rule S-REC here.

The basic intuition about the nominal unfolding rules is that, in order to deal with negative occurrences of recursive type variables, such as in $\mu\alpha.\,\alpha \to$ nat $\leq \mu\alpha.\,\alpha \to \top$ we need to unfold the recursive types at least twice to detect invalid subtyping statements. For instance, unfolding the previous example twice leads to $((\mu\alpha.\,\alpha \to \text{nat}) \to \text{nat}) \to \text{nat} \leq ((\mu\alpha.\,\alpha \to \top) \to \top) \to \top$, which is *not* a valid subtyping statement. Thus, the original subtyping statement should be rejected. The nominal unfolding rules leverage on this insight, while being terminating since the recursive types are replaced by non-recursive types that are in the same subtyping relation as the original types. The nominal unfolding rules have been shown by Zhou et al. [47] to have equivalent expressive power to the well-known (iso-recursive) Amber rules [12]. However, the nominal unfolding rules are easier to work with in terms of proofs, which is the reason why we employ them here. In particular, they enable us to prove transitivity, and to have a set of algorithmic rules (without transitivity built in). We refer interested readers to the work by Zhou et al. for the equivalence proofs with respect to the Amber rules and the theory of the nominal unfolding rules.

A toplike type, whose definition is shown as rule S-TOP, is both a supertype and a subtype of $\top$. In calculi with disjoint intersection types, the definition of toplike types plays an important role, since disjointness is defined in terms of toplike types. Allowing a larger set of toplike types enables more types to be disjoint. In particular, the motivation for λ_i to include rule TOP-ARROW in subtyping is to allow certain function types to be disjoint [6,28,33]. The rule TOP-ARROW itself is inspired from the well-known BCD-subtyping [4] relation, which also states that any function type that returns a toplike type is itself toplike. Rule TOP-ARROW was first adopted in calculi with disjoint intersection types by Bi et al. [6], and we follow that approach as well here. Without such rule two function types can never be disjoint, disallowing more than one function in a merge (where all expressions must have disjoint types). Similarly, in λ_i^μ the rule TOP-REC enables merges that can contain more than one expression with a recursive type.

Subtyping is reflexive and transitive:

Theorem 1 (Reflexivity). *If* $\vdash \Gamma$ *and* $\Gamma \vdash A$ *then* $\Gamma \vdash A \leq A$.

Theorem 2 (Transitivity). *If* $\Gamma \vdash A \leq B$ *and* $\Gamma \vdash B \leq C$ *then* $\Gamma \vdash A \leq C$.

Furthermore, we have also proved the unfolding lemma, which plays an important role in type preservation. The proof strategy is similar to the approach used in Zhou et al. [47].

Lemma 1 (Unfolding Lemma). *If* $\Gamma \vdash \mu\alpha.\ A \leq \mu\alpha.\ B$ *then* $\Gamma \vdash [\alpha \mapsto \mu\alpha.\ A]\ A \leq [\alpha \mapsto \mu\alpha.\ B]\ B$.

3.2 Decidability

Decidability of subtyping is a significant property, which is often problematic in many subtyping relations [27,37]. Fortunately, under our new iso-recursive subtyping rules with nominal unfoldings, decidability is easy to prove:

Theorem 3 (Decidability of Subtyping). *If* $\vdash \Gamma$, $\Gamma \vdash A$ *and* $\Gamma \vdash B$, *then* $\Gamma \vdash A \leq B$ *is decidable.*

Informally, looking at Fig. 2 we can identify two potential complications in deriving an algorithm from the subtyping relation and showing its termination. The first complication comes from the newly added intersection subtyping rules, which makes the relation not completely syntax directed. In particular, there is overlapping between all three intersection rules. However, this problem is well-known from the literature of intersection types. A standard solution, proposed by Davies and Pfenning [21], is to only apply rule S-ANDL and rule S-ANDR for $\Gamma \vdash A_1 \& A_2 \leq B$ when B is *ordinary* (i.e. not an intersection type). This removes the overlapping between rule S-AND and rules S-ANDR and S-ANDL. For the remaining overlapping between rules S-ANDR and S-ANDL backtracking is needed. The same approach can be adopted in an implementation of our subtyping relation. The second complication is that the relation is not structurally recursive because of rule S-REC. In rule S-REC the size of the types in the premise can actually grow. However, the key observation here is that the number of recursive binders will reach the peak and decreases after some unfoldings. We employ the same technique by Zhou et al. [47], to prove decidability with a nominal unfolding rule.

3.3 Disjointness

One of the core judgments of λ_i^μ is disjointness. The standard disjointness specification [33] states that two types A and B are disjoint if all common supertypes of A and B are toplike, as Definition 1 showed. In other words, A and B are disjoint if there are no non-toplike supertypes. While this definition of disjointness is concise, it is not algorithmic. Thus, a challenge in calculi with disjoint intersection types is to find an algorithmic set of rules that is sound and complete to the disjointness specification.

Figure 3 shows an algorithmic formulation of disjointness. Most rules are standard and follow from previous work [7,28,33]. Toplike types are disjoint with other types (rules DIS-TOPL and DIS-TOPR). Intersection types need to check the disjointness of every component (rules DIS-ANDL and DIS-ANDR). Two labelled types are disjoint if they have distinct labels or the types of the label are disjoint (rules DIS-RCDRCD and DIS-RCDRCDEQ). Two different variables are always disjoint (rule DIS-VARVAR). Rule DIS-ARRARR states that, for two function types, we just need to check if their output types are disjoint or not.

The most interesting one is the disjointness of recursive types. Without toplike types, it could be very simple: any two recursive types are not disjoint because $\mu\alpha. \top$ is a non toplike common supertype for all recursive types. However, the introduction of toplike types complicates the interaction between any two recursive types, as we described in Sect. 2. Nevertheless, rule DIS-RECREC is surprisingly simple: two recursive types are disjoint if their bodies are disjoint. Finally, two types with different type constructors (e.g. record types and recursive types) are disjoint (rule DIS-AXIOM).

Disjointness Soundness. The soundness lemma showing that our rules satisfy the specification is straightforward:

Lemma 2 (Soundness). *If $\Gamma \vdash A * B$ then $\Gamma \vdash A *_s B$.*

Proof. By induction on $\Gamma \vdash A * B$.

$$\boxed{\Gamma \vdash A * B} \hspace{5cm} (Disjointness)$$

DIS-TOPL
$$\frac{\rceil B \lceil}{\Gamma \vdash A * B}$$

DIS-TOPR
$$\frac{\rceil A \lceil}{\Gamma \vdash A * B}$$

DIS-ANDL
$$\frac{\Gamma \vdash A_1 * B \quad \Gamma \vdash A_2' * B}{\Gamma \vdash A_1 \& A_2 * B}$$

DIS-ANDR
$$\frac{\Gamma \vdash A * B_1 \quad \Gamma \vdash A * B_2}{\Gamma \vdash A * B_1 \& B_2}$$

DIS-VARVAR
$$\frac{\alpha \neq \beta}{\Gamma \vdash \alpha * \beta}$$

DIS-ARRARR
$$\frac{\Gamma \vdash A_2 * B_2}{\Gamma \vdash A_1 \to A_2 * B_1 \to B_2}$$

DIS-RCDRCD
$$\frac{\alpha \neq \beta}{\Gamma \vdash \{\alpha : A\} * \{\beta : B\}}$$

DIS-RCDRCDEQ
$$\frac{\Gamma \vdash A * B}{\Gamma \vdash \{\alpha : A\} * \{\alpha : B\}}$$

DIS-RECREC
$$\frac{\Gamma, \alpha \vdash A * B}{\Gamma \vdash \mu\alpha.\ A * \mu\alpha.\ B}$$

DIS-AXIOM
$$\frac{\Gamma \vdash A *_{axiom} B}{\Gamma \vdash A * B}$$

Fig. 3. Disjointness.

3.4   Completeness of Disjointness

The most challenging part of the formalization of λ_i^μ is to show that algorithmic disjointness is complete with respect to the specification. The difficulty is brought by rule DIS-RECREC. If two recursive types $\mu\alpha.\ A$ and $\mu\alpha.\ B$ satisfy the specification, then for any type C, $\Gamma \vdash \mu\alpha.\ A \leq C \wedge \Gamma \vdash \mu\alpha.\ B \leq C$ implies that C is toplike. By rule DIS-RECREC, we want to prove that any type D satisfying $\Gamma, \alpha \vdash A \leq D \wedge \Gamma, \alpha \vdash B \leq D$ implies that D is toplike. Clearly C and D should be related since in one case C is the supertype of two recursive types, and in the other case D is the supertype of the bodies of the two recursive types. However, the relation between C and D is intricate.

Lower Common Supertype. To help to relate C and D, we define a new function $\sqcup$, which is shown in Fig. 4. The function $\sqcup$ computes a lower supertype of type A and B. A simplification that we employ in our definition is that types of common supertypes in contravariant positions are all $\bot$. Strictly speaking this means that the supertype that we find is not the lowest one in the subtyping lattice. But in our setting this does not matter, because the disjointness of arrow types (see rule DIS-ARRARR) does not account for input types. If the input types did matter for disjointness then we would likely need a dual definition for finding greater common subtypes, making the definition more involved. We can prove some useful properties for $\sqcup$:

Lemma 3 ($\sqcup$ is supertype). *For any A and B, $\Gamma \vdash A \leq A \sqcup B$ and $\Gamma \vdash B \leq A \sqcup B$.*

Lemma 4. *If $\Gamma \vdash A \leq C$ and $\Gamma \vdash B \leq C$ and $A \sqcup B$ is toplike, then C is toplike.*

$$
\begin{aligned}
\top \sqcup A &= \top & A \sqcup \top &= \top \\
\alpha \sqcup \alpha &= \alpha & \alpha \sqcup \beta &= \top \ (\alpha \neq \beta) \\
A \sqcup B\&C &= A\&B \sqcup A\&C & A\&B \sqcup C &= A\&C \sqcup B\&C \\
\bot \sqcup \mu\alpha.\ A &= \mu\alpha.\ (\bot \sqcup A) & \mu\alpha.\ A \sqcup \bot &= \mu\alpha.\ (A \sqcup \bot) \\
\bot \sqcup \{\alpha : A\} &= \{\alpha : \bot \sqcup A\} & \{\alpha : A\} \sqcup \bot &= \{\alpha : A \sqcup \bot\} \\
\bot \sqcup A_1 \to A_2 &= \bot \to (\bot \sqcup A_2) & A_1 \to A_2 \sqcup \bot &= \bot \to (A_2 \sqcup \bot) \\
\mu\alpha.\ A \sqcup \mu\alpha.\ B &= \mu\alpha.\ (A \sqcup B) & \{\alpha : A\} \sqcup \{\beta : B\} &= \top \ (\alpha \neq \beta) \\
A_1 \to A_2 \sqcup B_1 \to B_2 &= \bot \to (A_2 \sqcup B_2) & \{\alpha : A\} \sqcup \{\alpha : B\} &= \{\alpha : A \sqcup B\}
\end{aligned}
$$

otherwise: $\bot \sqcup A = A, \ A \sqcup \bot = A, \ A \sqcup A = A, \ A \sqcup B = \top,$

Fig. 4. Lower common supertype.

Lemma 4 is the most important one: $A \sqcup B$ is not the least common supertype of A and B, but if it is toplike then all supertypes of A and B are toplike. With the previous lemmas we can prove the completeness lemma:

Lemma 5 (Completeness). *For types A and B, if $\Gamma \vdash A *_s B$ then $\Gamma \vdash A * B$.*

3.5   Bidirectional Typing

We use bidirectional type checking in λ_i^μ, following λ_i [29]. Bi-directional type-checking is helpful to eliminate a source of ambiguity (and non-determinism) that arises from an unrestricted subsumption rule in conventional type assignment systems in the presence of a concatenation/merge operator (a point which was also noted by Cardelli and Mitchell [15]). The typing rules are shown in Fig. 5. There are two standard modes: $\Gamma \vdash e \Rightarrow A$ synthesises the type A of expression e under the context Γ, and $\Gamma \vdash e \Leftarrow A$ checks if expression e has type A under the context Γ.

Many rules are standard. There are two rules for merge expressions, which follow from previous work [29]. Rule TYPING-MERGE employs a disjointness restriction, and only allows two expressions with disjoint types to be merged. The disjointness restriction prevents ambiguity that could arise merging types with common (non-toplike) supertypes. For instance, if $1,,2$ would be allowed, then in an expression like $(1,,2) + 3$ we could have two possible results: 4 and 5. The merge of duplicated values such as $1,,1$ is not harmful, since no ambiguity arises in this case, and such values can arise from reduction. Thus, there is also a rule TYPING-MERGEV, which allows merging two consistent values regardless of their types. The consistency relation is:

Definition 2 (Consistency). $v_1 \approx_{spec} v_2 \equiv \forall A, (v_1 \hookrightarrow_A v_1' \wedge v_2 \hookrightarrow_A v_2') \Rightarrow v_1' = v_2'$

In this relation, two values are consistent if for any type A casting of those two values under type A produces the same result. We introduce the casting relation $v_1 \hookrightarrow_A v_2$, which reduces the value v_1 to v_2 under the type A in Sect. 4.1. A key property relating consistency and disjointness is:

$$\boxed{\Gamma \vdash e \Leftrightarrow A}$$ *(Typing)*

TYPING-SUB
$$\frac{\Gamma \vdash e \Rightarrow A \quad \Gamma \vdash A \leq B}{\Gamma \vdash e \Leftarrow B}$$

TYPING-TOP
$$\frac{\vdash \Gamma}{\Gamma \vdash \top \Rightarrow \top}$$

TYPING-VAR
$$\frac{\vdash \Gamma \quad x : A \in \Gamma}{\Gamma \vdash x \Rightarrow A}$$

TYPING-APP
$$\frac{\Gamma \vdash e_1 \Rightarrow A_1 \rightarrow A_2 \quad \Gamma \vdash e_2 \Leftarrow A_1}{\Gamma \vdash e_1 \ e_2 \Rightarrow A_2}$$

TYPING-NAT
$$\frac{\vdash \Gamma}{\Gamma \vdash i \Rightarrow \mathbf{nat}}$$

TYPING-ANNO
$$\frac{\Gamma \vdash e \Leftarrow A}{\Gamma \vdash e : A \Rightarrow A}$$

TYPING-PROJ
$$\frac{\Gamma \vdash e \Rightarrow \{\alpha : A\}}{\Gamma \vdash e.\alpha \Rightarrow A}$$

TYPING-RCD
$$\frac{\Gamma \vdash e \Rightarrow A}{\Gamma \vdash \{\alpha = e\} \Rightarrow \{\alpha : A\}}$$

TYPING-ABS
$$\frac{\Gamma, x : A_1 \vdash e \Leftarrow A_2}{\Gamma \vdash \lambda x.e : A_1 \rightarrow A_2 \Rightarrow A_1 \rightarrow A_2}$$

TYPING-UNFOLD
$$\frac{\Gamma \vdash e \Leftarrow \mu\alpha.\ A}{\Gamma \vdash \mathsf{unfold}\ [\mu\alpha.\ A]\ e \Rightarrow [\alpha \mapsto \mu\alpha.\ A]\ A}$$

TYPING-FIX
$$\frac{\Gamma, x : A \vdash e \Leftarrow A}{\Gamma \vdash \mathsf{fix}\ x : A.\ e \Rightarrow A}$$

TYPING-MERGE
$$\frac{\Gamma \vdash e_1 \Rightarrow A \quad \Gamma \vdash e_2 \Rightarrow B \quad \Gamma \vdash A * B}{\Gamma \vdash e_1,, e_2 \Rightarrow A\&B}$$

TYPING-MERGEV
$$\frac{\cdot \vdash v_1 \Rightarrow A \quad \cdot \vdash v_2 \Rightarrow B \quad v_1 \approx_{spec} v_2}{\Gamma \vdash v_1,, v_2 \Rightarrow A\&B}$$

TYPING-FOLD
$$\frac{\Gamma \vdash e \Leftarrow [\alpha \mapsto \mu\alpha.\ A]\ A \quad \Gamma \vdash \mu\alpha.\ A}{\Gamma \vdash \mathsf{fold}\ [\mu\alpha.\ A]\ e \Rightarrow \mu\alpha.\ A}$$

Fig. 5. Typing.

Lemma 6 (Consistency of disjoint values). *If $\vdash v_1 \Rightarrow A$ and $\vdash v_2 \Rightarrow B$ and $\vdash A *_s B$ then $v_1 \approx_{spec} v_2$.*

4   Dynamic Semantics of λ_i^μ

We now introduce the Type-Directed Operational Semantics (TDOS) for λ_i^μ. TDOS, originally proposed by Huang et al. [28,29], is a variant of small-step operational semantics. In TDOS, type annotations are operationally relevant, since selecting values from merged values is type-directed. We show that λ_i^μ is deterministic and type sound.

4.1   A Type-Directed Operational Semantics for λ_i^μ

The defining feature of a TDOS is a relation called casting (originally called typed reduction by Huang et al.). Casting plays an important role: based on the contextual type information, values are further reduced to match the type

$$\boxed{v_1 \hookrightarrow_A v_2} \qquad\qquad\qquad\qquad\qquad\qquad\qquad\qquad \textit{(Casting)}$$

TRED-NAT

$$\frac{}{i \hookrightarrow_{\mathbf{nat}} i}$$

TRED-TOP

$$\frac{\mathbf{ord}\, A \qquad]A\lceil}{v \hookrightarrow_A A^\dagger}$$

TRED-MERGEL

$$\frac{v_1 \hookrightarrow_A v \qquad \mathbf{ord}\, A}{v_1,, v_2 \hookrightarrow_A v}$$

TRED-MERGER

$$\frac{v_2 \hookrightarrow_A v \qquad \mathbf{ord}\, A}{v_1,, v_2 \hookrightarrow_A v}$$

TRED-REC

$$\frac{\sim]\mu\alpha.\, B\lceil \qquad \cdot \vdash \mu\alpha.\, A \leq \mu\alpha.\, B}{\mathsf{fold}\, [\mu\alpha.\, A]\, v \hookrightarrow_{\mu\alpha.\, B} \mathsf{fold}\, [\mu\alpha.\, B]\, v}$$

TRED-ARROW

$$\frac{\sim]B_2\lceil \qquad \cdot \vdash B_1 \leq A_1 \qquad \cdot \vdash A_2 \leq B_2}{\lambda x.e : A_1 \to A_2 \hookrightarrow_{B_1 \to B_2} \lambda x.e : A_1 \to B_2}$$

TRED-AND

$$\frac{v \hookrightarrow_A v_1 \qquad v \hookrightarrow_B v_2}{v \hookrightarrow_{A\&B} v_1,, v_2}$$

TRED-RCD

$$\frac{v_1 \hookrightarrow_A v_2 \qquad \sim]\{\alpha : A\}\lceil}{\{\alpha = v_1\} \hookrightarrow_{\{\alpha:A\}} \{\alpha = v_2\}}$$

Fig. 6. Casting.

structure precisely. In many conventional operational semantics a value is the final result in a program, but with TDOS further reduction can happen if the type that is required for the value has a mismatch with the shape of the value. For example, if we have the merge $1,,' c'$ at type Int then casting will produce 1. However, the same value at type $Int\&Char$ would remain unchanged $(1,,' c')$.

The rules for casting are shown at the Fig. 6. All non-intersection types are ordinary types. Casting $v_1 \hookrightarrow_A v_2$ denotes that the value v_1 is reduced to v_2 under the type A. From the definitions, we can see that the A is the supertype of the principal type of v_1, and v_2 is the value compatible with A. The most special one is rule TRED-TOP: if the type is toplike, then a value will reduce to the corresponding top value, where the $A^\dagger$ is defined as:

$$(A \to B)^\dagger = \lambda x\,.\top : A \to B \quad (\mu\alpha.\, A)^\dagger = \mathsf{fold}\, [\mu\alpha.\, A]\, \top$$
$$\{\alpha : A\}^\dagger = \{\alpha : A^\dagger\} \qquad (A\&B)^\dagger = A^\dagger,, B^\dagger$$
$$\text{otherwise:} A^\dagger = \top$$

4.2 Reduction

The definition of reduction is shown at the Fig. 7. Most rules are standard. Casting is used in rule STEP-BETA for adjusting the argument value to the expected type for the input of the function. Casting is also used in rule STEP-ANNOV for annotations. Rules STEP-FLD and STEP-FLDT are for unfold expressions. Finally, there is also a special rule STEP-FLDM for recursive types as well as intersection types.

4.3 Determinism

One of the properties of our semantics is determinism: expressions will always reduce to the same value. Lemma 7 says that if a válue can be type-checked, then it reduces to a same value under the type A. Lemma 8 says that if an expression can be type-checked, then it reduces to a unique expression.

$$\boxed{e_1 \rightsquigarrow e_2} \qquad\qquad\qquad\qquad\qquad\qquad\qquad\qquad\qquad \text{(Reduction)}$$

STEP-BETA
$$\frac{v_1 \hookrightarrow_{A_1} v_2}{(\lambda x.e : A_1 \to A_2)\ v_1 \rightsquigarrow ([x \mapsto v_2]\ e) : A_2}$$

STEP-APPL
$$\frac{e_1 \rightsquigarrow e_1'}{e_1\ e_2 \rightsquigarrow e_1'\ e_2}$$

STEP-APPR
$$\frac{e_2 \rightsquigarrow e_2'}{v_1\ e_2 \rightsquigarrow v_1\ e_2'}$$

STEP-PROJ
$$\frac{e \rightsquigarrow e'}{e.\alpha \rightsquigarrow e'.\alpha}$$

STEP-MERGEL
$$\frac{e_1 \rightsquigarrow e_1'}{e_1,,e_2 \rightsquigarrow e_1',,e_2}$$

STEP-MERGER
$$\frac{e_2 \rightsquigarrow e_2'}{v_1,,e_2 \rightsquigarrow v_1,,e_2'}$$

STEP-ANNO
$$\frac{e \rightsquigarrow e'}{e : A \rightsquigarrow e' : A}$$

STEP-ANNOV
$$\frac{v \hookrightarrow_A v'}{v : A \rightsquigarrow v'}$$

STEP-FIX
$$\overline{\text{fix } x : A.\ e \rightsquigarrow (e\ (\text{fix } x : A.\ e)) : A}$$

STEP-FOLD
$$\frac{e \rightsquigarrow e'}{\text{fold } [A]\ e \rightsquigarrow \text{fold } [A]\ e'}$$

STEP-RCD
$$\frac{e \rightsquigarrow e'}{\{\alpha = e\} \rightsquigarrow \{\alpha = e'\}}$$

STEP-UNFOLD
$$\frac{e \rightsquigarrow e'}{\text{unfold } [A]\ e \rightsquigarrow \text{unfold } [A]\ e'}$$

STEP-FLD
$$\frac{v_1 \hookrightarrow_{[\alpha \mapsto \mu\alpha.\ A]\ A} v_2 \qquad \sim\rceil\mu\alpha.\ A\lceil}{\text{unfold } [\mu\alpha.\ A]\ (\text{fold } [\mu\alpha.\ B]\ v_1) \rightsquigarrow v_2}$$

STEP-FLDM
$$\frac{v_1,,v_2 \hookrightarrow_{\mu\alpha.\ A} v \qquad \sim\rceil\mu\alpha.\ A\lceil}{\text{unfold } [\mu\alpha.\ A]\ (v_1,,v_2) \rightsquigarrow \text{unfold } [\mu\alpha.\ A]\ v}$$

STEP-FLDT
$$\frac{v_1 \hookrightarrow_{[\alpha \mapsto \mu\alpha.\ A]\ A} v_2 \qquad \rceil\mu\alpha.\ A\lceil}{\text{unfold } [\mu\alpha.\ A]\ v_1 \rightsquigarrow v_2}$$

STEP-PROJRCD
$$\overline{\{\alpha = v\}.\alpha \rightsquigarrow v}$$

Fig. 7. Small-step semantics.

Lemma 7 (Determinism of $\hookrightarrow$). *If $\Gamma \vdash v \Rightarrow B$ and $v \hookrightarrow_A v_1$ and $v \hookrightarrow_A v_2$ then $v_1 = v_2$.*

Proof. By induction on $v \hookrightarrow_A v_1$.

Lemma 8 (Determinism of $\rightsquigarrow$). *If $\Gamma \vdash e \Leftrightarrow A$ and $e \rightsquigarrow e_1$ and $e \rightsquigarrow e_2$ then $e_1 = e_2$.*

Proof. By induction on $e \rightsquigarrow e_1$.

4.4   Type Safety

We prove type safety following a similar approach to the previous work [29], and by showing progress and preservation theorems. The following lemmas and theorems show that our system is type-safe.

Theorem 4 (Preservation). *If $\vdash e_1 \Leftrightarrow A$ and $e_1 \rightsquigarrow e_2$ then $\vdash e_2 \Leftarrow A$.*

Proof. By induction on $\vdash e_1 \Leftrightarrow A$.

Lemma 9. (Progress of $\hookrightarrow$). *If $\vdash v_1 \Leftarrow A$ then $\exists v_2,\ v_1 \hookrightarrow_A v_2$.*

Proof. By induction on A.

Theorem 5 (Progress). *If $\vdash e_1 \Leftrightarrow A$ then e_1 is a value or $\exists e_2,\ e_1 \rightsquigarrow e_2$.*

Proof. By induction on $\vdash e_1 \Leftrightarrow A$.

5   Discussion and Related Work

Throughout the paper, we have already reviewed some of the closest related work in detail. In this section, we will discuss other related work.

Disjoint Intersection Types and Record Calculi with Concatenation. Disjoint intersection types were originally proposed by Oliveira et al. [33]. Such calculi have intersection types as well as a merge operator [22,40] with a disjointness restriction to ensure the determinism of the language. Follow-up work [2,5,6] provides more advanced features, such as *disjoint polymorphism* and *distributive subtyping* and *first-class traits*, built upon the original work. With all these features together, an alternative paradigm called *Compositional Programming* (CP) is proposed [7,45]. CP allows for a very modular programming style where the Expression Problem [43] can be solved naturally. A limitation of existing calculi with disjoint intersection types is that they do not support recursive types, which are important to encode *binary methods* [9] or, more generally, recursive object types. The λ_i^μ calculus addresses this limitation and shows, for the first time, a calculus with disjoint intersection types and recursive types.

The merge operator generalizes concatenation by allowing values of any types (not just record types) to be merged. As we described in the introduction the interaction between subtyping and record concatenation is quite tricky. Cardelli and Mitchell observed the problem [15], but did not provide a solution. Instead, they decided to use record extension and restriction operators instead of concatenation. One solution adopted by some calculi [26,34,38,39] is to distinguish between records that can be concatenated, and records that have subtyping. The choice is mutually exclusive: records that can be concatenated cannot have subtyping and vice-versa. Such an approach would prevent Cardelli and Mitchell's f2 example in the introduction from type-checking. Calculi with disjoint intersection types, including λ_i^μ, offer a different solution by adopting a type-directed semantics, which ensures that fields hidden by subtyping are also hidden at runtime. This allows concatenation and subtyping to be used together.

As far as we know, no full formalization of a calculus supports subtyping, record concatenation and recursive subtyping at the same time. In Cardelli's $F_{<:\rho}$ calculus [13] equi-recursive subtyping is assumed to be an extension to record subtyping and record concatenation but no proofs were provided. Palsberg and Zhao's work [34] shows supporting subtyping, record concatenation and recursive types (but no recursive subtyping) together for type inference is NP-complete.

Alternative Models for Typed Objects. There are alternative ways to model objects without having records and record concatenation. Perhaps the most famous one are Abadi and Cardelli's object calculi [1]. In their work, objects are modelled directly. No form of concatenation is provided, but the fields of objects can be updated in object calculi. Besides, they also provide declarative type systems (with a transitivity rule built-in) to support recursive subtyping.

Another alternative approach, which has received a lot of attention recently, are calculi with dependent object types (DOT) [41], which aims to capture the essence of Scala. Many variants of DOT include intersection types, a form of recursive types and subtyping. However, there are no records and record concatenation, since objects are directly modelled rather than being encoded via records. The subtyping rules for intersection types are similar to ours. Moreover, the rules for recursive types employed in some variants of DOT [25,41,44] are mostly structural and employ an inductive definition of subtyping. The key subtyping rules in the DOT variant by [41] are shown next:

$$\frac{\Gamma, z : T_1^z \vdash T_1^z <: T_2^z}{\Gamma \vdash \mu z.\ T_1^z <: \mu z.\ T_2^z} \text{ BindX} \qquad \frac{\Gamma, z : T_1^z \vdash T_1^z <: T_2}{\Gamma \vdash \mu z.\ T_1^z <: T_2} \text{ BindI}$$

$$\frac{\Gamma \vdash x : T^x}{\Gamma \vdash x : \mu z.\ T^z} \text{ VarPack} \qquad \frac{\Gamma \vdash x : \mu z.\ T^z}{\Gamma \vdash x : T^x} \text{ VarUnpack}$$

We adapt the notation employed by [41] for recursive types to our notation. In the rules, T^z denotes that variable z is free in type T. Rule BINDX is in essence a one-step finite unfolding of the recursive type, leading to an inductive definition of subtyping. The second rule for recursive types (rule BINDI) is a special case where a recursive type $\mu z.\ T_1^z$ is a subtype of another type T_2 if T_2 does not contain the recursive variable z. A difference between recursive types $\mu z.\ T^z$ in DOT and the ones in this paper is that in DOT z is a *term* variable instead of a type variable. In DOT, recursive types can be used in combination with *path-dependent types* [3], to denote types such as $z.L$, where z represents a (possibly recursive) term with a type member L. Because of this design, the typing rules that introduce and eliminate recursive types [41], are defined on variables. Unlike our formulation of subtyping, which is algorithmic, DOT's formulation of subtyping is usually presented in a declarative form. Undecidability is an important problem with DOT's formulation of subtyping [27], and the existing decidable fragments of DOT lack transitivity [27,31].

Semantic Subtyping with Intersection Types and Equi-Recursive Types. Semantic subtyping [16,24], provides a set-theoretic point of view for type systems. In that approach, (equi-)recursive types and intersection types are interpreted as subsets of the model, the subtyping relation is decidable, and some important properties, such as transitivity, are derived naturally. Although semantic subtyping approaches have many advantages, they can be technically more involved, while the metatheory of syntactic formulations is simpler and generally easier to extend. Damm [20] explored a type system with equi-recursive types and intersection types. His subtyping relation is quite expressive, as it supports equi-recursive types and distributivity rules for subtyping. However, he does not follow the conventional syntactic formulations of subtyping, such as the one in this paper or those employed in DOT. Instead, types are encoded as regular tree expressions/set constraints. In contrast, our formulation is more conventional and supports iso-recursive types instead. Unlike our work Damm does not consider extensible records with concatenation.

Other Languages with Recursive Types and Intersection Types. Some languages employ recursive subtyping as well as intersection types, like Typescript [32] and Whiley [36]. Typescript has a rich type system but no formal document provided. [8] has formalized a subset of Typescript and proved that is safe, but · unfortunately, no intersection types are supported. Whiley is an experimental language that supports recursive types, intersection types and subtyping. However, no work formalizes all the features together, lacking either recursive types [35] or intersection types [30].

6   Conclusion

Recursive types, extensible record types and intersection types are important features in many OOP languages, since object types can be modelled with recursive records and multiple inheritance can be modelled via intersection types [17] and record concatenation. Our λ_i^μ calculus illustrates that the 3 features can be put together in a single calculus and therefore can be used to provide simple encodings for objects. There are a few interesting directions for future work. One is to add polymorphism and bounded quantification to λ_i^μ, which is a significant feature for real world languages. Another one is to investigate distributive subtyping for iso-recursive subtyping. With distributivity, we can model a form of family polymorphism [23].

Acknowledgement. We thank the anonymous reviewers for their helpful comments. This work has been sponsored by Hong Kong Research Grant Council projects number 17209519, 17209520 and 17209821.

References

1. Abadi, M., Cardelli, L.: A Theory of Objects. Springer, New York (1996). https://doi.org/10.1007/978-1-4419-8598-9
2. Alpuim, J., Oliveira, B.C.S., Shi, Z.: Disjoint polymorphism. In: Yang, H. (ed.) ESOP 2017. LNCS, vol. 10201, pp. 1–28. Springer, Heidelberg (2017). https://doi.org/10.1007/978-3-662-54434-1_1
3. Amin, N., Rompf, T., Odersky, M.: Foundations of path-dependent types. In: Proceedings of the 2014 ACM International Conference on Object Oriented Programming, Systems, Languages, and Applications. OOPSLA 2014. Association for Computing Machinery (2014)
4. Barendregt, H., Coppo, M., Dezani-Ciancaglini, M.: A filter lambda model and the completeness of type assignment. J. Symb. Logic **48**(4), 931–940 (1983)

5. Bi, X., Oliveira, B.C.d.S.: Typed first-class traits. In: 32nd European Conference on Object-Oriented Programming (ECOOP 2018) (2018)
6. Bi, X., Oliveira, B.C.d.S., Schrijvers, T.: The essence of nested composition. In: 32nd European Conference on Object-Oriented Programming (ECOOP 2018) (2018)
7. Bi, X., Xie, N., Oliveira, B.C.S., Schrijvers, T.: Distributive disjoint polymorphism for compositional programming. In: Caires, L. (ed.) ESOP 2019. LNCS, vol. 11423, pp. 381–409. Springer, Cham (2019). https://doi.org/10.1007/978-3-030-17184-1_14
8. Bierman, G., Abadi, M., Torgersen, M.: Understanding typescript. In: Jones, R. (ed.) ECOOP 2014. LNCS, vol. 8586, pp. 257–281. Springer, Heidelberg (2014). https://doi.org/10.1007/978-3-662-44202-9_11
9. Bruce, K., Cardeli, L., Castagna, G., Group, T.H.O., Leavens, G.T., Pierce, B.: On binary methods. Theory Pract. Object Syst. 1(3) (1996)
10. Bruce, K.B., Cardelli, L., Pierce, B.C.: Comparing object encodings 155(1/2), 108–133 (1999). http://www.cis.upenn.edu/bcpierce/papers/compobj.ps
11. Cardelli, L.: A semantics of multiple inheritance. In: Semantics of Data Types (1984)
12. Cardelli, L.: Amber. In: Cousineau, G., Curien, P.-L., Robinet, B. (eds.) LITP 1985. LNCS, vol. 242, pp. 21–47. Springer, Heidelberg (1986). https://doi.org/10.1007/3-540-17184-3_38
13. Cardelli, L.: Extensible Records in a Pure Calculus of Subtyping. Digital, Systems Research Center (1992)
14. Cardelli, L.: A language with distributed scope. In: Proceedings of the 22nd ACM SIGPLAN-SIGACT Symposium on Principles of Programming Languages. POPL 1995, pp. 286–297 (1995)
15. Cardelli, L., Mitchell, J.C.: Operations on records. Math. Struct. Comput. Sci. 1(1), 3–48 (1991)
16. Castagna, G., Frisch, A.: A gentle introduction to semantic subtyping. In: Proceedings of the 7th ACM SIGPLAN International Conference on Principles and Practice of Declarative Programming, pp. 198–199 (2005)
17. Compagnoni, A.B., Pierce, B.C.: Higher-order intersection types and multiple inheritance. Math. Struct. Comput. Sci. (MSCS) 6(5), 469–501 (1996)
18. Cook, W.R., Hill, W., Canning, P.S.: Inheritance is not subtyping. In: Proceedings of the 17th ACM SIGPLAN-SIGACT Symposium on Principles of Programming Languages. POPL 1990, pp. 125–135 (1989)
19. Cook, W.R., Palsberg, J.: A denotational semantics of inheritance and its correctness. In: Object-Oriented Programming: Systems, Languages and Applications (OOPSLA) (1989)
20. Damm, F.M.: Subtyping with union types, intersection types and recursive types. In: Hagiya, M., Mitchell, J.C. (eds.) TACS 1994. LNCS, vol. 789, pp. 687–706. Springer, Heidelberg (1994). https://doi.org/10.1007/3-540-57887-0_121
21. Davies, R., Pfenning, F.: Intersection types and computational effects. In: International Conference on Functional Programming (ICFP) (2000)
22. Dunfield, J.: Elaborating intersection and union types. J. Funct. Program. 24(2–3), 133–165 (2014)
23. Ernst, E.: Family polymorphism. In: Knudsen, J.L. (ed.) ECOOP 2001. LNCS, vol. 2072, pp. 303–326. Springer, Heidelberg (2001). https://doi.org/10.1007/3-540-45337-7_17
24. Frisch, A., Castagna, G., Benzaken, V.: Semantic subtyping. In: Proceedings 17th Annual IEEE Symposium on Logic in Computer Science, pp. 137–146. IEEE (2002)

25. Giarrusso, P.G., Stefanesco, L., Timany, A., Birkedal, L., Krebbers, R.: Scala step-by-step: soundness for dot with step-indexed logical relations in iris. Proc. ACM Program. Lang. **4**(ICFP) (2020)
26. Glew, N.: An efficient class and object encoding. In: Proceedings of the 15th ACM SIGPLAN Conference on Object-Oriented Programming, Systems, Languages, and Applications. OOPSLA 2000, pp. 311–324. Association for Computing Machinery (2000)
27. Hu, J.Z., Lhoták, O.: Undecidability of DSUB and its decidable fragments. Proc. ACM Program. Lang. **4**(POPL), 1–30 (2019)
28. Huang, X., Oliveira, B.C.d.S.: A type-directed operational semantics for a calculus with a merge operator. In: 34th European Conference on Object-Oriented Programming (ECOOP 2020), vol. 166 (2020). https://doi.org/10.4230/LIPIcs.ECOOP.2020.26
29. Huang, X., Zhao, J., Oliveira, B.C.d.S.: Taming the merge operator: a type-directed operational semantics approach. J. Funct. Program. (2021)
30. Jones, T., Pearce, D.J.: A mechanical soundness proof for subtyping over recursive types. In: Proceedings of the 18th Workshop on Formal Techniques for Java-like Programs, pp. 1–6 (2016)
31. Mackay, J., Potanin, A., Aldrich, J., Groves, L.: Decidable subtyping for path dependent types. Proc. ACM Program. Lang. **4**(POPL), 1–27 (2019)
32. Microsoft: Typescript (2021). https://www.typescriptlang.org/
33. Oliveira, B.C.d.S., Shi, Z., Alpuim, J.: Disjoint intersection types. In: Proceedings of the 21st ACM SIGPLAN International Conference on Functional Programming, pp. 364–377 (2016)
34. Palsberg, J., Zhao, T.: Type inference for record concatenation and subtyping. Inf. Comput. **189**(1) (2004)
35. Pearce, D.J.: Rewriting for sound and complete union, intersection and negation types. ACM SIGPLAN Not. **52**(12), 117–130 (2017)
36. Pearce, D.J., Groves, L.: Whiley: a platform for research in software verification. In: Erwig, M., Paige, R.F., Van Wyk, E. (eds.) SLE 2013. LNCS, vol. 8225, pp. 238–248. Springer, Cham (2013). https://doi.org/10.1007/978-3-319-02654-1_13
37. Pierce, B.C.: Bounded quantification is undecidable. Inf. Comput. **112**(1), 131–165 (1994)
38. Pottier, F.: A 3-part type inference engine. In: Smolka, G. (ed.) ESOP 2000. LNCS, vol. 1782, pp. 320–335. Springer, Heidelberg (2000). https://doi.org/10.1007/3-540-46425-5_21
39. Rémy, D.: A case study of typechecking with constrained types: typing record concatenation (1995). Presented at the Workshop on Advances in Types for Computer Science at the Newton Institute, Cambridge, UK
40. Reynolds, J.C.: Preliminary design of the programming language Forsythe (1988)
41. Rompf, T., Amin, N.: Type soundness for dependent object types (DOT). In: Proceedings of the 2016 ACM SIGPLAN International Conference on Object-Oriented Programming, Systems, Languages, and Applications, pp. 624–641 (2016)
42. The CoQ Development Team: CoQ (2019). https://coq.inria.fr
43. Wadler, P.: The expression problem (1998). Discussion on the Java Genericity mailing list
44. Wang, F., Rompf, T.: Towards strong normalization for dependent object types (DOT). In: 31st European Conference on Object-Oriented Programming (ECOOP 2017). Schloss Dagstuhl-Leibniz-Zentrum fuer Informatik (2017)
45. Zhang, W., Sun, Y., Oliveira, B.C.d.S.: Compositional programming. ACM Trans. Program. Lang. Syst. (TOPLAS), 1–60 (2021)

46. Zhou, Y., Oliveira, B.C.d.S., Fan, A.: A calculus with recursive types, record concatenation and subtyping (artifact) (2022). https://doi.org/10.5281/zenodo.7003284
47. Zhou, Y., Zhao, J., Oliveira, B.C.d.S.: Revisiting ISO-recursive subtyping. ACM Trans. Program. Lang. Syst. (TOPLAS) (2022). https://doi.org/10.1145/3549537

Novice Type Error Diagnosis with Natural Language Models

Chuqin Geng[1,2(✉)] , Haolin Ye[1] , Yixuan Li[1] , Tianyu Han[1] ,
Brigitte Pientka[1] , and Xujie Si[1,2,3(✉)]

[1] McGill University, Montreal, Canada
{chuqin.geng,haolin.ye,yixuan.li,tianyu.han2}@mail.mcgill.ca,
{bpientka,xsi}@cs.mcgill.ca
[2] Mila - Quebec Institute, Montreal, Canada
[3] CIFAR AI Research Chair, Montreal, Canada

Abstract. Strong static type systems help programmers eliminate many errors without much burden of supplying type annotations. However, this flexibility makes it highly non-trivial to diagnose ill-typed programs, especially for novice programmers. Compared to classic constraint solving and optimization-based approaches, the data-driven approach has shown great promise in identifying the root causes of type errors with higher accuracy. Instead of relying on hand-engineered features, this work explores natural language models for type error localization, which can be trained in an end-to-end fashion without requiring any features. We demonstrate that, for novice type error diagnosis, the language model-based approach significantly outperforms the previous state-of-the-art data-driven approach. Specifically, our model could predict type errors correctly 62% of the time, outperforming the state-of-the-art NATE's data-driven model by 11%, under a more rigorous accuracy metric. Furthermore, we also apply structural probes to explain the performance difference between different language models.

Keywords: Type error diagnosis · Language model · Natural language processing · Type system

1 Introduction

Diagnosing type errors has received much attention from both industry and academia due to its potential of reducing efforts in computer software development. Existing approaches such as standard compilers with type systems, report type errors through type checking and constraint analysis. Thus, they merely point to locations where the constraint inconsistencies can occur and such locations might be far away from the true error source. Moreover, type error localization would require programmers to understand the functionality of type systems and check which part of the code contradicts their intent. Languages such as C

© The Author(s), under exclusive license to Springer Nature Switzerland AG 2022
I. Sergey (Ed.): APLAS 2022, LNCS 13658, pp. 196–214, 2022.
https://doi.org/10.1007/978-3-031-21037-2_10

and Java force programmers to write annotations which make the code neat. It also makes it easier to find the roots of type errors. Strongly typed functional languages such as OCaml and Haskell, however, programmers need not bother with annotations, since type systems automatically synthesize the types. The absence of type annotation comes at a price: novices could easily get lost in debugging their programs and locations of constraint inconsistencies from error messages can be misleading.

Joosten et al. [7] suggests that beginners usually pay more attention to underlined error locations rather than error messages themselves when fixing programs. Therefore it is necessary to ameliorate the localizing performance of these type systems. Let us consider an OCaml ill-type program in Fig. 1a. Although the programmer intends to write a function that sums up all numbers from a list, they mistakenly put the empty list, [], at line 3 as a base case. This should instead be 0 as shown in Fig. 1b. The compiler identifies the type error in line 5 saying that the head of the list, h, has type list rather than integer as required by the integer addition operator.

```
1        let rec sumList xs =
2        match xs with
3        | [] -> [] (* root cause *)
4        | h :: [] -> h
5        | h :: t -> h + sumList t (* misleading complaint *)
6        this expression has type 'a list but was expected of type int
7
```

(a) an ill-typed OCaml program that aims to sum all the elements from a list

```
1        match xs with
2        | [] -> 0 (* <= correct fix *)
3        | h :: [] -> h
4        | h :: t -> h + sumList t
```

(b) the fixed version of the OCaml code above

Fig. 1. A simple example of OCaml type error and its relevant fix.

This illustrates that programmer's intent plays an important role in localizing type errors. To tackle this issue, NATE [18] proposes to use data-driven models to diagnose type errors. In this way, programmers' intent can be learned and incorporated into machine learning models. NATE 's best model could achieve over 90% accuracy in diagnosing type errors. Although this is an exciting result, NATE 's models are evaluated with a rather loose metric and heavily rely on a considerable amount of hand-designed feature engineering. In addition, these features are designed in an ad-hoc fashion which prevents them from being directly applied to other language compilers.

Our approach adopts transformer-based language models to avoid considerable feature engineering. As we treat programs as natural language texts, these models do not rely on any knowledge or features about the specific programming language, thus they can be easily applied on any language. This method may seem to ignore the syntactic structure of a given programming language. However, we use structural probes [11] to demonstrate the structure is embedded implicitly in the deep learning models' vector geometry in Sect. 4. We also propose a more rigorous metric, and show language models outperform not only standard OCaml compiler and constraints-based approaches but also the state-of-the-art NATE 's models under the new metric.

Transformer-based models have achieved great success in a wide range of domains in computer science including natural language processing. BERT [4] and GPT [1,15], popular transformer variants, have shown incredible capability of understanding natural languages. Together with its pre-training and fine-tuning paradigm, these models can transfer knowledge learned from a large text corpus to many downstream tasks such as token classification and next sentence prediction. Empirical results suggest that the performance of these language models even exceeds the human level in several benchmarks. In this work, we show how to take advantage of these powerful language models to localize type errors. First, we process programs as if they were natural language text and decompose the processed programs at the term or subterm level into token sequences so that they can be fed to language models. This allows us to turn the type error diagnosis problem into a token classification problem. In this way, language models can learn how to localize type errors in an end-to-end fashion.

Contributions. We propose a natural language model-based approach to the type error localization problem. Our main contributions are as follows:

- Without any feature engineering or constraints analysis, we apply different language models including BERT, CodeBERT, and Bidirectional LSTM to type error localization.
- We study training methodology such as positive/negative transfer to improve our models' performance. Instead of using a loose evaluation metric as proposed in previous work, we define a more rigorous, yet realistic, accuracy metric of type error diagnosis.
- Empirical results suggest that our best model can correctly predict expressions responsible for type error 62% of the time, 24 points higher than SHErrLoc and 11 points higher than the state-of-the-art NATE tool.
- We study the interpretability of our models using structural probes and identify the link between language models' performance with their ability of encoding structural information of programs such as AST.

We start by presenting the baseline, our model architecture and the structural probe in Sect. 2. Section 3 introduces the dataset and evaluation metric, while Sect. 4 presents the experiential results and our discussion. Then, Sect. 5 gives an overview of related work. Finally, Sect. 6 concludes the whole paper and proposes some directions for future work.

2 Approach

In this section, we introduce deep learning-based language models including RNN, BERT, and CodeBERT. We take advantage of the pre-training and fine-tuning paradigm of language models and show how to transform the type error diagnosis problem to a token classification problem, a common downstream task in fine-tuning. We also present the structural probe which allows us to find the embedded structural information of programs from models' vector geometry.

2.1 Language Models

Deep learning has achieved great success in modelling languages since the invention of recurrent neural networks (RNNs) [9]. RNNs adopt "internal memory" to retain information of prior states to facilitate the computation of the current state. Unlike traditional deep neural networks, the output of RNNs depends on the prior elements within the sequence which make them ideal for processing sequential inputs such as natural languages and programs.

In this study, we also choose a bidirectional long-short term memory (Bidirectional LSTM) [16] as our baseline model. However, RNNs are known to have several drawbacks such as a lack of parallelization and weak long-range dependencies. These two limitations are later addressed by the self-attention mechanism introduced by the transformer. Self attention [20] is an attention mechanism relating different positions of a single sequence in order to compute a representation of the sequence. Transformers also follow an encoder-decoder architecture as other successful neural sequential models. Both its encoder and decoder have been studied and shown great capabilities for modelling natural languages and solving many downstream tasks.

BERT, which stands for Bidirectional Encoder Representations from Transformers takes advantage of the encoder part of the transformer while the GPT-n series are based on the decoder. In this work, we focus on BERT rather than GPT-3 [1] for several reasons. First, BERT requires a fine-tuning process which alters the pre-trained model for specific downstream tasks. This fits our formalization of treating type error diagnosis as a downstream task. Second, the size of GPT-3 is enormous compared to BERT, making it hard to train and infer. Third, BERT is an open-source tool and easily available for users to access while GPT-3 is not open-sourced.

2.2 The Pre-training and Fine-Tuning Scheme

The pre-training and fine-tuning scheme allows machine learning models to apply knowledge gained from solving one task to different yet related tasks. Compared to fine-tuning, pre-training is more essential as it determines what knowledge is learned and stored in machine learning models. As a result, there are some recent works on improving the pre-training scheme of language models.

BERT stands out by proposing two critical unsupervised tasks during pre-training - Masked Language Modeling (MLM) and Next Sentence Prediction

(NSP) [4]. MLM requires the model to predict masked-out tokens conditioned on other tokens within sentences whereas NSP forces the model to predict if the input two sentences are next to each other in the original document. These two training tasks or objectives allow the model to understand the natural language from a statistical perspective, and empirical results of BERT have shown that pre-training on large text corpus using these two objectives facilitates a wide range of downstream tasks.

2.3   Type Error Diagnosis as Token Classification

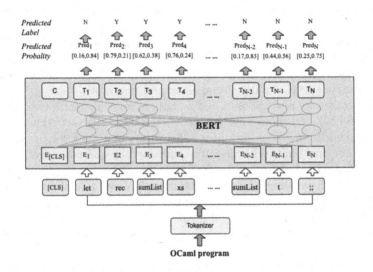

Fig. 2. The type error diagnosis as a token classification task. After an input program is split into a sequence of tokens by a tokenizer, each token is fed into BERT to get an embedding representation. A simple classification head takes each token representation and outputs a predicted probability which indicates the model's belief of the current token being related to type error.

Token classification [4] is a downstream task which uses a pre-trained Bert model with a token classification head on top to make a prediction for each token in a sentence. One of the most common token classification tasks is Named Entity Recognition (NER). The goal of NER is to find a label for each entity in a sentence, such as a person, location or organization. Type error diagnosis can be naturally viewed as a token classification problem. Note that type error diagnosis attempts to find type error locations within a piece of code, so we can reformulate it to a token classification task if we assign label 1 to all the tokens that contribute to the type error and label 0 to those tokens that are unrelated to type error. Figure 2 gives an overview of using token classification to achieve type error diagnosis. As a fine-tuning task, token classification requires labelled data to provide ground truth to help the model learn. In the context of type error diagnosis, this means we need to have a dataset consisting of many ill-typed programs along with their true type error locations. We will discuss our dataset more in Sect. 3.

Given that large language models are extremely expensive to train, even for industrial companies, a common practice is to fine-tune pre-trained large language models on a new dataset. In our case, we choose different configurations of BERT to explore the optimal model for type error diagnosis. Our models are as follows:

- **Bidirectional LSTM**: The model is trained directly on the fine-tuned dataset from scratch. This model serves as our baseline.
- **BERT from scratch**: To compare with Bidirectional LSTM, we train the BERT to do token classification from scratch, without any pre-training process.
- **BERT Small, BERT Medium, BERT Base, and BERT Large**: As the name suggests, these four models are different in terms of size. Although they are pre-trained on the same dataset, we hypothesize that the size would affect the representation power of models and therefore would affect the performance of type error diagnosis.
- **CodeBERT**: CodeBert [5] is a pre-trained bimodal model for programming language (PL) and natural language (NL). It is pre-trained on several programming languages including Ruby, Javascript, Go, Python, Java, and PHP. As it is pre-trained on such programming languages that ask programmers to specify the type, we postulate that it may not work well on OCaml programs. However, we are still curious to see if these programming languages may share some patterns with OCaml which can enhance its error localization ability during the fine-tuning process.
- **BERT pre-trained on OCaml**: Since BERT is pre-trained on natural language texts which do not contain OCaml programs, we collect two datasets of OCaml programs, one from industry and the other one from students' homework submission. Then we pre-train BERT Base and BERT Large on them with the same training objectives. This technique is also called domain shift which could help the model perform better on downstream tasks which have different data distribution from that of the original input. Together with CodeBERT, these models allow us to explore how domain shift affects models' performance.

2.4 Structural Probe

We attempt to use the structural probe method [11] to find structural information embedded implicitly in the deep learning models' vector geometry.

In deep learning, each token has a vector representation after feeding into the model. The method finds a distance metric that can approximate the result of the distance metric defined by the syntax tree from applying to any two tokens

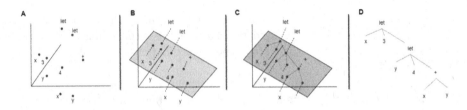

Fig. 3. Syntax tree of example OCaml program "let x = 3 in let y = 4 in x + y"

of a program. More specifically, it defines a linear transform of the space in which squared L_2 distance between vectors best reconstructs tree path distance, and thus the structure of the tree is demonstrated by the geometry of the vector space. Figure 3 gives an overview of using the structural probe to reconstruct tree structure information of programs.

3   Dataset and Evaluation Metric

In this section, we present the datasets and the evaluation metric that we use in our work. The training datasets that we use are the same ones used in the baseline. However, we propose a different metric of accuracy. Notice this metric has been applied to every model, so data produced by NATE's models may look different from their original paper. To explore the capability of language models, we also create two pre-training datasets consisting of over 370,000 OCaml programs in total.

Table 1. Statistics of pre-training and fine-tuning datasets

	Num. of programs	Average num. of tokens	Has ground-truth label	Usage
NATE SP14	2,712	136	Yes	Fine-tuning (training and testing)
FA15	2,365	133	Yes	
GitHub	350,000	121	N/A	Pre-training
Homework	20,000	99	N/A	

3.1   Pre-training Dataset

The pre-training procedure plays an important role in transformer-based language models. The purpose of pre-training is to train the model on large-text corpus in an unsupervised fashion. After pre-training, models should have weights that encode the probabilities of a given sequence of words occurring in sentences.

The success of modern language models is often attributed to large pre-training datasets. Motivated by this observation, we collect the following two datasets.

- **GitHub-OCaml dataset:** Based on the default ranking configuration provided by GitHub, we collected top-500 OCaml GitHub repositories, which has been identified as an instance of "fair use" [13]. Given that most samples of our GitHub dataset are from the industry, we perform some post-processing work by filtering out programs that are automatically generated by lexer and parser. Even though, some of them are still quite different from programs written by novice programmers. The resulting dataset contains over 350,000 OCaml programs.
- **Student-OCaml dataset:** To collect OCaml programs written by novice programmers, we collected around 2, 000 homework submissions made by over 350 students from an undergraduate programming languages course taught at McGill University. Each homework submission consists of 10 subtasks (e.g., functions for a specific coding question) on average. This gives us 20,000 OCaml data samples.

In Sect. 4, we study how pre-training on these two datasets affects the performance of type error diagnosis.

3.2   Fine-Tuning Dataset

Fine-tuning, on the other hand, requires labelled data as supervision to facilitate model learning. This means we need a set of ill-typed programs along with the correct locations of type errors as ground truth. Manual ground truth annotation and ill-typed program collection can be troublesome. Fortunately, NATE provides a dataset consisting of 5,000 labelled programs that cover many types and locations of the errors that beginners make in practice, together with the corresponding fixes.

NATE's dataset was collected from an undergraduate Programming Languages course at UC San Diego in Spring 2014 and Fall 2015, which are named SP14 and FA15 respectively. Besides providing supervision, NATE's dataset can also be used as a test-bed so we can compare our models with NATE's fairly.

3.3   Evaluation Metric

NATE processes programs to sub-tree sets and then filters the sub-trees that are not related to type errors to get true error locations — the ground truths. As a consequence, if a large sub-tree, T, is the ground truth, many of its sub-trees are treated as true error locations as well. Then, if a model predicts any of these sub-trees, the prediction accuracy would be 100% under the NATE's metric. We illustrate this using an example as shown in Fig. 4. As we can see in 4a, the model blames the token, clone, which happens to match the error token, clone, in 4b. It is not easy to see why clone is an error location because we only

```
1 let rec clone x n = if n <= 0 then []
2                           else x :: (clone x (n - 1))
3 let rec helper x = if x = 0 then 1 else 10 * helper (x - 1)
4 let padZero l1 l2 =
5   if (List.length l1) < (List.length l2)
6   then (( clone  "0"  List.length  l2) - (List.length l1)) :: l1
7   else (( clone  "0" List.length l1) - (List.length l2)) :: l2
```

(a) An ill-typed OCaml program. Highlighted tokens on line 6 and 7 are predictions made by NATE's model.

```
1 let rec clone x n = if n <= 0 then []
2                           else x :: (clone x (n - 1))
3 (*let rec helper x = if x = 0 then 1 else 10 * helper (x -
      1) *)
4 let padZero l1 l2 =
5   if (List.length l1) < (List.length l2)
6   then  (((clone 0 ((List.length l2) - (List.length l1))) @ l1), l2)
7   else  (((clone 0 ((List.length l1) - (List.length l2))) @ l2), l1)
```

(b) Fixed version of the OCaml program above. Highlighted tokens on line 6 and 7 form the ground truth, whereas the change on line 3 does not.

Fig. 4. An ill-typed OCaml program and its corresponding fix.

highlighted the union of all error spans. It ends up to be one since it is a strongly-related subtree of the ground truth highlighted in blue at line 6. Therefore, the prediction matches to the ground truth, resulting in an accuracy of 100% under NATE's metric. However, such prediction is merely a tiny portion of the union of all error spans highlighted in blue which makes this an over-evaluation.

As a result, NATE's metric overestimates the prediction accuracy of not only its own machine learning models but also our language models. To visualize the over-evaluation from a data point of view, we test NATE's models and some of our models under NATE's metric. We use BERT Small, Base and Large models, and they achieve Top-3 accuracies of 80%, 84% and 87% respectively. Generally speaking, they are comparable to NATE's models, whose accuracies range from 84% to 90%.

We solve the overestimation issue by treating programs as consecutive token sequences rather than trees. Hence by counting the number of correctly predicted tokens, we can get a more precise and strict accuracy between 0% and 100% rather than just 0 (miss) or 1 (hit). To be more specific, our models estimate the probabilities of type error blame for each token in a binary classification setting. By converting predicted probabilities to label 0 or 1 using a default threshold value of 0.5, gives us a collection of predicted token sequences, P. By transforming the ground truth denoted by L to token sequences as well, the correctly predicted token set is simply the intersection of them, $P \wedge L$. However, a trivial prediction which simply predicates each token as type error, i.e. $P = \{1, 1, 1, ..., 1, 1\}$, could achieve 100% accuracy due to $P \wedge L = L$. To prevent this from happening, we divide the size of $P \wedge L$ by that of $P \vee L$.

$$Accuracy(P, L) = \frac{|P \wedge L|}{|P \vee L|}$$

4 Evaluation

In this section, we empirically evaluate several approaches to type error diagnosis with particular focus on the following research questions:[1]

RQ1: How well do language models and other baseline methods perform on type error diagnosis?

RQ2: To what extent do model size and transfer learning affect models' performance?

RQ3: How well do language models generalize to unseen data?

RQ4: Does the model's ability of encoding structure information contribute to prediction accuracy?

Implementation and Training. We implement our experiments using PyTorch, Tensorflow and HuggingFace library. We use a batch size of 32 for both pre-training and fine-tuning processes. For pre-training, we pre-train BERT Base and BERT Large on both pre-training datasets for 10 epochs. For fine-tuning, all BERT models are fine-tuned on NATE's training dataset for 30 epochs. We set the initial learning rate to 0.00003 and use a scheduler to alter the learning rate during fine-tuning. To avoid stochasticity, we run each experiment three times and take the average. All our models are trained on a Tesla P100-PCIE-16GB GPU.

Configurations of Language Models. We explore different configurations of BERT to find the best model. We call BERT Base and BERT Large (BERT+) pre-trained on the homework OCaml dataset OCamlBERT Base (OBERT) and OCamlBERT Large (OBERT+). As for the BERT Base pretrained on the GitHub OCaml dataset, we call it BERT pre-GitHub (PBERT). We also trained a BERT Base from scratch without leveraging pre-trained weights and name it BERT Init (IBERT).

Baselines. We compare our language model-based approach with three baselines as follows:

- OCAML, which extracts the type error location from the error message from the standard OCaml compiler. It is worth noting that the standard OCaml compiler stops compiling immediately when any type check fails and thus cannot report multiple errors.
- SHERRLOC, which identifies the minimum set of locations to patch a type error using Bayesian inference [10].
- NATE, which predicts the top-K most likely ASTs that contribute to the type errors based on 282 hand-designed features [18]. Specifically, NATE uses five different machine learning models — logistic regression (LOGISTIC), decision

---

[1] Our artifact is available at [6].

tree (TREE), random forests (FOREST), and two multi-layer perception models (MLP-10 and MLP-500) with a single hidden layer of 10 and 500 neurons, respectively.

4.1 Performance of Different Models (RQ1)

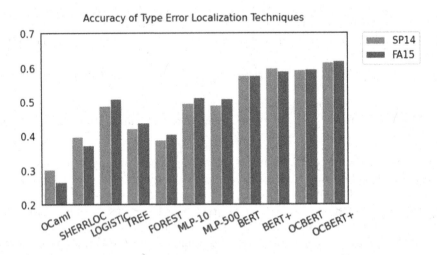

Fig. 5. Comparison of accuracy of type error diagnosis methods.

Figure5 summarizes our main results. We observe that both optimization-based approaches like SHErrLoc and data-driven based approaches like Nate and various language models (i.e., BERT, BERT+, OCBERT, OCBERT+) outperform the standard OCaml compiler in terms of localizing root causes of type errors. Furthermore, data-driven approaches generally outperform optimization-based approaches, indicating that data plays a more important role compared to the pure optimization algorithm as adopted by SHErrLoc. Among the five models used by Nate, it is a bit surprising that Logistic achieves similar performance as multi-layer perceptrons. We believe this is due to the rich hand-designed features which make simple models like logistic regression very effective.

Nevertheless, we observe that our language model-based approaches significantly outperform Nate, which suggests that the embeddings learned in an end-to-end fashion are more effective than hand-designed features.

Both Nate's and BERTs' output can be interpreted as a probability. Normally, we set the threshold to be 0.5, so if the output probability is greater than 0.5, the prediction will be 1, and 0 otherwise. The change in accuracy of models along with varying thresholds is reported in Fig. 6. We notice that if we increase the threshold, BERTs' accuracy is robust whereas Nate drops significantly. This suggests that BERT models are much more confident with their predictions compared to Nate.

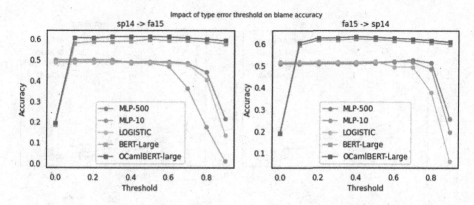

Fig. 6. Impact of different thresholds on accuracy.

4.2 Effectiveness of Model Sizes and Transfer Learning (RQ2).

Larger Model Leads to Higher Accuracy (not overfitting) . To study the effectiveness of different model sizes, we evaluate four modes of different sizes — Small (L = 4, H = 256), Medium (L = 8, H = 512), Base (L = 12, H = 768), and Large (L = 16, H = 1024). Figure 7(a) presents training loss curves of the four models of different sizes. This is somewhat expected since larger models usually tend to have lower training loss but may have an overfitting concern. This then may not lead to better accuracy.

We further evaluate the testing accuracies of models of different sizes, which is summarized in Table 2. The top half of Table 2 shows the testing accuracies of four BERT models on four different train/test setups. The accuracy increases consistently when the model size increases on all train/test setups. This is very interesting because the train/test dataset is fixed with only the model size increasing, that is, with the same dataset, the larger model usually leads to higher accuracy instead of overfitting.

Positive/Negative Transfer of Learning. To study this objective, we focus on BERT, BERT pre-GitHub, CodeBERT, and OCamlBERT. Figure 7(b) presents the training loss curves of these four models. Since OCamlBERT is pretrained on only 20k code samples whereas BERT pre-GitHub is pretrained on 350k samples, it is quite surprising to notice that OCamlBERT has the lowest training loss whereas BERT pre-GitHub has the highest one. This is kind of counter-intuitive as models usually perform better when trained on a larger dataset. The bottom part of Table 2 shows the testing accuracies of four BERT models on four different train/test setups. BERT pre-GitHub reports 51% accuracy, 8 points lower than OCamlBERT which is consistent with training loss curves. The difference in accuracy could be explained by the positive/negative transfer of learning effect. As OCamlBERT is pretrained on code samples written by students/novice programmers (although from different universities working on different programming assignments), the similar data distribution in the fine-tuning process affects positively on accuracy [22]. On the other hand, transfer

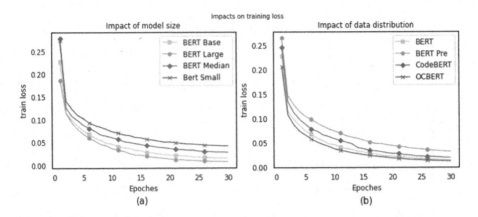

Fig. 7. Impact on training loss. (a) shows how model size affects training loss while (b) illustrates how data distribution affects training loss.

learning impacts CodeBERT's and BERT pre-GitHub's accuracy due to disparate data distribution.

Table 2. Accuracies of different models evaluated on four train/test setups.

	SP14/SP14 (Acc)	FA15/FA15 (Acc)	SP14/FA15 (Acc)	FA15/SP14 (Acc)
BERT Small	68.83	63.05	50.45	51.37
BERT Medium	71.53	65.08	53.39	53.52
BERT Base	74.10	69.89	57.62	57.52
BERT Large	77.57	74.36	59.72	58.89
Bi-LSTM	44.15	40.51	7.25	8.79
BERT Init	60.70	57.02	45.37	43.98
BERT pre-GitHub	68.52	59.59	51.84	51.43
CODEBERT	71.94	69.35	56.40	55.98
OCAMLBERT Base	74.72	70.11	59.24	59.34
OCAMLBERT Large	78.76	74.78	61.40	61.84

4.3   Generalization Ability of Language Models (RQ3)

The generalization ability is an important property of our models as it measures how well a trained model performs on unseen program questions [12].

To study this property, we focus on accuracy drops when evaluating different program problem sets, for instance, training on SP14 yet evaluating on FA15.

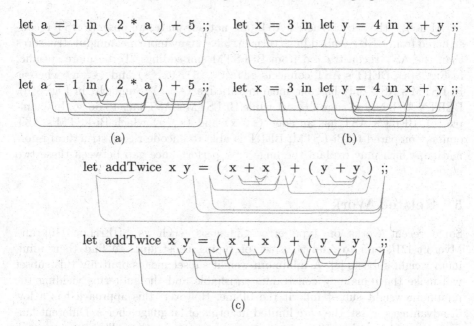

(a)   (b)

(c)

Fig. 8. AST edge reconstruction from learned embeddings (edges in red are reconstructed by BERT Large model; edges in blue are reconstructed by Bidirectional LSTM model). (Color figure online)

We calculate accuracy drops using the difference between the first and last two columns of Table 2. We observe that relatively simple language models such as the Bidirectional LSTM model (Bi-LSTM) experience a large accuracy drop of over 30% on unseen data. In addition, it achieves only 7.25% and 8.79% accuracies on the generalization tasks, which makes it almost useless in the real world. In contrast, the severest accuracy drop of BERTs accuracy is merely 17%. This indicates that BERTs may have learned more robust and critical features which facilitate localizing type errors compared to Bi-LSTM.

In short, we should always consider large and powerful language models rather than small and simple ones when solving difficult tasks such as type error diagnosis.

4.4 Explaining Performance Difference by the Structural Probe (RQ4)

We use the structural probe to reconstruct structural information of programs based on both BERT's and Bi-LSTM's embedding representation. We hypothesize the difference in the ability of encoding structure information of programs could explain the performance gap between these two models. To gain some insights, we conduct a number of qualitative case studies. Figure 8 shows three examples of reconstructed AST of OCaml program using the structural probe.

Although the reconstructed ASTs are not adequate, we observe AST reconstructed from BERT embeddings turns to have many more meaningful structures than the AST reconstructed from Bi-LSTM embeddings. To be more specific, in Fig. 8(a), BERT's AST connects edge (+, 5), (2, *) and (*, a) whereas Bi-LSTM's AST only has one meaningful edge (*, a). Similarly, in Fig. 8(b), BERT's AST has an edge (+, y) while Bi-LSTM's AST fails to do so. In example (c), BERT's AST has an edge (+, x) and (+, y) which Bi-LSTM's AST omits. Compared to Bi-LSTM, BERT is able to encode richer structural information, which may explain the huge 54% performance gap between these two models.

5   Related Work

Some recent works on type error diagnosis, such as SHErrLoc [10] and Mycroft [21], aim to analyze a set of typing constraints to find their minimum weight subsets [8]. A minimum weight subset means omitting this subset will make the remaining constraints satisfiable and the subterms yielding the minimum weight subset inherit the blame. However, this approach has a few disadvantages. First, they are limited in terms of language choice. Different languages tend to employ different type systems and constraints. Thus, an approach designed for one type system can be hard to transfer to others. Secondly, the weights assigned are based on researchers' prior knowledge of the most likely errors instead of the most likely mistakes in practice [10]. Moreover, constraint-based approaches could blame a number of locations equally without taking the author's intent into account.

In contrast, data-driven approaches such as NATE employ machine learning models to learn to localize type error from a large data set. While constraint analysis is not mandatory, NATE's machine learning models require considerable feature engineering. To be more specific, NATE employs over 282 hand-designed features annotated by human experts which are then fed into machine learning models to make the final prediction. However, NATE and other data-driven approaches still suffer from some disadvantages mentioned above. Although NATE doesn't perform constraint analysis, feature engineering also requires prior knowledge, making it difficult to transfer to other type systems. In addition, data-driven methods may implicitly consider the programmer's intent when making predictions, but there is no guarantee that such intent can be understood by models. In our study, we also show that the accuracy metric of NATE can be problematic in certain conditions.

There are also approaches that provide instructions to help novice programmers debug. Seidel et al. creates a dynamic model that generates counterexample witness inputs to show how the program goes wrong [17]. When given a function with type errors, the algorithm symbolically executes the program and synthesizes witness the wrong values. Then the procedure is extended to a graph that shows the witness execution. Experimental results suggest their algorithm can generate witnesses 88% of the time and in these successful programs, the algorithm yields counterexample successfully 81% of the time. The advantage of this algorithm is that by using graphs and counterexamples, students can learn how to write code easily and understand the logic of the programming language. However, people who are familiar with the language but not that skilled, do not need such detailed suggestions. All they need is the precise location of the error. Chen et al. develops a type debugging system that asks programmers to provide type specifications during the debugging process and then generate suggestions that help to fix the type error [2]. The advantage of this system is instead of aiming exclusively at the removal of type errors, it collects user feedback about result types to give useful suggestions, which include almost all possible corrections. This will help novices to debug more easily as they only need to choose from options given by the system. However, to achieve their goal, the authors systematically generate all potential type changes, which, when compared to our model, is more time-consuming in construction and needs more human judgment to make corrections.

There are also approaches which adopt SAT and SMT solvers to solve the type error localization. Pavlinovic et al. designs an algorithm that finds all minimum error sources, where 'minimum' is defined in terms of a compiler-specific ranking criterion [14]. With these error sources, a compiler is able to offer more useful reports. Then the authors try to reduce the search for minimum error sources to an optimization problem by implementing weighted maximum satisfiability modulo theories (MaxSMT). In this way, they leverage SMT solvers, making it easier to extend to multiple type systems and abstract from the concrete criterion that is used for ranking the error sources. The evaluation results on existing OCaml benchmarks for type error localization are also quite promising. In another work [8], Jose et al. aims to reduce the error localization problem to a maximal satisfiability problem (MAX-SAT), which finds the maximum number of clauses that are simultaneously satisfied by an assignment. Three steps are involved when an error should be reported. First, it encodes the denotation of a bounded unrolling of the program to a boolean formula. Then they construct an unsatisfiable formula for the failing program execution. In the last step, a MAX-SAT solver is used to find the largest set of clauses that can be satisfied at the same time, after which they output complement set as result, which is treated as potential locations of type error. Experimental results suggest the algorithm can find a few lines of code that are probable to be blamed for type error. Compared with our algorithm, the location it gives is too general. For novices, it is difficult for them to find the precise location of the type error when given such a large span of possible locations.

There are some other works that aim to diagnose the root causes of programs with typing errors. Chitil et al. uses a compositional type explanation graph created based on the Hindley-Milner type system [3]. More specifically, this work relies on structural type information such as trees with principal typings. Tsushima et al. builds a type debugger without implementing any dedicated type inferencer [19]. The type debugger avoids re-implementing an independent type inference algorithm by leveraging the compiler's type inference engine. In contrast to their work, we train natural language models to capture patterns in code changes. Our models do not require additional information beyond the code and can predict multiple error locations simultaneously. Our approach provides an orthogonal angle for (novice) type error diagnosis, and we believe that incorporating explicit type information can further improve our current approach.

6 Conclusions and Future Work

Many techniques have been developed to address the type error localization problem. While most of them employ static analysis on programs such as SHER-RLOC, NATE's success suggests that data-driven methods are also promising. Our experimental results suggest transformer-based language models outperform the state-of-art NATE and SHERRLOC under a stricter yet more realistic accuracy metric.

Although being a black-box model, we show that language models can encode structural information of programs which may explain their better performance. Moreover, our models simply view a program as a sequence of tokens, thus they do not rely on any special knowledge of OCaml. It is the large amount of data (programs in our context) that plays an essential role in the performance. Since no feature engineering and constraints analysis are required, our approach can be transferred to other programming languages easily. We plan to investigate the effectiveness of our model on new languages like Go and Rust in the future. Through experiments, we identify several factors which help improve model accuracy such as size and positive transfer. We believe these factors may also be beneficial to solving other programming language-related tasks using language models.

In this work, our approach treats programs as natural language texts. This, however, fails to utilize the structural information of programs. Although we show language models could encode some structures, it is unclear how the encoded structural information leads to the final prediction. In contrast, constraint-based approaches such as SHERRLOC take advantage of structural information and have much better interpretability. We plan to explore how to combine language models and the structural information of programs in our future work.

Acknowledgement. We thank the anonymous reviewers for their insightful comments. This work was supported, in part, by Individual Discovery Grants from the Natural Sciences and Engineering Research Council of Canada, the Canada CIFAR AI Chair Program, and Social Sciences and Humanities Research Council (SSHRC).

References

1. Brown, T.B., et al.: Language models are few-shot learners. CoRR abs/2005.14165 (2020). https://arxiv.org/abs/2005.14165
2. Chen, S., Erwig, M.: Guided type debugging. In: Codish, M., Sumii, E. (eds.) FLOPS 2014. LNCS, vol. 8475, pp. 35–51. Springer, Cham (2014). https://doi.org/10.1007/978-3-319-07151-0_3

3. Chitil, O.: Compositional explanation of types and algorithmic debugging of type errors. SIGPLAN Not. **36**(10), 193–204 (2001). https://doi.org/10.1145/507669. 507659

4. Devlin, J., Chang, M., Lee, K., Toutanova, K.: BERT: pre-training of deep bidirectional transformers for language understanding. In: Burstein, J., Doran, C., Solorio, T. (eds.) Proceedings of the 2019 Conference of the North American Chapter of the Association for Computational Linguistics: Human Language Technologies, NAACL-HLT 2019, Minneapolis, MN, USA, 2–7 June 2019, Vol. 1 (Long and Short Papers), pp. 4171–4186. Association for Computational Linguistics (2019). https://doi.org/10.18653/v1/n19-1423

5. Feng, Z., et al.: CodeBERT: a pre-trained model for programming and natural languages. In: Cohn, T., He, Y., Liu, Y. (eds.) Findings of the Association for Computational Linguistics: EMNLP 2020, Online Event, 16–20 November 2020. Findings of ACL, vol. EMNLP 2020, pp. 1536–1547. Association for Computational Linguistics (2020). https://doi.org/10.18653/v1/2020.findings-emnlp.139

6. Geng, C., Ye, H., Li, Y., Han, T., Pientka, B., Si, X.: Novice Type Error Diagnosis with Natural Language Models - Artifacts (2022). https://doi.org/10.5281/zenodo.7055133

7. Joosten, S., van den Berg, K., van Der Hoeven, G.: Teaching functional programming to first-year students. J. Funct. Program. **3**(1), 49–65 (1993). https://doi.org/10.1017/S0956796800000599

8. Jose, M., Majumdar, R.: Cause clue clauses: error localization using maximum satisfiability. In: Hall, M.W., Padua, D.A. (eds.) Proceedings of the 32nd ACM SIGPLAN Conference on Programming Language Design and Implementation, PLDI 2011, San Jose, CA, USA, 4–8 June 2011, pp. 437–446. ACM (2011). https://doi.org/10.1145/1993498.1993550

9. Li, H.: Deep learning for natural language processing: advantages and challenges. Natl. Sci. Rev. **5**(1), 24–26 (2017). https://doi.org/10.1093/nsr/nwx110

10. Loncaric, C., Chandra, S., Schlesinger, C., Sridharan, M.: A practical framework for type inference error explanation. In: Visser, E., Smaragdakis, Y. (eds.) Proceedings of the 2016 ACM SIGPLAN International Conference on Object-Oriented Programming, Systems, Languages, and Applications, OOPSLA 2016, part of SPLASH 2016, Amsterdam, The Netherlands, 30 October - 4 November 2016, pp. 781–799. ACM (2016). https://doi.org/10.1145/2983990.2983994

11. Manning, C.D., Clark, K., Hewitt, J., Khandelwal, U., Levy, O.: Emergent linguistic structure in artificial neural networks trained by self-supervision. Proc. Natl. Acad. Sci. U.S.A. **117**(48), 30046–30054 (2020). https://doi.org/10.1073/pnas.1907367117

12. Neyshabur, B., Bhojanapalli, S., McAllester, D., Srebro, N.: Exploring generalization in deep learning. In: Guyon, I., et al. (eds.) Advances in Neural Information Processing Systems 30: Annual Conference on Neural Information Processing Systems 2017(December), pp. 4–9, 2017. Long Beach, CA, USA. pp. 5947–5956 (2017). https://proceedings.neurips.cc/paper/2017/hash/10ce03a1ed01077e3e289f3e53c72813-Abstract.html

13. O'Keefe, C., Lansky, D., Clark, J., Payne, C.: Comment regarding request for comments on intellectual property protection for artificial intelligence innovation (2019). https://perma.cc/ZS7G-2QWF

14. Pavlinovic, Z., King, T., Wies, T.: Finding minimum type error sources. In: Black, A.P., Millstein, T.D. (eds.) Proceedings of the 2014 ACM International Conference on Object Oriented Programming Systems Languages & Applications, OOPSLA 2014, part of SPLASH 2014, Portland, OR, USA, 20–24 October 2014, pp. 525–542. ACM (2014). https://doi.org/10.1145/2660193.2660230

15. Radford, A., Wu, J., Child, R., Luan, D., Amodei, D., Sutskever, I.: Language models are unsupervised multitask learners (2019)

16. Schuster, M., Paliwal, K.: Bidirectional recurrent neural networks. IEEE Trans. Signal Process. 45(11), 2673–2681 (1997). https://doi.org/10.1109/78.650093

17. Seidel, E.L., Jhala, R., Weimer, W.: Dynamic witnesses for static type errors (or, ill-typed programs usually go wrong). In: Garrigue, J., Keller, G., Sumii, E. (eds.) Proceedings of the 21st ACM SIGPLAN International Conference on Functional Programming, ICFP 2016, Nara, Japan, 18–22 September 2016, pp. 228–242. ACM (2016). https://doi.org/10.1145/2951913.2951915

18. Seidel, E.L., Sibghat, H., Chaudhuri, K., Weimer, W., Jhala, R.: Learning to blame: localizing novice type errors with data-driven diagnosis. Proc. ACM Program. Lang. 1(OOPSLA), 1–27 (2017). https://doi.org/10.1145/3138818

19. Tsushima, K., Asai, K.: An embedded type debugger. In: Hinze, R. (ed.) IFL 2012. LNCS, vol. 8241, pp. 190–206. Springer, Heidelberg (2013). https://doi.org/10.1007/978-3-642-41582-1_12

20. Vaswani, A., et al.: Attention is all you need. In: Guyon, I., et al. (eds.) Advances in Neural Information Processing Systems 30: Annual Conference on Neural Information Processing Systems 2017(December), pp. 4–9, 2017. Long Beach, CA, USA. pp. 5998–6008 (2017). https://proceedings.neurips.cc/paper/2017/hash/3f5ee243547dee91fbd053c1c4a845aa-Abstract.html

21. Zhang, D., Myers, A.C.: Toward general diagnosis of static errors. In: Jagannathan, S., Sewell, P. (eds.) The 41st Annual ACM SIGPLAN-SIGACT Symposium on Principles of Programming Languages, POPL '14, San Diego, CA, USA, 20–21, January 2014. pp. 569–582. ACM (2014). https://doi.org/10.1145/2535838.2535870

22. Zhuang, F., et al.: A comprehensive survey on transfer learning. Proc. IEEE 109(1), 43–76 (2021). https://doi.org/10.1109/JPROC.2020.3004555

Author Index

Arceri, Vincenzo   25

Becker, Mike   110

Cagne, Pierre   135
Chin, Wei-Ngan   88

Delaware, Benjamin   67
Dickerson, Robert   67
Dvir, Yotam   3

Fan, Andong   175
Foo, Darius   88

Geng, Chuqin   196

Han, Tianyu   196

Johann, Patricia   135

Kammar, Ohad   3

Lahav, Ori   3
Li, Yixuan   196

Mastroeni, Isabella   25
Meyer, Roland   110

Oliveira, Bruno C. d. S.   155, 175

Pientka, Brigitte   196

Runge, Tobias   110

Schaefer, Ina   110
Schöpp, Ulrich   45
Si, Xujie   196
Song, Yahui   88

van der Wall, Sören   110

Wolff, Sebastian   110

Xie, Ningning   155
Xu, Chuangjie   45
Xue, Xu   155

Ye, Haolin   196
Ye, Qianchuan   67

Zaffanella, Enea   25
Zhang, Michael K.   67
Zhou, Yaoda   175

Printed in the United States
by Baker & Taylor Publisher Services